GREENING AFRICA'S INDUSTRIALIZATION

ECONOMIC REPORT ON AFRICA

United Nations
Economic Commission for Africa

2016

Ordering information

To order copies of Greening Africa's Industrialization, Economic Report on Africa by the Economic Commission for Africa, please contact:

Publications
Economic Commission for Africa
P.O. Box 3001
Addis Ababa, Ethiopia

Tel: +251 11 544-9900
Fax: +251 11 551-4416
E-mail: ecainfo@uneca.org
Web: www.uneca.org

First printing March 2016

Sales no.: E.16.II.K.3
ISBN: 978-92-1-125126-5
eISBN: 978-92-1-057921-6

Cover design, layout and graphics: Karen Knols, Carolina Rodriguez and Tessa Schlechtriem

CONTENTS

LIST OF FIGURES, TABLES & BOXES

CHAPTER 1

BOXES

FIGURES

CHAPTER 1 (CONT)

CHAPTER 2

CHAPTER 3

CHAPTER 4

CHAPTER 4 (CONT)

FIGURES

TABLES

CHAPTER 5

BOXES

FIGURES

CHAPTER 5 (CONT)

ANNEX

CHAPTER 6

BOXES

FIGURES

TABLES

CHAPTER 7

LIST OF ABREVIATIONS USED

AfDB	African Development Bank
AIDA	Accelerated Industrial Development of Africa
AMU	Arab Maghreb Union
APHRC	African Population and Health Research Center
AREI	Africa Renewable Energy Initiative
AUC	African Union Commission
BAU	Business as Usual
BEE	Black Economic Empowerment
BRICS	Brazil, Russia, India, China and South Africa
CAADP	Comprehensive African Agricultural Development Program
CAR	Central African Republic
CDKN	Climate and Development Knowledge Network
CDP	Carbon Disclosure Project
CEN-SAD	Community of Sahel- Saharan States
CFA	Communauté Financière d'Afrique
CLMRS	Child Labour Monitoring and Remediation Systems
CO_2	Carbon dioxide
COMESA	Common Market for Eastern and Southern Africa
COP	Conference of the Parties
COP21	United Nations 21st Conference of the Parties
CRGE	Climate-Resilient Green Economy
CSIR	Council for Scientific and Industrial Research (South Africa)
CSOs	Civil Society Organizations
CSP	Concentrated Solar Power
DAC	Development Assistance Committee
DRC	Democratic Republic of the Congo
EAC	East African Community
ECA	United Nations Economic Commission for Africa
ECCAS	Economic Community of Central African States
ECOWAS	Economic Community of West African States
EDPRS	Economic Development Poverty Reduction Strategy
EIB	European Investment Bank
EIU	Economist Intelligence Unit
EIZ	Engineering Institute of Zambia
ERA	Economic Report on Africa
EU	European Union
FAO	Food and Agriculture Organization of the United
FDI	Foreign direct investment
FFF	Forest and Farm Facility
FGLG	Forest Governance Learning Group

FSC	Forest Stewardship Council
GA	Green Agenda
GDC	Geothermal Development Company
GDP	Gross Domestic Product
GE	Green Economy
GEC	Green Economy Coalition
GESIP	Green Economy Strategy and Implementation Plan (Kenya)
GFTN	Global Forest and Trade Network
GGGF	Global Green Growth Forum
GGGI	Global Green Growth Institute
GGKP	Green Growth Knowledge Platform
GHG	Greenhouse gas
GIZ	German Corporation for International Cooperation
GMP	Green Morocco Plan
GNI	Gross National Income
GVC	Global Value Chains
GW	Gigawatts
GWh	Gigawatts Hours
HDI	Human Development Index
ICA	Infrastructure Consortium in Africa
ICRAF	International Centre for Research in Agroforestry
ICT	Information and communications technology
IEA	International Energy Agency
IF	International Futures
IFC	International Finance Corporation
IGAD	Intergovernmental Authority on Development
ILO	International Labour Organization
IMF	International Monetary Fund
IMO	International Maritime Organization
IRENA	International Renewable Energy Agency
ISIC	International Standard Industrial Classification
kWh	Kilowatt Hours
LDCs	Least-Developed Countries
LED	Light-Emitting Diode
LIU	Leather Industries of Uganda Ltd.
MARPOL	Marian Pollution
MASEN	Moroccan Agency for Solar Energy
MDGs	Millennium Development Goals
MED TEST	Transfer of Environmentally Sound Technologies (Mediterranean)
MID	Maurice Ile Durable
MVA	Manufacturing Value Added
MW	Megawatt
NCE	New Climate Economy
NCP	Nestlé Cocoa Plan
NDB	New Development Bank BRICS Development Bank
NEPAD	New Partnership for Africa's Development

NRI	Natural Resources Institute
ODA	Overseas Development Assistance
OECD	Organisation for Economic Cooperation and Development
OKACOM	Permanent Okavango River Basin Commission
OPEC	Organization of the Petroleum Exporting Countries
PEP	Poverty-Environment Partnership
PIDA	Programme for Infrastructure Development in Africa
PRB	Population Reference Bureau
R&D	Research and development
RDI	Relative Decoupling Index
REC	Regional Economic Communities
RECPR	Resource-efficient and cleaner production
REFIT	Renewable Energy Feed-in Tariff
REIPPPP	Renewable Energy Independent Power Producer Procurement Programme
SADC	Southern African Development Community
SDGs	Sustainable Development Goals
SE4ALL	Sustainable Energy for All
SIPRA	Société Ivoirienne de Productions Animales
SITC	Standard International Trade Classification
SME	Small and medium-sized enterprise
SOLAS	Safety of Life at Sea
STCW	Standards of Training, Certification and Watchkeeping for Seafarers
TNCs	Trans-National Corporations
UK	United Kingdom
UN	United Nations
UNCTAD	United Nations Conference on Trade and Development
UN-DESA	United Nations Department of Economic and Social Affairs
UNDP	United Nations Development Programme
UNECA	United Nations Economic Commission for Africa
UNEP	United Nations Environment Program
UNESCO	United Nations Educational, Scientific and Cultural Organization
UNFCCC	United Nations Framework Convention on Climate Change
UNIDO	United Nations Industrial Development Organization
UN-PAGE	Partnership for Action on Green Economy
UNSD	United Nations Statistics Division
US	United States
USAID	United States Agency for International Development
WBCSD	World Business Council for Sustainable Development
WDI	World Development Indicators
WHO	United Nations World Health Organization
WIEGO	Women in Informal Employment: Globalizing and Organizing
WTO	World Trade Organization
WWF	World Wide Fund for Nature
ZESCO	Zambia Electricity Supply Corporation

ACKNOWLEDGEMENTS

The Economic Report on Africa 2016—a publication of the United Nations Economic Commission for Africa (ECA)—was prepared under the leadership of Carlos Lopes, ECA's Executive Secretary, with the close involvement of Abdalla Hamdok, Deputy Executive Secretary and Chief Economist of ECA. The report team benefited from the guidance and supervision of Adam Elhiraika, Director of Macroeconomic Policy Division, ECA, and Fatima Denton, Director, Special Initiatives Division, ECA.

The ECA core team comprised Yesuf Mohammednur Awel, Hopestone Chavula, Adrian Gauci, Bartholomew Armah, Mama Keita, Mongameli Mehlwana, Johnson Nkem, Saurabh Sinha and Heini Suominen.

The Report benefited from substantive contributions by Camilla Toulmin, Senior Fellow, International Institute for Environment and Development, who also contributed significantly to its content editing; Professor Raphael Kaplinsky of the University of Sussex; Belynda Petrie of One World, Cape Town, South Africa; and Ralph Luken of the United Nations Industrial Development Organization.

The report team is grateful to Tessa Adamson, Charles Akong, Andrew Allieu, Nassirou Ba, Derrese Degefa, Ngone Diop, Adama Ekberg Coulibaly, Susannah Fisher, Diane Guerrier, George Kararach, Yacouba Gnégné, Abbi Kedir, Deniz Kellecioglu, Mamo Girma, Louis Lubango, Iris Macculi, El Helepi Medhat, Linus Mofor, William Muhawava, Maimouna Hama Natama, Guy Ranaivomanana, Gideon Rutaremwa, John Rwirihira, Semia Guermas Tapia, Edlam Abera Yemeru and Jack Jones Zulu for their input to the Report.

Ten country case studies were undertaken by Tessa Adamson and Susanna Fisher (Kenya), Abbi Kedir (Ethiopia), Andrew Allieu (South Africa), Charles Akong (Nigeria), Susannah Fisher (Rwanda), Linus Mofor (Ghana), Johnson Nkem (Malawi), Louis Lubango (Mauritius) and Yacouba Gnégné (Côte d'Ivoire and Tunisia).

Constructive comments and suggestions were received from staff in various divisions and subregional offices of ECA and from external reviewers: Wassie Berhanu, Atlaw Alemu Addis Ababa University; Dr. Vicente Jose D.A. Costa Pinto de Andrade, Lusia University of Angola; Dr. Sarah N. Ssewanyana, Economic Policy Research Centre, Uganda; Dr. Christopher W. Guta, Press Corporation, Malawi; Dr. Atewamba Calvin, United Nations University–Institute for Natural Resources in Africa; Dr. Desta Mebratu, United Nations Environment Programme, Nairobi; Dr. Theresa Moyo, University of Limpopo, South Africa; Mr. Michel Phan, Pioneer Food Cannery, Ghana; Dr. Lankoande Gountien, Researcher,

Burkina Faso; Dr. Tadele Agaje Ferede, Addis Ababa University; Mr. Jean Bakole, United Nations Industrial Development Organization, Ethiopia; and Mr. Girma Balcha, Climate Change Forum, Ethiopia.

The Report would not have been possible without the contribution of the following: Collen Kelapile, Jimmy Ocitti, Demba Diarra, Charles Ndungu, Teshome Yohannes, Menkir Girma, Henok Legesse, Robel Tsegaye, Mercy Wambui, Agare Kassahun, Yetinayet Mengistu, Solomon Wedere, Bekele Demissie, Melkamu Gebre Ezigiabher of ECA; Bruce Ross-Larson and Joe Caponio of Communications Development Incorporated, editors; and Karen Knols, Tessa Schlechtriem, Carolina Rodriguez of Dilucidar Incorporated, infographic design consultants.

FOREWORD

In recent years the continent has made some significant strides in all dimensions of economic and human development, comparable with other regions of the world on similar economic trajectories, having registered some of the fastest growing economies in a constrained global economy. However, although the drivers of growth are diversifying, the continent continues to rely heavily on the production and export of raw commodities, and the share of manufacturing stagnated at around 11 per cent over the last decade. As a result many African economies are vulnerable to fluctuations in commodity prices, and the continent remains home to the world's highest proportion of poor people and to a growing youth population.

Industrialization is an imperative for Africa to meet the objectives of Agenda 2063 within a global economy constrained by climate change and driven by competitive supply chains and complex supply and demand dynamics. Indeed, accelerated and profound economic structural transformation, through reallocating economic activities from less productive to more productive sectors for sustainable and inclusive growth, is the only means to address chronic poverty on the continent.

African industrialization has to focus on the regional market through increased trade before it extends to the global supply chain, with special emphasis on agro-processed products and value addition to mineral exports. For example, transforming our mineral export volume by just 5 per cent before exporting them can create 5 million jobs a year. Recent estimates show that African countries spend some $30 billion a year to import processed food. This trend can be reversed through value added agro-processing, creating countless jobs, especially for our growing youth population.

How should Africa pursue its industrialization? Many pathways exist, but as a latecomer it can learn from others' experiences while defining and designing its own pathway—based on its own realities and learning from history and the experiences of other regions—to leapfrog traditional, carbon-intensive methods of growth and champion a low-carbon development trajectory. The continent can take advantage of new innovations, technologies and business models on a pathway that uses our natural resources optimally and efficiently as inputs to an industrialization process powered by our endowments of clean sources of energy.

This is why the ECA has seized the opportunity this year to herald the era for Africa to pursue a different pathway to industrialization, in short, one that enables the region to green its industrialization. In so doing Africa will pursue its development agenda along a pathway that ensures that economic growth is truly sustainable and inclusive through green jobs and positive spillovers. It is this new niche that we recognize as a winning formula, a "no regret" option that will secure Africa a central space in the world economy. Such a transformation will make significant productivity gains in rural areas with vibrant hubs of agri-business and linkages to industrial activity.

Through case studies this report shows that there is good news on greening industrialization in Africa. A number of countries have already put in place policies and regulatory frameworks for green industrialization. A good number of enterprises are taking the lead to implement green measures, driven by legal requirements and opportunities for economic returns on their investments, as well as the need for a long-term sustainable business model. But more need to follow suit, and this report is an entry point for shared learning and the replication of good practice on how we develop a low-carbon pathway.

ERA 2016 on green industrialization is well informed by primary data drawn from 12 African countries where green industrialization is gaining strong momentum. It complements several recent editions of the ERA by focusing both on the quality of industrialization and on the opportunities for upgrading throughout the value chain. And it adopts a systemic approach to green industrialization using examples from value chains in key sectors, including agriculture, energy, extractives, manufacturing, transport, and water to make a credible case for green industrialization.

Several forward-looking lessons emerge from the report. The costs of industrializing on a business-as-usual approach are unacceptably high. Industrialization must adopt a low-carbon and inclusive pathway. Indeed, the report shows that doing so creates jobs, increases returns on investment, uses finite resources efficiently, reduces harm to the environment, increases global competitiveness and ensures the long-term business sustainability of enterprises. But this transition requires a step-wise change, recognizing that changes at the margins will not transform African economies or bring about the desired inclusive growth that can give agency and confidence to communities that have long stood at periphery of development.

Structural transformation based on green industrialization will not happen spontaneously. It needs coherent policies entrenched in a coherent development strategy, enlightened by a transformative leadership. The report makes the case that governments need to take bold measures now and put in place the necessary interventions. This can happen through seven key actions.

First is for countries to review their national development plans and strategies to identify opportunities and entry points for green industrialization, and thus develop an economy-wide green growth vision. Second is to identify clear, consistent and coherent policies and interventions, involving all key stakeholders. Third is to build partnerships and leverage limited public resources to mobilize investments from the private sector and various sources aligned with national priorities. Fourth is to invest in innovation, infrastructure, collaborative research, regional integration and trade as key enablers for green industrialization. Fifth is to adopt a learning-by-doing approach through sharing best practices and learning from the experiences of other countries to leapfrog the green industrialization agenda. Sixth is to build and strengthen national institutional and human capacities to drive the green growth vision. And seventh is to regularly monitor and review national green visions and policy instruments for continual improvement.

I trust that this report will serve as the catalyst for driving this new order and giving our citizens the Africa we want. The time for Africa has come. It is within our reach to wean ourselves from our dependency on fossil fuels and to opt for a new, cleaner and more efficient growth formula that will result in a shared prosperity for our people. The window of opportunity is wide open, and the continent and its people can leap forward to seize it.

Carlos Lopes

United Nations Under-Secretary-General and Executive Secretary
Economic Commission for Africa

EXECUTIVE SUMMARY

Structural transformation in Africa's economies remains the highest priority, and industrialization is the top strategy for achieving it in practice. Achieving the African Union's Agenda 2063 and fulfilling the Sustainable Development Goals will demand a major re-design of growth strategies across the continent.

The big opportunity for Africa in 2016, as a latecomer to industrialization, is in adopting alternative economic pathways to industrialization. This requires governments to take on-board the drivers, challenges, and trade-offs in pushing for a greening of industrialization—and to build them into the vision and route-map for action. Seizing the momentum of the Paris Climate Agreement and the SDGs provides the ideal timing for such a shift in economic strategy.

Dispelling the myths currently surrounding green growth will promote the re-shaping of Africa's economic growth in favour of sustainable development. Investing in environmental standards should be seen not as an obstacle to competitive manufacturing, but as underpinning competitiveness, making more efficient use of energy, and de-coupling resource use from output growth. While some individual countries have taken the lead, there would be far greater benefits from a regional approach to greening the essential infrastructure, industrial structures, and major trade flows that span each region.

Africa's growth has been characterized by heavy reliance on natural resources and low productivity across most sectors. It has been accompanied by high energy and material intensities, as well as waste generation. These factors drive the resource scarcity and contribute to the high production costs that undermine the global competitiveness of Africa's industrial sector.

Greening industrialization is an opportunity for Africa to achieve the type of structural transformation that yields sustainable and inclusive growth, creating jobs while safeguarding the productivity of natural resource assets. Growth in the region has been largely jobless and associated with the degradation of Africa's valuable natural capital. Structural transformation through industrialization will inevitably and justifiably increase the uptake of resources. But a strategy for greening this process, in its many dimensions, will deliver a more competitive and resource-efficient industrial sector—one that provides employment, is climate resilient and is decoupled from environmental degradation. There is now a growing commitment among African countries to pursue inclusive green development. A collective commitment from across the African Union would strengthen the speed and effectiveness of such a strategic shift.

Governments are central in mapping out the pathway to green industrialization. Long term, consistent, and clear directions are required of policy makers to provide the institutional design and credible incentives at the heart of this structural transformation. Such a shift in economic strategy requires not a marginal tweaking of current policy tools, but a step-change in direction. Leadership at the highest level of government is needed to confirm this step-change. In addition to the adoption of effective inclusive green economy policies and strategies, greening industrialization will need relevant measures to create a policy environment characterized by good governance and institutions, available financial resources and technologies, and high quality human capacities. But this is not just a task for government. Indeed, it will be achieved only by a partnership between government, business, civil society, producer groups, neighbourhood organizations, municipal government, researchers and technical experts.

Greening industrialization provides the impetus for turning current supply chains linking natural resources to markets, into value chains that diversify Africa's economies and ensure greater value added. In an era of growing scarcity, resource-rich Africa must shift away from being a marginal supplier of raw commodities, to harness the full potential of natural resources by diversification into greater value addition, through processing and marketing. The Africa Mining Vision offers a good example for making this step-change.

Taking stock of current economic trends, global economic growth slowed in 2015, reflecting a range of problems in the euro area, China, Brazil, and the Russian Federation, combined with the collapse of oil prices. This slowdown among Africa's largest trading partners has inevitably hit economic performance on the continent, with growth moderating from 3.9 per cent in 2014 to 3.7 per cent in 2015. Africa's reliance on exports of raw materials to other regions of the world has led to falling revenues for government and a decline in investment. Growth in many African countries has been underpinned by increased private consumption over the last few years, due to rising domestic demand, stemming from increased government spending in infrastructure projects and growing incomes among the middle class. An increase in inward investment has also spurred growth, thanks to improvements in the commercial environment and lower costs of doing business. But falling commodity prices now mean that most countries are experiencing growing fiscal deficits, especially those reliant on oil and gas exports, and will have to revise government spending plans.

Africa's vulnerability to these external shocks calls for a rethink of its growth and broader development strategy along four critical dimensions.

- First, economic growth in Africa has not been inclusive: the number of Africans in absolute poverty has risen, and inequality remains a major concern.
- Second, growth has been associated with increased exploitation of non-renewable natural resources, incurring heavy costs to the soils, water, forests and biodiversity which make up Africa's rich and diverse natural resource base.
- Third, the structures of African economies have remained largely based on raw material extraction, with very little value addition and limited employment generation.
- Fourth, Africa trades more with other parts of the world than within the continent. A strategic re-think across Africa's regions could build much stronger domestic and regional linkages—reducing large and growing food imports, greatly improving the use of renewable resources, particularly water and energy, and establishing competitive industrial activity.

The challenge facing African leaders is to transform their patterns of production, and to build system-wide infrastructure in order to ensure secure supplies of water, food and energy. Green and inclusive industrialization provides a pathway to attain such goals. And since most African countries share common environmental challenges, greening Africa's development would promote regional integration, cooperation and the growth of continent-wide innovation capabilities, putting Africa's development on a more robust, technologically smart and sustainable foundation.

The time has never been better for African countries to follow this route to development. The past year has seen three landmark global agreements that align well with Africa's need to industrialize, by generating greener and more inclusive growth. The first was the 21st annual Conference of the Parties (COP21) during the United Nations Climate Change Conference in Paris in December 2015. At COP21 all nations signed an agreement that—if the terms are carried out—will lead to a worldwide low-carbon economy and a shift away from fossil fuels. The agreement puts the global economy on course for transforming its energy systems. All countries have pledged "to keep a global temperature rise this century well below 2°C and to drive efforts to limit the temperature increase even further to 1.5°C, above pre-industrial levels" (UNFCCC, 2015). All countries of the world have submitted plans laying out their intended contribution to achieving the global target of less than 2°C, and those plans will be subject to five-year review to ratchet up the ambition gradually. The second agreement—on the Sustainable Development Goals (SDGs), in September 2015—places equality, sustainability and universal basic needs at the heart of our common global economic strategy. The Addis Ababa Action Agenda, the outcome of the Financing for Development summit in Addis Ababa in July 2015, offers a comprehensive framework for financing Africa's industrialization and structural transformation, with an emphasis on domestic resource mobilization.

Properly aligned, these global agreements set the stage for international and regional partnerships that can transform Africa's growth prospects. They confirm a shift in the direction of the global economy towards a sustainable, low-carbon future based on green and inclusive growth.

Africa is blessed with abundant land, water and energy sources and with a young and increasingly better educated population. Such abundance, when combined with capital investment, can generate the prosperity, employment and sustainability needed to achieve the promise laid out in the African Union's Vision 2063. Some African countries are making good progress, with a focus on water, energy and agriculture, systematically building low-carbon development and climate resilience into their plans and decision-making. But many countries have yet to focus on how best to harness the post-2015 momentum in climate and sustainability and use it to accelerate their own plans for growth, structural transformation and sustainable industrialization. The year 2016 is the ideal time to redesign long-term growth plans to deliver green and inclusive industrialization.

A low-carbon economic pathway must be followed worldwide if the world is to keep the mean global temperature increase to less than 2°C. A perspective to 2050 and beyond means that all countries should plan their routes to deep de-carbonization to achieve 80 per cent emission cuts by 2050 and net zero carbon by 2070. African nations have contributed very little to global greenhouse gas emissions, and perhaps should not, therefore, be expected to take the lead on low-carbon development.

African countries can stand back and watch others take the lead in building a green economy—or they can benefit from their current low-carbon position and leapfrog the process. Following the latter strategy means that many African economies can get it right the first time; infrastructure does not have to be retrofitted to make it climate resilient, and high dependence on volatile fossil fuels can be avoided, bringing significant co-benefits for health and energy security.

Africa's move to greener industrialization is not just a step towards meeting global carbon emission targets—it is a precondition for sustainable and inclusive growth. The Intended Nationally Determined Contributions, prepared by each country in advance of COP21, offer the ideal framework for practical steps over the next 5 to 10 years, aligning with long-term goals of de-carbonizing, building climate resilience and delivering sustainable development.

Africa can explore many ways to achieve green industrialization—starting with existing enterprises. Because of current high levels of waste and inefficiency at the plant level, supporting business to become more resource-efficient provides multiple opportunities for win-wins. And working at the systems level offers big opportunities for greening supply chains, infrastructure and, above all, energy generation.

Government has the central role in taking the long view—out to 2030 and beyond. Policy stability, effective pubic institutions and consistent implementation make all the difference in creating credible incentives to unlock private investment by small, medium and large enterprises. And while government must take the lead, it cannot hope to design, fund and achieve a green and inclusive economy on its own. Strong, long-term partnerships are needed with business, civil society organizations, community groups, municipal government, finance and research sectors. Each one brings its own skills, networks and interests to construct a shared vision for an inclusive green economy.

Africa has a bright future that is within reach. The continent is a 'gold mine,' a world region with very significant natural resource assets, and significant growth and industrialization opportunities. Building on previous editions, this report emphasizes effective policy frameworks and actions that will enable Africa to leapfrog in the industrialization process, particularly through good resource use and governance and the construction of green infrastructure. This report's work on alternative scenarios makes this starkly clear. Africa is also fortunate to have excellent examples of what bold, informed decisions about green industrialization can achieve.

How best to stimulate growth and ensure it is both inclusive and environmentally sustainable? Africa cannot continue on a business-as-usual (BAU) trajectory if it truly wishes to industrialize and scale up broad-based development. Looking forward to 2050, and using a set of green agenda policy tools, many of the supply-demand gaps in energy close considerably if major investments tap into Africa's vast renewable energy resources. Even water scarcity becomes manageable, largely as a result of improved governance, regional integration and green infrastructure. Critically, urban populations generate big dividends where investment is made in green infrastructure, and enhanced skills and innovation.

African governments have clear policy options to follow.

- First, they need leadership at the highest level to achieve this structural change. This leadership needs to translate a broad vision into strategy and policies. A credible and long-term plan is vital, which is shared and communicated clearly.
- Second, while current capacity may be limited, steps should be taken to build the ability to deliver. This means investing in domestic resources and learning lessons on greening industrialization from elsewhere. Many other governments are pursuing similar challenges—so there is much to be learned.
- Third, if governments really seek a step-change in economic strategy, some interests are bound to block progress. Inevitably, such a shift in strategy will not please everyone, and government needs to be ready for this.
- Fourth, the enormous size of the informal sector means it cannot be wished away. Instead, government needs to find ways of engaging and bringing its energy and innovative capacity on board.

- Fifth, it can sometimes be tempting to consider large-scale initiatives as the only ones that really count. But in practice, lots of small initiatives add up to a big impact. A decentralized pattern of economic innovation can also be more resilient to shocks than a small number of large enterprises.
- Sixth, if government policy is to be credible, some fundamental institutions have to be in strengthened—among them, local government administration, land and property rights, and access to law.
- Seventh, it is important to decentralize economic activity across the country to avoid having everything happen in the capital city. In practice, much of the innovation is likely to be at the local level, since this is the arena where people, enterprise and the government administration have the closest connection.
- Eighth, if policy is to adjust to circumstance, there must be means to assess progress through regular data collection, review and adjustment to the strategy.

Central in all this is an approach focused on decoupling energy. Many industrial energy decoupling programmes in Africa show the scale of savings achievable in energy use. In Tunisia and South Africa big savings offer profitable opportunities to industries, and broader targets for greening in government strategies.

At the heart of green industrialization is infrastructure investment. Greening Africa's infrastructure enables leapfrogging in the green industrialization process. Decisions today will have long-lasting impacts on patterns of growth and consumption. So getting it right the first time is vital to avoid retro-fits, which are always more expensive. It is also a no-regret investment option under any scenario or growth pathway for Africa, since at a minimum it will build Africa's resilience to climate change. Bold expansion of renewable energy can help resolve Africa's energy deficit, providing a cornerstone for Africa's industrialization.

Greening African cities is another cornerstone of Africa's green industrialization and another opportunity to leapfrog the green industrialization process. Cities bring together social innovation, skills, infrastructure, and energy, food and water security, making them a natural focal point for fueling green industrialization while making urbanization inclusive.

The year 2016 offers a valuable opportunity for a step-change in the direction taken by any African economies, in favour of structural transformation which delivers green, inclusive growth which builds industrial capacity, value added and quality employment.

CHAPTER 1

RECENT ECONOMIC AND SOCIAL DEVELOPMENTS IN AFRICA

Global economic growth slipped from 2.6 per cent in 2014 to 2.4 per cent in 2015, reflecting subdued growth in gross fixed capital formation (investment) and households' final consumption. Growth moderation in China and declining economic activity in Brazil, the Russian Federation and other commodity-exporting countries weighed on global growth (box 1.1).

Africa's economic growth also declined moderately amid these global headwinds. Growth in many of the continent's countries was underpinned by increased private consumption owing to greater domestic demand (reflecting increased government spending on infrastructure projects and the rising middle class) and greater investment encouraged by an improved business environment and lower cost of doing business. Most African countries, however, experienced wider fiscal deficits: for commodity exporters, mainly because of less fiscal revenue from commodities as prices declined; for many countries, because of expansionary fiscal policies through increased expenditure on infrastructure development; and for countries with presidential and parliamentary elections, because of election-related outlays.

All the African subregions and economic groups had current account deficits in 2015, driven in part by declining commodity prices. Most African countries exercised tight monetary policy as global headwinds buffeted the region, mainly to curb rising inflation and high fiscal and current account deficits. Inflation increased mainly owing to weaker domestic currencies on declining commodity prices and to rising food prices.

FIGURE 1.1 ECONOMIC GROWTH IN AFRICA AND EMERGING AND DEVELOPING COUNTRIES, 2010–2015

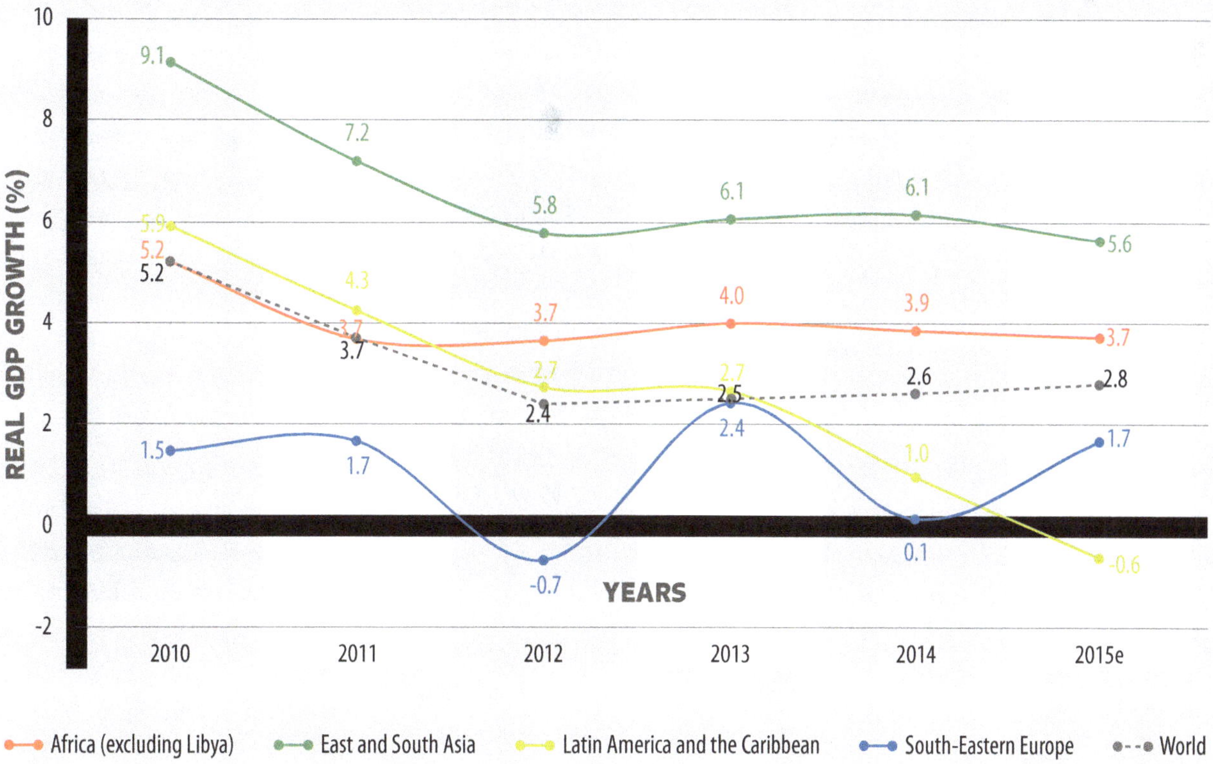

SOURCE: ECA CALCULATIONS BASED ON UN-DESA (2015) AND EIU (2015).
NOTE: e=ESTIMATES.

BOX 1.1 KEY DEVELOPMENTS IN THE WORLD ECONOMY IN 2015

Growth

Gross domestic product (GDP) growth in developed economies edged up from 1.7 per cent in 2014 to 1.9 per cent in 2015 and is expected to rise to 2.2 per cent in 2016, driven mainly by faster growth in the United States (US) and the euro area.

In the US, growth in 2015 stayed at around 2014's 2.4 per cent, but is expected to inch up to 2.6 per cent in 2016, driven by a combination of factors such as increased private consumption—which benefited from steady job creation in every sector, income growth, lower oil prices and improved consumer confidence—and a lower unemployment rate (IMF, 2015). The unemployment rate declined steadily from 7.9 per cent in 2013 to 6.2 per cent in 2014 and to 5.9 per cent in 2015; it is projected to reach 5.5 per cent in 2016 (ILO, 2015a).

In Japan, growth is estimated at 0.5 per cent in 2015, a switch from a 0.5 percent contraction in 2014. It is projected to reach 1.3 per cent in 2016, supported by the fall in oil prices and real wage gains. But a planned increase in the consumption tax in 2017 and rising spending owing to continued population aging (and shrinkage) will crimp GDP growth in the medium and long terms.

Developed economies continued to rely on highly accommodative monetary policy to deliver growth in 2015. Over the forecast period, the vast majority of central banks in developed countries—the Federal Reserve of the United States aside—are expected to maintain this stance. This divergence has been linked to a strong US dollar appreciation against other developed-economy currencies, and is expected to lead to a substantial redistribution of real net exports from the United States to Japan and Europe. Low commodity prices have generally supported the outlook in developed economies, except the oil-heavy economies of Canada and Norway, where investment in the hydrocarbon sector has stalled and economic prospects have deteriorated markedly.

In the euro area, growth edged up from 1.4 per cent in 2014 to 1.9 per cent in 2015, bolstered by improved business and consumer confidence, and a recovering banking sector but also by increased consumption supported by lower oil prices, higher net exports and tapering fiscal consolidation. Despite the illegal migration crisis, growth is projected to continue on its positive path, marginally improving to 2.0 per cent in 2016.

In emerging and developing economies, GDP growth declined from 4.3 per cent in 2014 to 3.8 per cent in 2015, underpinned by weaker export demand, lower commodity prices, lower capital inflows and sluggish investment. In some cases, military conflicts, natural disasters and adverse weather effects on agricultural output put downward pressure on growth. But stronger demand from developed countries and stabilizing commodity prices are expected to nudge growth up to 4.3 per cent in 2016 and 4.8 per cent in 2017. The decelerating Chinese economy, political tensions in Russia, declining confidence and lower oil prices point to a further short and medium-term GDP growth slowdown in this group. Growth in East and South Asia was 5.6 per cent in 2015 and is expected to rise only marginally to 5.8 per cent in 2016, mainly on concerns over the Chinese economy's health. Heightened volatility in financial markets coupled with strong capital outflows from China will continue weighing on regional GDP growth, particularly in Hong Kong and Taiwan (China), given their strong ties to China's economy.

Latin America and the Caribbean moved from 1.0 per cent growth in 2014 to a 0.6 per cent contraction in 2015, marking worsening economic activity for the third year, driven by slowing commodity exports from Bolivia, Brazil, Colombia, Chile, Ecuador and Venezuela. Lower commodity prices and subdued global trade, the economic slowdown in China and expectations of normalizing US monetary policy are the main factors affecting the region. The outlook is positive, however, with growth projected to recover to around 0.7 per cent in 2016.

Unemployment

Global unemployment—at 203 million—is estimated to have risen by 2 million in 2015, with an estimated youth unemployment rate of 13.1 per cent, (almost three times higher than adults), increasing from 13 per cent in 2014. Moderate economic growth in recent years has failed to create enough jobs to lower the high unemployment rate stemming from the global financial crisis. A total of 280 million jobs will be needed to bridge this gap (due to the crisis) over the next five years when taking into account new entrants in the labour market (ILO, 2015a). Global unemployment improved to 7.5 per cent in 2015 from 7.8 per cent in 2014 owing to the recovery in growth, though developed economies will continue to face a higher unemployment rate. In Africa and the Middle East, the unemployment rate was estimated at more than 15 per cent in 2015 and is projected to rise further.

In 2014, global unemployment stood at 201.3 million in 2014, up by 1.2 million from 2013 and by about 31 million from 2007. In 2014, close to 5.9 per cent of the labour force was without a job, with wide variations across countries. Some countries in Africa and the Middle East have up to 30 per cent unemployment (ILO, 2015a). There will be no relief among countries in the Middle East and North Africa, which have the world's highest unemployment rates. Africa as a whole, despite a relatively good performance less affected by the global economy's difficulties, will not see any real decline in its unemployment rate, stuck at around 10 per cent.

The global number of employed youth has been steadily decreasing for reasons beyond the business cycle. The global youth employment-to-population ratio—the share of the working-age population that is employed—declined by 2.7 percentage points between 2007 and 2014 (to 41.2 per cent). This ratio is declining in all regions except in Central, East, Southern and West Africa, which showed an increase from 46.9 per cent in 2000 to 48.0 per cent in 2014 (ILO, 2015b). But youth unemployment rates are expected to decline gradually in developed economies, particularly in the European Union (EU).

Inflation

Global inflation declined from 3.1 per cent in 2014 to 2.6 per cent in 2015, reflecting declines in commodity prices, especially oil, and weakened demand in many emerging and advanced economies. In developed economies, inflation is projected at 1.2 per cent in 2016, up from 0.3 per cent in 2015. Low inflation in Japan and the euro area is partly due to declining demand. In emerging and developing economies, domestic currencies depreciated because of low commodity prices, a strong US dollar and high food prices (which account for a large share in most countries' consumer price indices), lifting inflation from 6.7 per cent in 2014 to 7.7 per cent in 2015. The rise in inflation has been more pronounced in Africa's oil-exporting countries.

Commodity prices

Since mid-2014, global commodity prices have declined sharply. The global commodity price index of the International Monetary Fund (IMF) slid from 175 to 131 between August and December 2014 and to below 90.5 in December 2015, with crude oil prices tumbling to less than $37 a barrel. The fall in the oil price was driven by supply increases in oil production (including shale oil, mainly in the United States) and the subsequent shift in the strategy of the Organization of the Petroleum Exporting Countries (OPEC) of not easing production, alongside production increases outside OPEC and demand weakness in emerging market economies.

Average annual metal prices declined by 17 per cent in 2015 and are expected to continue falling in 2016, mainly driven by the slowdown in China's construction sector. Despite the overall decline of agricultural commodity prices—down 16 per cent in 2015 from 2014—global tea prices climbed slightly, supported by dry-weather concerns in Kenya and parts of Southern Africa. Overall food prices are expected to further increase in 2016 while vegetable oil prices, particularly those of wheat and soybeans, are projected to decline slightly (UN-DESA, 2016).

World trade and current account balance

At 2.6 per cent in 2015, world trade growth was at its slowest since the global financial crisis, reflecting a mix of factors: weak aggregate demand in emerging and developed economies, especially China and the euro area; the US dollar's appreciation; and rising geopolitical tensions in Iraq, Syria, Russia and Ukraine. They affected trade in developing countries, such as those in Africa. China, for example, accounts for more than 12 per cent of global merchandise exports and about 10 per cent of merchandise imports, so its demand slowdown has hit hard global demand for some commodities. China accounted for an estimated 20 per cent of the slowdown in developing and emerging economies' import growth between 2014 and 2015 (UN-DESA, 2016). In 2016, however, global trade growth is projected to accelerate to 4.0 per cent, due to strengthening demand from developed countries, which is expected to lift exports of developing countries in Latin America and Asia.

Global current account imbalances stayed stable in 2015 compared with 2014 and are projected to follow the same trend in the short term, despite weakening commodity prices. Growth in global net foreign direct investment (FDI) rose slightly in 2015, underpinned by an increase in net FDI in low-income developing countries of 5.3 per cent against 4.8 per cent growth in 2014 (World Bank, 2015a).

Risks

The global outlook in the short term is on balance slightly positive, with growth projected at 2.9 per cent in 2016. But persistent macroeconomic uncertainties and commodity-price volatility will continue shaping the medium-term outlook. Exchange rate volatility has become more pronounced against a backdrop of falling commodity prices, subdued global growth patterns, declining trade flows, declining capital flows and diverging monetary policies (UN-DESA, 2016).

Still, continuing lower oil prices may be good on balance for Africa given the number of oil importers, though oil exporters may well see their current account balances deteriorate and their currencies depreciate.

The overall impact on Africa will strongly depend on the recovery momentum in China and the euro area (Africa's main trading partners). Political tensions in Syria and elsewhere in the Middle East and massive illegal migration to the euro area are also serious concerns since they will directly affect demand from trading partners. Continued US monetary policy tightening will also have a tendency to attract capital from developing and emerging economies.

Africa's medium-term prospects remain positive, despite downside risks such as the drought in the Eastern and Southern parts of the region, which might seriously hit agricultural production since most of the economies are based on agriculture. A still-weak global economy, monetary tightening in the United States (US) and concerns over security and political instability in some countries remain challenges.

The task confronting Africa is not only to maintain rapid economic growth but also to transform into sustained and inclusive development, based on economic diversification that creates jobs, enhances access to basic services, reduces inequality and contributes to poverty eradication while not undermining the natural resource base. This challenge underlies renewed calls by countries for a structural transformation that fosters sustained and inclusive growth. Africa's industrialization and structural transformation should involve factor accumulation (including investment in natural capital), factor reallocation and organization, technological knowledge and innovation to drive the emergence of new, dynamic green activities, and an increase in the importance to national economies of green sectors such as organic agriculture, renewable energy and ecotourism.

Greening Africa's industrialization can be a major source of growth, providing opportunities to create jobs. The green sector can improve Africa's trade balance by reducing energy imports, and raise foreign exchange by exporting green goods and services. With most African countries sharing common environmental challenges, such greening would promote regional integration and cooperation and the growth of continent-wide innovation capabilities.

The rapid growth of the working age population (aged 25–64), increasing urbanization and the dominance of informal employment have weighty implications for the continent's structural transformation. While young people provide a valuable resource to be harnessed in national development, they can drive green industrialization only if they have green jobs in different sectors. And since most of these jobs are in urban areas, cities must also be included in Africa's green agenda.

The task confronting Africa is not only to maintain rapid economic growth but also to transform into sustained and inclusive development...

1.1 RECENT ECONOMIC DEVELOPMENTS IN AFRICA

Africa's growth rate declined slightly from 3.9 per cent in 2014 to 3.7 per cent in 2015 (figure 1.1), an average that masks high growth in several large economies, including Kenya (6.4 per cent) and Ethiopia (7.3 per cent). South Africa maintained its slow growth (1.8 per cent).

Growth in Africa remains driven by private consumption and investment (figure 1.2). Growth in private consumption is propelled by increased consumer confidence and an expanding middle class. Investment is stimulated mainly by an improved business environment and lower costs of doing business. Continued government spending on infrastructure has also contributed to growth. Net exports, hit by weak and volatile commodity prices, crimped growth.

PRIVATE CONSUMPTION REMAINS AFRICA'S MAIN GROWTH DRIVER

Relative to GDP, private consumption's growth increased from 1.6 per cent in 2014 to 2.7 per cent in 2015, representing 73 per cent of total GDP growth in the later year (figure 1.2). Despite increased African infrastructure development, gross fixed capital formation grew at only 1.0 per cent relative to GDP, accounting for 27 per cent of total GDP growth in 2015 (as in 2014). This was mainly because of the reduction in capital inflows tied to a slowing global economy, especially among Africa's development partners in the euro area and some emerging economies such as Brazil, China and the Russian Federation.

FIGURE 1.2 AFRICA'S GDP GROWTH AND ASSOCIATED COMPONENTS, 2013–2015

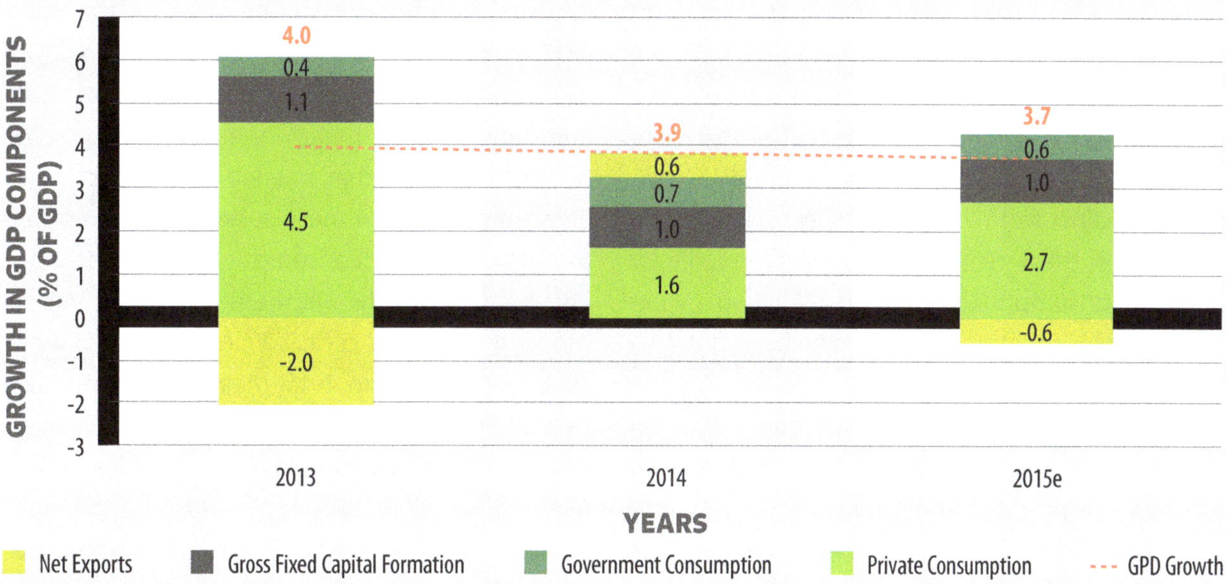

SOURCE: ECA CALCULATIONS BASED ON UN-DESA (2015) AND EIU (2015).
NOTE: e=ESTIMATES.

FIGURE 1.3 AFRICA'S GROWTH PERFORMANCE BY ECONOMIC GROUP, 2012–2015

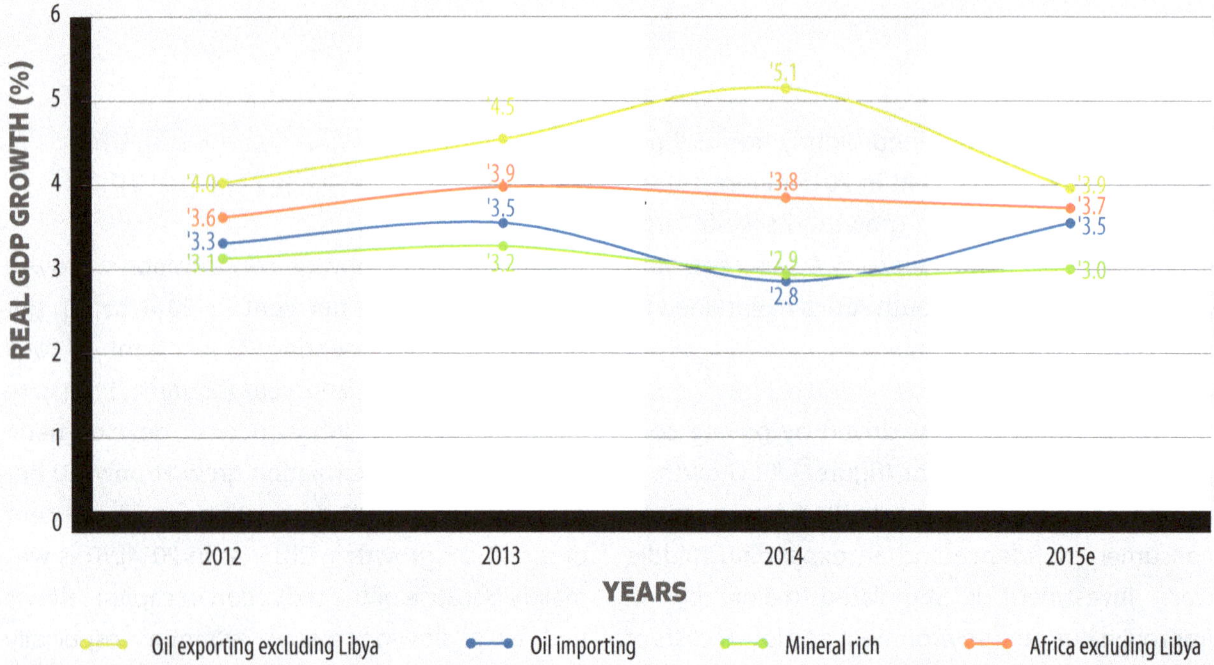

SOURCE: ECA CALCULATIONS, BASED ON UN-DESA (2015).
NOTE: e = ESTIMATES.

Despite low oil prices, oil-exporting countries, at 3.9 per cent growth, continue to perform well (as declining oil prices are partly cushioned by healthy dynamics in the non-oil sectors in some countries, such as increased investment in the agriculture, electricity, construction and technology sectors) compared with both oil-importing (3.5 per cent) and mineral-rich (3.0 per cent) countries, (figure 1.3). Mineral-rich countries saw a near-doubling in investment, from 0.7 per cent in 2014 to 1.3 per cent in 2015, and oil-exporting countries a marginal decline, from 1.6 per cent to 1.5 per cent. Growth in these two groups is driven mainly by private consumption, increasing at 2.5 and 3.2 per cent relative to total GDP, respectively (figure 1.4).

Growth in oil-importing countries moved up from 2.8 per cent in 2014 to 3.5 per cent in 2015; that in oil-exporting countries slid from 5.1 per cent to 3.9 per cent; and that in mineral-rich countries recorded a marginal increase from 2.9 per cent to 3.0 per cent. ECA analysis using monthly data from January 2000 to October 2015 shows that oil prices have had a statistically significant positive impact in oil-importing and mineral-rich countries, but a negative and insignificant impact on oil-exporting countries. The overall effect of low oil prices on Africa's growth thus appears marginal (box 1.2).

Private consumption continued to be the main GDP growth driver across subregions in 2015, despite the decline in its share to growth in East and Central Africa, mainly due to the global economic slowdown that has led to a reduction in investment flows to these subregions. Compared to GDP, private consumption increased significantly in North, Southern and West Africa, growing at 2.2 per cent, 2.1 per cent and 3.4 per cent, respectively, in 2015. Meanwhile, compared to total GDP, gross capital formation also increased significantly in the East and North Africa subregions, growing at 1.8 per cent and 1.6 per cent relative to GDP, respectively, mainly as a result of increased investments in infrastructure projects in both subregions.

BOX 1.2 LOW OIL PRICES HAVE A MARGINAL EFFECT ON OVERALL AFRICAN GROWTH

Crude oil prices continued to decline at a 4.1 per cent monthly average from June 2014 to October 2015. Higher supplies alongside lower demand (owing to the global economic slowdown) largely account for the decline (IMF, 2015).

BOX FIGURE 1.1 CRUDE OIL PRICE AND AFRICA'S GDP GROWTH, JANUARY 2007–OCTOBER 2015

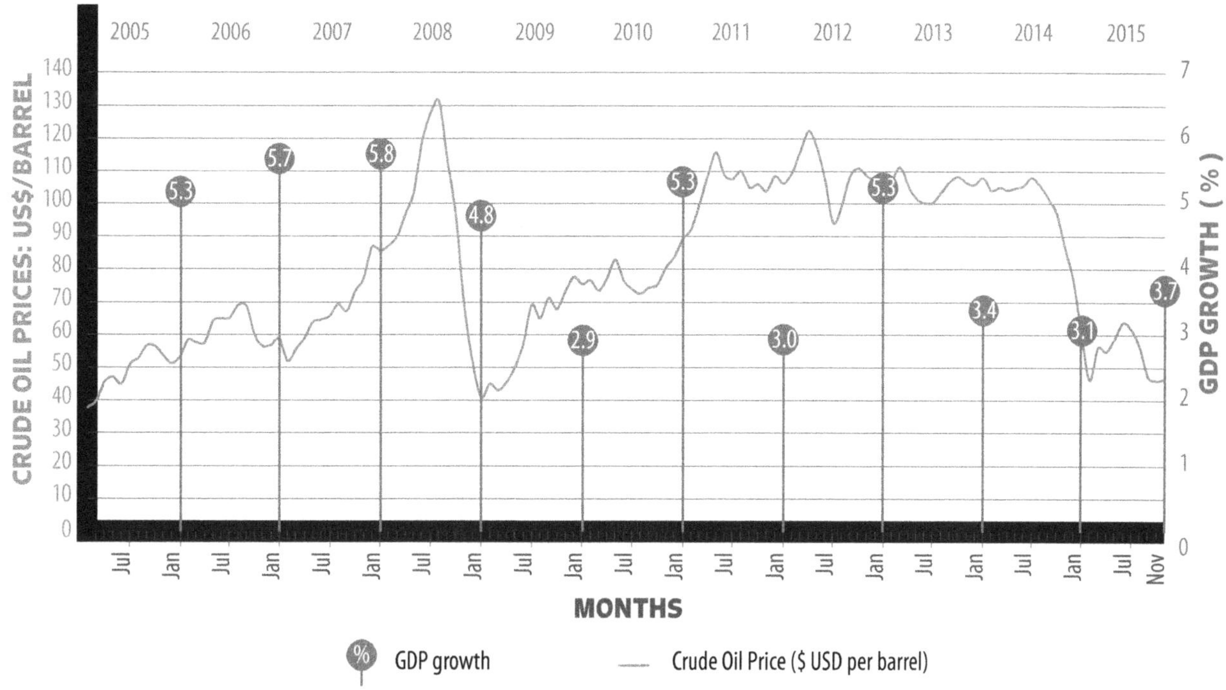

SOURCE: IMF (2015) AND UN-DESA (2015).

The oil decline's impact on Africa's growth is found to be marginal, since it contributed only about 0.08 percentage points to Africa's growth from January 2000 to October 2015; the oil-price shock contributed marginally to growth in the subperiod from June 2014 to October 2015.

By economic group, oil prices had a marginal negative impact on oil-exporting countries' growth, contributing 0.3 percentage points over the period January 2000-October 2015, but a positive and significant contribution to growth in oil-importing and mineral-rich countries, of 0.14 percentage points and 0.15 percentage points, respectively. This is despite the decline in oil prices having a marginal but insignificant negative impact on both oil-importing and mineral-rich countries in the subperiod from June 2014 to October 2015.

This marginal impact of the oil price decline emphasizes the importance of African countries continuing to diversify their economies, especially into non-oil sectors, and the impact of improved macroeconomic management and associated fiscal policies.

FIGURE 1.4 AFRICA'S GDP GROWTH AND ITS COMPONENTS BY ECONOMIC GROUP, 2013–2015

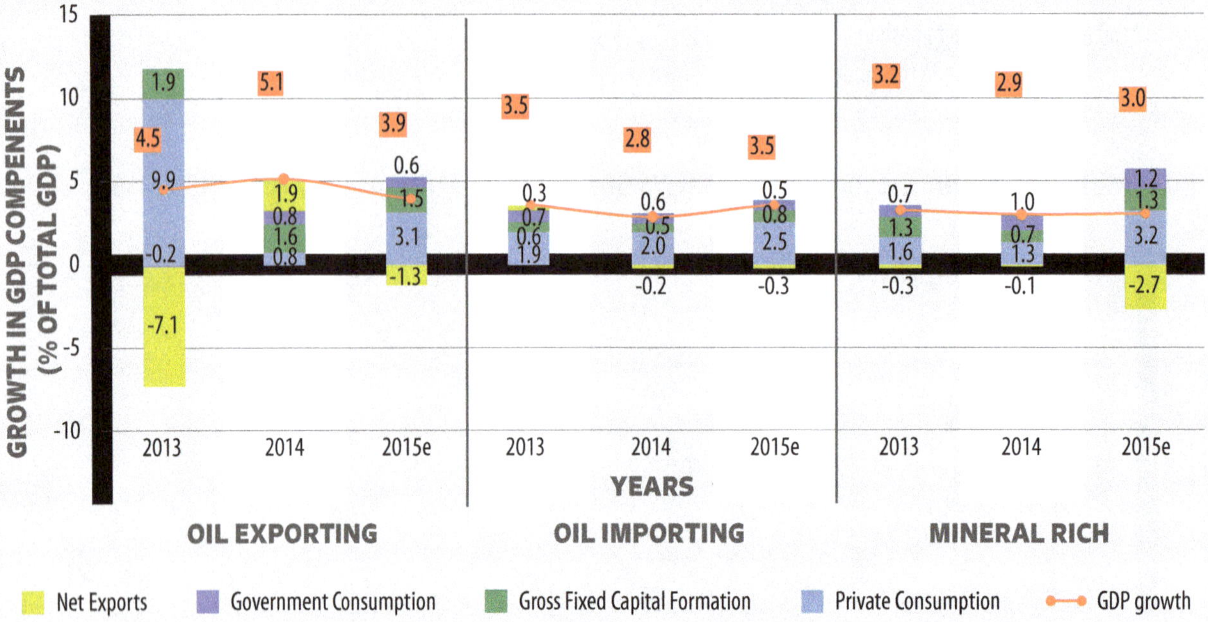

SOURCE: ECA CALCULATIONS, BASED ON EIU (2015).

NOTE: e = ESTIMATES.

VARYING GROWTH PERFORMANCE AMONG SUBREGIONS

East Africa maintained the highest growth rate in the region, at 6.2 per cent in 2015, despite a decline from 7.0 per cent in 2014 owing to slower growth in Ethiopia and Democratic Republic of Congo (DRC). Ethiopia's net exports suffered from low commodity prices and an increase in imports of capital goods and construction-related services. Its drought is one of the risks facing the country, particularly for food security. In DRC, the growing service sector and the dominant mining sector still drive growth, though political uncertainties in that country weigh on subregional growth. Infrastructure development, robust private consumption and exports drive growth in Ethiopia, Kenya and Tanzania.

Growth in West Africa slowed to 4.4 per cent in 2015, from 5.7 per cent in 2014, mainly because of slower growth in Nigeria, emanating from weaker oil prices, uncertainty surrounding the March 2015 elections, power outages and the war against Boko Haram. In Ghana, lower cocoa production and energy challenges slowed growth, while in Côte d'Ivoire continued public infrastructure investment and robust performance in services and agriculture supported growth. The Ebola outbreak's consequences in the three most affected countries—Guinea, Liberia and Sierra Leone—hit their expansion, even if Guinea and Liberia returned to positive growth.

In Central Africa, overall growth slipped from 3.5 per cent in 2014 to 3.4 per cent in 2015, despite improved mining performance. Most countries maintained relatively high growth, but security concerns in the Central African Republic (CAR) and lower oil production in Equatorial Guinea contributed to a decline in subregional GDP.

Growth in North Africa (excluding Libya) accelerated from 2.8 per cent in 2014 to 3.6 per cent in

2015, helped by improved political and economic stability, and a subsequent increase in business confidence, especially in Egypt and Tunisia. Heavy external aid to Egypt raised public expenditure and boosted investment in large infrastructure projects, such as the Suez Canal's expansion. The gradual recovery of export markets and hopes for improved security should support growth, especially through tourism. Algeria's oil production picked up for the first time in eight years and is boosting growth. Mauritania still has the fastest (and steadiest) growth in the region, supported by sound macroeconomic and structural policies. Growth was buttressed by mining and construction, and by private consumption and investment—exceptionally high investment of about 45 per cent of GDP bodes well for the future. Continuing political challenges in Libya continue to hurt political and economic governance in the subregion.

Southern Africa's growth increased marginally from 2.4 per cent in 2014 to 2.5 per cent in 2015, heavily influenced by poor growth in the subregion's largest economy, South Africa. Weak export demand and low prices for key raw materials, as well as electricity shortages, subdued South Africa's performance. In Angola, GDP growth remained strong despite low oil prices, as the government embarked on investing in strategic non-oil sectors such as electricity, construction and technology. Mozambique and Zambia recorded the highest growth in the region, driven respectively by large infrastructure projects and FDI in mining.

LOW COMMODITY PRICES AND LARGE INVESTMENT PROJECTS EXPLAIN GROWING FISCAL DEFICITS

Africa's aggregate fiscal deficit increased from 5.1 per cent of GDP in 2014 to 5.6 per cent in 2015 (figure 1.5). The continuing decline of oil prices and other volatile (and largely declining) commodity

In Angola, GDP growth remained strong despite low oil prices, as the government embarked on investing in strategic non-oil sectors such as electricity, construction and technology.

prices reduced fiscal revenue in many countries, whereas high spending on infrastructure, fiscal loosening and higher spending in the lead-up to elections in some countries raised government spending. The fiscal deficit is expected to narrow in 2016 to 4.6 per cent of GDP as growth in emerging and developed economies, and commodity prices (of some commodities in the near term), are expected to pick up (UN-DESA 2016).

The fiscal deficit was the largest in the North African subregion, widening from 9.7 per cent of GDP in 2014 to 10.0 per cent in 2015. Increased spending on large public investments, continued subsidies for basic goods (in, for example, Morocco and Tunisia) and election-related expenditure (in Morocco) continued to exert pressure on public spending.

In West Africa, the fiscal deficit widened from 2.0 per cent in 2014 to 2.5 per cent in 2015, mainly driven by deteriorating fiscal balances in Nigeria and Ghana. But in Nigeria, low oil prices' impact on fiscal balance is, to some extent, offset by the use of the buffers from oil-revenue savings and improved non-oil sector performance led by the services sector. In East Africa, the deficit increased from 3.8 to 4.6 per cent due to expansionary fiscal policies, mainly through increased spending on infrastructure and mining activities in Ethiopia, Kenya, Madagascar, Tanzania and Uganda.

FIGURE 1.5 AVERAGE BUDGET BALANCE BY SUBREGION, 2012–2016

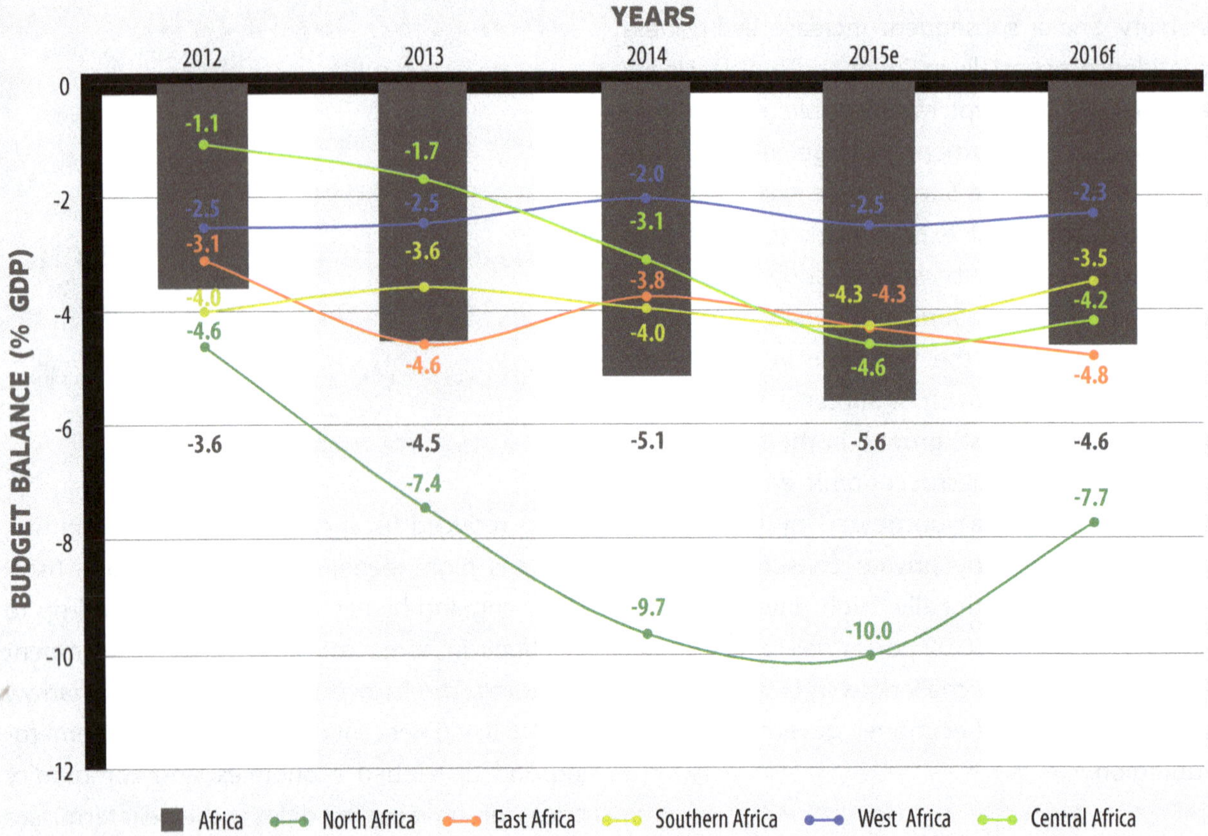

SOURCE: ECA CALCULATIONS, BASED ON EIU (2015).

NOTE: e = ESTIMATES; f = FORECASTS.

FIGURE 1.6 AVERAGE BUDGET BALANCE BY ECONOMIC GROUP, 2012–2016

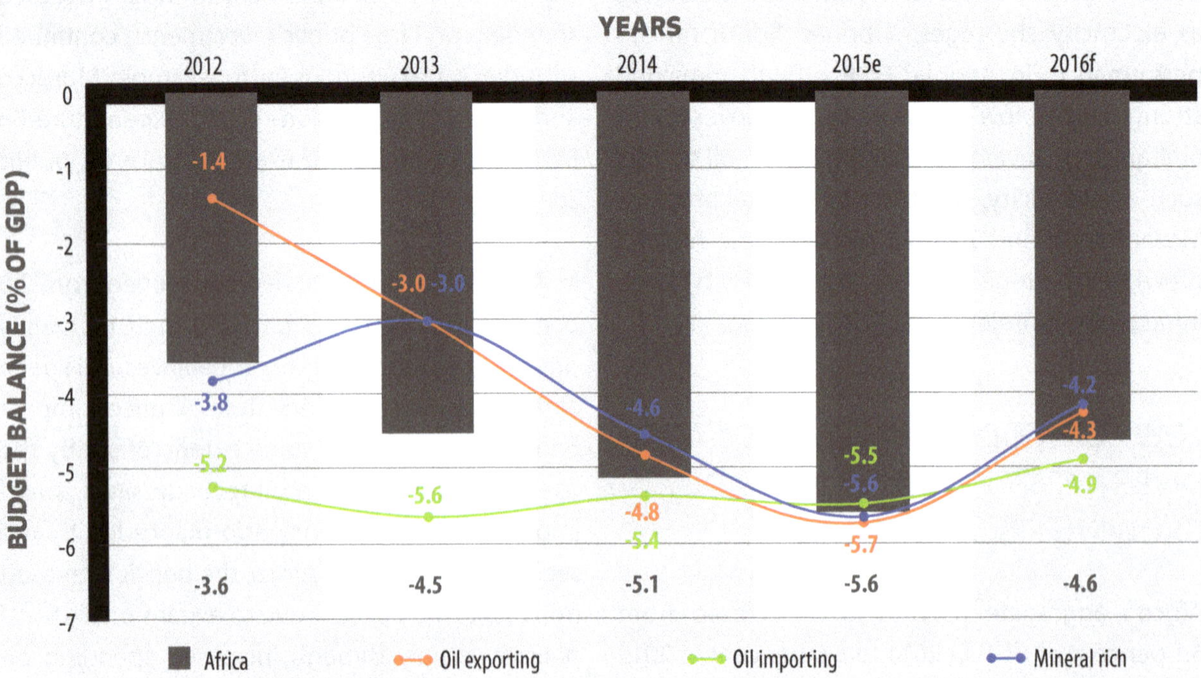

SOURCE: ECA CALCULATIONS, BASED ON EIU (2015).

NOTE: e = ESTIMATES; f = FORECASTS.

FIGURE 1.7 INFLATION BY ECONOMIC GROUP, 2012–2016

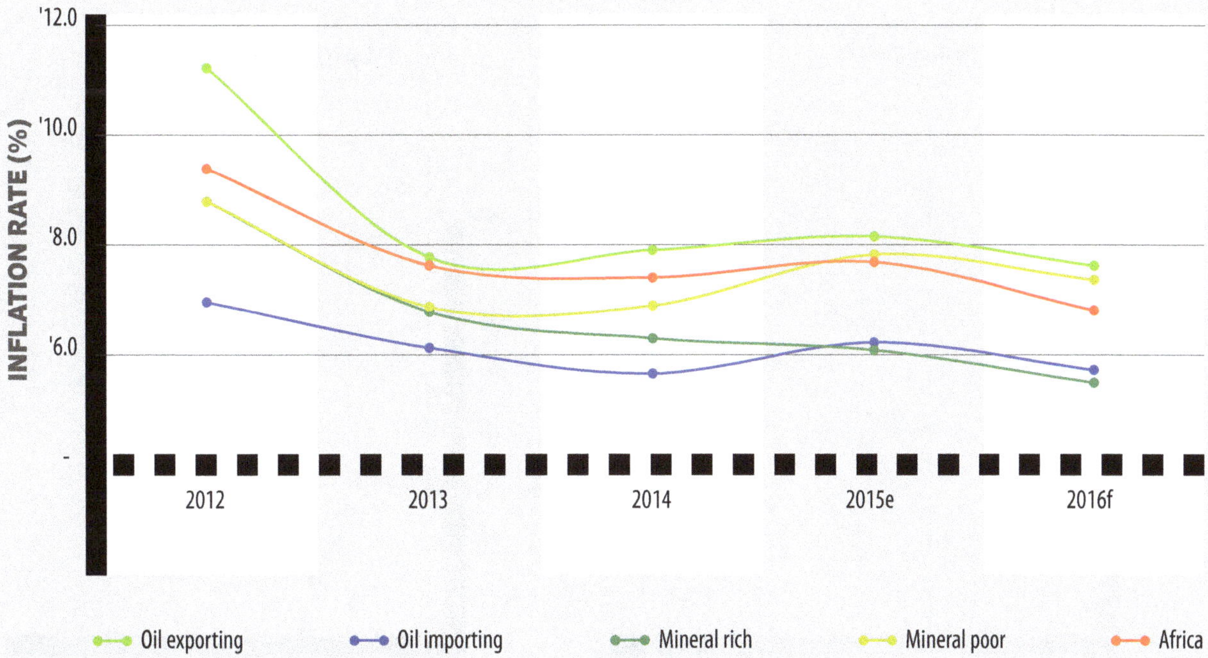

SOURCE: ECA CALCULATIONS, BASED ON UN-DESA (2015).
NOTE: e = ESTIMATES; f = FORECASTS.

Central Africa saw its fiscal balance deteriorate the most, from 3.1 per cent to 4.6 per cent, mirroring expansionary fiscal policies, including infrastructure development in Cameroon, Chad, Republic of Congo and Equatorial Guinea (though with swinging cuts in recurrent expenditure) and election spending in Chad and Republic of Congo. In Southern Africa, the deficit expanded from 4.0 per cent to 4.3 per cent of GDP, largely in response to low commodity prices, which have affected the mining sector in Botswana, South Africa and Zambia and the oil sector in Angola.

Fiscal deficits are expected to improve in 2016 to 4.6 per cent of GDP, and in all subregions except East Africa, where the deficit is forecast to widen to 4.8 per cent. Despite efforts to mobilize tax revenue and restrain expenditure in Rwanda, security concerns in Kenya weigh on tourism, the country's main source of foreign exchange.

Largely driven by low oil prices, oil-exporting countries' fiscal deficits reached their widest as a share of GDP (since 2012) at 5.7 per cent, but they are projected to narrow to 4.3 per cent in 2016, with prices of some commodities (in the near term) are envisaged to recover and as some oil-exporters remove subsidies to alleviate pressure on their national budgets (figure 1.6). But with oil prices projected to remain low, fiscal revenue is not expected to move back to earlier levels in oil-exporting countries.

MONETARY POLICY WAS TIGHTENED AMID FALLING COMMODITY PRICES AND DECLINING REVENUE

African countries exercised tight monetary policy in response to inflationary pressure and high fiscal and current account deficits. Inflation rose from 7.0 per cent in 2014 to 7.5 per cent in 2015 (figure 1.7). A strong US dollar and high food prices exerted inflationary pressure on the region despite partly offsetting weak global growth and low commod-

FIGURE 1.8 REAL EXCHANGE RATE AND EXPORTS AND IMPORTS OF GOODS AND SERVICES, AS PERCENTAGE OF GDP, AFRICA, 2000–2014

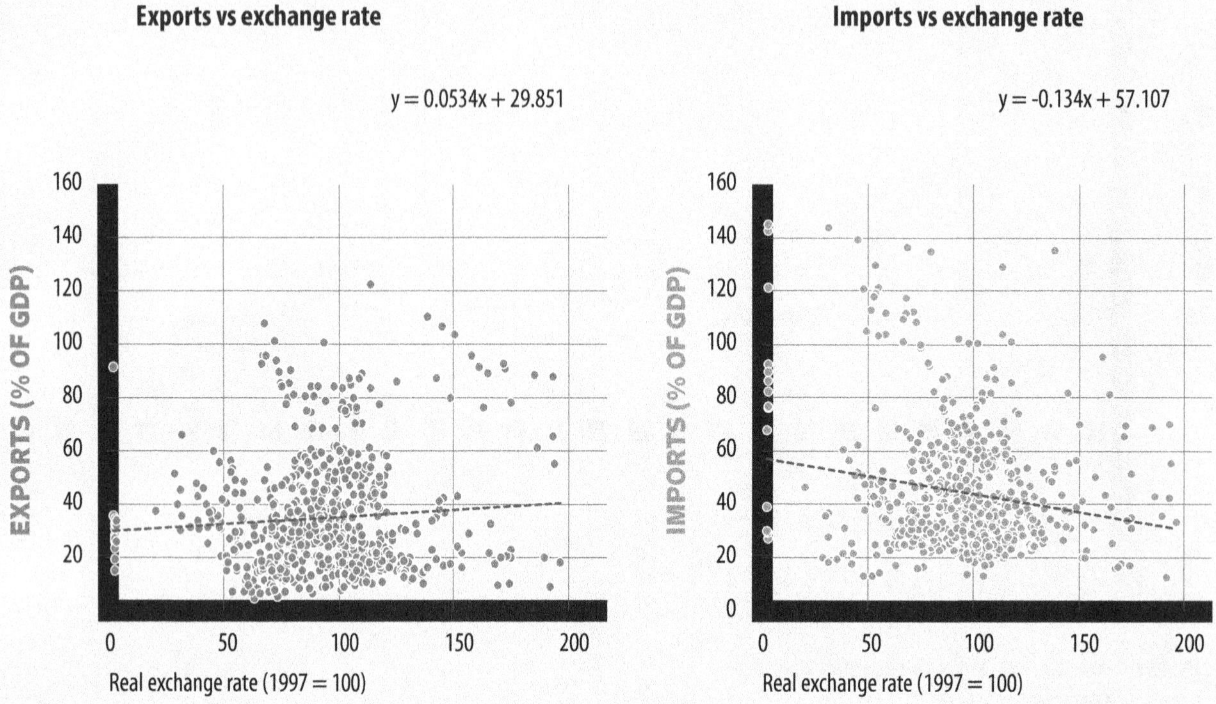

SOURCE: ECA CALCULATIONS BASED ON EIU (2015) AND WORLD BANK (2015b).

NOTE: AN INCREASE IN THE EXCHANGE RATE INDEX INDICATES AN APPRECIATION OF THE CURRENCY.

ity prices. Currency depreciation, especially in oil-rich countries, amid falling oil prices and declining revenue and exports contributed to African inflation. Countries hiking policy rates to keep inflation in check included Angola, Ghana, Kenya, Malawi, South Africa and Uganda.

EXCHANGE RATES DEPRECIATED, THOUGH GENERALLY FAILED TO LIFT EXPORTS

Most African currencies depreciated in 2015, continuing a trend from 2014, driven partly by low oil prices, a strong US dollar and the expected tightening of US monetary policy. Currency depreciation should in theory see increased exports and decreased imports, but for African countries that association seems either weak or non-existent (figure 1.8).

This link's weakness could point to other factors behind Africa's lack of competitiveness, undermining depreciation's benefits. The decline in imports *and* exports during an exchange rate depreciation may suggest a lack of production diversification (since there are no local substitutes for expensive imports in terms of production inputs and final goods) and of value added, even if the cost of doing business in Africa has fallen.

For some of the continent's larger economies including Kenya, Nigeria and South Africa, the association between the real exchange rate depreciation and increased exports becomes stronger (figure 1.9). But the relationship between imports and the real exchange rate remains negative for Nigeria and South Africa, possibly reflecting reliance on imported inputs. For Kenya, the relationship is positive, as expected.

FIGURE 1.9 REAL EXCHANGE RATE AND EXPORTS AND IMPORTS OF GOODS AND SERVICES, AS A PERCENTAGE OF GDP, KENYA, NIGERIA AND SOUTH AFRICA, 2000–2014

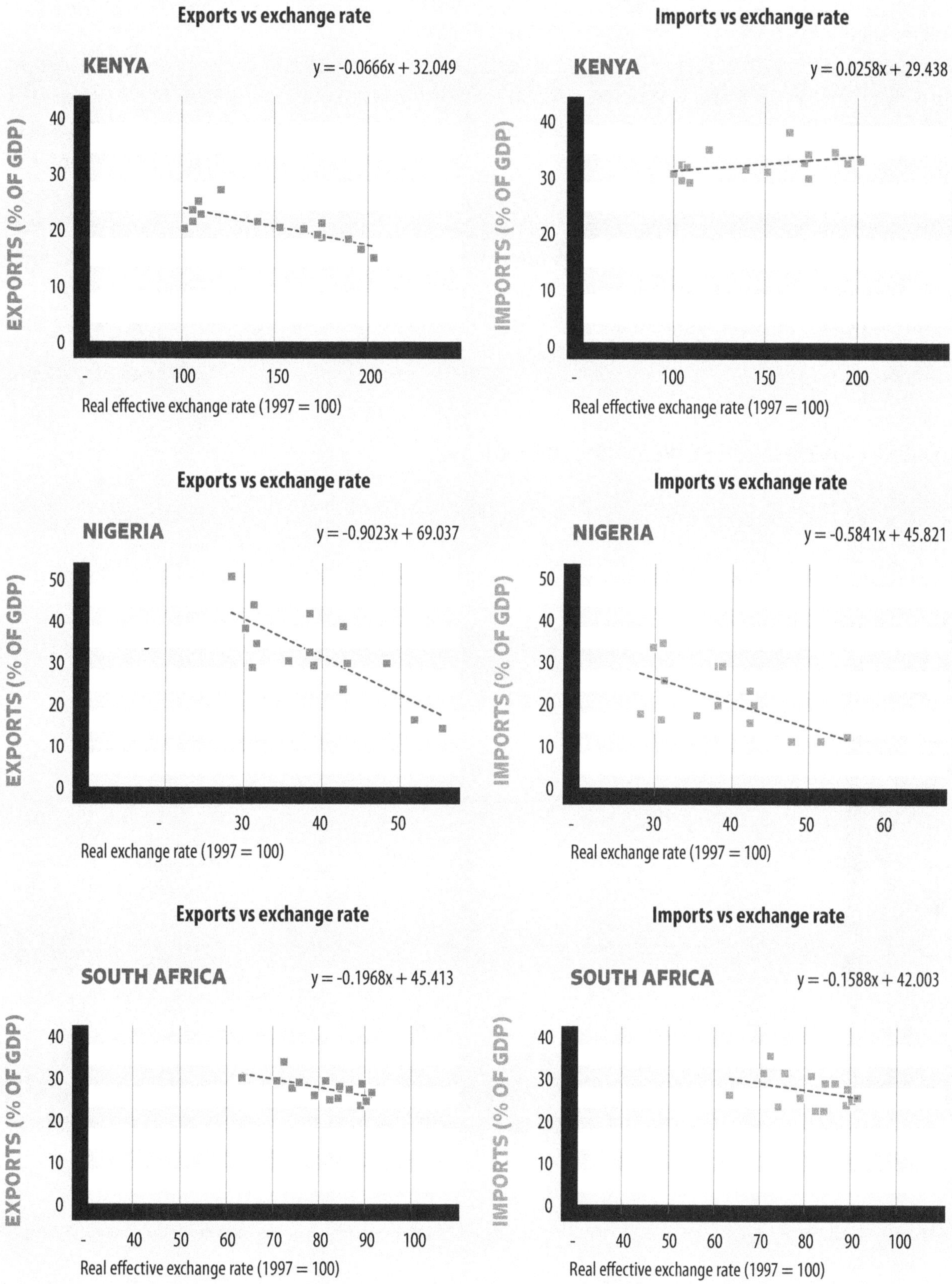

SOURCE: ECA CALCULATIONS BASED ON EIU (2015) AND WORLD BANK (2015b).

REGIONAL INFLATION REMAINED STABLE WITH LOW OIL PRICES

Regional inflation reached 7.5 per cent in 2015 up from 7.2 per cent in 2014, but is forecast to decline to 6.7 per cent in 2016 and 6.3 per cent in 2017 (figure 1.10). Inflationary pressure was reduced by lower global oil prices and the continuing fall in food prices since 2011 (estimated at a further 14 per cent drop in 2015),[1] while currency depreciations increased the risk of imported inflation. Prudent monetary policy in countries such as Kenya and South Africa have moderated inflation. Slightly lower inflation is expected in 2016 because of lower food and energy prices, improved security and diminished impacts of subsidy cuts in 2014.

Inflation increased in all the subregions except North Africa, where it declined from 9.3 per cent in 2014 to 8.4 per cent in 2015. Inflation in Sudan tumbled from 37.7 per cent to 22.0 per cent, but remained stable (or increased) in all other countries in the subregion. The fall in Sudan was driven by the decline in international food prices (as food items constitute the largest proportion of the country's total imports) and central bank measures to contain inflation.

FIGURE 1.10 INFLATION BY SUBREGION, 2012–2016

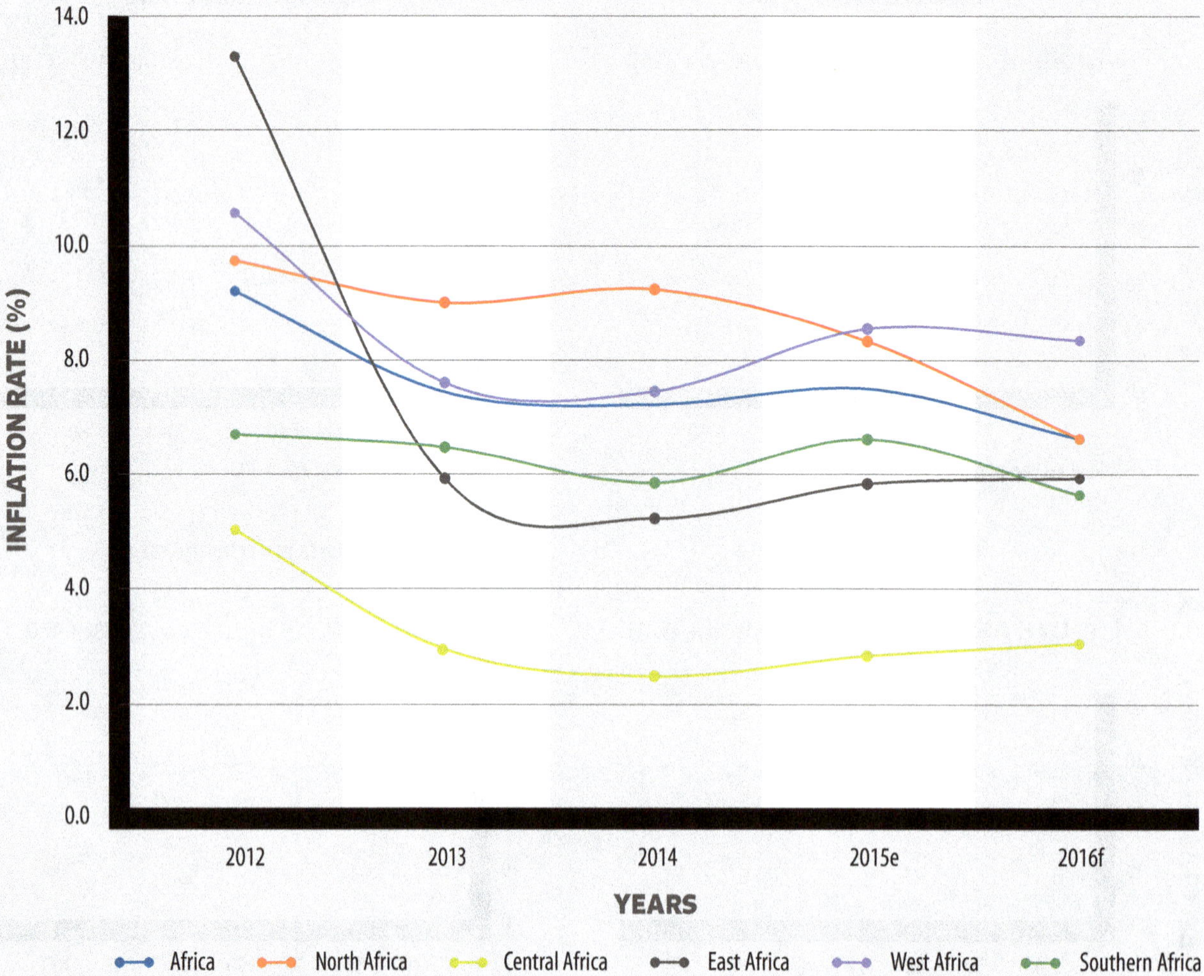

SOURCE: UN-DESA (2015).
NOTE: e = ESTIMATES; f = FORECASTS.

Inflation in East Africa rose from 5.3 per cent in 2014 to 5.9 per cent in 2015. In Kenya, it went down from 6.9 to 6.3 per cent and remained unchanged in Tanzania at 6.1 per cent. But it climbed steeply in Burundi (from 4.4 to 7.4 per cent), Ethiopia (from 7.4 to 10 per cent) and Uganda (from 4.3 to 5.7 per cent), respectively, reflecting, political instability, weather-related shocks and consequent increases in domestic food prices, and a depreciation of the domestic currency and rise in domestic food prices.

The euro's depreciation against the dollar depreciated the CFA franc in 2015, feeding a rise in West African inflation from 7.5 per cent in 2014 to 8.6 per cent. Public spending in Nigeria and currency depreciations in Ghana and Nigeria also added to subregional inflationary pressure.

Inflation was 6.6 per cent in Southern Africa in 2015, up from 5.9 per cent the previous year. While many countries in the subregion recorded falling inflation, the rise in inflation in Angola (from 7.5 to 11.0 per cent), Mozambique (from 2.6 to 4.5 per cent) and South Africa (from 5.3 to 5.9 per cent) stoked subregional inflationary pressure. Inflation was fueled mainly by currency depreciations, reductions of subsidies or rises in regulated fuel and utility prices (as in Angola, Malawi and Mozambique). Low oil prices and prudent monetary policy softened South Africa's inflationary pressure.

In Central Africa inflation remained fairly stable, edging up from 2.5 per cent in 2014 to 2.8 per cent in 2015, largely on the declines in oil prices and global demand.

The continent's imports are dominated by consumer goods, its exports by primary commodities: fuels, bituminous minerals and agricultural products such as cocoa, fruits, fertilizers and vegetables.

ALL ECONOMIC GROUPS AND SUBREGIONS RECORDED CURRENT ACCOUNT DEFICITS

The continent's current account deficit widened from 3.9 per cent of GDP in 2014 to 5.0 per cent in 2015, with all economic groups reporting deficits (figure 1.11). Declining commodity prices and global demand especially in emerging economies were major factors, with oil-exporting African countries together recording their first current account deficit since 2009 in 2014 (of 2.1 per cent), and a deficit of 5.1 per cent in 2015. Low oil prices narrowed oil importers' aggregate deficit. Of the subregions, the current account deficit was largest for Central Africa (8.1 per cent), followed by East Africa (7.4 per cent), Southern Africa (5.7 per cent), North Africa (5.3 per cent) and West Africa (3.1 per cent).

Africa's total exports of goods and services fell by 3.2 per cent in 2013 and by 5.2 per cent in 2014, while total imports grew by 3.0 per cent and by 1.7 per cent over the two years. The continent's imports are dominated by consumer goods, its exports by primary commodities: fuels, bituminous minerals and agricultural products such as cocoa, fruits, fertilizers and vegetables. By value,

FIGURE 1.11 CURRENT ACCOUNT BALANCE, 2013–2016

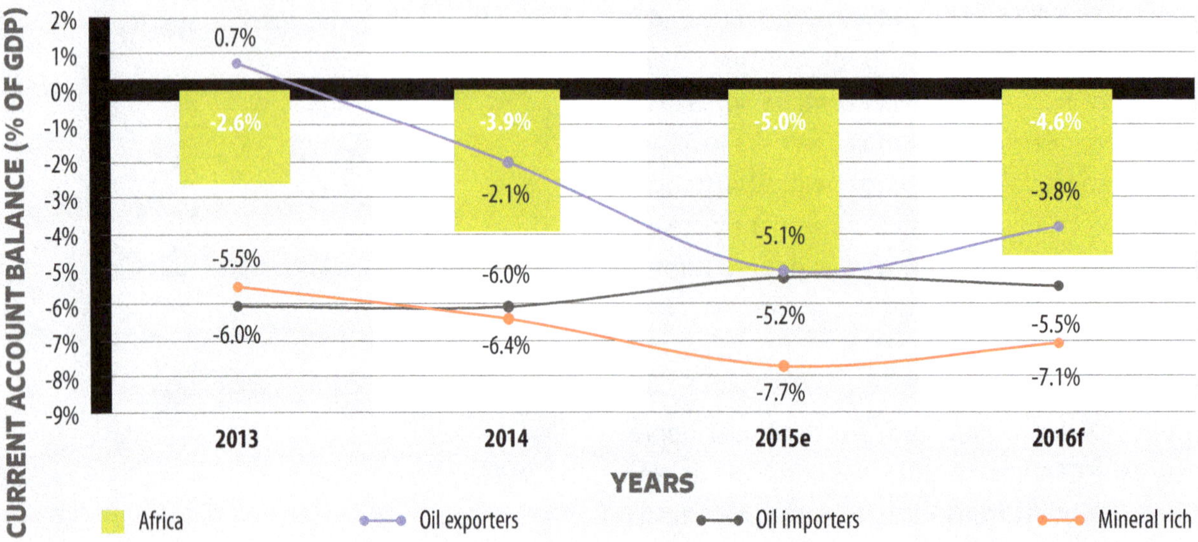

SOURCE: ECA CALCULATIONS BASED ON EIU (2015).
NOTE: e = ESTIMATES; f = FORECASTS.

fuel exports fell by 13.2 per cent and ore and metal exports by 8.2 per cent in 2014. On a positive note, whereas Africa's exports to most of its trading partners have stagnated or even declined since the global economic crisis, intra-African trade remains relatively strong by volume, and diversified towards manufactured products and services (ECA, 2015a). Manufactured goods as a proportion of total intra-African merchandise exports stood at 41 per cent in 2014, down from 44 per cent in 2013, while fuel exports stood at 31 per cent in 2014, up from 29 per cent in 2013.[2]

Heavy dependence on natural capital, coupled with the high growth needed for the continent to achieve its economic and social development goals (including industrialization and structural transformation) will raise energy demand and greenhouse gas emissions. These outcomes will harm the environment unless African nations adopt green growth strategies, particularly renewable energy technologies to cut carbon emissions. Indeed, the uptake of renewables is a primary means of cutting carbon emissions globally, even though the continent (excluding South Africa) accounts for less than 1 per cent of global carbon emissions, owing to its low electricity consumption (ICA, 2011). As highlighted in this report's thematic part, Africa has an enormous opportunity for greening its industrialization, mainly through the electricity subsector.

NET DEBT INCREASES ON THE BACK OF LOWER LENDING BY OIL-EXPORTING COUNTRIES; FDI REMAINS STABLE

Falling oil and other commodity prices drew down African countries' international reserves, to 15.8 per cent of GDP in 2015, from 17.1 per cent the year before. They also raised their net debt sharply, from 5.8 per cent of GDP in 2014 to 9.9 per cent in 2015, up from a mere 1.6 per cent in 2013 (figure 1.12). The main reason was a sharp fall in net lending of countries in North Africa and the oil-exporting countries. Central Africa's net debt jumped from 4.0 to 12.0 per cent of GDP, as net debt doubled as a share of GDP in Cameroon and Gabon, and net lending fell to a third for Republic of Congo. Total African debt rose from 22.9 per cent of GDP to 25.7 per cent in 2015, and is forecast to rise further to 26.3 per cent in 2016 (figure 1.13).

FIGURE 1.12 NET AFRICAN DEBT, 2014–2016

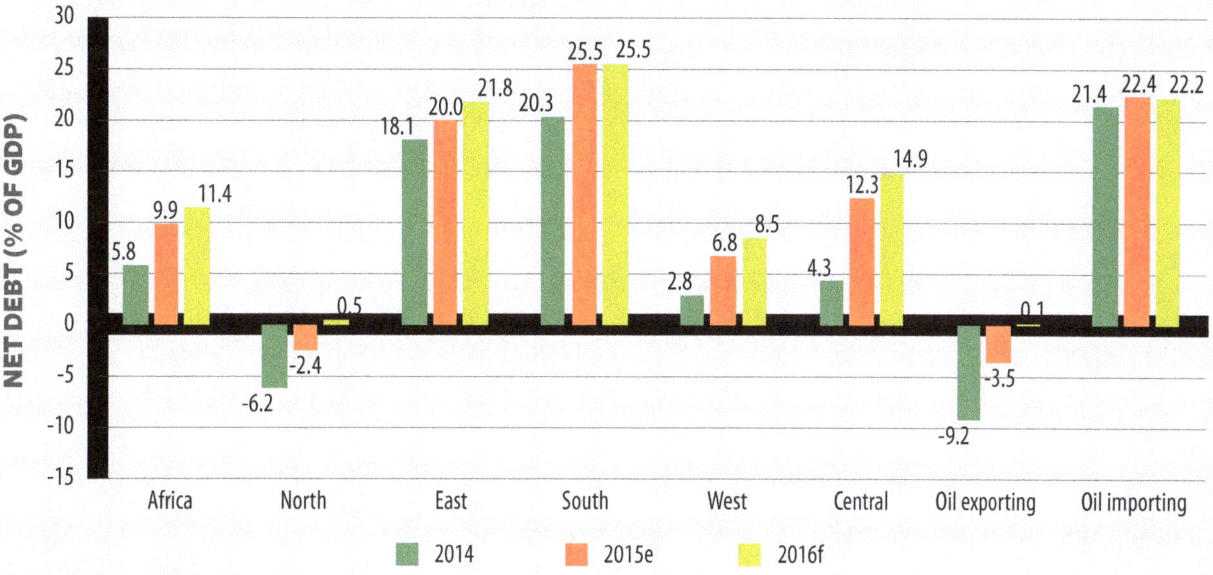

SOURCE: ECA CALCULATIONS BASED ON EIU (2015).
NOTE: E = ESTIMATES; F = FORECASTS.

FIGURE 1.13 TOTAL AFRICAN DEBT, 2014–2016

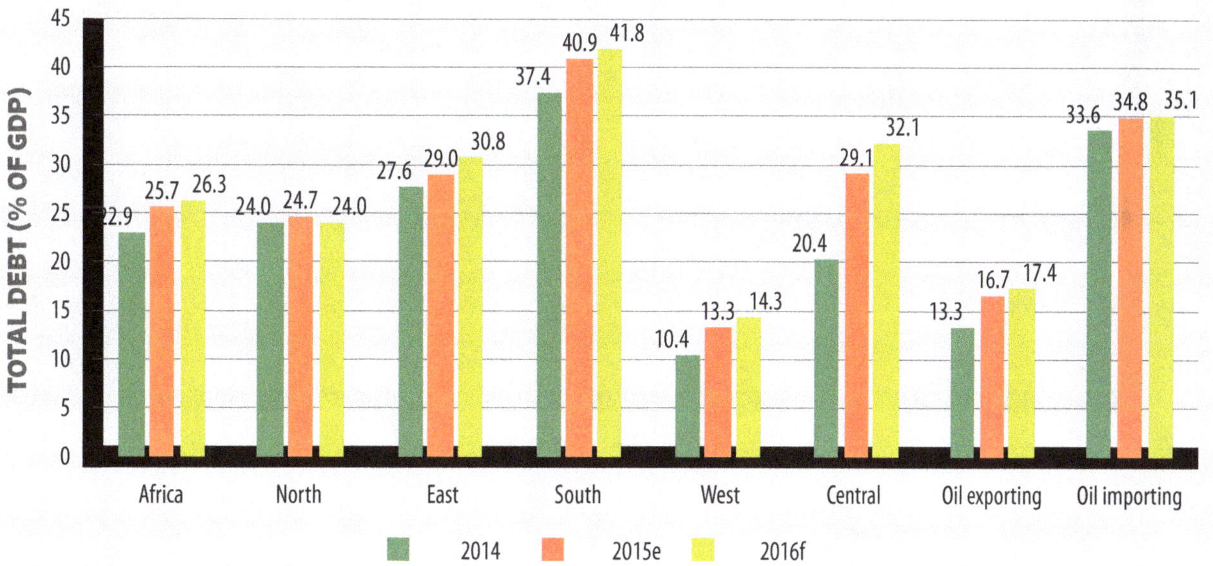

SOURCE: ECA CALCULATIONS BASED ON EIU (2015).
NOTE: E = ESTIMATES; F = FORECASTS.

African countries' incoming FDI, stable in 2015 at around 3 per cent of GDP, is expected to remain around this rate in 2016 and 2017 (UNCTAD, 2016). A North African recovery was reflected in the pickup of FDI inflows, from 1.4 per cent to 1.7 per cent growth. Southern Africa (particularly Angola, Mozambique, South Africa and Zambia) and Central Africa have been the main FDI destinations, with East Africa (particularly Ethiopia, Kenya and Tanzania) also attracting substantial flows.

Manufacturing is the destination of one-third of FDI by function, an encouraging sign of the changing perceptions of Africa, though extraction remains the target, with 26.0 per cent and construction 14.0 per cent of the total. Coal, oil and natural gas dominate at 38.0 per cent of the total, showing scope for investment to diversify from primary commodities and construction. FDI into Africa has been driven partly by strong economic growth in key economies and by low interest rates in Europe and the United States. With US monetary tightening expected to continue in 2016, some capital flows may switch to mature markets.

FIGURE 1.14 AFRICA'S GROWTH BY ECONOMIC GROUP, 2014–2017

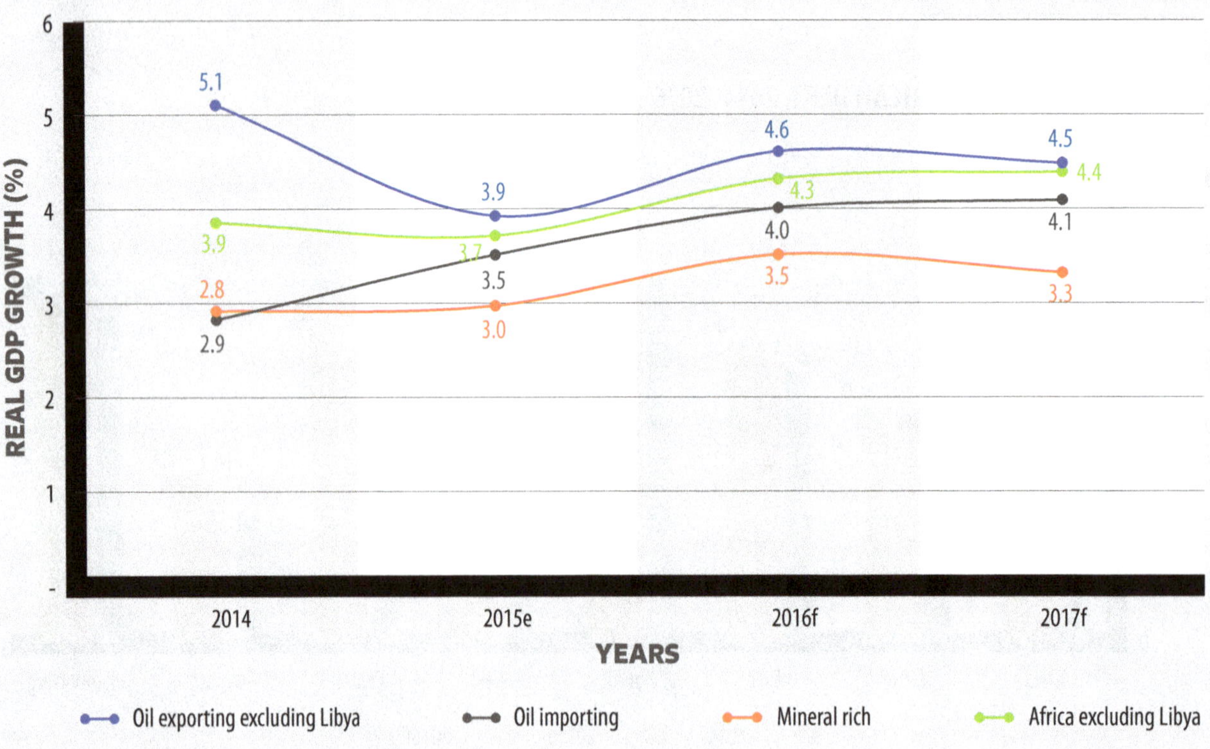

SOURCE: ECA CALCULATIONS BASED ON UN-DESA (2015).
NOTE: e = ESTIMATES; f = FORECASTS.

1.2 MEDIUM-TERM PROSPECTS AND A CHANCE TO CHANGE

GROWTH PROSPECTS

Africa's real GDP growth is expected to increase by about 4.3 per cent in 2016 and 4.4 per cent in 2017 (figure 1.14), led by strong domestic demand and by investment, particularly in infrastructure. The buoyant service sector and oil-exporting economies' focus on non-oil sectors mitigate the impact of the oil price decline, contributing to better medium-term prospects. Increasing trade and investment ties within Africa and between Africa and emerging economies, and the recovery of traditional export markets, particularly in the euro area, also lift the outlook.

At the subregional level, Southern and West Africa are expected to enjoy real GDP growth in both forecast years, but Central, East and North Africa are forecast to see a rise in 2016 and a slight decline in 2017 (figure 1.15).

West Africa's growth is projected to increase to about 5.2 per cent in 2016 and 5.3 per cent in 2017, boosted mainly by an improving economic performance in Nigeria, with its emphasis on diversifying investments into non-oil sectors. In Southern Africa, growth is forecast to increase to 3.0 per cent in 2016 and 3.3 per cent in 2017, mainly because of expected investment increases in strategic non-oil

FIGURE 1.15 AFRICA'S GROWTH PROSPECTS BY SUBREGION, 2014–2017

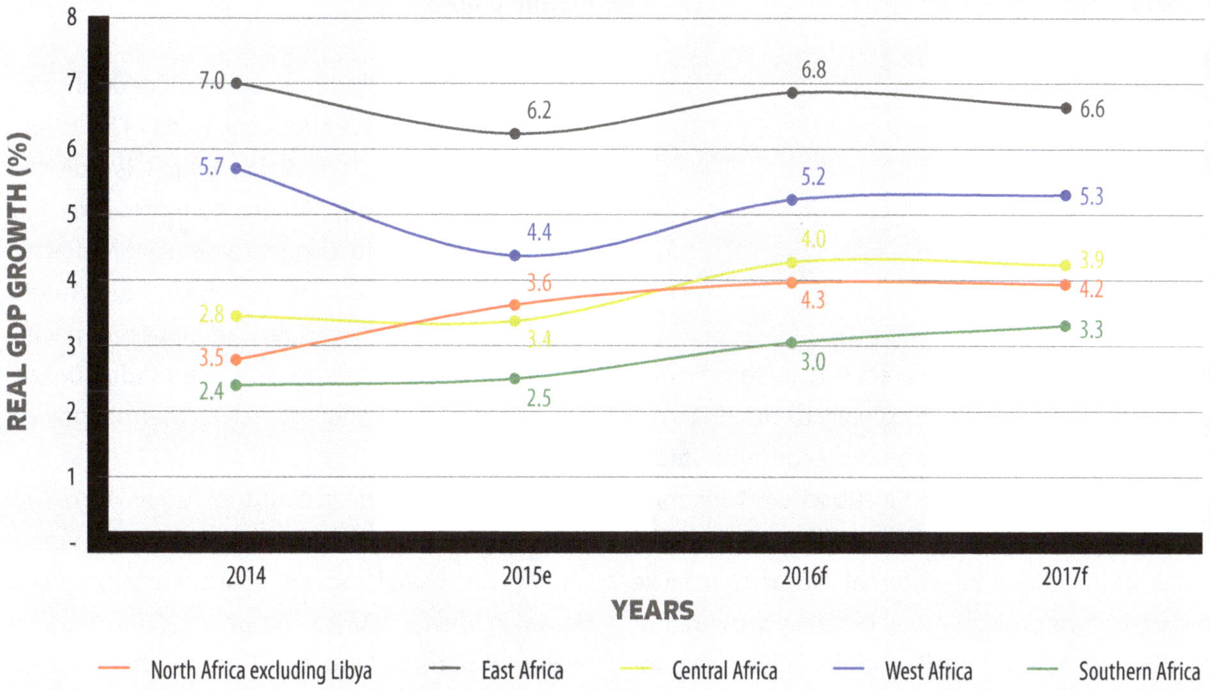

SOURCE: ECA CALCULATIONS BASED ON UN-DESA (2015).

NOTE: e = ESTIMATES; f = FORECASTS.

sectors, such as electricity, construction and technology, in large infrastructure projects and in mining.

East Africa's growth is set to lead the rest of the subregions, rising by 6.8 per cent in 2016 and 6.6 per cent in 2017, bucked by robust growth in countries such as Ethiopia, Rwanda and Tanzania—this despite low commodity prices, rising imports of capital goods for infrastructure (instead of productive capacities) and the aftermath of the recent drought. Central Africa is expected to see growth rise to 4.3 per cent in 2016, driven by investment in energy and infrastructure and strong service sector performance.

Low oil prices will hurt hydrocarbon-exporting countries, but on balance may be positive for Africa as a whole.

In North Africa, growth is forecast to increase to 4.3 per cent in 2016 before marginally declining to 4.2 per cent. Improved political and economic stability in the subregion—and a subsequent increase in business confidence (especially in Egypt and Tunisia), in inflows of external aid and in large infrastructure projects—will buttress growth. But continuing political challenges in Libya will continue to affect the subregion's political and economic governance.

RISKS

The global economy's weak recovery affects Africa's performance through trade, investment and remittances. Besides China's economic deceleration, the Eurozone's subdued (though improving) performance is a concern. Likely solid performance by India and Africa may, however, buffer the trade impact. Low oil prices will hurt hydrocarbon-exporting countries, but on balance may be positive for Africa as a whole. The depreciation of major African currencies, while possibly beneficial for exports (see the earlier discussion, "Exchange rates depreciated, though generally failed to lift exports") is likely to put pressure on monetary stability through imported inflation.

FDI flows are expected to remain steady at about 3 per cent of GDP, but the Federal Reserve's monetary policy presents a risk over the medium term. Low interest rates have increased speculative investors' appetite for emerging markets, and US policy rate rises may divert some flows back to mature markets.

Regional risks include weather-related shocks. Drought in East Africa and some parts of Southern Africa could hurt agriculture, which is still the main employer in most African countries (box 1.3). Poor harvests would also increase risk of inflation through higher food prices. And the drought may affect the hydropower generation capacity, threatening the greening of Africa's industrialization as economic agents switch to thermal power.

Security in some African countries remains an issue, especially in Egypt, Kenya, Libya and Tunisia, where security concerns have hurt tourism receipts. Boko Haram in Western Africa and political unrest in, for example, Burkina Faso and Burundi, may disrupt domestic economic activity and reduce foreign investment.

BOX 1.3 DROUGHT IN SOUTHERN AFRICA AND THE HORN OF AFRICA—IMPACT ON GROWTH

Both the direct and indirect impacts of climate change are felt in many parts of the world, including Africa. With El Niño's recent increase in intensity, high temperatures are likely to continue in 2016, affecting most of Africa's large and fast-growing economies.

The Horn of Africa and Southern Africa, where some countries have grown fast over the past 15 years (box figure 1.2), are experiencing severe drought and may well continue to do so with rising carbon emissions (Oxfam, 2015). South Africa, Africa's second-largest economy, declared five of its nine provinces drought-disaster areas in late 2015. In Ethiopia—the fastest-growing economy in the world (with Turkmenistan) in 2014, at 10.3 per cent—severe drought is decimating crops, livestock and water, leaving 4.5 million people in need of food relief in August 2015.

The impact of the drought is likely to hurt African economies because 94 per cent of their agricultural output is rain fed, and the major source of energy generation is hydroelectricity (WWF, 2011). Forecasters predict little rain in the months ahead.

BOX FIGURE 1.2 AVERAGE ANNUAL GDP GROWTH, 2000–2014

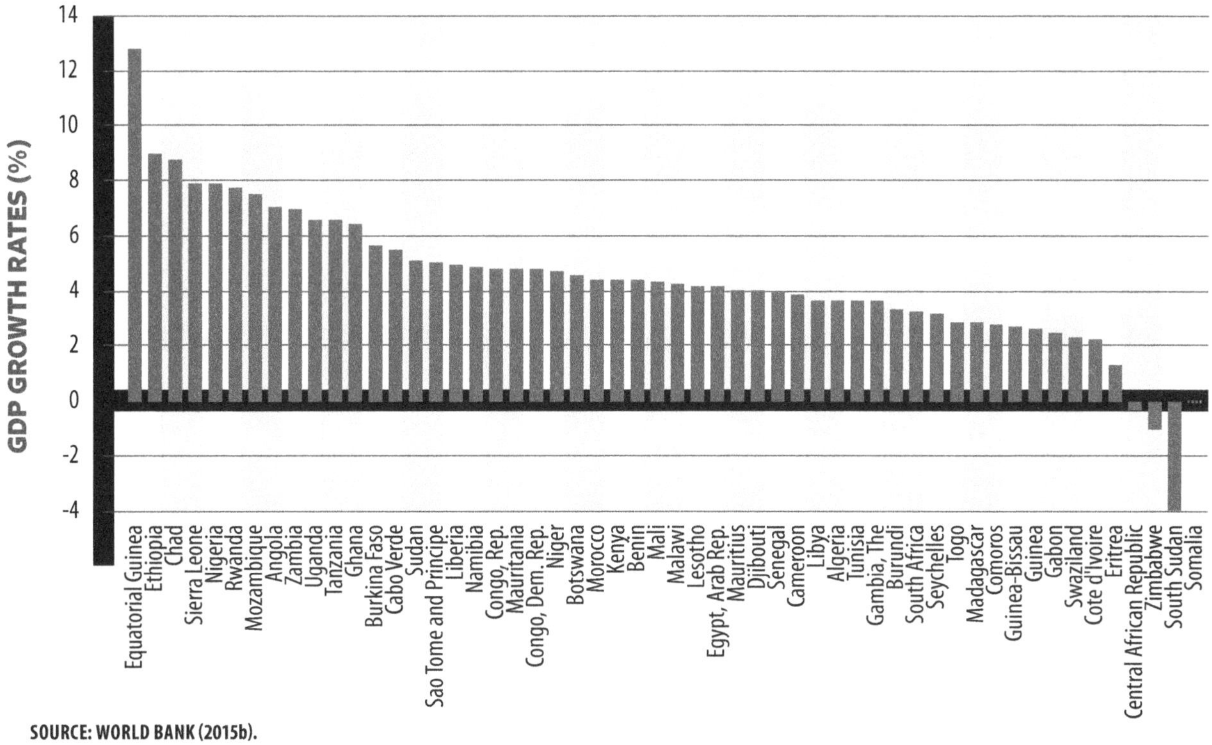

SOURCE: WORLD BANK (2015b).

STRUCTURAL TRANSFORMATION AND GREEN GROWTH—IT MUST BE "WHEN?" NOT "IF"

African economies face risks that require special attention from policymakers, including turbulence in the global economy. Africa's vulnerability calls for a rethink of its broader development strategy. Despite healthy economic growth (often higher than elsewhere in the world over the last decade), it has rarely been inclusive: the number of Africans in absolute poverty has risen and inequality remains a major issue. And because Africa's growth has been largely tied to exploiting non-re-

FIGURE 1.16 AFRICA'S VALUE ADDED BY SECTOR, 2010–2016

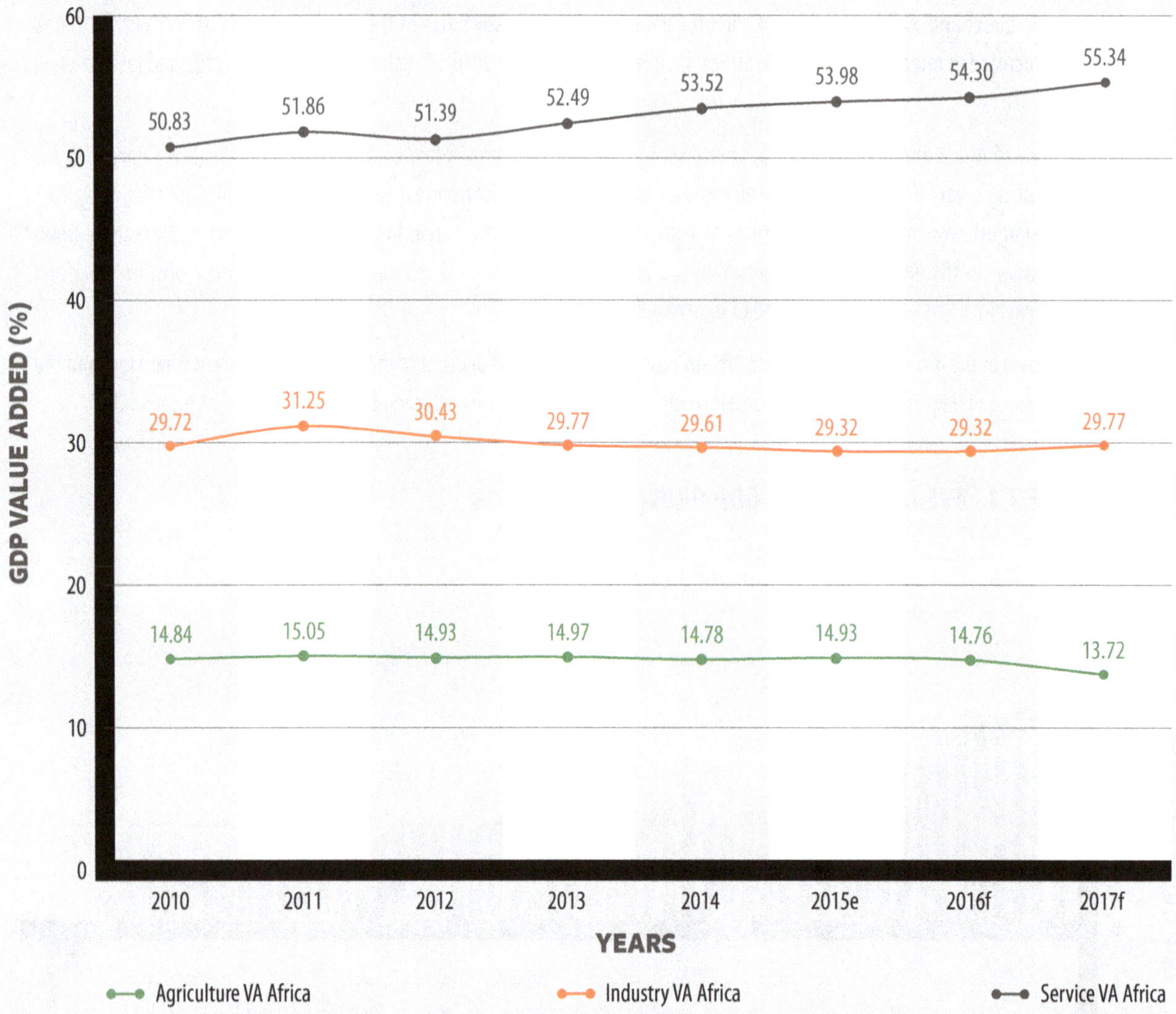

SOURCE: ECA CALCULATIONS BASED ON EIU (2015).
NOTE: e = ESTIMATES; f = FORECASTS.

newable natural resources—with minimal value added and employment generation—sustainable growth has been undermined. Services dominate African economies' valued added as a share of GDP (figure 1.16).

These three strands—macroeconomic vulnerability, social inequality and natural resource dominance—weave into the argument that industrialization is critical for Africa's structural transformation and efforts to create jobs, raise value added and increase incomes. Current developing-country models of economic growth, as exemplified by China and India, rarely account for the social and environmental externalities that exacerbate poverty in developing countries, Africa included. Given the commodity domination of its exports, its drive for industrialization and structural transformation, and its greater energy needs, Africa's imperative is to adopt green growth.

A green economy is considered to improve human well-being and social equity, while sharply curtailing environmental risks and ecological scarcities. It integrates economic, social and environmental policies and focuses on new opportunities for economic growth that reduce pressure on the quality and quantity of natural capital systems (UNEP, 2011).

A green growth pathway will put Africa's development on a more robust and sustainable foundation, since it not only accommodates growth of the economy but also prioritizes the need for restoring or increasing environmental and social assets. Environmental protection's contribution to economic growth is relatively straightforward to analyse, enhancing as it does the quality of natural capital—a critical input into production processes—and increasing income. As Africa's GDP grows, the continent will have to better manage its scarce natural resources, such as water and fertile land. The economic system cannot be separated from the environment, so the benefits of rapid industrialization have to be seen as part of wider ecological and social systems. (Social trends are reviewed in the next section.) Modern economic growth must thus cease stoking environmental pressures. Box 3.1 in Chapter 3 outlines the main concepts and definitions surrounding Industrialization, Structural Transformation, Greening and their inter-linkages.

1.3 RECENT SOCIAL DEVELOPMENTS IN AFRICA

Africa has made considerable progress towards achieving the Millennium Development Goals (MDGs). The baseline, generally 1990 for most MDGs, was low relative to that for other developing regions. The direction is positive overall, with widely varying progress among goals and countries, and within countries.

PROGRESS TOWARDS THE MDGS

In Central, East, Southern and West Africa , poverty rates declined, though slowly, from 56.5 to 48.4 per cent from 1990 to 2010 (ECA, 2015b). A similarly meagre improvement was seen in the share of the population facing hunger and malnutrition, which fell by 8 per cent from 1990 to 2013. In Central Africa, unfavourable extreme weather shifts drive food insecurity and malnutrition and economic performance has not been robust enough to really dent poverty and create jobs.

In education, Africa is close to achieving universal primary enrolment, with over 68 percent of the 25 countries (with data) achieving net enrolment of at least 75 per cent in 2013. Completion rates, however, are still only 67 per cent. Education quality also lags behind quantitative gains. Gender parity in primary schooling improved from 0.86 before 2012 to 0.93 after 2012, though both secondary and tertiary gender parity remain below the 0.93 benchmark, at 0.91 and 0.87 ((ECA, 2015b).

In Central Africa, unfavourable extreme weather shifts drive food insecurity and malnutrition and economic performance has not been robust enough to really dent poverty and create jobs.

Under-five mortality fell from 146 deaths per 1,000 live births in 1990 to 65 in 2012, an improvement of 55.5 per cent against the MDG 4 target of a two-thirds reduction by 2015. The efforts to combat HIV/AIDS, malaria and tuberculosis have yielded some achievements in incidence, prevalence and mortality.

Progress towards the environmental goal has been lacklustre. Only a quarter of Africa's population has gained access to an improved water source, the lowest rate globally (ECA, 2015b). Similarly, the proportion of people with access to improved sanitation rose from 24 per cent in 1990 to 30 per cent in 2012. But the disaggregated figure of both indicators is skewed towards urban areas, in part driving health hazards and reducing economic activity. This inadequate attention to rural areas, combined with population growth, degrades land and reduces agricultural productivity, lowering incomes and food security (UNEP, 2008).

Impressively, the MDG target to bring about a significant improvement in the lives of at least 100 million slum dwellers by 2020 was achieved 10 years in advance and then surpassed, by 100 million. But the absolute number of slum dwellers climbed, to 863 million by 2013 (UN-Habitat, 2013). More than 60 per cent of Africa's urban populations still live in slum areas in precarious conditions, lacking basic services, infrastructure and secure tenure.

PROGRESS GOOD BUT INEQUITIES PERSIST

Progress seems to reflect income, gender, ethnicity and location. For example, only 23 per cent of poor rural girls in Central, East, Southern and West Africa complete their primary education (UN, 2014). In some countries, children in the poorest 20 per cent of the population are three times more likely not to be enrolled in primary school than children from the wealthiest 20 per cent. In 2007, girls accounted for 54 per cent of the world's out-of-school population.

Similarly, health-related costs affect low-income groups disproportionately. Cost-sharing mechanisms in health delivery can be as high as 90 per cent of the costs borne by households, causing them inordinate problems, at times driving them into poverty. Some urban slum dwellers face greater health and literacy disadvantages than rural dwellers (UN-Habitat, 2006). The inequalities of access to improved human capital carry over to income inequalities, perpetuating poverty and

TABLE 1.1 HDI AND INEQUALITY-ADJUSTED HDI, SELECTED REGIONS

	HDI value	Inequality-adjusted HDI value	Loss due to inequality (%)
Central, East, Southern and West Africa	0.518	0.345	33.3
Latin America	0.748	0.570	23.7
South Asia	0.607	0.433	28.7

SOURCE: UNDP (2015).

BOX 1.4 THE SUSTAINABLE DEVELOPMENT GOALS

The Sustainable Development Goals are an array of development instruments to spur innovation and move economies towards greater efficiency in the use of resources, including energy.

The goal of environmental sustainability reflects global public concern about the need to decouple economic growth and development from environmental degradation and the effects of climate change and environmental degradation—to ensure green growth. This provides scope for an elaboration of the possible interlinkages among the 17 goal sets, the possible sequencing of chains and the strata of the national system of innovation with which they are most likely to engage.

In a green economy, income growth and employment are driven by investments that cut carbon emissions and pollution, that widen biodiversity and that improve efficiency of resource use.

vulnerability across generations, a pattern particularly evident in access to formal employment in Africa.

The inequalities of opportunities are reflected in inequalities of outcomes. The Human Development Index (HDI), which measures average achievements in three basic dimensions of human development—a long and healthy life, knowledge and a decent standard of living—puts most African countries in the lower ranks of human development. The inequality-adjusted indicator in the HDI shows a 33 per cent fall from the HDI value, the steepest globally (table 1.1).

The inequalities are partly responsible for the slow pace of social improvement and the transformations inherent in the 2030 Agenda for Sustainable Development (and related Sustainable Development Goals—box 1.4) and Agenda 2063 of the African Union. These are the reverse side of the coin of greening industrialization, which for Africa is enmeshed with greater employment opportunities tied to improving skills and education, managing population and youth issues, and urbanizing successfully.

EMPLOYMENT AND SKILLS

Africa's human capital, though improving, is not linked tightly enough to industrialization, and certainly not to the green economy as endorsed in the 2030 Agenda and Agenda 2063. These agendas aim to transform economies by tackling their structural vulnerabilities and by including all their citizens, building sustainability on solid social, economic and environmental foundations.

Unemployment rates for Central, East, Southern and West Africa were 6.9 per cent for males and 8.8 per cent for females in 2014 (ILO, 2015a), marking marginal declines of 0.2 and 0.1 percentage points from 2009. Economic growth has not kept pace with employment growth, largely because it has been driven by capital-intensive sectors, such as mining and oil, and by exports of primary commodities, adding little value.

Africa is plagued by the twin problems of unemployment and underemployment, mutually reinforcing and exacerbating widespread informality in countries. The highest unemployment rates in countries with data in 2012 were Mauritania (31 per cent), Reunion (28.5 per cent), Lesotho (26.5 per cent) and Gabon (20.3 per cent). Women had higher unemployment rates than men in Egypt, Gabon, Lesotho and Reunion (figure 1.17), in part reflecting the different access to labour markets for women.

Underemployment is taking root in African labour markets because of structural barriers that hinder labour to flow to the areas where it is most needed. For example, time-related underemployment as a share of total employment for male and female youths aged 15 years and above was 9.2 per cent in Morocco, 6.4 per cent in Namibia, 4.6 per cent in Botswana and 3.9 per cent in South Africa. Most jobs in Africa, particularly for youth and women, are generated outside the formal economy. Nine of 10 rural and urban workers have informal jobs in Africa, and most employees are women and youth. Over the next decade or so, at best only one in four youths will find a wage job, and only a small fraction of those jobs will be formal in modern enterprises (AfDB, 2013). The informal economy absorbs nearly 70 per cent of workers in Central, East, Southern and West Africa and 62 per cent in North Africa (figure 1.18).

FIGURE 1.17 UNEMPLOYMENT RATES BY SEX, 2012

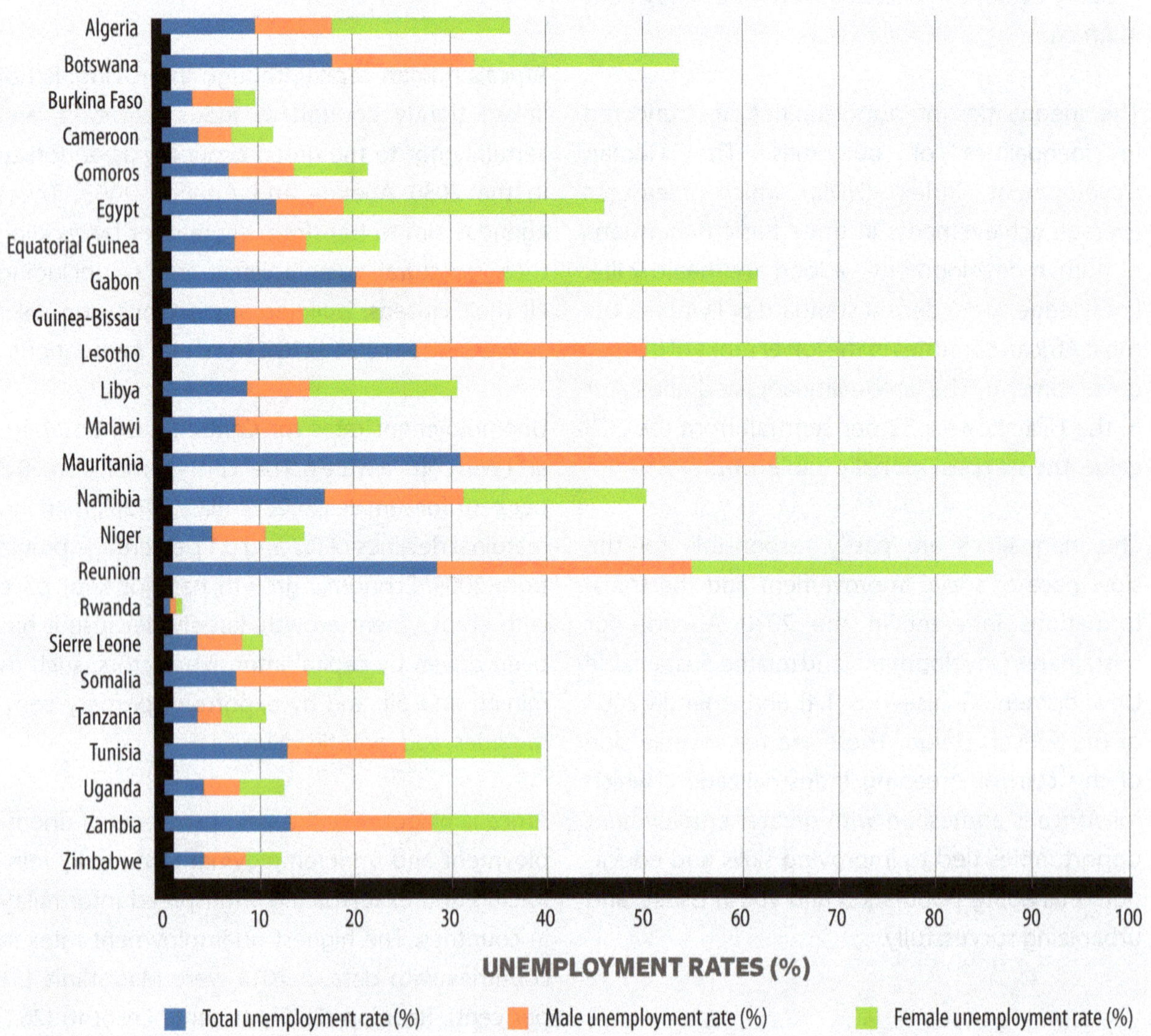

SOURCE: ILO (2014).

FIGURE 1.18 INFORMAL EMPLOYMENT AS A PERCENTAGE OF NONAGRICULTURAL EMPLOYMENT BY SEX, SELECTED AFRICAN COUNTRIES

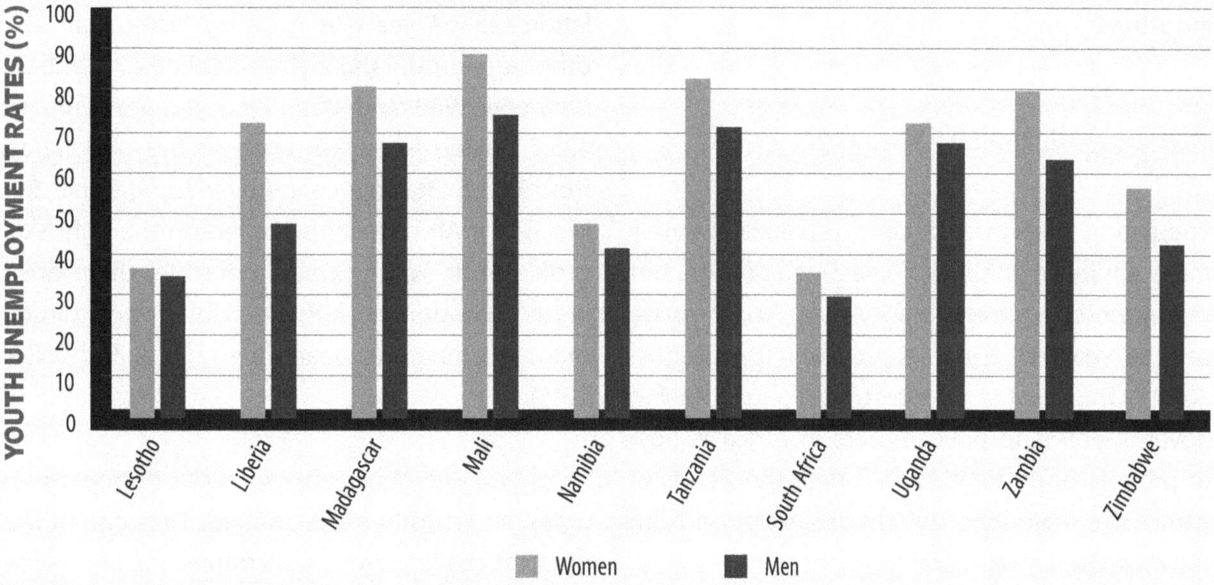

SOURCE: ECA (2016).

Informal workers, particularly women and youth, are vulnerable because of limited social protection, poor working conditions and low incomes. Economic empowerment through a level playing field for jobs, backed by access to land and credit, is needed for women and youth. Improved gender parity in Africa and significant gains in parliamentary representation seem to be decoupled from skill profiles adequate for participating fully in the labour market.

The skill profile for greening industrialization, more technically and technologically intensive than today's, reduces demand for unskilled workers—of particular importance in sustainable development. Given the current emphasis on primary education, the new development agenda for secondary education needs to be technically aligned to green industrialization. The benefits of green jobs cannot be overstated, particularly in light of the climatic changes threatening to reverse Africa's hard-won economic and social gains.

Given this threat and the unsustainably high environmental costs associated with a business-as-usual economic model, the International Labour Organization proposes a transition to green jobs with profound effects on production and consumption, on enterprises and workers, and on employment and incomes.[3] Africa cannot remain a passive bystander. It needs to explore the opportunities for green jobs while pursuing low-carbon growth within its structural transformation and inclusive development agenda, in line with the Rio+20 agenda.

Adopting green technology has challenges, including steep costs of innovations, new technologies and new jobs and institutions. Since most jobs in Africa are informal, all key stakeholders must appreciate and contribute to the targeted support needed for such adoption, possibly through a phased and differentiated approach, starting with countries whose initial conditions are amenable to new technologies. More fundamentally, African countries should be supported with institutional and financial capacity to embrace and sustain the economic transformation towards green jobs and industries.

POPULATION AND YOUTH

Population growth and rapid urbanization may make it hard to attain inclusive green growth, but the potential contribution of Africa's youth bulge can be realized if harnessed well (Babatunde, 2014). One of the greatest challenges facing governments and policymakers in Africa is how to provide opportunities and meet the needs of youth, the majority of whom are excluded from the mainstream economy.

A further challenge is the changing population structure (figure 1.19). The working-age population (25–64 years) is growing faster than any other age group, more than trebling in numbers between 1980 and 2015, from 123.7 million to 425.7 million—or as a share of the population from 33.3 to 36.5 per cent. Any "demographic dividend" for Africa must be based on the right skill profile of its youth population to let them drive industrialization through green jobs in agriculture, manufacturing and clean energy (ECA and UNEP, 2015).

Youth are energetic, keen to adopt new technologies, and mostly well-schooled. Thus one of the greatest challenges for governments is to provide opportunities and meet the needs of youth. To ensure that youth are empowered to lead decent

FIGURE 1.19 AFRICA'S POPULATION BY AGE GROUP, 1980–2065

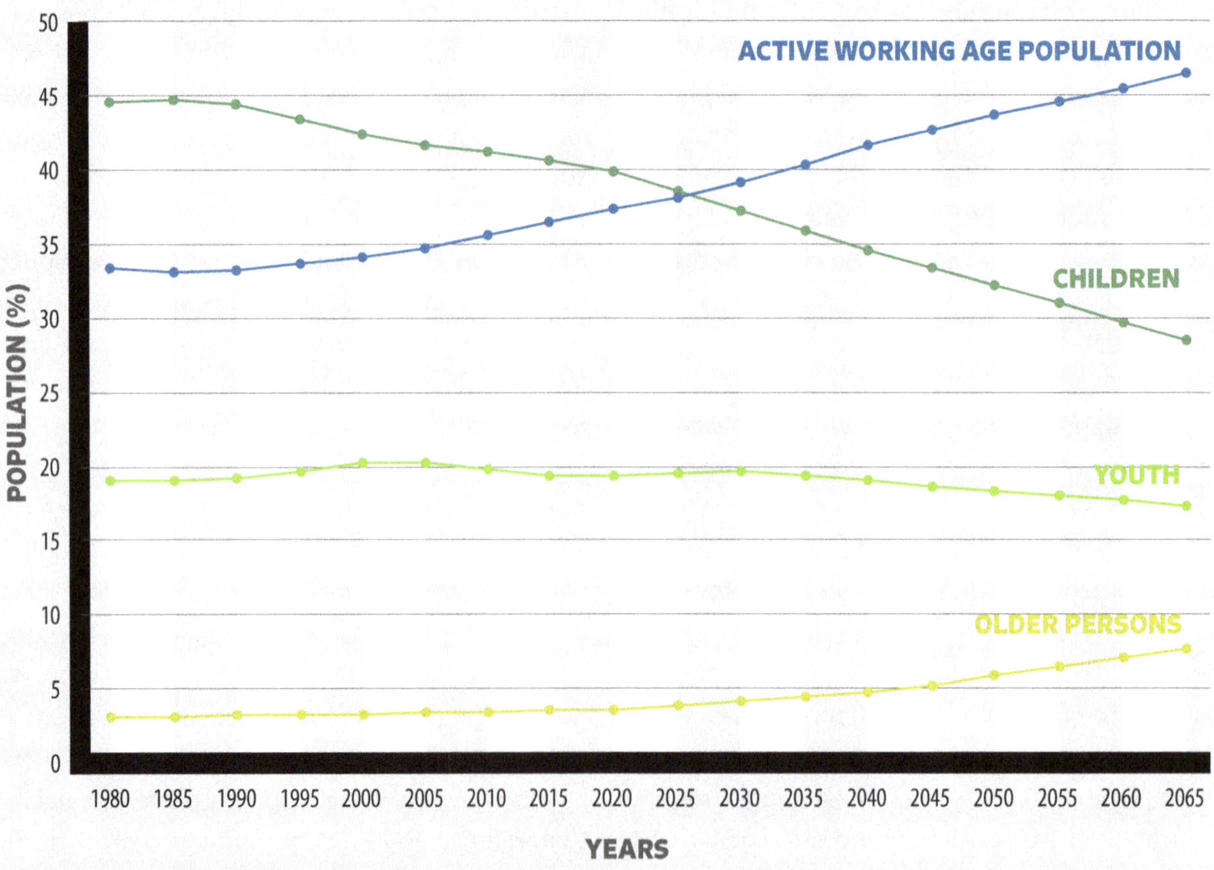

SOURCE: ECA CALCULATIONS BASED ON UN-DESA (2015).

FIGURE 1.20 AFRICAN URBAN AND RURAL POPULATIONS, 1980–2050

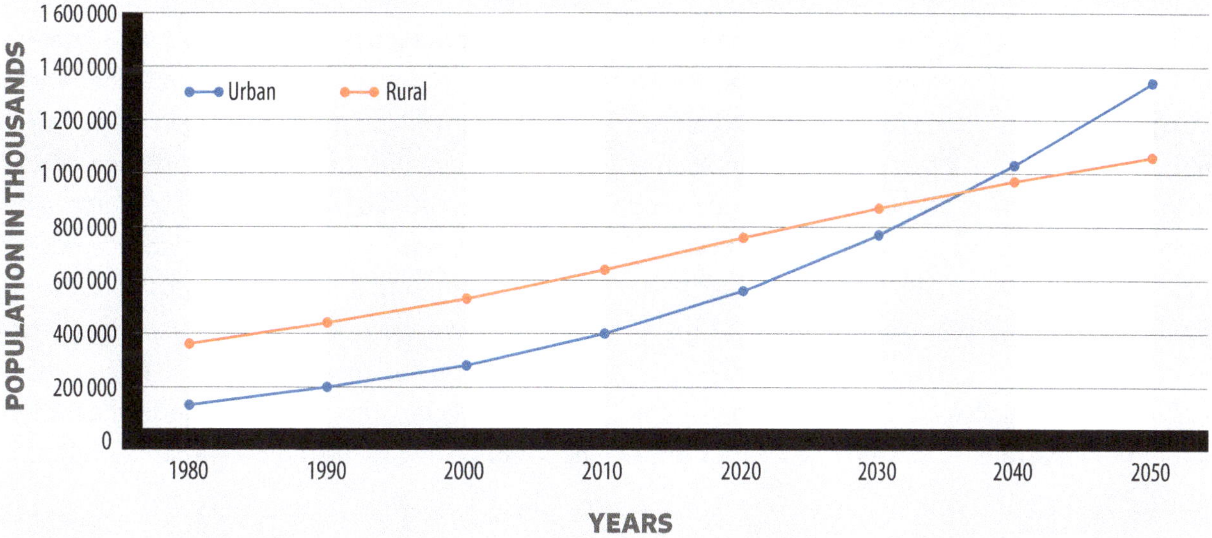

SOURCE: ECA CALCULATIONS BASED ON UN-DESA (2014).

lives and contribute to the socioeconomic development of their countries, policymakers need to draft and enforce economic policies and programmes that facilitate their full participation.

URBANIZATION

Over 2015–20, Africa will have the world's highest annual rate of urban growth (3.4 per cent, against the global rate of 1.84 per cent). The share of the continent's population that is urban climbed from 27 per cent in 1980 to 40 per cent in 2015, and is expected to pass 50 per cent by 2035 (ECA and UNEP, 2015). In absolute terms, Africa's urban population is projected to more than double between 2015 and 2040, reaching 1.02 billion and surpassing the rural population (figure 1.20). This will be matched by a considerable rise in demand for urban services, infrastructure and employment, whose provision is already severely constrained.

Urban areas account for more than 55 per cent of African GDP (AfDB, 2012), though their economic role is largely one of consumption rather than production. Unlike other parts of the world, Africa's urbanization is not linked to industrialization, leading to "consumption cities" populated mainly by workers in nontradable services (Gollin et al., 2014). Urban consumption is expected to continue rising. By 2020, Africa's largest consumer markets—Alexandria, Cairo, Cape Town, Johannesburg and Lagos—are expected to have $25 billion in household spending, and in 2030, the continent's 18 largest cities may have a combined spending power of $1.3 trillion (McKinsey Global Institute 2010). African cities also remain largely informal: More than 60 per cent of their populations are in slums, and employment is concentrated in the informal sector. These are worrying factors given the youth bulge in the region and the concomitant need to create decent jobs.

Urban growth is expected to be paced by greater energy and resource demands. Globally, urban areas account for over 70 per cent of greenhouse gas emissions (UN-Habitat, 2011). African cities have lower carbon dioxide emissions than the world average, but these volumes are projected to surge without strategies for boosting efficiency in urban resource and energy use (Godfrey and Zhao, 2015). Environmental impacts can be mitigated and resource efficiency and productivity enhanced through, for example, more compact cities (UNEP, 2013; UN-Habitat, 2012). As the least urbanized region globally, Africa has a unique opportunity to minimize its cities' carbon footprint, including through infrastructure and land-use practices that promote urban density and lower car dependence (and thus less fossil-fuel consumption).

Africa's current and future massive urban infrastructure investments present vast opportunities to exploit urban agglomeration, leading to resource efficiency and economies of scale in industrial production through intra- and inter-industry interactions—as illustrated in China, where the government has promoted urban clustering to enhance economies of scale (World Bank, 2009). Africa's industrialization—to be resource and energy efficient—requires a proficient framework of urban centres that produce industrial goods and high-value services, embedded in transport networks linking national economies to regional and global markets. Greening Africa's industrialization needs to be tied to the region's urban transition.

1.4 CONCLUSIONS AND POLICY RECOMMENDATIONS

African countries have made notable gains in the regional business environment. With greater economic and political stability across most subregions, these advances have supported growth through higher private consumption and increased public and private investment. Recent commodity price developments have, however, highlighted many economies' persistent structural weaknesses, particularly in government revenues, exchange rates and current account balances. Stronger emphasis is required on strategic non-oil sectors such as electricity, construction and technology, particularly in economies heavily dependent on oil revenue, such as Nigeria.

The global economic environment underlines the need for prudent, counter-cyclical macroeconomic management. Continued low commodity prices offer an opportunity for improved fiscal management and consolidation through further cutting of subsidies to utilities. Spending should instead target high-priority sectors for accelerated structural transformation. Countries should also focus on mobilizing domestic resources to fund public investment, by issuing Eurobonds, for example. African countries still have high international reserves that could be used for investment. Exchange rate depreciation can also enhance exports, particularly in oil-dependent countries.

Intra-African trade represents a low share of Africa's exports, but since it is more diversified than that with the rest of the world, it too provides an opportunity for diversifying production. Diversified trade can also shore up resilience to external shocks. Africa continued to grow in and after the global financial crisis, while traditional markets have seen very slow recoveries, limiting Africa's export opportunities. African countries should therefore seek to enhance intra-African trade by strengthening regional integration, lowering trade costs and the nonphysical barriers to trade and pledging stronger commitments to the Continental Free Trade Area under negotiation.

Africa's industrialization has the potential to create green jobs, and its structural transformation should expand its fiscal space, enabling countries to increase their investment in social sectors essential to strengthening human capital, and exposing women to green skills and technologies on the way to achieving inclusive, equitable and sustainable green industrialization. (Green jobs will not automatically benefit women unless governments take steps to recognize and resolve the inequities they face.)

The links between education and employment, population shifts and urbanization as the continent "green industrializes" must be understood to ensure sustainability. Growth in income and employment is driven by reallocating factors from unsustainable industries to ones that build human skills, enhance energy and resource efficiency and prevent biodiversity loss. The growth of an unplanned urban Africa with a youthful population needs to be matched with industrialization that provides skills demanded by the labour market and efficient services required by the public. A focus on largely young and female informal sector workers to drive the new agenda is a key aspect of industrialization. The informal sector can be leveraged to provide training, access to credit and social protection to increase productivity and welfare, including manufacturing in micro, small and medium enterprises (AfDB, 2013).

Urban planning to foster environmentally friendly infrastructure and smart cities is also needed, encompassing related industries when policymakers select and promote greener technologies (Freire, 2013). Such planning will help mitigate environmental degradation, informal and unregulated settlements, haphazard disposal of waste and industrial products, unsustainable transport systems, high demand for energy (especially fossil fuels) and unregulated use of land and natural resources. Well-planned urban agglomeration can help ensure energy efficiency and facilitate resource efficiency in industrial production by enabling intra- and inter-industry interactions.

Africa's various industrial and urban and regional development policies need to evolve in tandem, so as to optimize efficiency and sustainability gains from agglomeration, drawing on the experience of other formerly developing parts of the world, such as countries in East Asia. Mainstreaming urbanization into national development planning will create the framework to optimize the spatial dimension of industrialization towards green economies.

Africa's industrialization has the potential to create green jobs,...

..., and exposing women to green skills and technologies on the way to achieving inclusive, equitable and sustainable green industrialization.

The close of the MDGs in 2015 provided some important messages on the transition towards the SDGs and Agenda 2063, particularly the link between growth and social development. Africa's positive but slow pace in improving social outcomes masks many idiosyncrasies: Aggregate gains in health and education have often excluded low-income households, women and rural dwellers. For these reasons, among others, addressing industrialization's environmental implications offers a strong incentive for developing socially inclusive green technologies, for enhancing local systems of innovation on climate change mitigation and adaptation, and for improving resource-use efficiency—as discussed in the next chapter.

1.5 REFERENCES

AfDB (African Development Bank). 2012. *Urban Development Strategy: Transforming Africa's Cities and Towns into Engines of Economic Growth and Social Development. Abidjan, Côte d'Ivoire: African Development Bank Group.* http://www.afdb.org/fileadmin/uploads/afdb/Documents/Policy-Documents/Urban-Development%20Strategy-Rev%201.pdf. Accessed January 2016.

———. 2013. "Recognizing Africa's Informal Sector." Abidjan, Côte d'Ivoire: African Development Bank Group. http://www.afdb.org/en/blogs/afdb-championing-inclusive-growth-across-africa/post/recognizing-africas-informal-sector-11645/. Accessed January 2016.

Babatunde, O. 2014. *Inclusive Green Growth in Africa: Rationale, Challenges and Opportunities*. New York: United Nations Population Fund.

ECA (United Nations Economic Commission for Africa). 2015a. Industrializing through Trade. Economic Report on Africa, March. Addis Ababa, Ethiopia: ECA

———. 2015b. Demographic Profile of Africa. Mimeo. Addis Ababa, Ethiopia: ECA.

———. (2016) Informality and inequality:The African Social Development Report, forthcoming, Addis Ababa.,ECA EIU (Economic Intelligence Unit). 2015. *EIU Country Data.* London: Economist Intelligence Unit.

EIU (Economic Intelligence Unit). 2015. EIU Country Data. London: Economist Intelligence Unit.

Freire, M. 2013. "Africa's Urbanization Challenge: An Opportunity for Green Growth." Policy Brief 11, The Growth Dialogue, Washington, DC.

Godfrey, N., and X. Zhao. 2015. *The Contribution of African Cities to the Economy and Climate: Population, Economic Growth, and Carbon Emission Dynamics*. Technical Note. The New Climate Economy.

Gollin, D., R. Jedwab and D. Vollrath. 2014. "Urbanization with and without Industrialization." Background paper, presented in April at World Bank-George Washington University Conference on Urbanization and Poverty Reduction.

Infrastructure Consortium in Africa (ICA). 2011. *Regional Power Status in African Power Pools. Tunis, Tunisia: AfDB.*

International Labour Organization (ILO). 2014. *Key Indicators of the Labour Market 8th Edition*. Geneva: ILO.

———. 2015a. *World Employment and Social Outlook: Trends 2015*. Geneva: ILO.

———. 2015b. *Global Employment Trends for Youth 2015: scaling up investments in decent jobs for youth*. Geneva: ILO.

International Monetary Fund (IMF). 2015. *World Economic Outlook: Uneven Growth Short- and Long-Term Factors*. Washington, DC: IMF.

McKinsey Global Institute. 2010. *Lions on the move: The progress and potential of African economies*. http://www.mckinsey.com/insights/africa/lions_on_the_move. Accessed January 2016.

Oxfam. 2015. *Entering Uncharted Waters: El Niño and the threat to food security*. Oxfam Media Briefing, 1 October 2015, Oxford, UK.

United Nations (UN). 2014. *Millennium Development Goals Report*. New York: UN.

United Nations Department of Economic and Social Affairs (UN-DESA). 2014. *World Urbanization Prospects: The 2014 Revision, Highlights*. New York: UN.

———. 2015. *World Economic Situation and Prospects 2015*. New York: UN.

———. 2016. *World Economic Situation and Prospects 2015*. New York: UN.

United Nations Development Programme (UNDP). 2015. *Human Development Report*. New York: UNDP.

———. 2015a. *Industrializing through Trade*. Economic Report on Africa, March. Addis Ababa, Ethiopia: ECA.

———. 2015b. *Demographic Profile of Africa*. Mimeo. Addis Ababa, Ethiopia: ECA.

United Nations Economic Commission for Africa (ECA) and United Nations Environment Programme (UNEP). 2015. *BRICS-Africa Partnership for Development: Driving Inclusive Growth and Transformational Change*. Addis Ababa, Ethiopia and Nairobi, Kenya: ECA.

United Nations Environment Programme (UNEP). 2008. *Global Environmental Outlook*. Paris: UNEP.

———. 2011. *Towards a Green Economy: Pathways to Sustainable Development and Poverty Eradication*. Paris: UNEP.

———. 2013. *City-Level Decoupling: Urban resource flows and the governance of infrastructure transitions*. Paris: UNEP.

United Nations Human Settlements Programme (UN-Habitat (2006) State of the World Cities, U.K.

———. 2007. *State of the Worlds Cities 2006/7: The Millennium Development Goals and Urban Sustainability: 30 Years of Shaping the Habitat Agenda*. Nairobi, Kenya: UN-Habitat.

———.2011. Cities and Climate change: Global Report on Human Settlements, Nairobi.

———. 2012. *Urban Patterns for a Green Economy: Working with Nature*. Nairobi, Kenya: UN-Habitat.

———. 2013. *State of the World's Cities 2012/2013*. Nairobi, Kenya: UN-Habitat.

United Nations Conference on Trade and Development (UNCTAD). 2016. "UNCTADStat." Geneva: UNCTAD. http://unctadstat.unctad.org/wds/ReportFolders/reportFolders.aspx. Accessed January 2016.

World Bank. 2009. "Harnessing Urbanization for Growth and Poverty Alleviation." Washington, DC: World Bank. http://www-wds.worldbank.org/external/default/WDSContentServer/WDSP/IB/2009/12/17/000333038_20091217003914/Rendered/PDF/520080BRI0IDA110Box345548B01PUBLIC1.pdf. Accessed January 2016.

———. 2015a. *Global Monitoring Report 2014/2015: Ending Poverty and Sharing Prosperity*. Washington, DC: World Bank.

———. 2015b. *World Development Indicators 2015*. Washington, DC: World Bank. wdi.worldbank.org/tables. Accessed October 26, 2015.

World Wide Fund for Nature (WWF). 2011. *The Energy Report: 100 % Renewable Energy by 2050*. Gland, Switzerland: WWF International.

1.6 ENDNOTES

1 ECA calculations, based on EIU (2015).

2 ECA calculations, based on United Nations Conference on Trade and Development (UNCTAD), 2016.

3 http://www.ilo.org/wcmsp5/groups/public/---dgreports/---dcomm/---publ/documents/publication/wcms_153458.pdf.

CHAPTER 2

GLOBAL AND CONTINENTAL DEVELOPMENT FRAMEWORKS FOR GREEN INDUSTRIALIZATION

Green industrialization can advance the broader objective of sustainable development in Africa. It is an opportunity for the continent to keep down its greenhouse gas emissions and to protect its biodiversity and ecological systems while reaping the benefits of long-term, socially inclusive economic growth.

The commitments in recently adopted global and continental frameworks—such as the Addis Ababa Action Agenda, the United Nations 21st Conference of the Parties (COP21), Agenda 2063 of the African Union, and the 2030 Agenda for Sustainable Development (Agenda 2030) focused on the Sustainable Development Goals (SDGs)—provide a supportive backdrop for adopting and following through on green industrialization initiatives. These frameworks should also support African countries' efforts to integrate their diverse development policies and strategies.

The commitments in recently adopted global and continental frameworks... ... provide a supportive backdrop for adopting and following through on green industrialization initiatives

Africa's aspiration for inclusive structural transformation, underpinned by commodity-based industrialization, remains largely unmet despite positive trends in socioeconomic indicators. The gross domestic product (GDP) of most African countries is dominated by services and agriculture, with only a small contribution from manufacturing. That leaves most African economies undiversified and vulnerable to shocks. While real GDP growth has exceeded the global average over the last decade, it remains below the 7 per cent benchmark generally considered necessary to eradicate extreme poverty (ECA (1999)). It also masks the continued depletion of the natural resource base, measured by the adjusted net savings indicator (ECA and UNEP 2013).

On the social front, despite improvements in access to primary education and health services, the quality of services remains a concern—evidenced, in part, by the still relatively high rates of maternal and child mortality. Access to safe drinking water and basic sanitation is low in Africa, with rural–urban disparities and performance gaps between North Africa and the rest of the continent. Social exclusion—typified by declining but high levels of spatial and horizontal inequalities in income and access to basic social services—also remains a challenge (Armah et al., 2014). Underlying these issues is the continent's vulnerability to environmental hazards and stresses, heightened by climate change.

Collectively, these problems call into question the sustainability of growth and development in Africa. They also call for re-examining Africa's industrialization through the lens of social, economic and environmental sustainability.

Recent global and regional developments point to an increasingly supportive environment for Africa's sustainable development. Globally, Agenda 2030, and regionally, Agenda 2063, have committed the international community to a set of global interventions and resources. Similarly, the agreements reached at December 2015's COP21 conference heightened awareness about the environmental fall-outs of the current global growth trajectory and proposed concrete measures that should inform the continent's agenda for structural transformation.

This chapter examines the opportunities for promoting green industrialization in the context of these frameworks, identifying commitments that can leverage industrial greening in Africa.

2.1 GLOBAL AND REGIONAL DEVELOPMENT AGENDAS FOR SUSTAINABLE DEVELOPMENT

The Millennium Development Goals (MDGs) galvanized the international community and resources around a core set of global issues such as poverty, hunger, HIV/AIDS and maternal and child health. During their 15-year span (2000–2015), Africa witnessed sharp declines in poverty, significant reductions in maternal and child deaths, improvements in primary school enrolment and declines in malaria, TB and HIV-related deaths (ECA et al., 2015)—as well as the representation of women in national parliaments and the continued emissions of low carbon dioxide. Africa's performance on the MDGs was particularly striking given its low initial conditions. That said, the continent is unlikely to

FIGURE 2.1 CARBON DIOXIDE EMISSIONS (METRIC TONNES PER CAPITA), VARIOUS YEARS

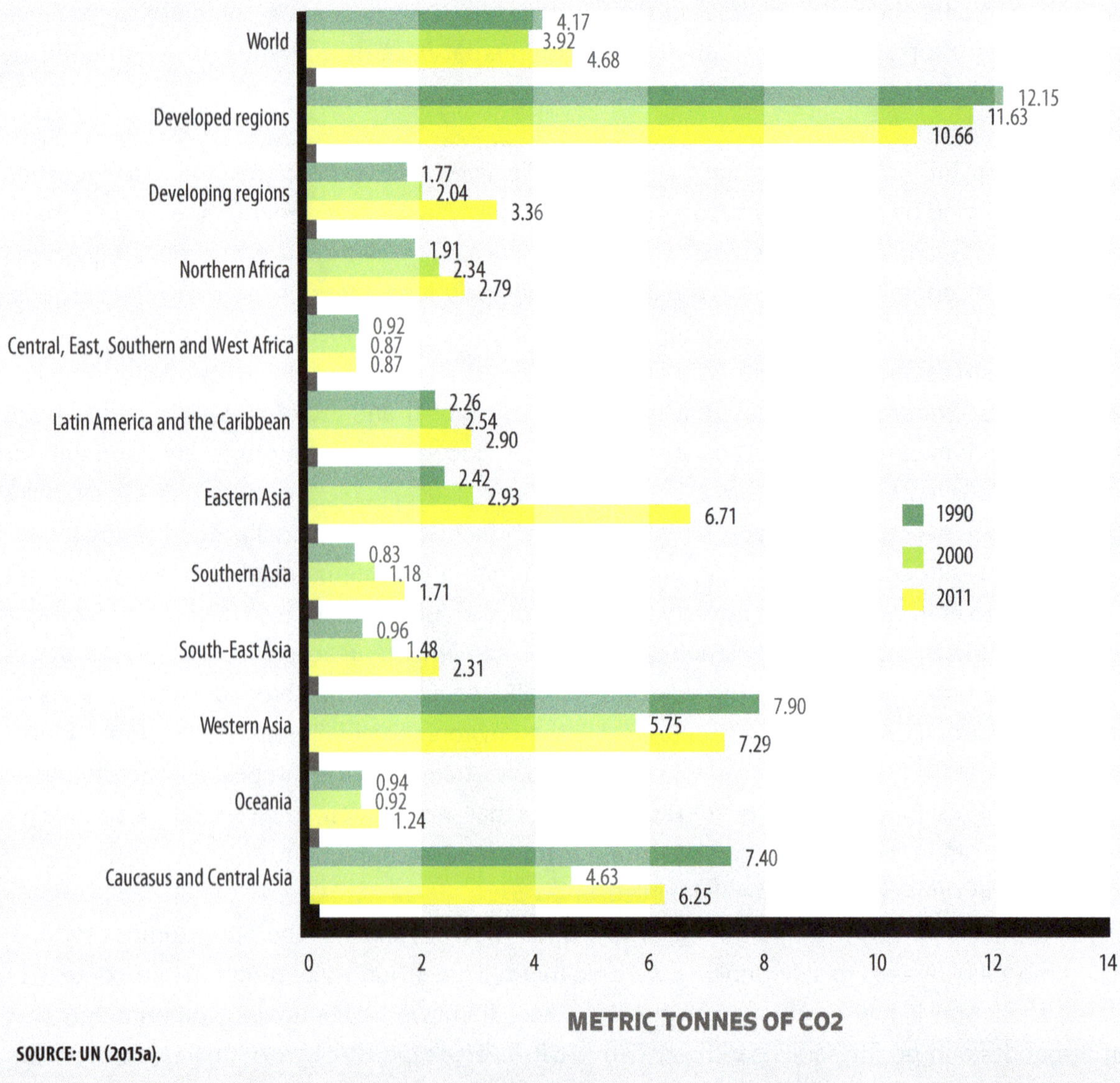

SOURCE: UN (2015a).

achieve all the MDGs by the end of 2015. With mounting concerns about climate change, natural resource depletion and vulnerabilities to economic shocks, the successor development agenda has reoriented the discourse towards environmental sustainability and conservation of natural assets.

AFRICA'S CONTRIBUTION TO ENVIRONMENTAL DEGRADATION IS LOW

Africa's contribution to global environmental degradation is insignificant, but the continent is highly vulnerable to climatic hazards. Carbon dioxide emissions in metric tonnes of CO_2 per capita in Central, East, Southern and West Africa in 2011 were much lower than the global and developing country average: 0.87 metric tonnes of CO_2 per capita compared with 4.68 globally and 3.36 for developing regions as a whole; the figures were slightly higher in North Africa, which averaged 2.79 (figure 2.1). Similarly, Africa's consumption of ozone-depleting substances is low. In Central, East, Southern and West Africa, such consumption was 1,371 tons of ozone-depletion potential in 2013, compared with 1,661 tons in Southern Asia and 17,675 tons in Eastern Asia (ECA et al., 2015).

Protected areas are essential to conserving species and ecosystems and a key element in climate change mitigation. The continent has performed comparatively well in protecting terrestrial and marine areas, controlling biodiversity loss, and slowing the pace of species extinction. Globally, 14 per cent of terrestrial and marine areas were protected in 2012; in Central, East, Southern and West Africa, protected area coverage increased from 10.7 per cent in 1990 to 15.2 per cent in 2012. In 2014, 32 African countries had reached the target of protecting at least 10 per cent of their territorial and marine areas, up from 19 countries in 1990 (ECA et al., 2015). On average, 96.9 per cent of the continent's species, in Central, East, Southern and West Africa, are not at risk of extinction, against 91.7 per cent of those in developing countries and 91.3 per cent in the world as a whole.

AFRICA IS HIGHLY VULNERABLE TO ENVIRONMENTAL AND CLIMATIC HAZARDS

Notwithstanding their limited contribution to environmental degradation and thus resource depletion, African countries (Schellnhuber et al., 2013) and regions (Turco et al., 2015) are hotspots of current and future climate impacts, which have already hit GDP growth. Extreme variations in rainfall patterns can disrupt commercial and industrial activities, damaging capital stocks or reducing income-generation capacity. In a study of the effects of precipitation on macroeconomic output, Barrios, Bertinelli and Strobl (2010) demonstrated that the paucity of rainfall was a "significant determinant of poor economic growth" in Africa during 1960–2000. The reliance on agriculture by many Africa countries for food, value added and employment further renders their economies particularly vulnerable to extreme droughts (World Bank 2015).

Africa's contribution to natural resource depletion is lower than the global average. For instance, Central, East, Southern and West Africa uses only 3 per cent of its total water resources, compared with 9.1 per cent for the developing world as a whole and 8.8 per cent for the planet.[1] The figure is, however, much higher for North Africa, at 78.8 per cent (ECA et al., 2015).

Even though the continent currently exploits only a small fraction of its natural resources, natural resource use as a share of gross national income (GNI) is high. Net adjusted savings is one measure of the intensity of resource use. It discounts total national savings for carbon dioxide emissions as well as the depletion of energy, forest and mineral resources. In Central, East, Southern and West Africa, net adjusted savings were negative during 2007–2009, and below the least-developed country average (figure 2.2). The net adjusted savings is even lower for natural resource–rich countries like Angola, Republic of Congo and Democratic Republic of Congo (figure 2.3).

The evidence suggests that Africa's contribution to global environmental degradation and natural resource depletion is relatively low. However, given the dependence of several African countries on natural resources, resource depletion accounts for a relatively high share of its gross national income. Consequently, if Africa should pursue an industrialization pathway based on "brown" technology, its contribution to greenhouse gas emissions will inevitably rise and further lower its net adjusted savings.

Africa's status as a latecomer to industrialization should be viewed as an opportunity to avoid the environmental mistakes of emerging countries like China. A green industrialization pathway that promotes growth, creates employment and reduces poverty will sustain development and increase net adjusted savings.

Still, advancing green industrialization in Africa will not be cost-neutral: it will require a boost in domestic resource mobilization and the support of the international community in financial and technological resources. In line with this thinking, the Rio outcome document calls on the international community to facilitate the green economy by avoiding creation of new trade barriers and imposition of new conditions on aid and finance. It also urges development partners to support technological innovation in developing countries and to enhance their policy space to pursue their own paths to sustainable development (UN 2012).

FIGURE 2.2 ADJUSTED NET SAVINGS BY REGION (% GNI)

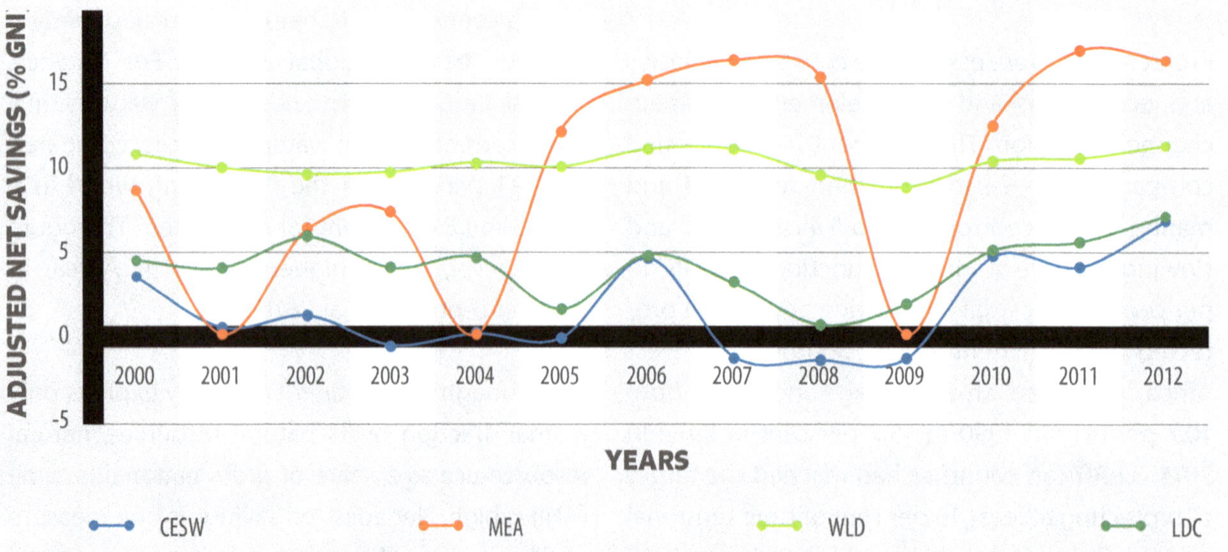

SOURCE: WORLD BANK (2015). CESW: CENTRAL, EAST, SOUTHERN AND WEST AFRICA; MEA: MIDDLE EAST AND NORTH AFRICA; WLD: WORLD; LDC: LEAST DEVELOPED COUNTRIES.

2.2 SUSTAINABLE DEVELOPMENT, THE GREEN ECONOMY AND GREEN INDUSTRIALIZATION: THE NEXUS

The recently adopted Sustainable Development Goals are anchored on the economic, social, and environmental dimensions of sustainable development and hence provide a framework for greening industrialization in the context of sustainable development.

Sustainable development and green industrialization are linked through the concept of a "green economy". It is generally accepted that greening the economy through a shift away from fossil fuel dependency to renewable energy is critical for sustainable development. The Rio outcome document for instance, acknowledges "the green economy as a means to achieve sustainable development" (UN, 2012). However, opinions differ on the appropriate mechanism for transitioning from green economy to sustainable development. The Rio document stresses the importance of sustainable consumption and production patterns and non-market approaches in the transition process. Other schools of thought place greater emphasis on market-led approaches such as a global carbon market and markets for ecosystems.

Despite differences in approach, broad consensus argues that greening the economy should facilitate improvements in human well-being and social equity, while reducing environmental risks and ecological scarcities. To the extent that the green economy is driven by green investments, such investments constitute one of the green-economy drivers (UNEP, 2011).

FIGURE 2.3 NET ADJUSTED SAVINGS IN SELECTED AFRICAN COUNTRIES (% OF GNI)

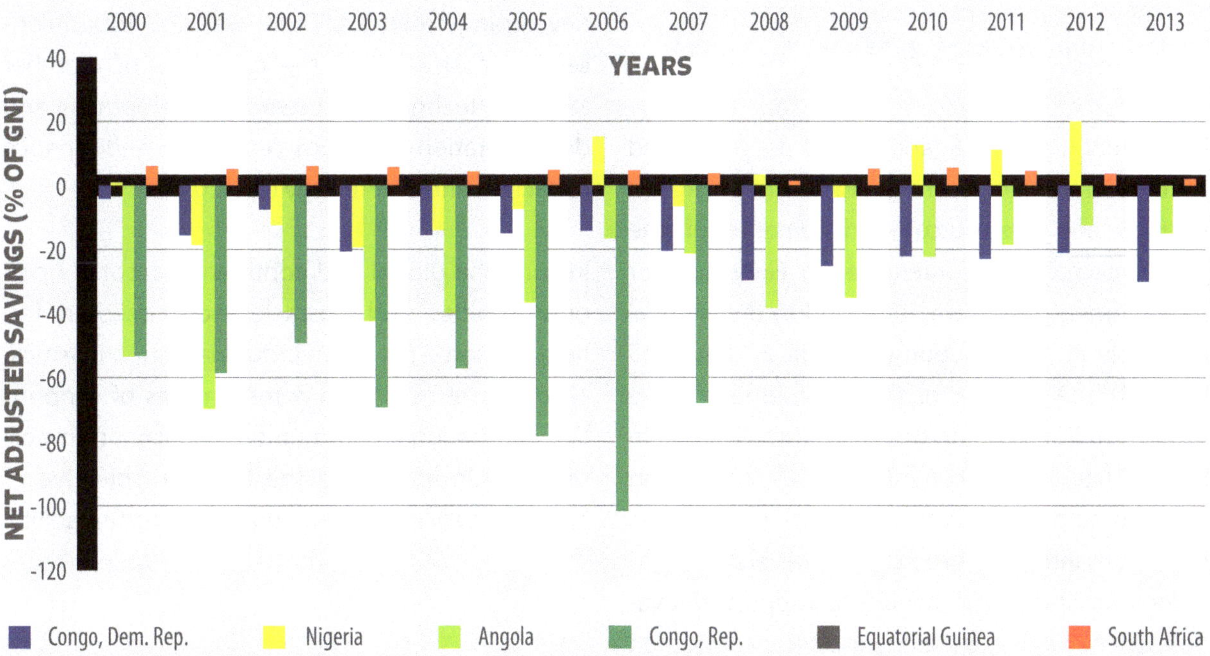

SOURCE: WORLD BANK (2015).

THE SUSTAINABLE DEVELOPMENT GOALS

The SDGs provide a framework for green industrialization because they embed industrial development in the larger context of environmental sustainability. Seven of the 17 SDGs have a direct bearing on environmental sustainability (table 2.1).

AGENDA 2063

Similar to the SDGs, Agenda 2063—Africa's blueprint for development—provides an enabling framework for green industrialization by prioritizing environmental sustainability (see table 2.1). It emerged from the 50th Anniversary (Golden Jubilee) of the AU in 2013, where the Heads of State rededicated themselves to the Pan-African vision. The Agenda has three key components: the vision itself, the transformation framework and the first 10-year implementation plan. Anchored by 7 aspirations, 20 goals and 34 priority areas, the framework spans the three dimensions of sustainable development, including the environmental (AUC, 2013).

THE ADDIS ABABA ACTION AGENDA

Implementation of Agenda 2030 is supported by the commitments in the Addis Ababa Action Agenda and the outcome documents of the Third International Conference on Financing for Development, which was endorsed by the General Assembly in its resolution 69/313 of 27 July 2015 (UN, 2015). A number of the commitments have broad implications for green industrialization in Africa. They include commitments to develop an infrastructure platform to coordinate investments in resilient infrastructure in Africa; develop a technology facilitation mechanism to support innovation, science and technology in Africa; strengthen international cooperation on tax matters to stem illicit financial outflows and ensure that Africa retains a fair share of the returns from private investments particularly in natural resources; and strengthen capacities for domestic resource mobilization. Collectively these commitments to boost investments in green industrial development in Africa.

COP21

The 21st Conference of the Parties in Paris in December 2015 reached agreement on issues tying economies to a pathway of environmental sustainability. The conference committed to holding the increase in the global average temperature to well below 2 degrees Celsius above pre-industrial levels and to pursue efforts to limit the temperature increase to 1.5 degrees Celsius. Countries were also urged to strengthen their capacities for adaptation and resilience to climate change and reduce greenhouse gas emissions. To this end, all parties were encouraged to devise and communicate their strategies for reducing greenhouse gas emission within the framework of intended nationally determined contributions. The conference agreed to provide at least $100 billion a year in climate financing for developing countries. There was also broad consensus to strengthen the capacities of member states in technology research, development and demonstration—and to enhance endogenous capacities and technology (UN, 2015c).

In sum, the global and continental accords open opportunities and obstacles—discussed in the next section—for green industrialization in Africa. Through set goals and commitments of support, the international community can play an important role in advancing the broader objective of economic, social and environmental sustainability.

TABLE 2.1 GREEN GOALS OF AGENDA 2063 AND AGENDA 2030

Agenda 2063	Agenda 2030
1. A high standard of living, quality of life and well-being for all Priority area 4: Modern and livable habitats and basic quality services	7. Ensure access to affordable, reliable sustainable and modern energy for all
	6. Ensure availability and sustainable management of water and sanitation for all
	12. Ensure sustainable consumption and production patterns
4. Transformed economies and job creation Priority area 4: Hospitality/tourism	14. Conserve and sustainably use the oceans, seas and marine resources for sustainable development
5. Modern agriculture for increased productivity and production Priority area 1: Agricultural productivity and production	1. End poverty in all its forms everywhere
	2. End hunger, achieve food security and improved nutrition and promote sustainable agriculture
	13. Take urgent action to combat climate change and its impacts
6. Blue/ocean economy for accelerated economic growth Priority area 1: Marine resources and energy	14. Conserve and sustainably use the oceans, seas and marine resources for sustainable development
	7. Ensure access to affordable, reliable, sustainable and modern energy for all
7. Environmentally sustainable climate resilient economies and communities Priority area 1: Biodiversity, conservation and sustainable natural resource management. Priority area 2: Water security Priority area 3: Climate resilience and natural disasters and preparedness	2. End hunger, achieve food security and improved nutrition and promote sustainable agriculture
	6. Ensure availability and sustainable management of water and sanitation for all
	14. Conserve and sustainably use the oceans, seas and marine resources for sustainable development
	15. Protect, restore and promote sustainable use of terrestrial ecosystems, sustainably manage forests, combat desertification, and halt and reverse land degradation and halt biodiversity loss
	11. Make cities and human settlements inclusive, safe, resilient and sustainable
	9. Build resilient infrastructure, promote inclusive and sustainable industrialization and foster innovation
	1. End poverty in all its forms everywhere
	3. Ensure healthy lives and promote well-being for all at all ages
	13. Take urgent action to combat climate change and its impacts
	7. Ensure access to affordable, reliable, sustainable and modern energy for all
	12. Ensure sustainable consumption and production patterns
12 Capable institutions and transformed leadership in place at all levels Priority area 2: Human rights, justice and the rule of law	12. Ensure sustainable consumption and production patterns
	16. Promote peaceful and inclusive societies for sustainable development, provide access to justice for all and build effective, accountable and inclusive institutions at all levels

SOURCE: AUC (2015); UN (2015b).

2.3 KEY ISSUES, CHALLENGES AND OPPORTUNITIES IN THE TRANSITION

After almost three years of intense global, regional and national consultations, in September 2015, the UN General Assembly adopted a new global development agenda, with features somewhat different from the MDGs. These elements create opportunities for the continent but also signal operational challenges. This section identifies those requiring attention from policy-makers, especially during the transition.

CONVERGENCE WITH AFRICA'S PRIORITIES WILL FOSTERS BUY-IN AND INTEGRATION IN NATIONAL FRAMEWORKS

Africa's proactive engagement coupled with the broadly consultative process that underpinned the development of Agenda 2030 allowed the continent's priorities to be reflected in the document, particularly by articulating a common position on the post-2015 agenda and by creating a political structure for that (the High Level Committee on the Post-2015 Development Agenda). This success will encourage member states to buy in to the agenda and help integrate it with national development frameworks.

THE AGENDA'S VERY COMPREHENSIVENESS PRESENTS IMPLEMENTATION AND FOLLOW-UP CHALLENGES

The more comprehensive nature of Agenda 2030 makes implementation and follow-up even more daunting process than for the MDGs (17 goals and 169 targets, up from 8 goals and 18 targets). This numerical surge reflects not only a desire to accommodate competing priorities of multiple interest groups but also a conscious effort to tackle emerging issues such as climate change and to direct the global spotlight to the root causes of poverty.[2]

Achieving and following up on all these goals and targets (with more than 200 indicators) will obviously be difficult, requiring states to have the capacity to identify interventions with multiplier effects on other goals and targets.

ACHIEVING THE SDGS WILL BE HARD

Unlike the MDGs, Agenda 2030 is anchored by the three dimensions of sustainable development: economic, environmental and social. The focus on sustainability adds yet another layer of complexity: countries must grow in a way consistent with environmental sustainability and social inclusion.

In effect, sustainable development has institutional and policy implications including: the choice of the drivers of growth (such as the role of crude oil or coal exports in the growth mix), the appropriate energy mix (renewable or nonrenewable) to drive growth; the requisite macroeconomic policy regime to promote inclusion and equitably redistribute the benefits of growth; and the institutional architecture to coordinate and operationalize the three dimensions.

COMPETITION FOR RESOURCES WILL INTENSIFY

The new development agenda applies to all countries and, unlike the MDGs, is not restricted to developing countries. Agenda 2030 erodes the exclusive attention enjoyed by developing countries during the MDG era. Developing countries must factor this "preference erosion" in their implementation strategy. Middle-income countries in particular will share the limelight of global attention with their poorer counterparts, affecting the volume of financial and nonfinancial resources directed to the latter.

CAPITALIZING ON THE MEANS OF IMPLEMENTATION IS ESSENTIAL

More positively, Agenda 2030 includes a "means of implementation" mechanism as well as a more elaborate architecture for follow-up. The means of implementation is explicitly linked to the outcome document of the Third International Conference on Financing for Development (the Addis Ababa Action Agenda) and underpinned by Goal 17 of Agenda 2030, which focuses on this issue. In addition, Agenda 2030 includes means of implementation for each of the 16 other goals (goal-specific means of implementation). The integration of the means of implementation in Agenda 2030 provides a more robust mechanism relative to the MDGs, to assess country performance against financial and nonfinancial support. But the outcomes of the Addis Ababa Action Agenda underscored the limited appetite by development partners to honour their existing commitments (especially the 1970 commitment by DAC countries to provide 0.7 percent of ODA/GNI to developing countries) and to commit new resources to the new development agenda, notwithstanding their expressed desire to craft an ambitious agenda. For instance, the Agenda made no new ODA commitments, and partners, except for the European Union (EU), did not agree a timeline to meet existing commitments. And even though the bloc committed to fulfilling the 0.7 per cent commitment of ODA/GNI by 2030, such resources will have an impact only if they are disbursed well before the end of the SDG cycle.

EXPLOITING SYNERGIES BETWEEN AGENDA 2030 AND AGENDA 2063

African countries are confronted by a dual transition: a global level transition from the MDGs to Agenda 2030 and a regional transition from New Partnership for Africa's Development (NEPAD) to Agenda 2063 (and its 10-year implementation plan). They must be coordinated to ensure coherence and pre-empt burdening policymakers with multiple development frameworks.

The agendas share a considerable overlap in part owing to the inclusion in both of several elements of the Common African Position in Agenda 2030. Both are comprehensive and address the social, economic and environmental dimensions of sustainable development. Both share a common aspiration of sustainable development. Both aim to improve the living standards of households through inclusive and sustainable growth. And both call for poverty eradication, greater equity in the distribution of economic and social assets and improvements in social service delivery for all social groups irrespective of gender, ethnicity, age or geography.

Yet several elements of Agenda 2063 are not in Agenda 2030, including Goal 8 on creating a United Africa: Goal 9 on the creation of continental financial and monetary institutions; Goal 15 on ensuring a fully functional and operational African Peace and Security Architecture; and Goal 19 on ensuring that Africa as a major partner in global affairs and peaceful co-existence.

2.4 FINANCING GREEN INDUSTRIALIZATION IN THE SUSTAINABLE DEVELOPMENT AGENDA

Successful transition towards a green economy requires huge financial investments by public and private investors, with a focus on renewable energies and resource-efficient technologies, water and waste management systems, conservation of resources in environmentally friendly agriculture and forestry, and prevention of climate-related disasters.

African governments recently stepped up their efforts to plug the financing gap, particularly that for infrastructure, estimated at $93 billion a year by the World Bank (African Development Bank 2010). Beyond the large investments already made in clean energy, Africa needs to invest more than $50 billion a year for transformative, inclusive and green growth (ECA, 2015). The estimated cost of all the projects in the Programme for Infrastructure Development in Africa to address the infrastructure needs through to 2040 is $360 billion, across energy, transport, information and communication technologies and trans-boundary water resources. The energy sector accounts for 60 per cent of that amount (ECA and AUC, 2012).

Renewable energy projects account for a third of the active energy portfolio of the African Development Bank, clean energy projects about half.

Renewable energy generation has become an important driver of green growth. By 2040, such resources are projected to provide more than 40 per cent of all power generation capacity in Africa (OECD and IEA, 2014). But efficiently harvesting the continent's renewables is costly, and requires mobilizing both domestic and external finances, including that through South–South cooperation, public–private partnerships and climate finance. Many countries face difficulties in domestically financing infrastructure owing to low domestic savings rates and tax revenues. Moreover, large renewable-energy projects and their financing depend on strong, long-term policy frameworks for renewable energy and their translation into reliable instruments. With domestic legal, structural and economic frameworks often too weak to allow the emergence of domestically financed market-based renewable energy development, investments in such projects are driven by international finance and development institutions (GIZ, 2014).

Renewable energy projects account for a third of the active energy portfolio of the African Development Bank, clean energy projects about half. In its effort to boost Africa's energy generation from renewables in the mid to long term, the Bank is acting as an implementing agency of the Clean Technology Fund and the Scaling Up Renewable Energy in Low Income Countries Program. It also supports 27 African countries through the Climate Investment Fund (AfDB, 2015a).

Appropriate policy instruments, incentive mechanisms and regulatory frameworks are essential for attracting private and public investments in renewable energy resources. Some African countries have embraced development options that can steer the continent towards green economies. For instance, Ethiopia and South Africa demonstrated how political will, supported by enabling partnerships and policy and regulatory frameworks, can readily mobilize and leverage domestic and foreign investments in transformative low-carbon energy and climate-resilient development. Public–private partnerships are also an important source of infrastructure funding. The full potential of such partnerships needs to be explored in more detail.

Part of South–South cooperation and investment, Chinese engagement in Africa's energy has grown considerably, with Central, East, Southern and West Africa receiving nearly $10 billion in official development assistance (ODA) from that country in 2005–2011. Chinese investment is not, however, evenly disbursed across the region, with Angola, Ethiopia, Nigeria, South Africa and Zimbabwe, for example, receiving greater shares. Chinese companies are among the largest investors in renewables across the continent, in major hydropower, solar, wind and biogas projects. For instance, China has provided, through its the Export-Import Bank, financing for transmission lines related to the Gilgel Gibe III hydropower project in Ethiopia and a $500 million project loan to the Transmission Company of Nigeria (OECD and IEA, 2014).

Access to climate finance remains a key challenge for Africa. However, some progress has been made in climate negotiations, which agreed to make finance flows consistent with a pathway towards low greenhouse gas emissions and climate resilient development. The agreement also sets a new collective floor of $100 billion a year in climate financing (UN, 2015c). However, the contention by developing countries that climate financing should not be double-counted as ODA has not been well received by development partners. Furthermore, questions remain about the adequacy and distribution of climate funding in general; financing is skewed towards mitigation as opposed to adaptation.

Africa regional banks are, however, stepping up to the plate. The African Development Bank aims to nearly triple its climate financing to reach $5 billion a year by 2020. Apart from increasing its own climate financing, the Bank will also pursue co-financing opportunities by mobilizing concessional climate financing from global funds such as the Climate Investment Funds, the Global Environment Facility and the Green Climate Fund (AfDB, 2015b).

The capacity of countries to achieve the SDGs will depend in part on their capacity to mobilize the requisite financial and nonfinancial resources to facilitate implementation. Strengthening capacities for domestic resource mobilization, stemming the tide of illicit financial flows and re-invigorating the manufacturing sectors will be key to enlarging Africa's fiscal envelope. Nevertheless, African countries and especially least developed countries and small island states will require a supportive global environment and technological support to transition to a green economy pathway. In this context, following through on the commitments to the means of implementing the SDGs will be vital for success.

2.5 CONCLUSIONS AND POLICY RECOMMENDATIONS

The global and continental frameworks provide a favourable context for sustainable development and green industrialization, yet exploiting them will require their integration with national planning frameworks. The convergence of Africa's priorities with the SDGs will likely consolidate support for implementation and follow up among African countries. Still, the broad scopes of Agenda 2030 and Agenda 2063 will create implementation and follow-up difficulties. Further, having developed (not just developing) countries in the agenda will engender greater competition for an ever-shrinking pool of ODA. Policymakers in Africa must work to resolve these issues.

Maintaining [the continent's] low greenhouse gas emissions will require heavy investments in green technology and renewable energy.

African countries will begin pursuing the agendas from some low initial conditions, notably industrial development. Continued dependence on natural resources and fossil fuels will expose the continent to the challenges faced by China and other fossil fuel–dependent emerging economies. Maintaining its low greenhouse gas emissions will require heavy investments in green technology and renewable energy.

Yet as a late industrializer, Africa has a unique opportunity to avoid the pitfalls of brown development, including costly environmental fall-outs, by leapfrogging to a green industrial development pathway. It will be aided by the recent global and regional development agendas that facilitate access to resources, encompassing climate financing, curbs on illicit financial outflows and domestic resource mobilization.

Policymakers must take full advantage of the commitments in the Addis Ababa Action Agenda on international tax cooperation and the technology facilitation mechanism to mobilize financial and non-financial resources. They must hold the international community accountable for their commitments.

Finally, investments in green infrastructure, particularly energy, will be vital for successful green industrialization, so policy-makers must engage the private sector as partners to fill the infrastructure financing gap.

2.6 REFERENCES

Armah, Bartholowmew et al., 2014. "Structural Transformation for Inclusive Development in Africa: The Role of Active Government Policies." *Development*, 57 (3–4). Society for International Development 1011-6370/15. www.sidint.net/development/.

African Union Commission (AUC). 2015. *Agenda 2063: The Africa We Want: First Ten-year Implementation Plan 2013–2023*. Addis Ababa, Ethiopia.

African Development Bank. 2010. "Infrastructure Deficit and Opportunities in Africa." Economic Brief Volume1, September 2010.

AfDB (African Development Bank), OECD (Organisation for Economic Co-operation and Development) and UNDP (United Nations Development Programme). 2015. *African Economic Outlook 2015: Regional Development for Spatial Inclusion*.

———. 2015a. "Climate Finance: Nurturing Africa's Green Growth". Bimonthly Newsletter 29, January–February 2015.

———. 2015b. "Climate Finance: On the Road to COP21". Bimonthly Newsletter 33, September–October 2015.

ECA. (United Nations Economic Commission for Africa). (1999). Economic report on Africa 1999 : the challenge of poverty reduction and sustainability, Addis Ababa.

----------. 2013. *Economic transformation in Africa: Drivers, Challenges and Options*. Issues Paper Prepared for the Third Meeting of the High Level Panel of Eminent Persons, Monrovia, 30th January to 1st February, 2013. Addis Ababa, Ethiopia.

———. 2015. *Innovative financing for the economic transformation of Africa*. Addis Ababa, Ethiopia.

ECA (United Nations Economic Commission for Africa), AUC (African Union Commission), AfDB (African Development Bank) and UNDP (United Nations Development Programme). 2015. *Assessing Progress in Africa toward the Millennium Development Goals*. Lessons learned in implementing the millennium development goals. Addis Ababa, Ethiopia.

ECA and AUC. 2012. Financing of the Programme for Infrastructure Development in Africa (PIDA), Meeting of the Committee of Experts of the 5th Joint Annual Meetings of the AU Conference of Ministers of Economy and Finance and ECA Conference of African Ministers of Finance, Planning and Economic Development, 22–25 March 2012, Addis Ababa, Ethiopia.

ECA and AUC. 2013. *Economic Report on Africa 2013: Making the Most of Africa's Commodities: industrialization for Growth, Jobs and Economic Transformation*. Addis Ababa, Ethiopia.

ECA and AUC. 2014. *Economic Report on Africa 2014: Dynamic Industrial Policy in Africa: Innovative Institutions, Effective Processes and Flexible Mechanisms*. Addis Ababa, Ethiopia.

ECA and UNEP. 2013. *Managing Africa's Natural Resource Base for Sustainable Growth and Development: Sustainable Development Report on Africa IV*. Addis Ababa, Ethiopia.

GIZ (Deutsche Gesellschaft für Internationale Zusammenarbeit [German Corporation for International Cooperation]). 2014. Financing Green Growth: A review of green financial sector policies in emerging and developing economies, November 2014, published on behalf of German Federal Ministry for Economic Cooperation and Development (BMZ), Eschborn, Germany.

ILO (International Labour Organization). 2015. *World Employment Social Outlook: The Changing Nature of Jobs*. Geneva. http://www.ilo.org/global/research/global-reports/weso/2015-changing-nature-of-jobs/WCMS_368626/lang--en/index.htm.

OECD (Organisation for Economic Co-operation and Development) and IEA (International Energy Agency). 2014. *Africa Energy Outlook: A Focus on Energy Prospects in Sub-Saharan Africa. World Energy Outlook Special Report*. Paris.

———. 2015. *Dataset: Aid (ODA) disbursements to countries and regions [DAC2a]*. OECD, Paris. http://stats.oecd.org/BrandedView.aspx?oecd_bv_id=dev-data-en&doi=data-00072-en#.

Turco, M., E. Palazzi, J. Von Hardenberg and A. Provenzale. 2015. "Observed Climate Change Hotspots". *Geophysical Research Letters*, 42: 1–8.

UN (United Nations). 2012. *The Future We Want*. Outcome document of the United Nations Conference on Sustainable Development, Rio de Janeiro, Brazil, 20–22 June 2012.

_______. 2015. Addis Ababa Action Agenda of the Third International Conference on Financing for Development. The final text of the outcome document adopted at the Third International Conference on Financing for Development Addis Ababa, Ethiopia, 13–16 July 2015) and endorsed by the General Assembly in its resolution 69/313 of 27 July 2015.

———. 2015a. Report of the Secretary General on the work of the Organization. New York. Accessed on October 20, 2015 at: http://www.un.org/en/ga/search/view_doc.asp?symbol=A/70/1

———. 2015b. Transforming our world: The 2030 Agenda for Sustainable Development. Outcome Document for the UN Summit on the Post 2015 Development Agenda.

———. 2015c. Adoption of the Paris Agreement. Conference of the Parties Twenty First Session, Paris, 30 November to 11 December. Distributed 12 December 2015.

______. 2016. World Economic Situation and Prospects. New York.

www.un.org/en/development/desa/policy/wesp

UNEP (United Nations Environment Programme). 2011. *Towards a Green Economy: Pathways to Sustainable Development and Poverty Eradication—A Synthesis for Policy Makers*. www.unep.org/greeneconomy.

———. 2011a. *The Transition to a Green Economy: Benefits, Challenges and Risks from a Sustainable Development Perspective*. Report by a Panel of Experts to Second Preparatory Committee Meeting for United Nations Conference on Sustainable Development. http://www.unep.org/greeneconomy/Portals/88/documents/research_products/UN-DESA,%20UNCTAD%20Transition%20GE.pdf.

World Bank. 2010. African Development Indicators. Washington, DC.

———. 2015. *World Development Indicators 2015*. Washington, DC: World Bank. wdi.worldbank.org/tables. Accessed January, 2016.

2.7 ENDNOTES

1 Defined as surface water and groundwater withdrawal as a share of total actual renewable water resources.

2 These factors include limited access to infrastructure; limited employment opportunities resulting from excessive dependence on primary commodity exports; weak governance systems; and conflict and insecurity.

CHAPTER 3

GREENING INDUSTRIALIZATION: RATIONALE AND CONCEPTS

African countries need to industrialize to increase incomes, create employment, raise value-added activity and diversify their economies. Industry has traditionally been a central source of generating employment—in developed and developing countries. In Africa, though, high rates of economic growth over the past decade have not translated into the structural transformation of the economy required. Manufacturing, also, has not made the expected contribution to aggregate output, trade or gross domestic product growth (ECA, 2014). African income levels are the lowest in the world, with 34 African nations among the least developed countries.

In Africa, though, high rates of economic growth over the past decade have not translated into the structural transformation of the economy required.

As described in Chapter 1, high economic growth in recent years has been based largely on commodity trade, especially oil and other extractive industries. African countries remain marginal players in domestic and international markets for manufacturing, and they provide a negligible share of manufactured exports in world markets. Tellingly, manufacturing often has a lower share of gross domestic product (GDP) today than it was 30 years ago. Given the ubiquity of market failures, industrial policy interventions are needed to address these failures, as markets are unable to generate the kinds of structural transformation needed to achieve the leap from low- to high-productivity activities.

As seen in the Economic Report on Africa 2014 (ECA, 2014), African governments have paid too little attention to the role of public authorities in achieving such a structural transformation. Policies and institutions are needed to focus on increasing investment, building higher-productivity economies and bringing public and private actors together in coalitions. Priority areas for government investment are education, infrastructure and technology innovation, set within a long-term development plan that demonstrates a consistent, but flexible, approach. Nothing can replace strong, high-level political leadership to demonstrate stability in macro-economic policy and the vision needed to generate domestic and international investment. From this can develop joint ventures and alliances between domestic and foreign firms, alongside an approach that celebrates innovation and technology cooperation (ECA, 2013).

The action plan for Accelerated Industrial Development of Africa—launched in 2008—presents national, regional and continental priorities, including the following:

- Mobilizing resources for regional infrastructure and heavy industry.
- Rallying the African diaspora to draw on their science and technology skills.
- Allocating 1 per cent of gross domestic product to research and development (R&D).
- Establishing university chairs in innovation and technology transfer centres.
- Building greater South–South collaboration.
- Harmonizing business and investment law.

A development-oriented state is central to such an action plan—one that is committed to mobilizing all stakeholders and has the welfare of the people at heart (ECA, 2013).

3.1 AFRICA'S IMPERATIVE TO ADOPT GREEN GROWTH

African countries risk being trapped at the bottom of the economic ladder, with activity focused on little processing, scarce high-value activity and raw-material and commodity production. This means continued reliance on imports of high-value products and weak linkages with products from the knowledge economy, research and development and enhanced technology.

Debate over the best strategy to escape this trap is appropriate, given the contraction in global "policy space" that is limiting the industrial policy measures countries can use. Some people argue that African countries should focus their investment on areas of comparative strength—especially agriculture and commodities—because that is where their skills and enterprise lie (see, for example, Lin and Monga, 2010). Other observers, however, argue that such a strategy leaves Africa in a low-income trap; hence, other countries will always be ahead in skills, incomes, market power and technology. In that case, African producers would remain junior partners in global value chains, in which power and profit are concentrated at higher levels in the chain (see, for example, Chang, 2015). Consequently, writers such as Chang recommend a "smart" industrial policy led by government that pushes the boundary of policy space, negotiates with lead firms in global value chains, identifies ways to create domestic linkages and invests in new activity areas in which the country can acquire comparative advantage gradually (Chang, 2015).

Africa needs smart industrial policies led by government to enhance value-addition and industrial upgrading

The global economic environment is more complex than such a binary strategy choice implies. Patents, value chains, economies of scale, global investment flows, transnational corporations and intellectual property rights all require that a country's chosen path consider what other countries—geographically near and far—are pursuing. The country also must determine its relative ability to attract the kind of investment it wants from international and domestic sources.

Although Africa has a few globally competitive enterprises (as in mining equipment in South Africa), many of its industries and manufacturing firms operate with significant inefficiency and high resource use (Chapter 4). Those inefficiencies, however, imply big opportunities for gains because investing in new technology should bring major financial and resource savings. In addition, the choice between following a natural resource pathway and knowledge-intensive manufacturing is less stark in practice. Multiple synergies exist between the two sectors. Also, many opportunities are available for increasing knowledge intensity not just of the mining sector but of the firms feeding inputs into the resource sector and processing its outputs (see, for example, Morris, Kaplinsky and Kaplan, 2011).

Chapter 1 flagged that global growth is tailing off, with a widespread slowdown in emerging markets and concerns about low growth in Europe and Japan. Commodity prices have been hit hard. Although the steep fall in oil prices since mid-2014 offers a windfall to oil importers and consumers, it also demonstrates the high-price volatility of primary commodity production. Building a more diverse economic structure makes sense for African countries. It potentially opens further opportunities for greater intra-African trade, in which manufactured products could play a larger role than in global trade. A regional approach to industrial policy also makes sense, alongside constructing the associated infrastructure—such as transport, water and energy—that lays the foundations for further growth.

In a world of uncertain market dynamics, one thing is certain. The future will be different from the past. As a consequence, countries need to build flexible and resilient economies. Although growth in the global economy will continue to reflect shifting patterns of investment, competition, and technology, shocks are also likely from bubbles in the financial and commodity sectors. Huge asymmetries exist in power, information and access to capital held by large investors, global corporations and major commodity brokers. Individually, African countries often are weaker parties in commercial negotiations, but they could gain greater leverage by working together.

Climate change will bring rising temperatures, increased risks of flood and drought, and greater shocks to agricultural systems. Following the 21st Conference of the Parties to the United Nations Framework Convention on Climate Change in Paris (UNFCCC), the necessary directions for future growth and investment are clear. Global leaders have agreed that all economies must shift from unabated use of fossil fuels. They have also pledged "intended nationally determined contributions" designed to set the global economy on a new course "to keep a global temperature rise this century well below 2 degrees Celsius and to drive efforts to limit the temperature increase even further to 1.5 degrees Celsius, above pre-industrial levels" (UNFCCC, 2015). African countries have a choice: Continue along a business as usual path, or seek to be among the leaders in designing the new global low-carbon economy (Denton, 2014). This post-Paris moment offers a time for critical reflection about where Africa's strategic advantage lies.

For all these reasons—the needs to pursue structural transformation, to increase the knowledge intensity in production, to sustain global competitiveness on a dynamic basis and to mitigate the impacts of climate change—Africa needs to adopt a green growth strategy in which green industrialization looms large. Box 3.1 below outlines the main concepts and definitions surrounding Industrialization, Structural Transformation, Greening and their inter-linkages.

GREENING INDUSTRIALIZATION: TRADE-OFFS OR WIN-WINS? SYNERGIES BETWEEN GROWTH, SUSTAINABILITY AND FAIRNESS

The growth–environment trade-off. A common assertion has been that greening the economy is a luxury that only richer countries can afford—that poor countries should develop first and clean up later (see, for example, Grossman, 1995). An equally common argument from neo-classical economists has been that social inclusion can be dealt with after the important business of economic growth has been achieved, through taxes and redistribution. In both cases, governments are urged to stand back and let the market economy operate without hindrance. This approach assumes that a hands-off approach to the environment will maximize growth and provide resources that more than compensate for the costs of environmental and social oversight. This trade-off is thus defined as the conflict between two desirable but incompatible objectives.

BOX 3.1 KEY CONCEPTS AND DEFINITIONS

Industrialization is the process during which a society or country transforms itself from a primarily agricultural society into one based on manufacturing goods and providing services. Individual manual labour often is replaced by mechanized production, and craftspeople are replaced by assembly lines. This transformation usually is accompanied by a set of other changes that enable industrialization, such as increased attention to skills development, accumulation of capital for investment and migration of people from rural to urban centres (and the loss of autonomy it brings). Although the terms *manufacturing* and *industry* often are used interchangeably, *industry* is defined as manufacturing, plus construction and utilities.

In the late 18th century in the United Kingdom, the first Industrial Revolution began with mechanizing the textile industry, based on harnessing water and coal power. Subsequent phases (see box figure 3.1) introduced the moving assembly line and the age of mass production. Further technological revolutions followed, including the digital age. Technology leaders are now exploring a set of techniques that could bring a radical shift in resource productivity and enable more sustainable production patterns based on biomimicry and nanotechnology.

Each phase or type of industrialization offers opportunities—and challenges—for sustainable and equitable growth. It affects not only how and where products are made and consumed but who gains the benefits. Substantial and unanticipated benefits from the new technology are likely. Examples of those benefits include the way banks, mobile phones and electronic identification cards have enhanced the capabilities of poor rural households to access information and services and thus improve their livelihoods.

Structural transformation is the reallocation of resources—especially through new investment—from lower- to higher-productivity activities, shifting typically from agriculture to industry and modern services and within each of these sectors from lower- to higher-productivity niches. It is closely linked to—and usually involves—industrialization and is associated with shifting people and resources into transforming and processing raw materials.

Greening describes a shift towards more resource-conserving activity, in which production and consumption patterns use fewer resources and create less waste over their life cycle. Typically, greening involves a combination of decoupling (maintaining production while using lower input, especially water and carbon-based energy), avoiding environmentally harmful impacts (including effluent spillage and noxious gas emissions) and supporting a diverse and sustainable biosphere.

Greening industrialization ensures that the structural transformation process avoids stranded assets; copes with accelerated urbanization; reduces resource inputs and increases efficiency in the production process; cuts back on harmful waste emissions, such as chemical effluents and poisonous gases; strengthens infrastructure to reduce environmental impacts (such as pollution and extreme weather events); and maintains or improves the natural resource base, including providing associated environmental goods and services.

A green economy ensures that environmental goods and bads are properly costed into individual, enterprise and government decisions. Given that environmental assets often are poorly valued, with unclear property rights, they are subject to generating many externalities, leading to overuse and damage. Interventions are therefore needed to ensure that environmental asset values are properly accounted for—collectively—as "natural capital" (the living and non-living aspects of nature that produce value and benefits to people and that underpin all other capital in economies and societies). Many examples of market failure exist, in which reliance on prices and markets to allocate goods and services over people, space and time is likely to generate unwanted social and environmental damage. Greenhouse gas emissions are the most obvious example, but a range of other environmental goods and services—such as threats to clean air, forests, water, biodiversity and genetic resources—require public action to correct market failure (see "Environmental damage means we need to green the economy," later in this chapter).

The United Nations Environment Programme's definition of a green economy is far broader and has social—not just environmental—objectives. By its definition the green economy "results in improved human well-being and social equity, while significantly reducing environmental risks and ecological scarcities. In its simplest expression, a green economy can be thought of as one that is low carbon, resource efficient and socially inclusive" (UNEP, 2011). In this report we keep separate the social and environmental dimensions, as they do not necessarily overlap and each demands different kinds of intervention.

BOX FIGURE 3.1 "NORMAL" PATTERNS OF INDUSTRIALIZATION

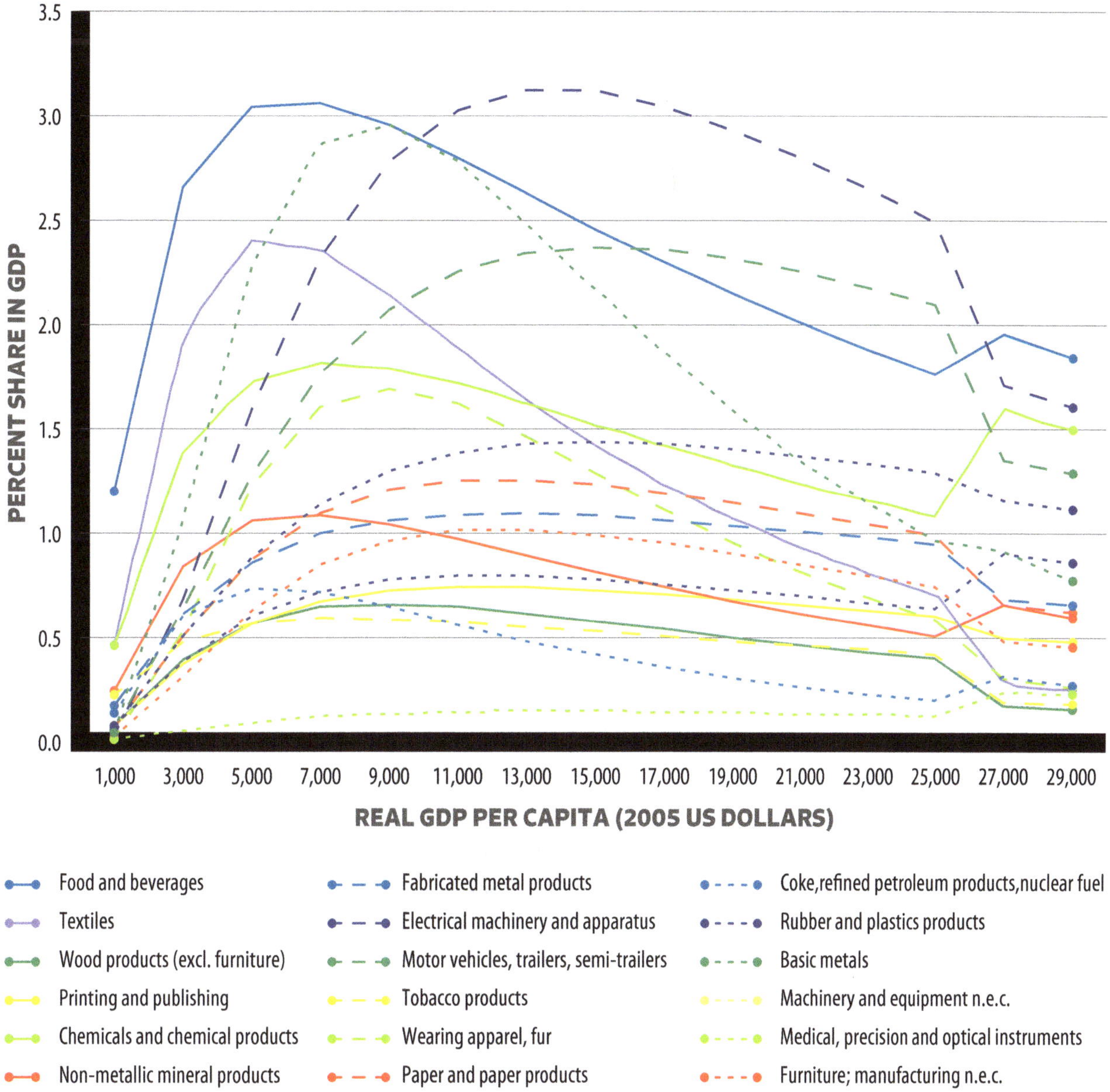

SOURCE: THE NATURAL EDGE PROJECT (2004).

Sustainable development is "a pattern of development that meets the needs of the present without compromising the ability of future generations to meet their own needs" (UN, 1987). Sustainable development promotes the idea that social, environmental and economic progress are attainable within the limits of Earth's natural resources if greater attention is paid to people's needs as opposed to their wants. Sustainable development approaches everything as connected through space, time and quality of life.

Growth–environment synergies or win-wins. Counter-posed to the trade-off argument is the idea of growth–environment synergies. According to this viewpoint, far from an environmental approach undermining the rate of growth, it makes a positive contribution to growth. For example, Perman and Stern (2003) show that the statistical basis for the growth–environment trade-off is not robust because, in particular, it ignores the consequences that neglecting the environment today may have by actively undermining current and future growth. The trade-off argument also does not consider that regulation tends to be more effective in higher-income nations than in middle and low income countries. In the latter countries, tackling pollution after it has occurred is largely ineffective.

Type of growth. The growth–environment trade-off does not involve only the rate of growth but the type of growth and the distribution of the fruits of growth. Conventional calculations of GDP provide little insight into the qualitative dimensions of the rate of growth, thus complicating the arguments for and against the existence of the growth–environment trade-offs and synergies or win-wins.

Time preferences. It is important to ask: over what period should the growth–environment trade-off be considered? How long might environmentally destructive growth be worthwhile before the fruits of rapid growth can be used to clean up the mess? Alternatively, if win-win synergies exist between growth and the environment, how long might those synergies take to emerge? Also, if a short-term investment is needed to achieve medium- to long-term gains, what is a reasonable payback period?

For Africa the costs to incomes, growth and health from business as usual will be heavy because of the rapid rise in demand from increased consumption across the continent (Chapter 5). Reparation of environmental damage is difficult and expensive. For example, soil lost by erosion often ends up in dams, reducing energy and irrigation capacity, and digging out soil from the reservoir and transporting it back to the lands from which it had been washed would be a hugely expensive task.

The politics of achieving an inclusive and green industrialization cannot be ducked. The language of "trade-offs" may be used by those who will not benefit from such change. For example, a government may want to invest in an electrified railway line to carry freight to and from its port but face opposition from major politicians who have already invested in a fleet of trucks and for whom freight transport is a big earner.

Sections of the rest of this report revisit the extent to which growth–environment synergies or trade-offs prevail, the quality of growth involved, and the optimum periods within which policymakers should consider these issues.

3.2 PROMOTING INDUSTRIALIZATION IN AFRICA

The three previous *Economic Reports on Africa* have focused the spotlight on how African governments can promote industrialization through commodities, trade and dynamic policy (ECA, 2013, 2014, 2015). They emphasized that countries seeking to accelerate industrialization must adopt a strong developmental mind-set and enact far-sighted, coherent efforts to address market failures and promote restructuring.

In a fast-changing world, African countries risk falling further behind in the competitiveness stakes as a result of weak institutions, infrastructure deficits and limited skills and technological achievements. Successful government action involves systematic coordination between the private and public sectors while avoiding risks of "capture" by interest groups. Structural change will inevitably involve the disruption of established industries and activities, hence the importance of the state ensuring policy independence (Oqubay, 2015).

Structural transformation has traditionally been seen as achieved by an economy "marching through the sectors," based on a snapshot of the economy at different levels of per capita income. On the basis of these data, the assumption is that all economies will move through a similar "normal pattern of industrialisation" (Kuznets, 1966; Syrquin and Chenery, 1989). An economy with an average GDP per capita of $3,000, for example, can expect to have an industrial sector dominated by food and beverages, textiles and several "lesser" activities. An economy with eight times that GDP per capita can expect to host a much more diverse pattern, in which electrical machinery and vehicle manufacturing are major elements but food and beverages are still important.

This traditional approach has been widely used to target sectors in industrial policy (Lin and Monga, 2010). A government would seek, for example, to target a level of per capita income somewhat above its existing level, analyse the "normal" pattern of economic structure at this higher income level (figure 3.1), and then promote investment in those identified growth-opportunity sectors that were close to its existing industrial structure.

A similar approach might be used to target greening of the industrial sector through the decoupling of growth from resource use. The priority sectors would be identified on the basis of their overall environmental footprint, however, rather than their association with levels of per capita income. Figure 3.2 illustrates how this approach might be used to lower energy intensity by inducing policymakers to direct investment from the metals, chemicals and non-metallic mineral sectors towards low energy–intensive sectors. If water scarcity is the principal environmental challenge, a government might promote economic activity that minimizes water use by moving out of food, textiles and leather goods and into electronics, biotechnology and pharmaceuticals.

This traditional approach of "marching through the sectors" suffers, however, from five main limitations, suggesting that while helpful at one level, it can only be a partial guide for achieving a green and inclusive vision.

- The "fallacy of composition" refers to an action or policy that offers returns only if a limited number of countries adopt the same policy. If many (or all) economies do so, a dearth of production will ensue in the vacated sectors and an excess of production in the targeted sectors.

FIGURE 3.1 WAVES OF INNOVATION AND STRUCTURAL TRANSFORMATION

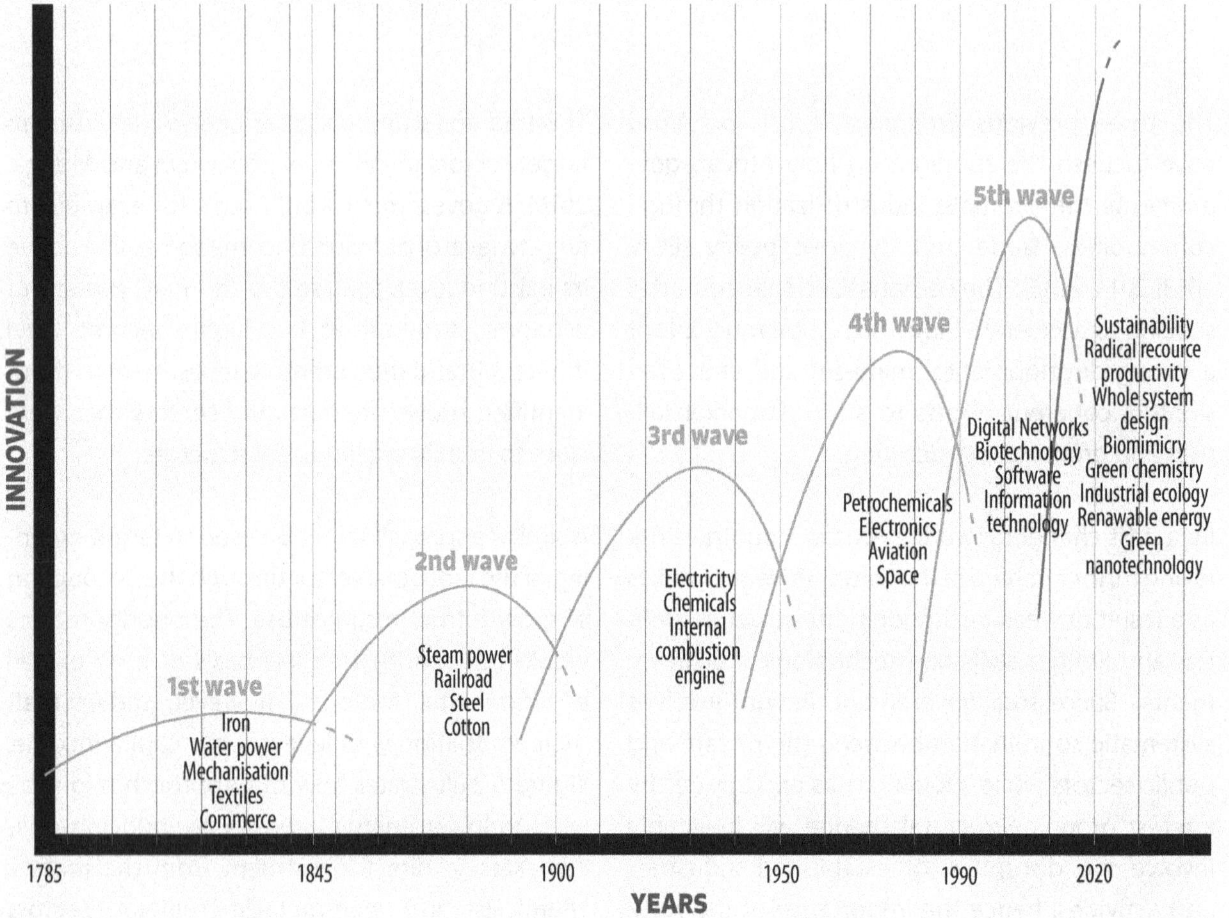

SOURCE: HARAGUCHI AND RESONJA (2010).

NOTE: GDP = GROSS DOMESTIC PRODUCT; N.E.C. = NOT ELSEWHERE CLASSIFIED.

- Even if a single economy acts alone to shift from environmentally damaging activity, without similar decisions in other economies, this move would not reduce the overall environmental impact—it would merely displace it. It is one of the weaknesses in the industrial economies' lauding the reduction of their environmental impact because of a reduction in energy intensity in their economies. In many cases this measures only the footprint of their own production rather than that of their consumption, ignoring the displacement of energy-intensive links to low- and middle-income economies.
- Because environmental impacts have no respect for national boundaries, the greening economy may be unable to avoid the negative externalities generated in the non-green sectors they are vacating. For example, water use in one economy may have profound impacts on water access and livelihoods in adjacent economies (box 4.6: Impacts of competition for scarce water).

FIGURE 3.2 INDUSTRIAL ENERGY CONSUMPTION, BY SECTOR, 1990–2008

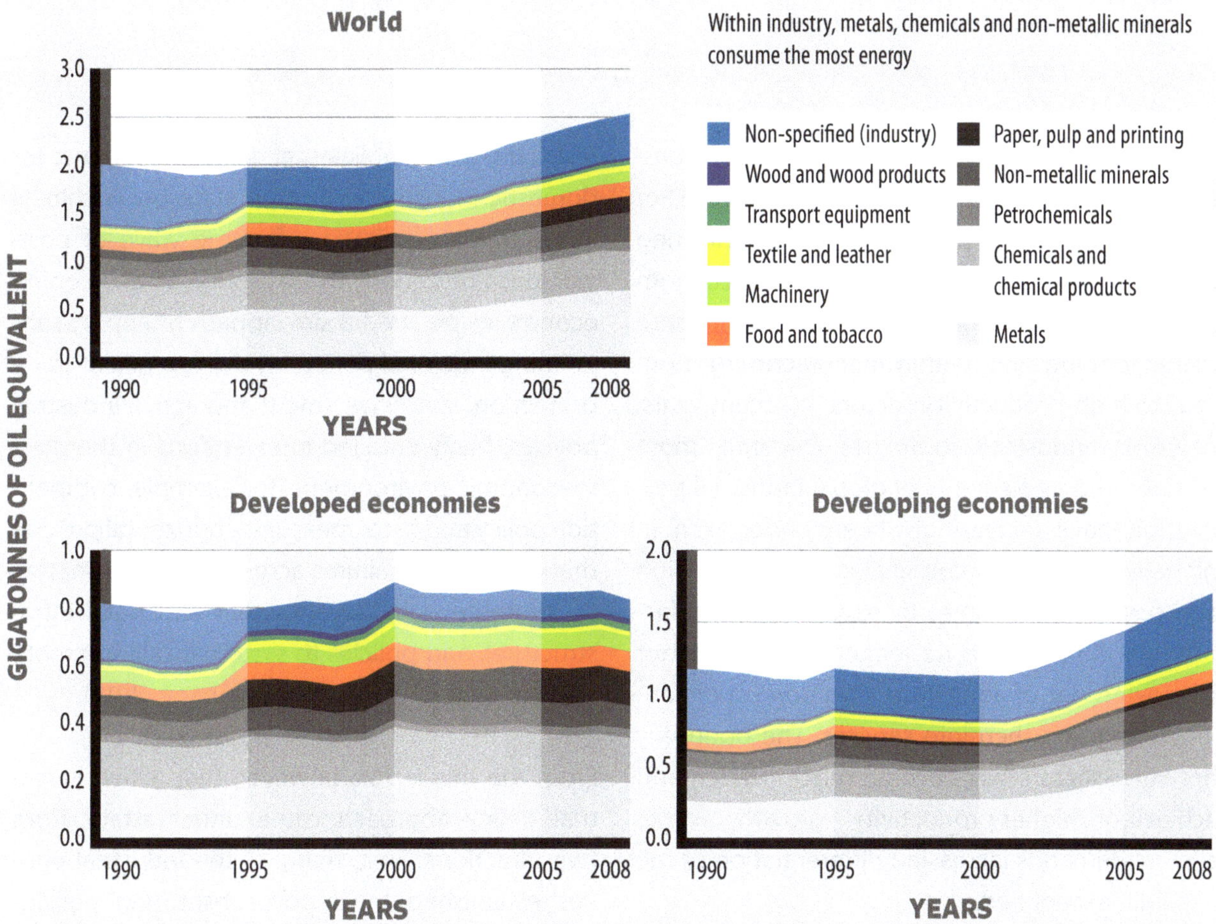

SOURCE: IEA (2010).

- Structural change may be as important within sectors as between sectors by, for example, introducing much more energy-efficient equipment to replace existing plants. This point is particularly relevant given the increasing spread of value chains as drivers of economic growth, nationally and globally.
- Some sectors are newly emerging and have little historical experience on which to draw in charting opportunities opened by new challenges. Newly industrializing economies have scope to leapfrog the structures of industrialized economies. An important emerging opportunity lies in producing capital goods and services for the green economy, as countries such as China and Germany have shown. Demand for green capital goods and services has a growth elasticity larger than 1 (that is, demand for these goods rises faster than the growth of the economy as a whole), so investment in this sector offers great potential.

3.3 CHANGING CONTEXT FOR INDUSTRIAL POLICY

Historically, *industrialization* and *structural transformation* have largely been synonymous. For many years, higher productivity, the wellspring of higher per capita incomes, has resulted from a structural transition out of agriculture into manufacturing and, within manufacturing, from low- to high-productivity sectors. In recent years, however, industrialization has become more complicated as elements of global industrial production have increasingly been undertaken in globally dispersed value chains. Achieving high and sustainable incomes by expanding manufacturing and industry is no longer a simple matter of moving out of agriculture into domestic manufacturing and then into services. The boundary between sectors has become much fuzzier, and achieving higher-productivity growth within sectors demands increasing differentiation of the capabilities required..

Industrial policy has a critical role to play in achieving green growth. Historically, advanced economies promoted their industrial transformation through active industrial policies that involved restrictive trade policies, active state support for domestic industry, and often state ownership of industry (Chang, 2015). After the wave of post-war decolonization, the majority of developing economies pursued a similar path of import-substituting industrial policy, involving a mix of trade protection, state investment and active industrial policies. Many entailed interventions in the macroeconomic environment (for example, competition policy and fiscal measures), horizontal policies that met market failures across a range of sectors (to promote skills development and build infrastructure), and policies to systematically promote specific sectors' development (Chang, 2015).

Achieving high and sustainable incomes ... ... is no longer a simple matter of moving out of agriculture into domestic manufacturing and then into services. The boundary between sectors has become much fuzzier,...

From the mid-1970s, however, that active industrial policy approach came under attack from two directions. First, many of the industrial entities established by import-substituting policies were marked by inefficiencies induced by lack of competition, low levels of scale and high rates of corruption, which led to growing balance-of-payments deficits, declining growth and rising debt. Second, the wave of neoliberalism that was surging through the advanced economies led to intense pressure on governments in Africa and elsewhere to sweep away their industrial policies. Proponents argued that the unleashing of market forces would allow industry to thrive in Africa and throughout the world. Support for this policy agenda was drawn from the export success of Asian economies, which was mistakenly characterized as driven almost entirely by market forces (Amsden, 1989; Chang, 2015; Wade, 1990).

The outcome for Africa did not meet the confident expectations of the neoliberal reformers. During the past 30 years in Africa, the abandonment of industrial policy has been linked to a decline in the share of manufacturing in GDP in virtually all the continent's economies and a fall in Africa's share of global manufacturing value added. At the same time, many of the formerly dominant advanced economies have increasingly become victims of deindustrialization, as the Asian economies—which had long used active public industrial policies—increased their competitiveness (Chang, 2015). Industrial policy and development of productive capacity have thus become increasingly recognized as needed now and once again are high on the policy agenda—not just in developing nations but in rich countries as well.

GLOBALIZATION AND THE RISE OF VALUE CHAINS

Many goods and services are now produced and distributed along global value chains, with different elements of the design, production and retail phases in (usually) widely separated locations. Differentiating "industrialization" from broader forms of "structural transformation" in the economy, therefore, is not easy. Many activities previously incorporated in manufacturing (for example, design and marketing) have now been outsourced to the service sector. Also, industry-related growth in the resource sector (including agriculture) cannot be easily distinguished from investments in services and agriculture. Following established practice, in this report we shall refer to this challenge of promoting higher-productivity growth as one of "industrialization," in the full knowledge that the pattern of structural change in contemporary economies cannot be captured by the expansion of manufacturing only.

The new industrial policy agenda, however, is of a different character. Many instruments of traditional industrial policy, such as trade policy protection and state ownership, are inhibited by international agreements, such as World Trade Organization (WTO) agreements and Economic Partnership Agreements. Instead, governments are increasingly focusing on promoting capabilities to enable their enterprises to compete in global value chains, promote technical and economic innovation (Mazzucato, 2013), develop new sectors (such as green industries), and diffuse new technologies (renewables, for example).

The complexity of the contemporary industrialization agenda is described in Chapter 4, particularly how it stems from, and is furthered by, extension of production in value chains.

ENVIRONMENTAL DAMAGE MEANS WE NEED TO GREEN THE ECONOMY

"Greening" the economy was an idea first introduced by David Pearce, Anil Markandya, and Edward Barbier (1989). These economists argued that governments needed to intervene in the economy to address market imperfections. A burgeoning literature on environmental economics has since evolved, suggesting ways to value unpriced environmental goods and services, to design instruments for addressing externalities and to recognize the essential role of public action and investment in public goods.

The past few decades have seen unprecedented—and accelerating—human impacts on the global environment, as shown by the global "human footprint" since 1960 (figure 3.3). This demonstrates that since the early 1970s, humankind has been taking more from the planet's resources than is sustainable in the long term, and that levels of consumption are "over-shooting" the ecological boundaries. It also shows that continuing on the current pattern of growth (Business as Usual), we overshoot the resources of two planet earths by 2040. If we are to sustain prosperity on this single planet, we need to follow a rapid reduction in resource use to achieve "one planet living" by 2050 (Global Footprint Network, 2015).

FIGURE 3.3 HOW MANY EARTHS DOES IT TAKE TO SUPPORT HUMANITY?

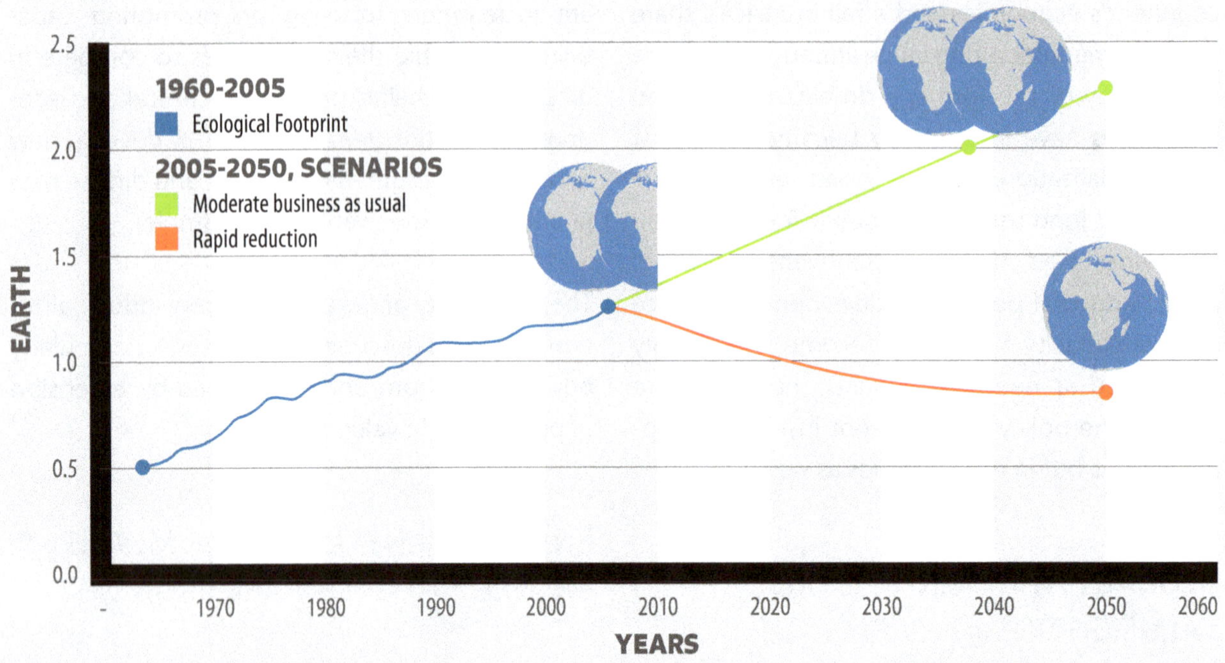

SOURCE: GLOBAL FOOTPRINT NETWORK (2015).

Given the scale and spread of human activity, we are changing the nature of the Earth's climate, its water and nitrogen systems, its ocean temperatures and chemistry, and its vitality and diversity of biological life. Scientists are now talking about the Earth having moved into a new geological era, called the Anthropocene, denoting an epoch in which humans (*Anthropos*) began to have an overwhelming impact on the earth's biological and chemical systems. Given the uncertainty we face over tipping points and the consequences of our cumulative impact, we must establish safe operating limits for key parameters (Rockstrom et al., 2009; Steffen et al., 2015). The decision to keep global warming to less than 2 degrees Celsius, made at the 21st Conference of the Parties (COP21) at the United Nations Conference on Climate Change in 2015, is one such agreed boundary, and identifying other boundaries will have to follow.

The current thinking on policy to achieve a green transition is summarized by Stern (2015), who reminds us of the six reasons for governments to address environmental market failures, especially regarding the climate:

- Greenhouse gases impose a negative externality because of the damage they inflict on others.
- Research, development and innovation are activities that are largely "public goods"; thus we will not likely see enough of them if they are left to the private sector.
- Capital markets are highly imperfect, short term and risk averse, and thus do not generate and allocate capital into the uncertain, long-term investments needed to address climate change.
- People operate with imperfect information about what others are likely to do, inducing coordination failure, which slows collective action.
- People also operate with imperfect information about the economic and technical oppor-

tunities open to them, especially in a time of rapid change. They benefit from access to information, training and learning platforms.

- Moving to a low-carbon economy generates multiple co-benefits, or positive externalities, but individuals are unlikely to harvest those benefits directly. Rather, as with improved air quality and better urban environments, the benefits cannot be appropriated and "sold" but benefit large numbers of people.

Governments must be involved in finding solutions to these market imperfections, and they must work with other actors—other governments, local and municipal governments, small and large businesses, civil society, R&D institutions—to achieve rapid, transformational change. Public policy must create credible, long-term signals for all agents to follow. Policy uncertainty holds back investment because those individuals with capital are not confident that their investment will bring returns. Given the scale of the green transformation required, the role of public action is especially critical. Small changes in prices will not be enough to achieve the scale of change required and will often have effects limited to individual sectors. Governments, then, need to understand how they can launch and sustain a holistic process of economic transformation, which greens the entire system, and drive the economy in a different manner from business as usual.

One key reason for the absence of environmental (and social) goods from the calculus of decision makers, whether government or business, is that those goods are not transacted in the marketplace and do not have a clear "price" at which they can be valued and included in the national accounts (UNEP, 2011). Consequently, the metrics we use to assess progress are limited to economic accounts, which ignore much of the informal sector and many environmental and social costs and benefits. Although many people have come to accept that GDP growth per capita is not a full measure of increased well-being, the absence of easy, comparable alternatives means that GDP continues to be accepted as the default metric. A further drawback of using GDP per capita as a measure of progress in a given country is the need to take due account of the distribution of incomes, as discussed in the next section. The Human Development Index—now in its 25th year—is one alternative. Others include the Global Happiness Index, the Global Ecological Footprint and a range of environmental indices.

WE MUST BUILD INCLUSION INTO THE GREEN ECONOMY

The need to promote more inclusive forms of economic growth—not just in Africa but in many other economies—is widely recognized. Commentary on the rise in inequality and exclusion over the past two decades has focused on incomes and assets, as well as on the jobless patterns of growth and capture of the political process by a small number of the very rich (Stiglitz, 2012). In many middle- and low-income countries, the majority of the population have been failed by the current

Policy uncertainty holds back investment because those individuals with capital are not confident that their investment will bring returns. Given the scale of the green transformation required, the role of public action is especially critical.

economic system—women and men who live and work in the informal economy, whose voices rarely count because they are poor—and the state provides little if any protection of their assets and property rights.

Africa is showing pervasive trends towards absolute and relative exclusion. Although African economies have grown at an unprecedentedly fast rate in recent years, the fruits of this growth have not been widely spread. The proportion of people living below the $1.25-a-day poverty line fell from 56.5 per cent in 1990 to 48.4 per cent in 2010, but because of population growth during that period, the absolute number of people living in poverty grew from 350 million to 505 million. Efforts at the country level to reduce poverty vary, however, with some countries reducing poverty rates much faster—Burkina Faso, Ethiopia, Gambia, Malawi, Niger, Rwanda, Swaziland, and Uganda—than others.

Exclusion is not just a factor affecting incomes and wealth. It also affects quality of life, nature and determinants of livelihoods, and access to basic services such as water, health services and education.

Inequality has grown over the same period, although data are patchy. Differences in inequality between African countries are marked: Botswana, Comoros Islands, Namibia and South Africa, exhibit the most unequal incomes, and Egypt, Ethiopia, Mali, and Niger the least. The growing gap between rich and poor is not unique to Africa, however, and has characterized growth in many other parts of the world (Piketty, 2014). The top 1 per cent of the global population is now estimated to own more than 50 per cent of total global wealth, with the bottom half owning less than 10 per cent (Credit Suisse, 2015).

Exclusion is not just a factor affecting incomes and wealth. It also affects quality of life, nature and determinants of livelihoods, and access to basic services such as water, health services and education. Access to formal employment in Africa is highly skewed and shows little sign of growth. Considering the proportion of people working outside agriculture, the informal economy is reckoned to account for 50–75 per cent of employment throughout the developing world. Within Africa, this differs significantly from South Africa at 33 per cent to Mali at more than 80 per cent (ILO, 2015). When agriculture is included, the informal sector constitutes the majority of working people in most of Africa, and much of it consists of small and medium-sized enterprises, often family run. Informal employment often means unsafe working conditions, with no protection over non-payment of wages, nor job protection. The informal sector only rarely offers social benefits, such as pensions, health insurance or sick pay. Often the most vulnerable groups—the poorest, migrants, women and children—work in the informal sector because of their limited formal qualifications.

For green growth and industrialization to really fulfil its promise, it also must focus on people—to tackle the poverty, inequality and exclusion that constrain growth and environmental sustainability, to realize women's and men's aspirations, to address the needs of different regions, and to gain broad political support. Without that broader support, neither the growth process as a whole nor specific stand-alone green-growth projects and investments will lead to real transformation.

BUILDING RESILIENCE TO CLIMATE CHANGE IS CENTRAL TO GREEN AND INCLUSIVE INDUSTRIALIZATION

Greening industrialization, as seen, involves much more than focusing on a low-carbon agenda, although the post-Paris momentum and the availability of financial resources mean that de-carbonization is now a powerful, fundamental driver. As will be seen in chapters 4 and 5, the sustainable management of the continent's environmental capital assets—land and soils, water, natural resources and energy—is central to providing food, shelter, and decent work; generating incomes, jobs and livelihoods; and ensuring well-being, health and dignity for all. Climate change will affect Africa's economic and social prospects, however.

Resilience has become the widespread term used to capture the capacity of social, economic and environmental systems to maintain their functions in the face of new external stresses imposed by climate change. A principal feature of climate change is a shift in the pattern and variability of the global water cycle, bringing more intense rainfall and droughts. Increased climate resilience hence requires, above all, investment in managing water—whether storing water to address long periods of drought or capturing and diverting floodwaters to limit damage to infrastructure, housing, soils and vegetation. A climate-resilient economy will need to adapt, reorganize and evolve into configurations that improve the sustainability of the system, better preparing it for future climate change impacts.

Greening and climate-resilient growth overlap but are not identical. Economies can be green yet not climate resilient, as when a low-carbon energy source, such as hydroelectric power, is highly vulnerable to a wide variability in rainfall and river flow (as in Zambia; see box 4.6). Conversely, economies can be climate resilient yet not greening, as when agricultural productivity is based on high levels of chemical fertilizer (whose manufacture relies on major fossil-fuel input and entails major emissions of the greenhouse gas nitrous oxide) to maintain yields variability in rainfall crises. Considerations of climate resilience might require a rethink of a country's irrigation options—for example, in Morocco, where investment has shifted into drip delivery of water for high-value fruit and vegetables and away from furrow irrigation of lower-value cereals and sugar.

Inclusive and climate resilient means building on an understanding of how climate-related shocks will not only exacerbate existing stresses faced by poor households but will also reinforce the underlying drivers of poverty. Repeated and long-term drought, for instance, will not only erode households' monetary income; it will also affect multidimensional indicators of poverty, including health, education and people's capability to participate in processes that are meaningful to them. Women and girls are among the most vulnerable to climate change impacts because they encounter multiple inequalities that hinder their ability to manage and recover from shocks and stresses. For instance, women tend to have lower incomes, fewer productive assets, greater responsibility for dependants and poorer access to education and climate-resilient livelihoods (Care International, 2010). With climate impacts set to worsen, the well-being of women and their dependants is under severe threat (Mearns and Norton, 2010).

Policy interventions must transform economic growth into climate-resilient and inclusive development to deliver poverty eradication and greater equity. A combination of social protection and climate-resilient investments can help to build the capability of poor and climate-vulnerable households to absorb or transfer risks (or both). Risk reduction through the preparation for and the recovery from climate-related disasters is part of building climate resilience.

3.4 GREENING INDUSTRIALIZATION AND INCLUSIVE GROWTH

Figure 3.4 presents the three public policy imperatives of industrialization, green growth and inclusive growth. As shown on the left-hand side, in most countries each of those goals has been pursued in isolation, with a different branch of government responsible for each area of policy design, implementation and funding. For example, the protection of industries such as cement manufacturing has been done with little thought either to the likely impacts on low-income groups or to environmental factors, such as pollution of water, energy and air. Equally, green growth can be pursued by a large company that practices sustainable timber production from a forest area, but it may exclude local people from access to and use of forest resources.

On the right-hand side of the figure, these three policy imperatives are brought together. Overlapping them offers a timely opportunity—first, to identify the synergies between industrialization, growth and inclusion; and second, to take steps to align the three policy areas closely. Such synergies will help strengthen win-win outcomes and minimize trade-offs between each policy objective.

BRINGING TOGETHER INDUSTRIALIZATION, GREENING AND INCLUSION

The green and inclusive industrialization agenda offers a valuable pathway to combine sustainable economic growth, more inclusive incomes and an enhanced environment within a broader green economy strategy. As noted by Jeffrey Sachs "Unless we combine economic growth with social

FIGURE 3.4 GREENING INDUSTRIALIZATION AND INCLUSIVE GROWTH

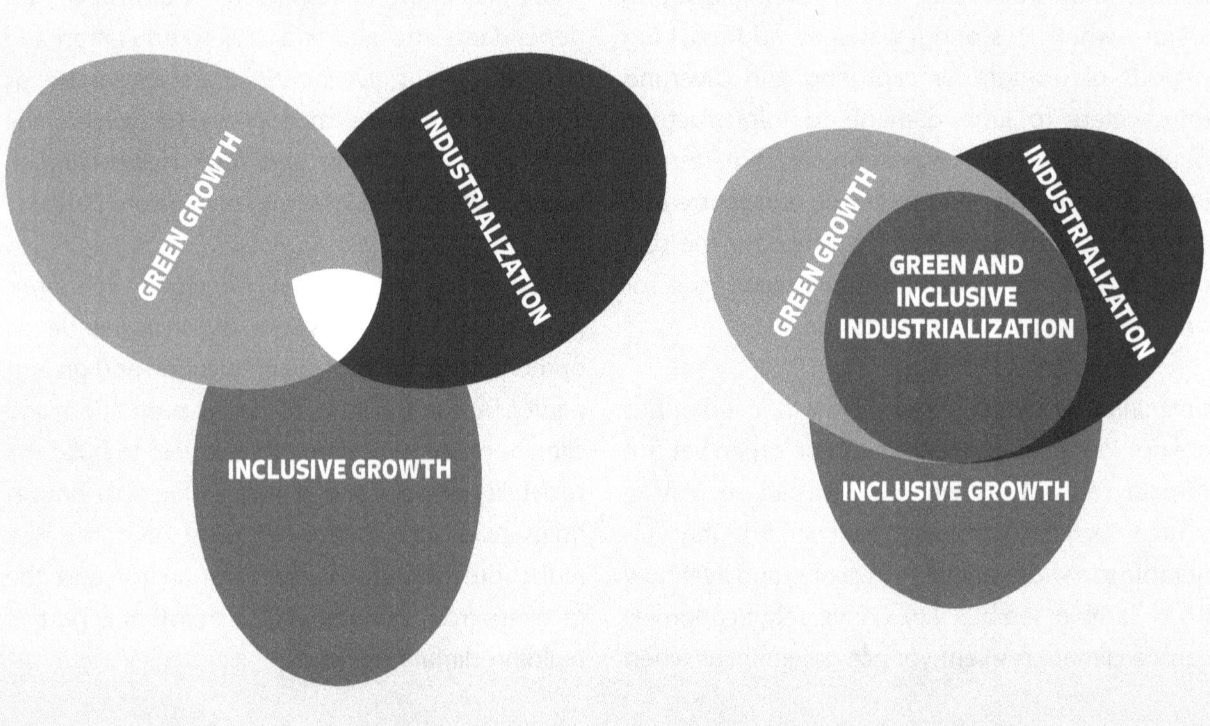

inclusion and environmental sustainability, the economic gains are likely to be short-lived, as they will be followed by social instability and a rising frequency of environmental catastrophes" (2015, p. 27).

Greening of industry can be achieved through three routes: transitioning out of brown industries; greening existing industries by increasing resource productivity, cutting pollution, and managing chemicals more safely; and creating new green enterprise, such as producing green capital goods, generating renewable energy and providing environmental advisory services.

Much of this transition can be classified as "decoupling"—that is, achieving economic growth with lower levels of materials intensity ("relative decoupling") or, better still, with a reduction in the overall use of materials ("absolute decoupling"). Decoupling can be achieved through a focus on increasing the efficiency of input use at the firm level and curbing environmental pollution from the production process. Equally, opportunities exist for systemic greening of production, including through the greening of value chains. (Africa's experience with decoupling and greening will be discussed in greater detail in Chapter 4). The greening of value chains requires collaboration among multiple actors, including governments, the private sector, civil society organizations and a range of multilateral institutions.

INCENTIVES FOR GREENING INDUSTRIALIZATION

The year 2015 was one of intense international diplomacy to build a more sustainable, fairer world. It witnessed many global processes and summits, including the Financing for Development meeting in June, agreement of the Sustainable Development Goals (SDGs) in September and the UNFCCC Conference of the Parties COP21 in December (see Chapter 2). At issue throughout the year was the acknowledged need to construct a more resource-efficient, inclusive and low-carbon global economy that simultaneously generates widespread growth in jobs and well-being while managing resource scarcities, building resilience to climate impacts and putting the global economy on a pathway towards zero net carbon emissions by 2050. The Paris Accord in December at the UNFCCC provided a solid agreement for building a low-carbon global economy.

Although the need to reduce carbon emissions globally clearly exists, developed and developing economies start from different points on emissions per head and levels of income. Because many African economies have low levels of industrial development, their contribution to global warming through carbon emissions has been small to date. Despite this difference in approach, given the collective threat, all African countries have agreed on common but differentiated responsibilities to meet the challenge of climate change through the "intended nationally determined contributions" announced by every country in the run-up to the Paris climate summit. All African economies readily acknowledge the need to join this critically important global agenda, as evidenced by their endorsement of the Paris Accord and a range of initiatives, such as those on renewable energy (see Chapter 4).

Greening of industry can be achieved through three routes: transitioning out of brown industries; greening existing industries...; and creating new green enterprise,...

Reducing carbon emissions to address the problem of global warming and climate change is one major incentive to move economies on to a greener industrialization trajectory, but other important factors also encourage such a shift:

- The green sector can be an important source of growth, providing the opportunity to increase GDP and to create productive employment (ILO, 2015).
- The green sector has the potential to improve Africa's trade balance sharply by reducing energy imports and earning foreign exchange through the export of green goods and services.
- Because many African economies share common environmental challenges, a shared green growth and industrialization agenda will promote regional integration, cooperation and the growth of continentwide innovation capabilities.
- African economies are relatively resource dependent. The processing of minerals, metals and energy resources is highly water and energy intensive and often produces harmful effluents. Hence, a resource-dependent growth path demands that more attention be paid to greater water and energy efficiencies plus pollution control.
- The green sector is relatively knowledge intensive, and its expansion can thus be an important source of structural transformation, productivity change and employment growth. Those types of growth are particularly important for Africa because, as seen in Chapter 1, behind the impressive growth experienced by many African economies, they still show little productivity growth and job creation.
- The greening of growth will improve the quality of development outcomes, particularly for health. Air pollution from diesel vehicles, coal- and oil-fired power stations, smoky cooking fires and industrial emissions increase mortality from respiratory diseases and heart problems. Globally, an estimated 7 million people die prematurely from indoor and outdoor air pollution, including 750,000 in Africa (WHO, 2014). A shift from fossil fuels promises substantial health gains.[1]
- A degrading biophysical environment reduces economic growth and renders livelihoods more insecure and vulnerable to shock. Such risks are a major political threat to individual African economies, for the continent as a whole and for the wider region, as recently flagged at the EU-Africa Valletta Summit on Migration, held in Malta in November 2015. Populations forced off their land by poverty, climate change impacts and conflict generate political difficulties domestically and, when translated into mass migration, within the wider region.
- The poor rely most heavily on natural capital and the services provided by land, water and biodiversity (PEP, 2005), rendering them particularly vulnerable to pollution of key assets and pressure on critical resources, such as water, forests and biodiversity.

Thus, the pathway to green and inclusive industrialization must be shaped by three considerations. First, the green growth agenda cannot be reduced to minimizing carbon emissions. Although it is an important part of green growth, so too is the need to protect Africa's scarce and fragile water resources, to minimize pollution and to enhance the quality of developmental outcomes on the quality of employment and of economic inclusion. Second, although some trade-offs will always exist between short-term economic growth and green industrialization, multiple opportunities will also emerge for green growth to bring win-win outcomes. If properly framed, green industrialization can contribute to faster, more equitable and more sustainable patterns of growth (Chapter 5). Third, the green growth agenda is not a "five-year" challenge. Many of its steps involve long-term policy and resource commitments, carried through consistently. Most policies require cooperation across ministerial divisions and economic sectors. Strategic vision and leadership at the highest level are thus critical to inclusive green industrialization.

If properly framed, green industrialization can contribute to faster, more equitable and more sustainable patterns of growth.

To be successful, governments have recourse to a range of possible policy measures, each with a specific consequence for distributional benefits. If inclusion is to be a key goal, consistent choices in policy design are needed to deliver pro-poor outcomes. If greening is to be more than policy rhetoric, a credible combination of regulations, fiscal measures and incentives are needed to provide private investment with clear and consistent messages about the government's intent to invest in a better environment and to curb environmental damage.

Crucially, alongside design of policy and institutions, governments must invest in the capacity to implement those policies. This will require a realistic assessment of what government can do best and where it needs to rely on private sector actors. It will also call for a learning approach to enable policy to be tweaked over time, in light of new information and changing circumstances. Public investment in education and basic infrastructure is critical, as is working within a regional and global context, to build most effectively on comparative advantage. Industrial policy must consider the right mix of production for domestic consumption and for exports to regional and global markets. This long-term vision for a given country must have a "starting point" that reflects the specific circumstances of an individual economy—including its resources, size and location—within the wider global context and the continuous evolution of international competition.

3.5 FROM POLICY TO PROCESS, PARTNERSHIPS AND LEARNING

This chapter has described the linkages between the green industrialization and inclusive growth agenda. Current policy debates recognize the growing strain on environmental resources as African economies grow and develop, and the need to generate better jobs and higher incomes for African citizens. Much of the impetus for green growth in other parts of the world has come from the need to cut greenhouse gas emissions. In the case of Africa, however, if growth is to be sustainable and inclusive, equal thought must be given to getting the best value from the agricultural sector and its associated environmental base—the minerals, oil and gas that have to date been more of a curse than a blessing, uncertain and poorly managed water supplies on which life depends, and the rapid growth in energy demand. Well-shaped green growth measures can offer good outcomes for all these challenges.

Such measures require the recognition that "policy" is no longer the monopoly of government. The neoliberal critique of industrial policy was based on the recognition of imperfect knowledge and corruption in government—state failure. In contrast, proponents of industrial policy argued that simultaneous patterns of imperfect knowledge exist in the private sector, complemented by a combination of short-termism and the failure of individual firms to promote systemic competitiveness in their value chains—private failure.

An important component of contemporary industrial policy thus seeks to promote collaboration between the private and public sectors, each recognizing its own weaknesses and strengths. In this way industrial policy is not made up of a series of documents, but instead is a process in which the key stakeholders—public, private and, in some cases, civil society—work together to achieve a structural transformation that promotes higher and more sustainable incomes. This process-oriented approach to industrial policy—recognizing the interdependence of the private and public realm and the significance of systemic efficiency—informs the green industrial policy agenda set out in Chapter 7, which is designed to achieve a win-win outcome to green growth in Africa.

Before identifying key policy agendas and suggesting roles for private and public actors in the pursuit of green and inclusive industrial growth, it is first necessary to understand the determinants of green industrialization and previous experiences with decoupling economic growth from environmental impacts (Chapter 4), the dangers of inaction for Africa's ability to meet current and future needs (Chapter 5), and experience from across Africa in addressing the systemic nature of the green industrialization agenda (Chapter 6).

3.6 REFERENCES

Amsden, Alice H. 1989. *Asia's Next Giant: South Korea and Late Industrialization*. New York: Oxford University Press.

Care International. 2010. "Adaptation, gender and women's empowerment." Care International Climate Change Brief. www.careclimatechange.org/files/adaptation/CARE_Gender_Brief_Oct2010.pdf.

Chang, Ha-Joon. 2015. *Smart industrial policy for Africa in the 21st century*. Addis Ababa, UNECA.

Credit Suisse. 2015. *Global Wealth Databook*. Zurich.

Denton, Fatima. 2014. A new development paradigm for Africa. Barbara Ward Lecture, International Institute for Environment and Development, London, November.

Grossman, Gene M. 1995. "Pollution and growth: what do we know?" In *The Economics of Sustainable Development,* Ian Goldin and L. Alan Winters, eds.. Cambridge: Cambridge University Press.

Haraguchi, Nobuya and Resonja, Gorazd. 2010. *In Search of General Patterns of Manufacturing Development.* Development Policy and Strategic Research Branch Working Paper 02/2010. Vienna, UNIDO.

IEA. 2010. *World Energy Outlook*. Paris, International Energy Agency.

International Labour Organization. 2015. *Decent Work, Green Jobs and the Sustainable Economy*. Geneva.

Kuznets, Simon. 1966. *Modern Economic Growth: Rate, Structure, and Spread.* New Haven: Yale University Press.

Lin, Justin Yifu and Celestin Monga. 2010. "Growth identification and facilitation: the role of the state in the dynamics of structural change." Policy Research Working Paper, No. 5313. Washington, D.C.: World Bank.

Mazzucato, Mariana. 2013. *The Entrepreneurial State: Debunking Public vs. Private Sector Myths.* Bath, UK: Anthem.

Mearns, Robin and Andrew Norton. 2010. "Equity and vulnerability in a warming world: introduction and overview." In *Social Dimensions of Climate Change: Equity and Vulnerability in a Warming World,* Robin Mearns and Andrew Norton, eds. Washington, D.C.: World Bank.

Morris, Mike; Kaplinsky, Raphael and Kaplan, David. 2011. "One thing leads to another. Commodities, linkages and industrial development: a conceptual overview." MMCP Discussion Paper No. 12, Milton Keynes, Open University.

The Natural Edge Project. 2004. Found on http://www.naturaledgeproject.net/Keynote.aspx. Accessed February, 2016.

Oqubay, Arkebe. 2015. *Made in Africa. Industrial Policy in Ethiopia.* Oxford: Oxford University Press.

Oxfam International. 2015. *Wealth: Having It All and Wanting More.* Oxford: Oxfam GB.

Pearce, David, Anil Markandya, and Edward Barbier. 1989. *Blueprint for a Green Economy.* London: Earthscan.

Perman, Roger and David I. Stern. 2003. "Evidence from panel unit root and cointegration tests that the environmental Kuznets curve does not exist." *Australian Journal of Agricultural and Resource Economics*, vol. 47 (September), pp. 325–347.

Piketty, Thomas. 2014. *Capital in the Twenty-First Century.* New York: Belknap Press.

PEP. 2005. *Investing in Environmental Wealth for Poverty Reduction.* Poverty Environment Partnership. New York, UNDP.

Rockstrom, J. et al. 2009. "Planetary boundaries: exploring the safe operating space for humanity." *Ecology and Society,* vol.14, No. 2, p. 32.

Sachs, Jeffrey D. 2015. *The Age of Sustainable Development.* New York: Columbia University Press.

Steffen, Will et al. 2015. "Planetary boundaries: guiding human development on a changing planet." *Science,* vol. 347, No. 6223 (13 February).

Stern, Nicholas. 2015. *Why Are We Waiting? The Logic, Urgency, and Promise of Tackling Climate Change.* Cambridge, MA: MIT Press.

Stiglitz, Joseph E. 2012. *The Price of Inequality: How Today's Divided Society Endangers Our Future.* New York: W. W. Norton & Company.

Syrquin, Moshe and Hollis B. Chenery. 1989. "Patterns of development: 1950–1985." Discussion paper No. 41. Washington, D.C.: World Bank.

United Nations. 1987. *Our Common Future*. The Brundtland report. New York.

United Nations, Economic Commission for Africa. 2013a. Making the most of Africa's commodities: industrializing for growth, jobs and economic transformation. *Economic Report on Africa*. Addis Ababa.

———. 2014. Dynamic industrial policy in Africa. *Economic Report on Africa*. Addis Ababa.

———. 2015. Industrializing through trade. *Economic Report on Africa*. Addis Ababa.

United Nations Environment programme. 2011. Green Economy Report. Nairobi.

Wade, Robert. 1990. *Governing the Market: Economic Theory and the Role of Government in East Asian Industrialization*. Princeton, NJ: Princeton University Press.

World Health Organization. 2014. Ambient (outdoor) air quality and health. Fact sheet No. 313. Geneva.

3.7 ENDNOTES

1 Much better data collection is needed, however, to track changes in air quality and associated health outcomes. For example, of 1,600 cities worldwide with data on particulate matter, only 11 were African.

CHAPTER

4

THE POLICY FRAMEWORK FOR GREENING INDUSTRIALIZATION IN AFRICA

Chapter 3 laid out the concepts, tools and thinking underlying Africa's industrialization and the pathway to make the process green and inclusive. It showed that governments must carve a decisive pathway, working closely with private sector actors—large and small—and civil society to set the direction for long-term investment in the continent's people and natural assets.

This chapter outlines the broader policy framework within which the shift to greening industrialization is happening, the close congruence of this greening with major regional and global policy directions, and evidence of current progress at the country level.

4.1 AFRICA'S GREEN GROWTH VISION

Environmental dimensions of economic development have been on the agenda for African countries since the first United Nations (UN) Conference on Environment and Development—or the Earth Summit— held in Rio de Janeiro, Brazil, in 1992. The period after the Earth Summit saw national sustainable development strategies drawn up, ministries of the environment set up, and global conventions—such as those on Climate Change, Biodiversity and Desertification—agreed to. African countries have been active in global negotiations, most recently in designing and agreeing to the Addis Ababa Action Agenda for financing development, the Sustainable Development Goals (SDGs) adopted by the UN General Assembly in September 2015, and the Paris Agreement on climate change reached at COP21 in December 2015.

The period after the Earth Summit saw national sustainable development strategies drawn up, ministries of the environment set up, and global conventions ... ... agreed to.

THE AFRICAN UNION AND GREEN GROWTH

At the continental level, there is strong adherence to an inclusive, green transformation of African economies. Agenda 2063 of the African Union (AU) outlines a high-level vision of "an integrated, prosperous and peaceful Africa, driven by its own citizens and representing a dynamic force in the global arena". The first aspiration is for "a prosperous Africa, based on inclusive growth and sustainable development" and seeks a context in which "the environment and ecosystems are healthy and preserved, and with climate resilient economies and communities". Such a vision builds on Africa's

BOX 4.1 INVESTING IN RENEWABLE ENERGY FOR ALL

The Africa Renewable Energy Initiative (AREI) is a transformative, Africa-led effort to accelerate the harnessing of the continent's huge renewable energy potential. Under the mandate of the AU and endorsed by African Heads of State, the initiative is set to achieve at least 10 gigawatts (GW) of new renewable energy generation capacity by 2020 and to realize African potential to generate at least 300 GW by 2030.

The AREI is firmly anchored in the context of sustainable development, climate change and zero-carbon development strategies in Africa. It also recognizes the critical importance of energy access for enhanced well-being, economic development and the fulfilment of, particularly, Sustainable Development Goal 7 on energy access.

The premise of the AREI is that all societies, including those in Africa, must transition to low- and zero-carbon energy systems to avoid catastrophic climate change. In accord with commitments and principles under the UNFCCC, such African efforts must be supported through international public climate finance, among other sources. It will build on the renewable energy components of other initiatives, such as the Africa Clean Energy Corridor of the International Renewable Energy Agency (IRENA), the Africa–European Union (EU) Energy Partnership, Power Africa, the Programme for Infrastructure Development in Africa (PIDA), Sustainable Energy for All (SE4ALL), one of the African Development Bank's "High-Fives" on lighting up and powering Africa, and numerous bilateral, civil society and community efforts.

The AREI seeks to address the needs of small-scale farming and micro-, small- and medium-scale enterprises on the quantity and quality of access to energy, and it entails a vision of electricity access beyond households' needs. The AREI will therefore promote unprecedented efforts to reach populations currently off the grid. The AREI envisions smart, distributed energy systems that can handle a mix of renewable energy generation. With a highly diversified ownership base compared with conventional, centralized energy systems, a vast number of households, communities, cooperatives and enterprises of all sizes will become producers and consumers of electricity, allowing Africa to leapfrog to the energy systems of the future. As such the AREI stands to contribute substantially to the green growth agenda in Africa.

position at the third international conference on sustainable development held in Rio de Janeiro in June 2012, and during the climate negotiations concluded at the COP21, at which African governments demonstrated their collective ambition to build a low-carbon future by mobilizing investments to more than double the installed electricity capacity on the continent by 2030, using renewable energy resources (box 4.1).

Agenda 2063 presents a determination to achieve structural transformation to deepen industrialization; develop modern and productive agriculture; and invest in science, technology and innovation. It recognizes sustainable management of water—including the vast ocean resources on the continent's doorstep[1]—as critical to Africa's transformation and growth (as well as management of land-based resources, which requires regional cooperation). Agenda 2063 also commits to pushing for major infrastructural investment in transport, energy and information and communications technology (ICT) through PIDA. It builds on the Action Plan for the Accelerated Industrial Development of Africa (AIDA; Chapter 3), which lays out national, regional and continental priorities.

The African Development Bank's Strategy for 2013–2022 (AfDB, 2013) aligns closely with the greening industrialization agenda, as it is underpinned by two central objectives to improve the quality of Africa's growth: inclusive growth and the transition to green growth. The first objective is based

BOX 4.2 AFRICAN GOVERNMENTS IN THE VANGUARD OF GREEN ECONOMY STRATEGIES

Country	Strategic framework for inclusive green economy
Ethiopia	Climate-Resilient Green Economy (CRGE) strategy. The vision is to achieve middle-income status by 2025 in a climate-resilient green economy. The country plans continued rapid economic growth, expanding industrialization and jobs but, by avoiding the conventional development pathway, Ethiopia aims to cut greenhouse gas emissions and shift to sustainable patterns of land, soil and water management. The CRGE makes Ethiopia a front runner in the green economy race.
Kenya	Green Economy Strategy and Implementation Plan (GESIP, 2015). The objective is to guide the transition to a green, low-carbon and climate-resilient economy. Scenario analysis shows that a green economy pathway delivers higher and more stable growth than business as usual (BAU). Building on Kenya Vision 2030 and the constitutional provisions of 2010, the GESIP promotes infrastructural investment, resilience and sustainable livelihoods. The priorities and approach were defined through an inclusive, participatory process.
Morocco	Green Morocco Plan (GMP). Launched in 2008, it has a focus on agriculture and the associated agrifood processing industry. It addresses the problem of increasing water scarcity through investment in drip irrigation technology and changes to agricultural water governance. Although the prospects for further growth in exporting agricultural produce to high-income markets in Europe has received much attention, the GMP recognizes that domestic urban growth and rising incomes are substantial new sources of growth for Moroccan agriculture.
Mozambique	Roadmap for a Green Economy in Mozambique: Accelerating sustainable economic, social, and environmental development. The vision for Mozambique is to become an inclusive middle-income country by 2030, based on protection, restoration and rational use of natural capital and its ecosystem services to guarantee development that is sustainable, inclusive and efficient within planetary limits.
Rwanda	Green Growth and Climate Resilience: National Strategy for Climate Change and Low Carbon Development 2011–2050 (2011). The vision is for Rwanda to be a developed, climate-resilient, low-carbon economy by 2050. Strategic objectives include achieving energy security and a low-carbon energy supply that supports development of green industry and services; and achieving social protection, improved health and disaster risk reduction that reduces vulnerability to climate change.
South Africa	Green Economy Accord (2011). This partnership was signed by organized labour, community constituents, businesses and government. It lays out 12 commitments to green the economy, including roll-out of solar water heaters and renewable energy; energy efficiency; biofuels; and waste recycling, reuse and recovery. Other commitments relate to clean coal initiatives, electrification of poor communities, and reduction of open fire cooking and heating. The partners also committed to promoting localization, youth employment, cooperatives and skills development.
Ghana	AKOBEN. The main responsibility for greening industrialization in Ghana at the government level lies with the Environmental Protection Agency (EPA) which implements this agenda through two units – the Ghana National Cleaner Production Centre, and the Manufacturing Industries Department. This department implements the EPA's AKOBEN Environmental Rating and Disclosure Programme that is used to assess the environmental performance of mining and manufacturing operations.

SOURCE: BASS (2015); AUTHORS' COMPILATION.

on the view that inclusive growth will unlock great, untapped potential and increase Africa's chances of reaping a demographic dividend that has been elusive so far. Green growth is seen as the means to ensure that inclusive growth is sustainable. The underlying assumption is that transitioning to green growth will protect livelihoods and improve water, energy and food security while promoting sustainable use of natural resources. Green growth is further believed to have the potential of fostering innovation, creating jobs and spurring economic development (AfDB, 2013).

SOME AFRICAN GOVERNMENTS ARE TAKING THE LEAD

Several African governments are ahead in designing and implementing an inclusive green economy (box 4.2). Such strategies combine focusing on energy access, creating high-quality jobs with rising incomes, investing in critical environmental assets—soil, water, biodiversity and forests—and designing resilience for cities and infrastructure.

In Kenya, the Green Economy and Strategy Implementation Plan carried out a scenario exercise (figure 4.1) that shows the huge importance of shifting from a Business as Usual (BAU) economic pathway to a new green-economy track. This exercise shows that a greener economy brings significant benefits in the medium to long term, but during the initial, investment phase, growth is slightly slower under the Green Economy (GE) scenario, than in the enhanced Business as Usual Scenarios. According to the analysis, the BAU or baseline scenario assumes no fundamental changes in policy or external conditions up to 2030; The BAU2% allocates an additional 2 per cent of GDP per annum as investments to the current BAU investment path; and the GE2% scenario assumes an additional 2 per cent of GDP per annum as green investments to the baseline (GESIP, 2015).

AFRICA IS NOT ALONE IN TARGETING GREEN GROWTH

A growing number of countries have recognized the need to promote inclusive green growth, not just as a counter to the harmful impacts of carbon emissions but also as a source of rapid economic growth, technical innovation and development benefits. Progress in addressing poverty, environment and economic growth has mainly been

FIGURE 4.1 TRENDS IN REAL GDP GROWTH IN BAU, BAU2% AND GE2% SCENARIOS FOR KENYA'S GREEN ECONOMY STRATEGY

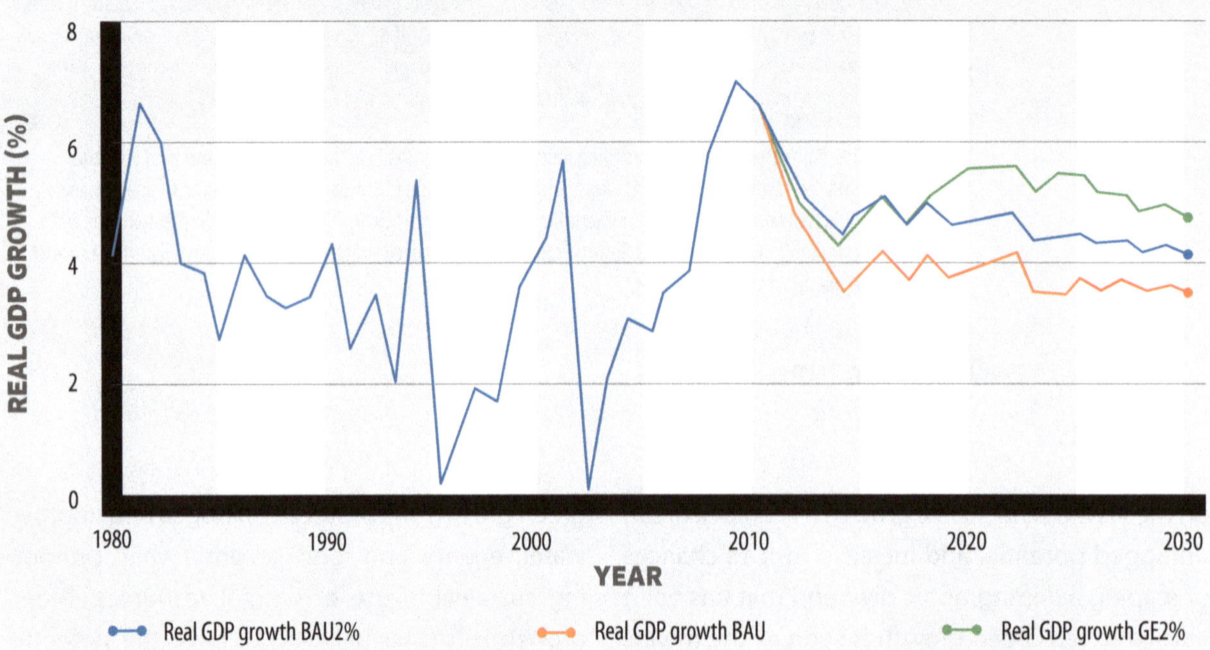

SOURCE: GOVERNMENT OF THE REPUBLIC OF KENYA (2015).

BOX 4.3 SOME GREEN ECONOMY ADVANCES

Indonesia: Phase-out of fossil fuel subsidies, complemented by social safety nets. For more than 30 years, fossil fuel subsidies formed a large part of the Indonesian government's economic programme. Those subsidies exceeded combined government spending on education, health and social protection. Given the huge financial costs and environmental impacts, the government has begun to phase them out. To support the welfare needs of its poorest citizens, Indonesia has built a stronger social safety net, including rice subsidies, public health insurance, cash assistance for school costs, and direct and conditional cash transfers. Those programs have all helped to support the poor while fossil fuel subsidies are removed.

Mexico: Renewable energy roll-out and fuel subsidy reform. Mexico has shown that a progressive legislative stance on climate change and strong consultative processes can deliver a renewable energy roll-out and fuel subsidy reform in ways that protect the poor. Incremental shifts in energy policy, along with alternative cash transfer mechanisms, have produced environmental improvements while mitigating negative impacts on marginalized groups. Robust consultation has been at the heart of designing the green growth policy, alongside supporting the social welfare of the poorest.

China: Green growth policies. These include a comprehensive range of laws, backed up by fiscal tools and research and development (R&D). These include the Renewable Energy Law (2006); the 12th Five-Year Plan for Energy Development, Energy Saving and New Energy Vehicle Development Plan (2011–2020); feed-in tariffs for solar and wind power; fiscal incentives to support R&D in manufacturing of renewable energies; concessional lending for renewable energy projects; subsidies for green technologies, including solar photovoltaic manufacturers; fuel-economy standards for the automotive industry; and cap-and-trade programmes in five cities—Beijing, Chongqing, Shanghai, Shenzhen and Tianjin—and the two provinces of Guangdong and Hubei. The Solar Roofs program and Golden Sun program provide investors with financial incentives for solar energy projects.

SOURCE: BASS (2015).

driven separately, by different institutions at both national and global levels. The fact that these are closely linked objectives, at the level of their causes and solutions, is now recognized much more substantially in the Sustainable Development Goals. These goals provide a touchstone for joint action on poverty reduction, inclusivity and environmental sustainability, given the high degree of consensus on them between countries and stakeholders.

Green growth is being pursued at global, regional, national and subnational levels. Globally, actions include the Green Economy Initiative of the United Nations Environment Programme (UNEP), the Green Growth Papers of the Organisation for Economic Co-operation and Development (OECD), the Global Green Growth Institute (GGGI), Green Growth Knowledge Platform (GGKP) and Global Green Growth Forum (GGGF), all of which have established themselves as centres for building knowledge and sharing lessons between government and business. The Green Economy Coalition (GEC) has created space for citizen engagement with greening debates and offered a platform for excluded voices.

Regionally, Europe has flagged its intent to roll out a green economy, by creating a circular economic system. Within the EU, Germany and the Scandinavian countries have been at the forefront of building a green economy. Policy in Germany has focused on achieving an energy transition (Energiewende) through rolling out decentralized renewable energy across the country. The factors leading to success have been loud, consistent and long-term leadership by government—with the required finance, innovation and infrastructure—alongside vocal, political demand from the population at large for the government to be ambitious in building a low-carbon economy. Households, industry and communities across the country have seen the benefit of being able to generate their own electricity, given generous feed-in tariffs and a secure energy supply.

The world now sees strong momentum for shifting economies onto a green growth pathway (box 4.3). Many strategies have been designed to be economically inclusive.

At the subnational level, a wave of green initiatives is under way in cities, states and national regions. These initiatives include the C40 initiative for cities, and the Transition Town movement. Similarly, a growing number of businesses seek to demonstrate their green credentials through a range of certification schemes, flagging the quality of their product to consumers. Although subnational governments lack the powers of the nation state, they often have considerable room for manoeuvre to test new ways of working, whether for transport, energy delivery or waste systems. City mayors often can make progress, even when inertia or special interests block the green agenda nationally.

4.2 WHY ACCELERATED GREENING MAKES SENSE FOR THE AFRICAN ECONOMY NOW

Despite having major differences in structure and context, most African economies confront four common challenges that frame their economic options and justify a strong, inclusive green growth agenda. Each challenge has implications for investment in appropriate infrastructure and for patterns of growth.

AGRICULTURE DOMINATES THE ECONOMY

Although agriculture's share of GDP has been falling in almost all African economies, it still contributes 32 per cent of continental GDP and remains the dominant sector for livelihoods and employment in most areas (AfDB, 2015). For more than two thirds of the population, it is their major source of income. Despite Africa's abundant agricultural potential, food imports have been on the rise and are an important drain on foreign exchange, although in an increasing number of economies agriculture has become a significant source of export earnings. Key continental policy initiatives have targeted growth in the agricultural sector, most particularly the African Union's 2003 Maputo Declaration on Agriculture and Food Security (see box 4.4). As shown in this box, it is easier to agree commitments than to carry them out.

Growth in food production is achievable in two ways: (1) raising agricultural yields in existing production systems, and (2) enabling entrepreneurship in new agribusiness sectors, such as those involving green technological innovation. Multiple examples show how agro-led industrialization can yield inclusive, green growth (such as the growth in aquaculture in Nigeria; Chapter 6).

BOX 4.4 AFRICAN AGRICULTURE—POLICY PLEDGES VS IMPLEMENTATION IN PRACTICE

At the AU summit in Maputo in July 2003, African leaders pledged to double spending on agriculture to reach at least 10 per cent of national budgets and to achieve at least 6 per cent annual growth in the sector. The Comprehensive African Agricultural Development Programme (CAADP), led by the New Partnership for Africa's Development (NEPAD), was drawn up to put this pledge into practice. Ten years on, however, only 10 of 54 countries had fulfilled their commitments, and growth in agriculture across the continent averaged less than one half the 6 per cent envisaged (2.6 per cent).

The AU's Agenda 2063 paints a vision of agriculture that is "modern and productive, using science, technology, innovation and indigenous knowledge. The hand hoe will be banished by 2025 and the sector will be modern, profitable and attractive to the continent's youth and women" (AU, 2013). Nigeria's example in the past three years shows the strong, positive benefits for the economy and trade balance from renewed investment in agriculture and food processing, with agricultural growth leading to a reported fall in the import bill from $11 billion in 2012 to $4.3 billion a year in 2013 (Chibuzor Emejor, 2014).

The African Development Bank launched a strategy, "Feeding Africa", in Dakar in October 2015. It seeks to make Africa food self-sufficient by 2025. With the goal of achieving rapid agricultural transformation across Africa, its 18-point plan includes better nutrition; increased research into raising agricultural productivity; affirmative action for women in Africa to de-risk financing to woman-owned businesses; and development of agro-allied industrial zones and agricultural corridors. New funding mechanisms will be developed, such as agribusiness diaspora bonds, as will ways to get greater support from private equity funds, sovereign wealth funds and pension funds to support long-term financing. Agro-input supplies to farmers will be scaled up, including African fertilizer production. Underlying emphasis will be on raising productivity, reducing production costs and expanding market outlets.

Moves to expand the green industrial sector require recognition of the strategic importance of agriculture in supply and demand factors. From the supply side, it requires critical inputs that are affected by patterns of growth—water, soil, biodiversity, infrastructure—as well as by climatic effects. From the demand side, agriculture feeds not only into local and national economies but also into regional and global markets. Each of those markets (Chapter 6) has its own characteristics; high-income markets in advanced economies, in particular, require producers to meet sustainability criteria along green supply chains (Potts et al., 2014). Given the high growth likely in Africa's urban demand for food over the next 10–20 years, African governments need to ensure that domestic producers can capture much of that growth, moving into higher value added food processing, and diverse fruit and vegetables. This growth in the food sector should generate jobs, reduce foreign exchange outflows on food imports, shift African economies from reliance on foreign foodstuffs and build positive domestic linkages between urban and rural income growth.

In building the industrial sector, expanding agri-food processing is infeasible without simultaneously building more sustainable management of the environmental assets (soils, water, biodiversity) that underlie agricultural growth. Further, because the sector is the source of livelihoods for much of the population, its future affects the inclusiveness of growth. Hence, strengthening local people's rights to land, water and other natural resources is a foundation for building an inclusive green economy, from which rural and urban people can benefit. Secure land rights provide the basis for greater investment and higher productivity by farmers, whether smallholders or large enterprises. In many rural settings, local people rely not only on their fields but also on the wider landscape of common property resources, including woodland, lakes and wetlands, and lands for grazing. Establishing clear rights to manage and control access to these collective resources often is as important as rights to household plots because the overall farming system relies on sound management of water, soil and nutrient flows between fallow bushland and farmland.

Natural capital is the stock of natural assets that yield critical services without which people (especially the poor) and economies cannot survive. As with financial capital, drawing down too much stock can run up a debt that must be repaid, such as allowing aquifers to replenish themselves. Poorly managed natural capital can thus become an ecological, not just a social and economic, liability. Sustainable agri-food processing relies on strong natural capital assets that provide flows of water and food, climate regulation and flood defences.

AFRICAN ECONOMIES ARE RESOURCE DEPENDENT

Chapter 1 pointed to the heavy dependence of many African economies on the extractive industries and other commodities. The Africa Mining Vision (box 4.5) points to the growth potential of linkages, with the resource sectors as a source of structural transformation, industrialization and economic growth.

As with agriculture, the expansion of the natural resource sector has important green growth linkages. Extraction of many resources, particularly minerals, oil and gas, often produces heavy spillages and pollution, with major adverse consequences for the health and livelihoods of people in the locality. The resource sector also is increasingly

BOX 4.5 THE AFRICA MINING VISION

After decades of falling commodity prices, the Asian economic boom from 2000 onwards provided an opportunity for African countries to use their mineral wealth to support more sustainable patterns of economic growth. The Africa Mining Vision (AU, 2009) laid out the interventions needed by government to ensure that mineral wealth translates into economic growth, diversification and well-being by:

- Strengthening governance of resource rents—so that tax regimes can exact an equitable share for the public purse;
- Establishing collateral use of resource-related infrastructure—to maximize economic development within the catchment;
- Taking advantage of downstream value added—to gain benefits from transformation of resources, including industrial and energy development, jobs, training, innovation and foreign exchange; and
- Capitalizing on upstream value added—by developing local-content requirements to benefit suppliers of goods and services and to achieve longer-term investment in knowledge-intensive activity.

However, the Vision has had only limited impact, with many mineral-rich countries continuing to suffer from the "resource curse". And the recent economic slowdown in Asia has now led to a slump in prices and activity, bringing big job cuts, mine shutdowns and many investments being mothballed.

FIGURE 4.2 THE STEEP FALL IN PRICE OF SILICON PHOTOVOLTAIC MODULES AS INSTALLED GLOBAL CAPACITY HAS GROWN, 1992–2014

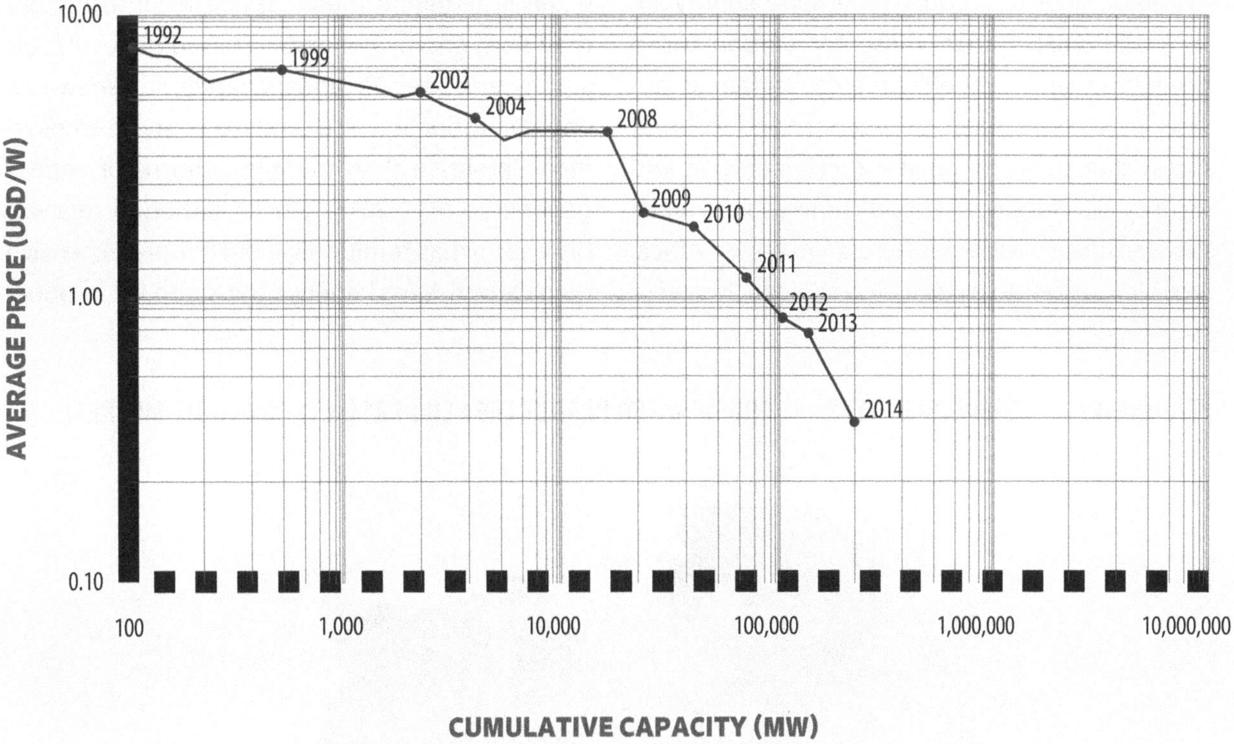

NOTE: MW = MEGAWATT; USD = US DOLLAR; W = WATT.
SOURCE: KING, DAVID, ET AL. 2015.

driven by the requirements of foreign markets, and those markets, as will be shown, demand a greening of supply chains and concomitant capabilities that also apply to many other sectors, offering the potential for spill-over benefits. Finally, because domestic and export-oriented resource sectors require transport, the greening of transport will be a necessary component if resource production is to expand in a sustainable manner. Early investment in low-carbon, climate-resilient infrastructure will avoid "lock-in" to systems of markets, urban density and distribution, which confer a heavy environmental burden and constrain future options.

READY ENERGY IS SCARCE AMID AN ABUNDANCE OF RENEWABLE ENERGY RESOURCES

Africa is blessed with bountiful energy potential—much of it renewable—but needs investment to unlock supplies that meet people's hunger for electric power. A great deal of policy on energy generation in advanced economies has focused on the need to reduce carbon emissions, and that focus has promoted major investments in developing and deploying renewable energy.

From the perspective of low- and middle-income economies, such as those in Africa, the renewable energy agenda offers important further economic advantages. In most African economies, imports of carbon-based energy are a major drain on foreign exchange, and the volatility in prices generates potential disruptions in fuel supply and distribution systems (as in Malawi; Chapter 6). The facilities to produce renewable energy are generally smaller than those for carbon-based generation, and they offer the combined advantage of decentralized production and off-grid access that supports greater social inclusion and security in supply. Off-grid renewables reach low-density populations across much of Africa, providing access to electricity in regions that were otherwise unlikely to gain access to grid supplies in the near future. The roll-out time for renewables is quick, requiring much less basic infrastructure than does energy generation based on fossil fuels and hydropower (Rwanda; Chapter 6). Renewable energy production also tends to be more employment intensive than traditional forms of energy generation (ILO, 2016). Finally, although renewable energy has traditionally been more expensive than carbon-based energy, the steep fall in prices

FIGURE 4.3 RENEWABLE INTERNAL FRESHWATER RESOURCES PER PERSON (1,000 CUBIC METRES)

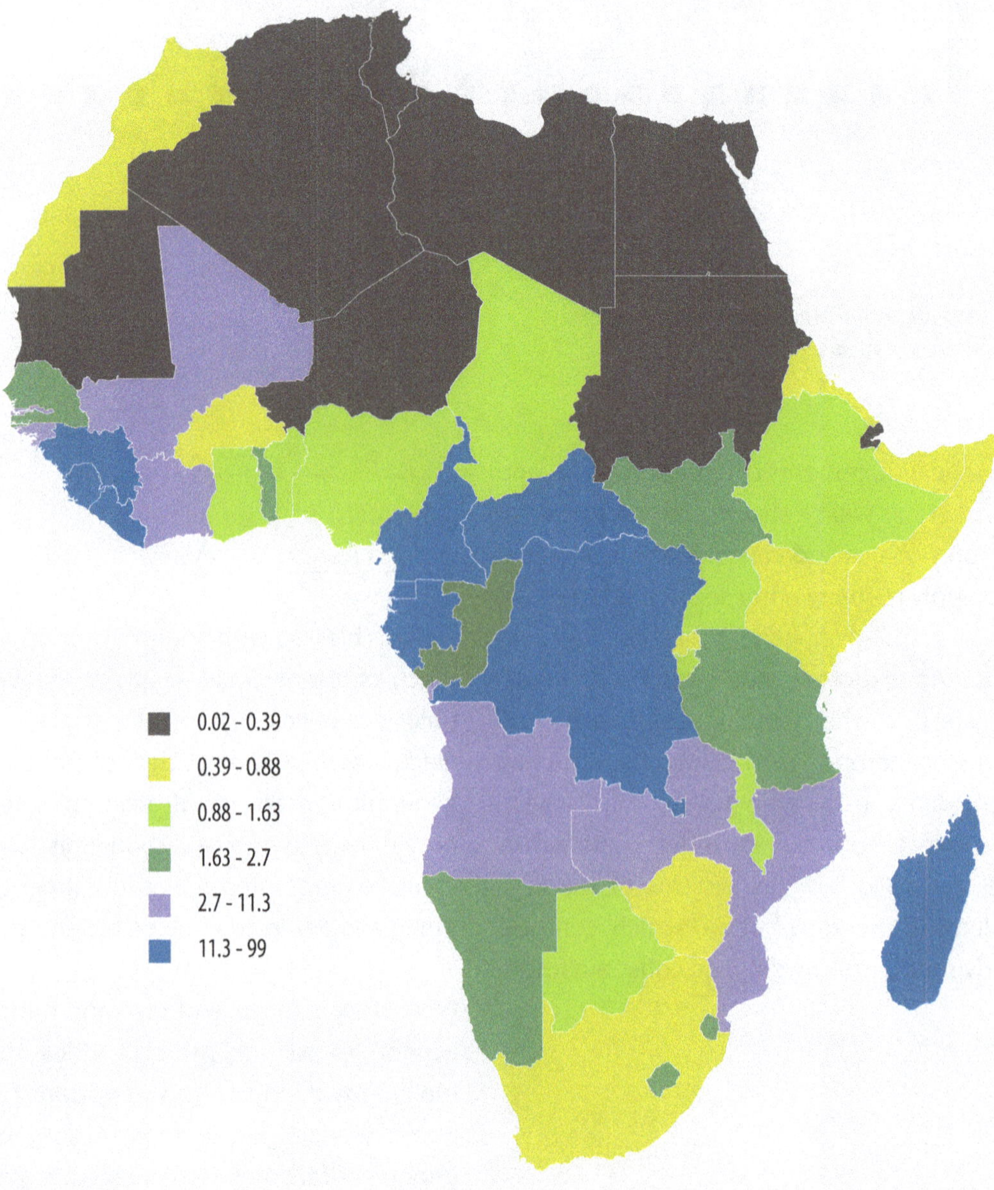

SOURCE: WORLD BANK (2015).

of photovoltaic panels (shown in figure 4.2) is making renewable energy cost competitive with high carbon sources in many countries. However, the take-up of renewable energy has been hindered in some countries by a policy regime that favours traditional, large electricity generating systems. Government action to address such hurdles is central to supporting investment in decentralized, smaller, renewable systems.

While the deployment of solar power has seen enormous growth in Africa, they are by no means the only significant source of renewable energy for the continent. Morocco has established an enormous concentrated solar power scheme, and Kenya has made major investments in geothermal power and also has the largest wind-powered array of turbines on the continent (Chapter 6). For decades, hydropower has been a major source of the baseload electricity supply for many African countries, and further large schemes are under construction. The combination of low rainfall, sediment from soil erosion, and fiercer competition for water, however, is causing major problems for hydropower generation in several African countries (box 4.6). Further investment is needed to incorporate climate uncertainty and better land management into the future design of big dams.

WATER CONSTRAINS AFRICAN GROWTH

The greening of industry and the wider economy often has been conflated with meeting carbon-reduction targets and lowering energy imports. Looking to 2050, though, water scarcity is the unacknowledged crisis confronting social, economic and political development in many economies. Water is the source of life and feeds directly into everyone's basic needs—rural and urban, producers and consumers—in all sectors of the economy. Even without the disruption to supply that will inevitably result from climate change, current levels of water abstraction in many regions are more than twice as high as those that offer long-term security of the supply.

Availability and volatility of the water supply in Africa vary hugely (figure 4.3). In North Africa, for example, the low rainfall and drying climate are leading to an absolute water shortage and, although extensive underground fossil water reserves exist, too great a reliance on such sources will place people and production at jeopardy in the near future. Much of Central, East and West Africa, by contrast, has substantial bodies of water—from rainfall, groundwater and rivers—that could be used for domestic and production purposes. The missing component is adequate infrastructure to capture and make more effective use of the resource and to ensure that it is channelled into high-value activities. Throughout Africa, little attention is paid to pricing water, which leads to misallocation and waste, and few, if any, controls limit the use of groundwater. Hence, Africa's water supply requires vast increases in investment and much more careful management if it is to meet the demands of a growing economy and population (Chapter 5).

Addressing water scarcity for greening industrialization requires complex and demanding policy responses. Because water provides the basis for life and survival, the scarcity, pollution and poor quality of water can generate strong political responses sub-nationally (sectors, locations and users) and between neighbouring countries. Water-scarce economies often show conflicting needs, as final consumers and agricultural producers compete for the same scarce resource. In Africa, agriculture gets the lion's share of water, for irrigation, with industry and domestic consumers sharing the remaining 15–20 per cent (UNESCO, 2009 p.99). Some irrigated crops are highly water intensive for both crop production and processing, such as cotton, which requires 4,000 cubic metres per ton of crop harvested and 9,980 per ton of finished textile, and fruits, vegetables and nuts, with almonds requiring 8,000 cubic metres for raw nuts, and 16,000 cubic metres per ton of shelled and peeled product (Mekonnen and Hoekstra, 2010). Countries facing water scarcity have important questions to resolve about how best to maximize the value from a limited water supply and about investing in much better water management. Morocco and its Green Plan aims to achieve savings of 20-50% water savings through a shift from furrow to drip irrigation, and improved public irrigation canal networks (EIB, 2015).

Coupled with changing rainfall patterns, competition for water has led in recent years to a water crisis in the Zambezi River Basin where, among other impacts, Victoria Falls has seen lower water volumes (box 4.6). The problems of water spanning national boundaries provide an additional layer of complexity.

BOX 4.6 DAMS AND IMPACTS OF COMPETITION FOR SCARCE WATER

In Zambia in recent months, ZESCO (the national electricity utility) has been increasing its rationing of electricity throughout the country as a result of insufficient water in the reservoirs at Lake Kariba and Itezhi Tezhi because of below average rainfall in the 2014/15 rainy season. At the end of December 2015, Kariba reservoir was about 14 per cent full, compared with 51 per cent a year earlier, and hydropower generation was at a minimum. Power cuts now average 10–14 hours a day, affecting industries, commerce and domestic customers. If the dry spell continues, it is likely to force a shutdown of hydropower plants (Business Report, South Africa 11 January 2016).

Low rainfall amounts and overuse of water by Zambia and Zimbabwe—the countries that share Lake Kariba—have caused water levels in the lake to drop, and electricity generation in Zambia has fallen by more than one half in a country that is 95 per cent dependent on hydropower for its electricity. This has led to public outcry and anger against the national utility, necessitating a fuller investigation of the cause (EIZ, 2015). Without a transboundary water management institution taking an effective lead, ZESCO assessed matters and concluded that both the low drought-related inflows (2014/15) and over-abstraction by the power plants at the Kariba Complex were the main factors. Tourism has been affected, with a fall in the amount of water going over the typically spectacular Victoria Falls. Mining companies in Zambia—Africa's second-biggest producer of copper—have had to reduce electricity use and buy expensive imported diesel fuel at a time of job losses and mothballing of mining operations.

Other hydropower investments around the Zambezi Basin, such as Batoka, are also failing to meet expected returns on investment, a trend likely to worsen as El Niño, exacerbated by climate change, continues to grip Southern and Eastern Africa.

In North Africa, a major loss of hydropower capacity has been caused by sedimentation of the reservoir because of soil erosion in the catchment area. In Morocco, many dams have lost 10–40 per cent of their capacity since construction, and some are now filled with silt. Similarly, in the Rift Valley, the Koka Reservoir in Ethiopia is threatened by siltation. Dredging is possible, but it is extremely expensive. In the future, hydropower investments must be more carefully designed and planned. Beyond sedimentation, hydropower—representing a good baseload supply of low-carbon energy—is also vulnerable to increasing rainfall volatility.

Improved transboundary water governance to manage dams and river basins is the solution to competing priorities between nation states so that they can agree on a process for managing scarcity. At the national level, priorities for the use of scarce water require careful thought for the long-term consequences of such trade-offs.

4.3 ENTRY POINTS TO EMBED GREENING IN INDUSTRIALIZATION

The greening of industrialization can become reality in Africa via four major entry points: changing price incentives; regulating environmental standards; greening public infrastructure; and reducing the resource intensity of industrial growth, a process called "decoupling".

> **The greening agenda, ..., requires a sharp cut in the use of fossil-fuel energy sources in the absence of efficient capture and sequestration of all greenhouse gas emissions.**

CHANGING PRICE INCENTIVES—SHIFTING FROM FOSSIL FUEL SUBSIDIES

Energy is a critical environmental input to the industrialization process. It provides the motive power for machinery, enables delivery of multiple inputs into production, is required in the processing of industrial outputs and is critical to the distribution and use of industrial goods and services. Industry uses a variety of energy sources, and its choices are largely determined by price. The greening agenda, which focuses on mitigating global warming and climate change, requires a sharp cut in the use of fossil-fuel energy sources in the absence of efficient capture and sequestration of all greenhouse gas emissions.

Energy pricing should, in principle, cover three sets of costs. The first set is the *capital cost* of providing the energy-generating capacity, which includes the cost of infrastructure, the cost of equipment and the cost of construction. The second set includes those costs involved in running the capital equipment—the *recurrent costs* of production. Finally, the third set, and the most difficult one to measure, are the *environmental externalities* generated in energy production and use. These costs include a welter of tangible and intangible spillovers, ranging from carbon dioxide emissions (which generate global climate change) to various pollutant emissions (which blight many urban lives).

The pricing problem arises because most countries gear energy pricing primarily to meet the recurrent costs of production. Many of the capital costs are subsidized by a range of mechanisms, and in most countries the full depreciation cost is not factored into energy prices. Equally, very few countries have built externalities into the pricing of energy, although with growing awareness of the dangers of climate change and the health costs of pollution, this is beginning to change. The political shock in the United States (US) and Europe from carmaker Volkswagen's falsified emissions data has brought much greater awareness of the health costs associated with diesel vehicle emissions. It highlighted the need to take action to limit people's exposure to particulates—by regulation, price rises to shift away from use of diesel-powered vehicles, and by ensuring that energy prices include funds to repair the estimated social and environmental damage caused.

The International Monetary Fund (IMF) has laid out the heavy cost to government budgets of fossil-fuel subsidies. It estimated the total cost of fossil fuel subsidies globally to be the equivalent of $5.3 trillion (6.5 per cent of global GDP). The IMF notes that fossil fuel subsidies damage the environment, causing premature deaths through local air pollution, exacerbating congestion and other adverse side effects of vehicle use, and increasing atmospheric greenhouse gas concentrations (IMF, 2015). Fossil fuel subsidies also impose steep fiscal costs, which must be financed by a combination of higher public debt, higher tax burdens, and crowding out of potentially productive public spending (on, for example, health, education and infrastructure), all of which can slow economic growth. Fossil fuel subsidies discourage needed investments in energy efficiency, renewables and energy infrastructure and increase the vulnerability of countries to volatile international energy prices. Finally, fossil fuel subsidies are a highly inefficient way to help low-income households because rich households typically capture most of those benefits.

By comparison, the International Energy Agency (IEA) (2014b) estimates that subsidies to low-carbon and renewable energy amounted to $121 billion globally—a tiny sum compared with fossil fuel subsidies. The urgent need to reduce greenhouse gas emissions emphasizes the clear need to level the playing field and ensure that fossil fuel production and consumption bear the true cost of use so that governments no longer favour exploration, production and consumption of high-carbon fuels.

In Central, East, Southern and West Africa, estimates of fossil fuel subsidies—including subsidies related to electricity—for 30 countries were $32 billion for 2013 (Bridle, Kitson and Wooders, 2014). Countries providing subsidies for fossil fuels worth more than $1 billion in 2015 include Angola, Côte d'Ivoire, Mozambique, Nigeria, South Africa,

FIGURE 4.4 PUBLIC HEALTH EXPENDITURE AND FOSSIL-FUEL SUBSIDIES IN FIVE AFRICAN COUNTRIES, 2013

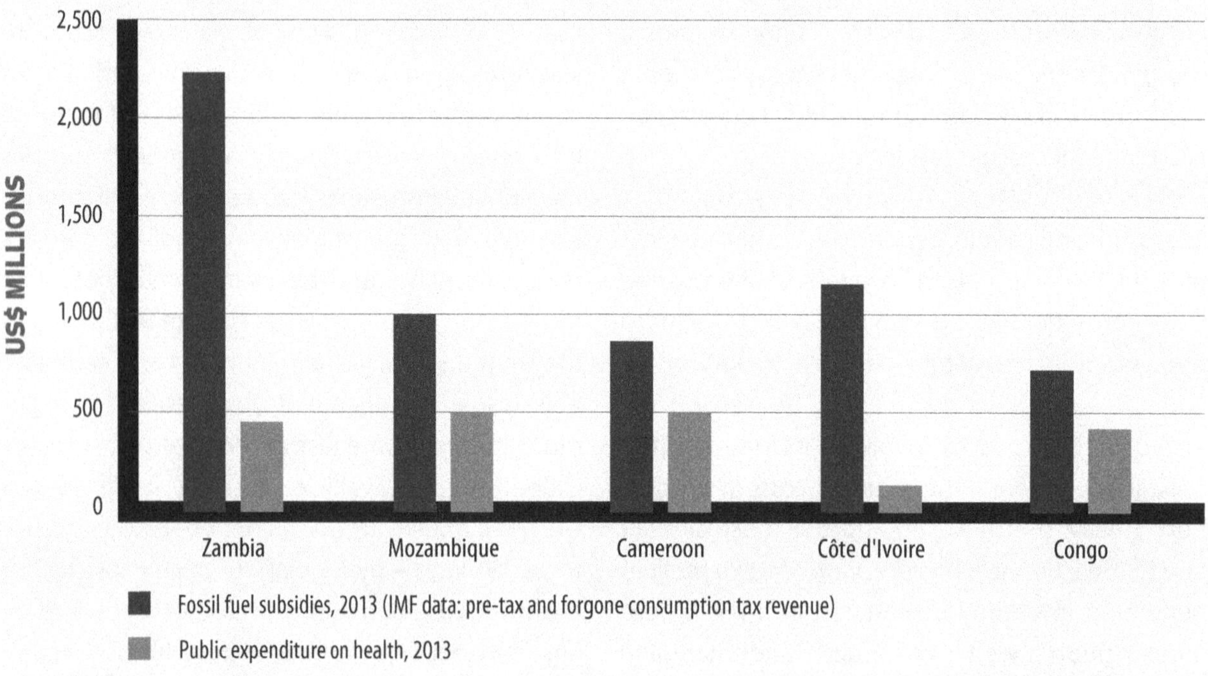

SOURCE: WHITLEY AND VAN DER BURGH (2015).

Tanzania, Zambia and Zimbabwe. Several North African countries exhibit much greater levels of fossil fuel subsidies, measured as a percentage of GDP. Fossil fuel subsidies in Egypt are reported to be among the highest in the world, as a share of GDP, reaching 10.2 per cent in 2012, or $16.9 billion (IEA, 2014a). Although the motivation on the social side may have been to provide the population with access to affordable energy, the benefits accrue primarily to the well-off (Bridle, Kitson, and Wooders, 2014).

Comparing the amount of government spending on fossil fuel subsidies with that on health is a somber exercise (figure 4.4). The enormous differences show how fuel subsidies tend to become locked into government spending—because of their political sensitivity—and are rarely reviewed relative to other expenditure. In the past three years, however, governments in Angola, Nigeria and Uganda have made efforts to cut fuel subsidies, often phasing in such changes and providing targeted assistance to poorer sections of the population.

REGULATING ENVIRONMENTAL STANDARDS

Government regulation is intended to tackle the social and environmental damage generated by productive activity. Because public authorities have a responsibility to represent fairly the interests of current and future citizens, they must find ways to correct market failures, ensure a fair balance between the interests of different groups and achieve a level playing field with rules that apply to all. In greening industrialization, the principal regulatory measures open to governments include the following:

- Setting standards for products, such as energy efficiency for electrical goods and fuel efficiency for cars and lorries;

Government regulation is intended to tackle the social and environmental damage generated by productive activity.

- Setting standards for air and water quality, which oblige enterprises to address the pollution they generate and to clean up the air and water they use before releasing it back to the atmosphere and rivers; and
- Establishing regulations for handling chemicals, waste, oil spills and other hazardous materials.

Regulation has the particular merit of setting a clear standard for an environmental good or service against which performance can be measured, but its effectiveness depends on credible enforcement. Enterprises must know that they will face sanctions if they breach the limits. An effective system for monitoring and enforcement is thus critical. Where regulation is weak, the law fails, often because of limited numbers and quality of staff and equipment and the potential for bribery, as businesses pay enforcement agencies to ignore breaches. Achieving regulation of the informal sector is especially difficult given the very large number of small enterprises and the absence of documented business ownership.

Limits to regulation have led governments to turn to other measures, such as creating incentives for private sector investment in energy supply by offering assured tariffs for renewable energy; investing in R&D; and encouraging universities to set up centres for joint technology development with local enterprises, to "incubate" new businesses. Governments can also use their own funds to promote greener products through green public procurement. In construction, for example, governments can set targets for energy conservation, forcing building firms to achieve higher standards for energy efficiency.

GREENING PUBLIC INFRASTRUCTURE

The "greening" of public infrastructure means taking a more holistic approach to its design and finance and integrating climate resilience into its construction and standards. There are big plans to expand public infrastructure across the continent. In addition to PIDA, some of the regional economic communities have infrastructure plans and strategies to support industrialization (for example, SADC's Regional Infrastructure Development Master Plan, 2012), and many countries (such as Ethiopia and South Africa) have ambitious infrastructure development plans. The combined investment of these plans amounts to more than $500 billion—to address the existing infrastructure deficit and to ensure the scale of infrastructure to support industrial growth. All these plans have the added advantage of creating jobs while stimulating growth; for example, South Africa's Expanded Public Works Programme (2014–2019) was designed with as many as 6 million jobs by 2019 (South African Government, 2015).

The greening of Africa's infrastructure offers an immediate and longer-term opportunity to leapfrog because the infrastructure deficit is so great that, ..., Africa can avoid the expensive and difficult business of retrofitting current assets.

The greening of Africa's infrastructure offers an immediate and longer-term opportunity to leapfrog because the infrastructure deficit is so great that, in starting from a low base, Africa can avoid the expensive and difficult business of retrofitting current assets. Instead, the continent can build to leading-edge standards based on the latest information and practices, which consider the expected impacts of climate change not only on resource availability but on infrastructure assets. In planning for a different future, the two primary considerations for investing in green infrastructure are *environmental decoupling* — reducing the resource intensity of growth — and building *climate-change resilience*.

On the first point, Africa is reaching its environmental boundaries and faces a crucial need to reduce the effects of its development pathways (Chapter 5). Because of the lumpy investment that infrastructure projects represent and the lock-in effects they induce once the asset is built, long-lived infrastructure projects must be part of the continent's decoupling strategy over the long term and thereby support sustainable economic growth and access to services. Strategic environmental assessments and environmental impact assessments will be key in making the right choices in greening Africa's infrastructure.

On the second point, although infrastructure is crucial in fostering development, it is also highly vulnerable to the destructive impacts of climate events and natural disasters. Planning for and building climate-resilient infrastructure are essential to avoid "stranded assets" and to minimize climate damage to Africa's infrastructure (and the people using it). Roads and bridges in Africa's flood-prone regions are routinely washed away, having to be rebuilt at a steep cost. Dams and their facilities on the continent are facing closure given the El Niño, a threat that is compounded by the growing impacts of climate change, which are felt most keenly in Southern and Eastern Africa. Some of these big, expensive investments already are becoming stranded, losing most of their value as climate impacts bite. Africa's infrastructure investments must integrate climate change risks and opportunities with their design, management and operation, essentially, "climate proofing" (AfDB, 2015).

Adapting infrastructure in this way helps to reduce the physical damage to assets and interruptions in services while yielding benefits such as greater energy security, biodiversity and water conservation, and reduced greenhouse gases. Moreover, climate proofing through expanded public works programmes can stimulate job creation, promote green jobs and skills, and transfer this knowledge to other sectors.

Africa's high and accelerating rates of urbanization accentuate the need to ramp up the greening of urban infrastructure through environmental decoupling and climate proofing (Chapter 5). Cities around the world have been central actors in stimulating green infrastructure. In Africa, city governments are key to designing the hardware of city infrastructure, the building standards for private investors and the broader software of urban systems. Africa's municipal authorities have growing knowledge of what they can achieve by rethinking how they design buildings; public spaces; and energy, water, transport and waste systems. The city of Durban, South Africa, shows what can be done by careful planning for resilience to climate impacts in ways that generate jobs and security for the urban poor. Starting in 2004, Durban's Municipal Climate Protection Programme has prioritized the need to tackle the challenge of climate risk within the context of poverty, escalating urbanization and deteriorating environmental conditions, and has become a national and international leader in the field of climate change adaptation planning and implementations (Roberts, 2008). It has done this by integrating concern for climate change across the urban, peri-urban and rural areas within the local government boundaries, and enhancing the contributions of natural capital and ecosystem services to adaptation, mitigation and disaster risk reduction. The environmental sector has been able to show the city government that greening the city can generate good jobs, and thereby build firm political support for climate action. Durban's government has developed more capacity than some better resourced cities, but it also has other pressing development priorities that can make the necessary commitment to adaptation and mitigation difficult (Roberts and O'Donoghue, 2013).

Given expected huge urban growth, cities hold the key to generating greater ecological sustainability and represent another leapfrogging opportunity for Africa. As the continent shifts to having 55 per cent of its people in urban areas by 2050 (Chapter 5), city planning will need to meet this challenge through greening its public and ecological infrastructure with ambitious energy and water use reduction targets, best-practice urban planning, and innovative technologies. Jobs, enhanced skills and social inclusion are major co-benefits of this process.

DECOUPLING INDUSTRIAL GROWTH FROM ENVIRONMENTAL IMPACTS

CONCEPTS AND DATA

A primary objective for green growth is to reduce the use of environmental inputs, particularly energy and water, and minimize harmful pollution discharges by decoupling. Decoupling takes two forms (figure 4.5). *Absolute decoupling*, which is desirable but rare, implies a constant or absolute reduction in inputs despite growth in output. *Relative decoupling*, which is more common, implies positive growth in inputs or pollutant discharge but slower than the growth in output.

Ideally, the assessment of decoupling requires baseline data on resource use, preferably by country and industry. The decoupling of energy and materials use from industrial output requires a timeline of how they have changed. For any given country, the intensity of resource use, whether energy or water, is a function of population, land mass, infrastructure, technology development, economic development and industry mix. Thus, practical analysis of the intensity of energy and water use is generally expressed as a series of ratios: energy or water use per capita, or as a share of GDP or manufacturing value added (MVA). These ratios can be used to assess the trajectory of resource intensity in the economy over time and among countries or regions.

Efficiency is a concept separate from intensity and is a measure of the ratio of inputs to output for an activity or process. An efficiency gain is achieved either by a reduction in inputs for the same level of output, an increase in output for the same inputs, or a reduction in pollution for the same level of output. Ideally, efficiency gains should also capture qualitative changes in inputs or outputs, but they rarely do so. Industrial greening should be reflected over time as an upward trend in the efficiency with which materials and energy are used at the industrial or plant level.

Although the essential elements of the decoupling objective are clear and help to inform policy choices, data constraints hinder capacity to measure decoupling in its various dimensions. One problem is that many of the data on output are a gross measure of value added in the economy (for example, MVA). Second, the patchy data on gross output and value added often are at very high levels of aggregation, usually at the two-digit ISIC (industry) or SITC (trade) levels. Hence, the chemicals sector in one country at this level of aggregation may hide very large differences in the composition of activity and output within the sector and over time, making a comparison of that sector across economies and between two periods very hard.

A third and related problem is that many countries that report "progress" in decoupling may in fact merely have shifted the resource-intensive stages of their value chains abroad. Ideally, therefore, the decoupling measure should focus on resource use per unit of consumption rather than per unit of recorded production in an economy. Such measures are unavailable on an economy- or sector-wide basis, however. Fourth, although these data limitations apply to all economies, in Africa data are particularly inconsistent (Jerven, 2013), so measuring the progress of decoupling is harder still.

Finally, whereas data for energy use and carbon emissions exist, little or no data are available for water use and pollution. The production and cleaning processes in the iron and steel, textiles, leather, pulp and paper, and chemical sectors, among others, pose a severe threat to human health and water resources in several African countries. Some data are available at the plant or enterprise level,[2] but little quantitative evidence exists at the economy-wide level.

DECOUPLING FROM ENERGY USE: HOW DOES AFRICA COMPARE?

The world increased its total industrial energy consumption by about 60 per cent from 1990 to 2013. Most of the increase occurred in Asia, whereas Europe and the United States showed some degree of absolute energy decoupling in their productive sectors (although not necessarily in their consumption patterns because energy-intensive imports increased) in the 1990s and stabilization after 2000. In the same period, total energy consumption in Africa increased at a similar rate to the global average—60 per cent—although starting from a very low base (figure 4.6).

FIGURE 4.5 ABSOLUTE AND RELATIVE DECOUPLING

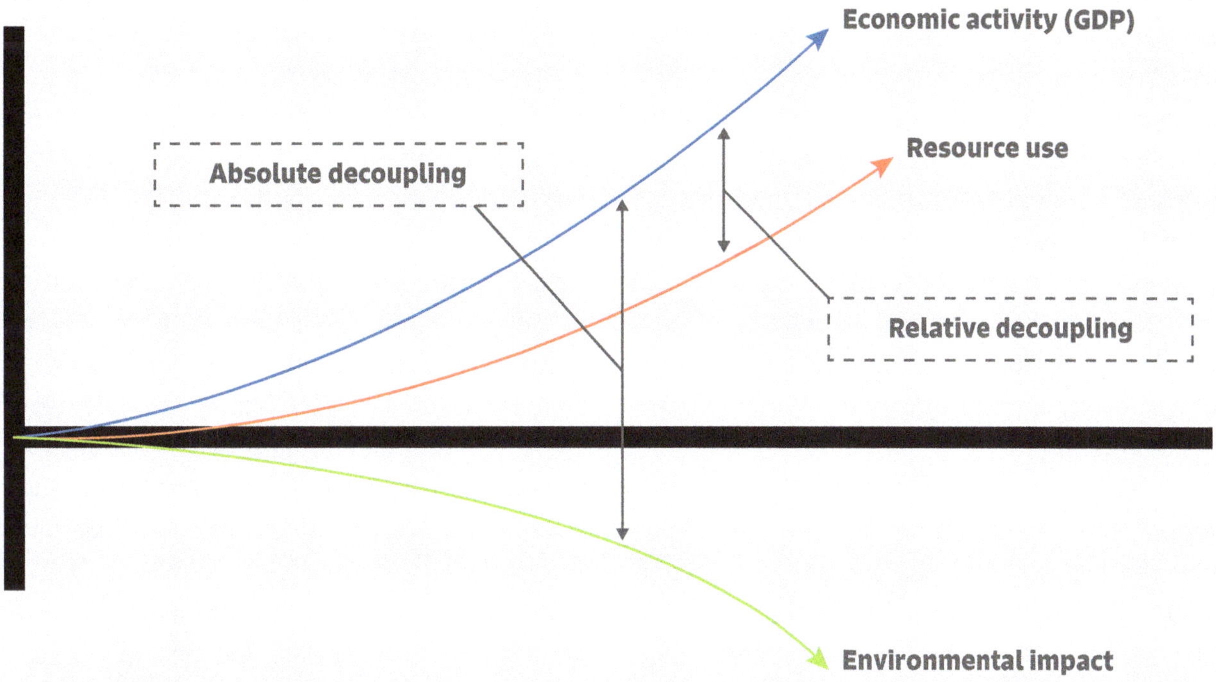

SOURCE: UNEP (2011).

FIGURE 4.6 GLOBAL ENERGY USE BY REGION (000 TONS OF OIL EQUIVALENT), 1990–2013

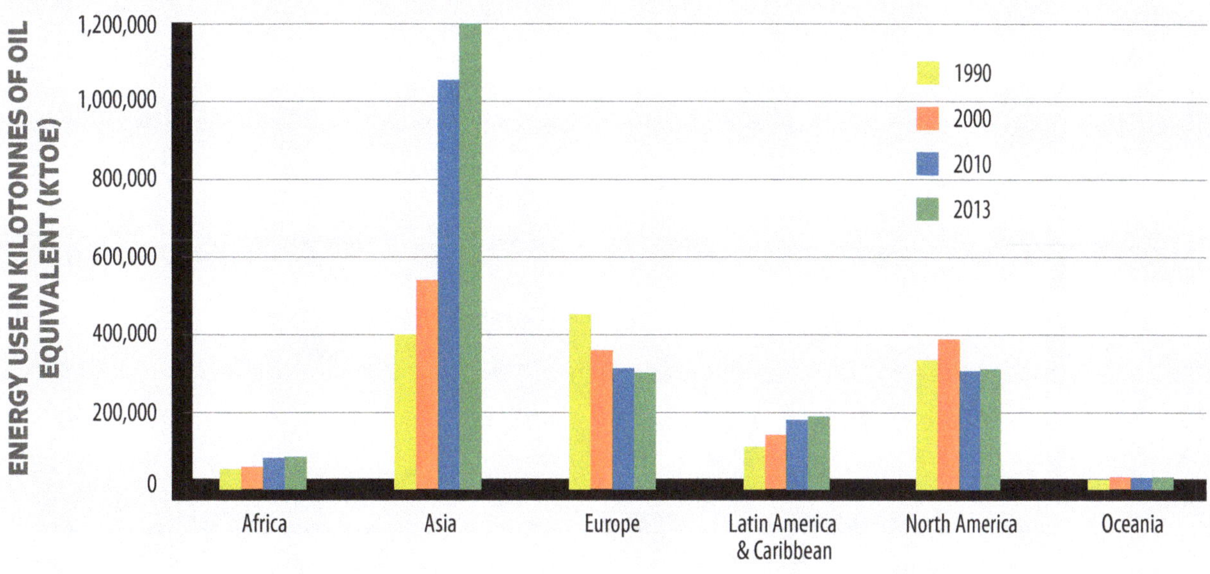

NOTE: KTOE = KILOTONNE OF OIL EQUIVALENT.

SOURCE: IEA (2015a, 2015b)

From 1990 to 2013, both the world economy and Africa recorded relative decoupling (table 4.1)—energy use rose at a slower rate than total output, as shown by falling energy intensity. Relative decoupling appears far higher for Africa than for the Asian and the Latin America and Caribbean regions. Although African energy intensity fell from 0.73 in 1990 to 0.64 in 2013, it remains the highest in the world, at 2.6 times the world average in 1990 and 2.7 times the world average in 2013, which suggests that Africa can save huge amounts of energy by introducing more energy-efficient technologies.

Among the five African regions, Southern Africa had the highest industrial energy consumption in 2013, of which South Africa accounted for 80 per cent and one third of Africa's total (figure 4.7). Countries with a higher degree of industrialization (South Africa and the North African countries) generally had the highest levels of energy use but lower levels of energy growth. In contrast, less industrialized regions experienced ever-increasing energy use over the same period, as reflected in their lack of decoupling. This pattern of energy growth is predictable because poorer countries establish greater levels of economic activity, and those with a stronger industrial sector seek to improve energy performance.

Table 4.2 shows selected African countries, ranked by their decoupling performance, from 1990 to 2013. Egypt, Tunisia, South Africa and Morocco—the four countries with the highest improvements in relative decoupling (that is, a negative relative decoupling index (RDI))—were also the top four countries for MVA in 2013. Although a definite correlation between relative decoupling and MVA or GDP could not be found for those African countries with the relevant data, the ranking of countries in Table 4.2 suggests that relatively strong economies in terms of GDP and MVA achieved the greatest decoupling between 1990 and 2013.

FIGURE 4.7 ENERGY USE, BY AFRICAN REGIONS, 1990–2013 (IN TONS OF OIL EQUIVALENT)

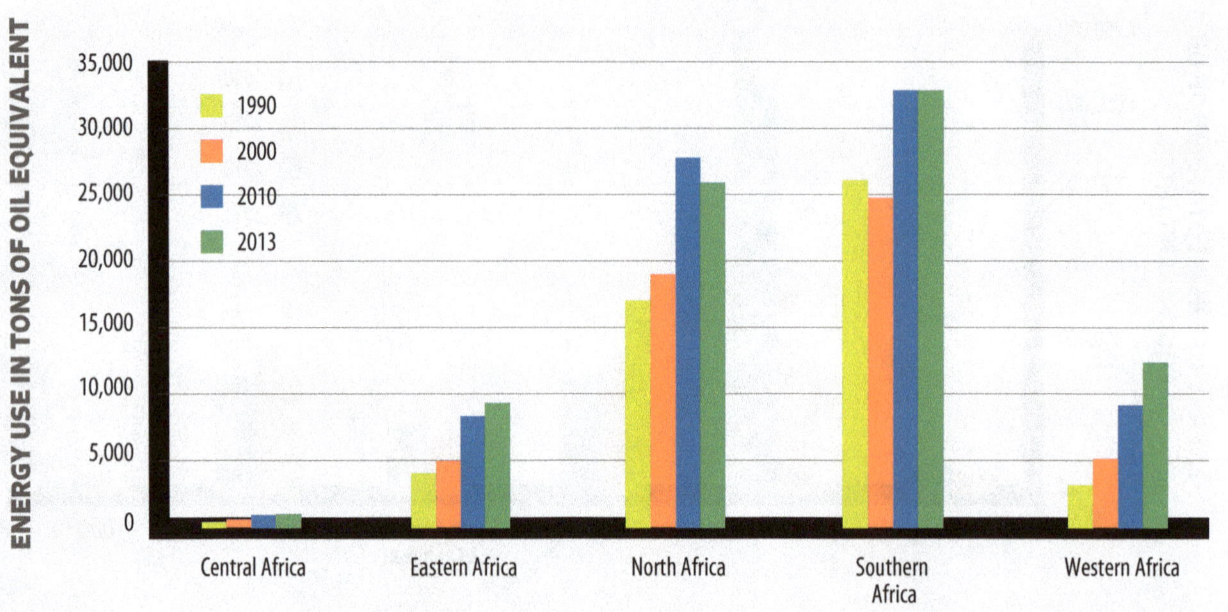

SOURCE: IEA (2015a).

TABLE 4.1 RDI AND ENERGY INTENSITY, REGIONAL AND GLOBAL, 1990–2013

	RDI	Energy intensity	
Region	1990 — 2013	1990	2013
Africa[1]	-0.12	0.73	0.64
Asia	0.03	0.31	0.32
Europe	-0.47	0.22	0.12
Latin America & Caribbean[2]	-0.01	0.37	0.36
North America[3]	-0.45	0.30	0.17
Oceania[4]	0.01	0.33	0.33
Total World	**-0.15**	**0.28**	**0.24**

1 28 countries out 54.
2 22 out 44 countries.
3 2 (USA, Canada) out 5 countries.
4 2 (Australia, New Zealand) out 26 countries.

SOURCE: IEA (2015a), UNIDO (2015a).

TABLE 4.2 RDI AND ENERGY INTENSITY, SELECTED AFRICAN COUNTRIES, 1990–2013

	RDI	Energy intensity	
Territorial Unit	1990 — 2013	1990	2013
World	**-0.15**	**0.28**	**0.24**
Africa[1]	-0.12	0.73	0.64
Egypt	-0.54	1.46	0.75
Tunisia	-0,40	0.51	0.32
South Africa	-0.21	0.71	0.61
Morocco	-0.12	0.33	0.28
Kenya	-0.05	0.39	0.47
Ghana	0.51	0.69	1.02
Nigeria	0.73	0.98	1.50
Senegal	0.83	0.15	0.26
Ivory Coast	0.90	0.08	0.15
Ethiopia	0.93	0.49	0.75

1 includes all African countries with available data.

SOURCE: IEA (2015a) AND UNIDO (2015a).

FIGURE 4.8 WATER USE, BY GLOBAL REGION AND SECTOR, 2010

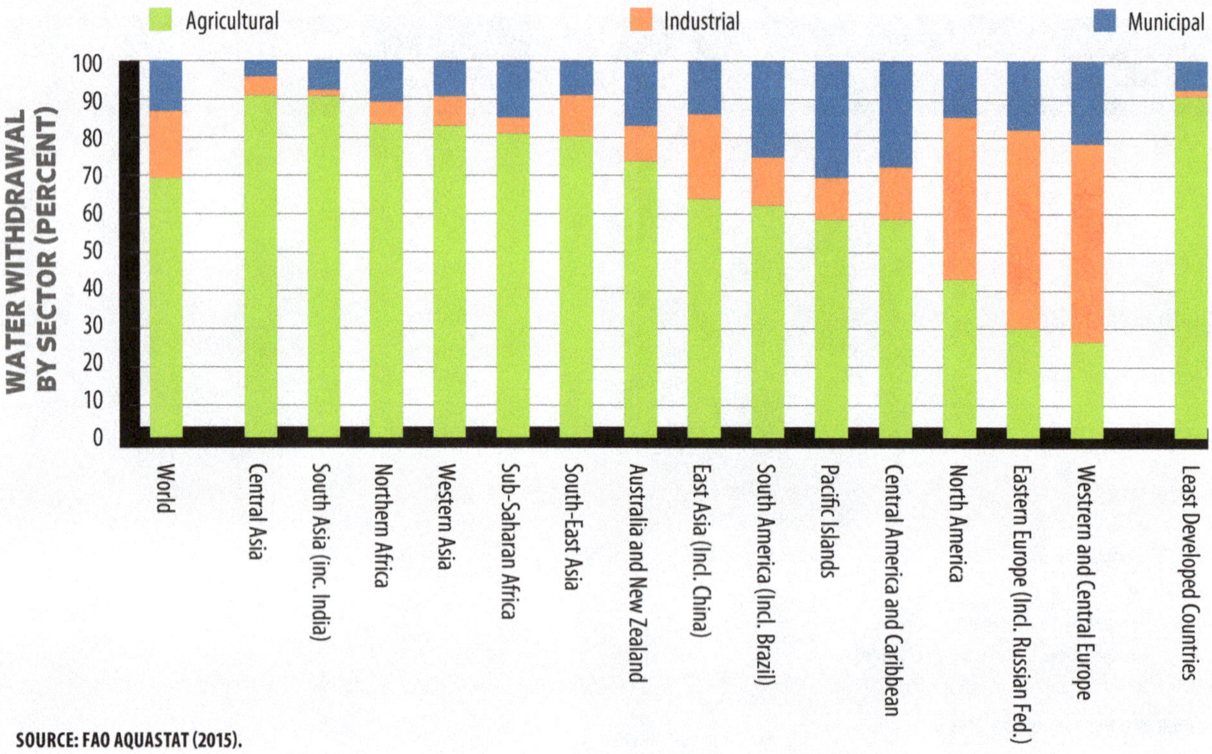

SOURCE: FAO AQUASTAT (2015).

FIGURE 4.9 RELATIVE WATER INTENSITY BY INDUSTRIAL SECTOR, GLOBAL

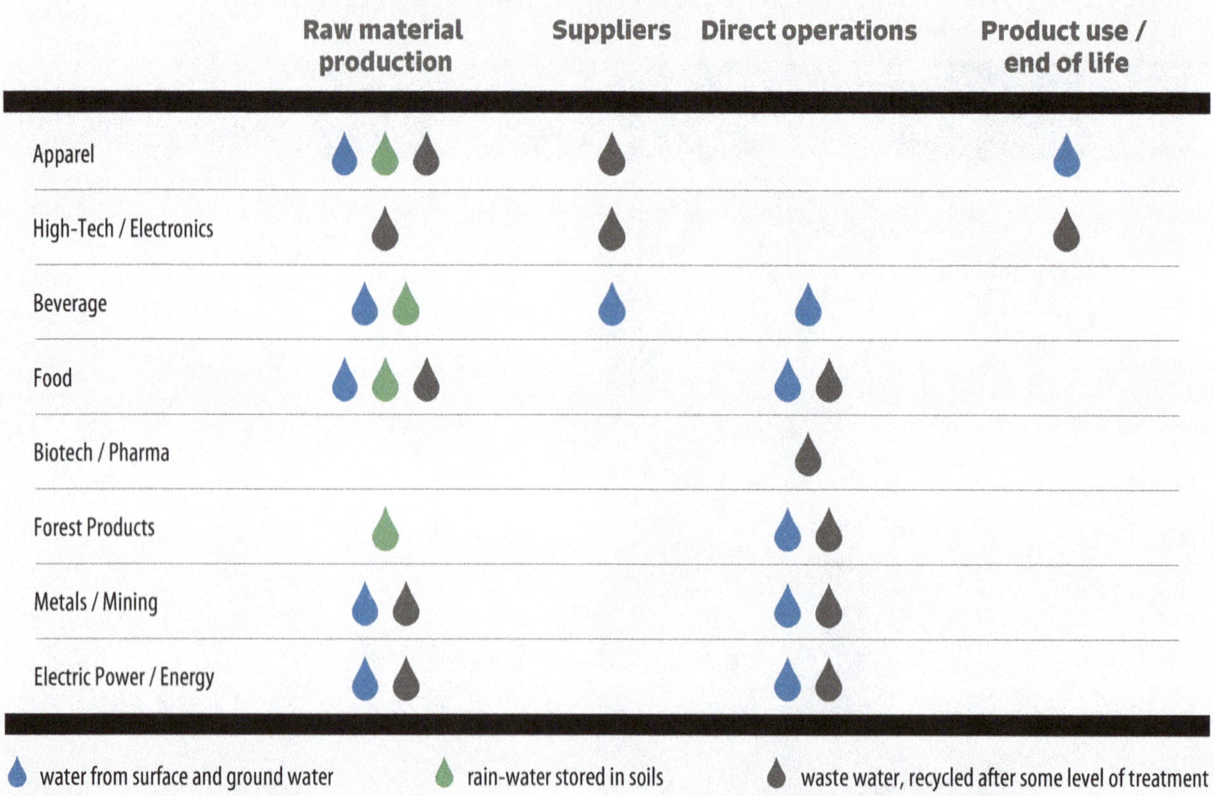

NOTE: WATER DROPS INDICATE THE VALUE CHAIN SEGMENTS THAT HAVE RELATIVELY HIGH BLUE, GREEN AND GRAY WATER FOOTPRINT INTENSITIES. BLUE REFERS TO WATER FROM SURFACE AND GROUND WATER; GREEN REFERS TO RAIN-WATER STORED IN SOILS; GRAY IS WASTE WATER, RECYCLED AFTER SOME LEVEL OF TREATMENT.

SOURCE: MORRISON ET AL., (2009), TABLE 3, P. 20, CITED IN UNESCO (2015), P. 62.

By contrast, Ghana, Nigeria, Senegal, Côte d'Ivoire and Ethiopia experienced an increase in their relative energy use over the period. The aggregate nature of the data, however, prevents one from concluding whether the figures reflect a deterioration in energy efficiency or a shift into more energy-intensive sectors.

INDUSTRIAL WATER-USE DECOUPLING IN AFRICA

Surprisingly little is known about industrial water use globally, especially in Africa. Although industrial water consumption accounts for about 20 per cent of the world's freshwater withdrawals, the proportion varies greatly among regions (figure 4.8). Those shares are only approximate, however, because water withdrawal by small and medium-sized industry often is conflated with domestic consumption (UNESCO, 2012, p. 59). In Africa, industrial water withdrawal accounts for about 5 per cent of the total, with agriculture using 85 per cent and human settlements 10 per cent (UNESCO, 2009, p. 99). This breakdown is consistent with the economic structure of the continent, given that much of the population still works in agriculture.

The production processes of some industrial sectors common in the African industrial landscape are water intensive, including apparel, beverage, food, and metals and mining (figure 4.9). The quality and coverage of the data do not permit an estimation of aggregate water use in Africa as a ratio of MVA, as was done for energy in table 4.2. An analysis of water use at the firm or plant level, however, suggests that considerable gains can result from large cuts in water use and effluent flows, offering payback periods of less than two years (Chapter 6).

4.4 GREENING INDUSTRIALIZATION AT THE SYSTEM LEVEL

Large gains in decoupling can be achieved by promoting greater resource efficiency at the establishment level, whether the manufacturing plant, farm or office (as will be shown in Chapter 6). Cleaner Production Centres, such as those established by UNEP and UNIDO in many African and Asian nations, have been instrumental in achieving these improvements. Although establishment-level changes are important, they meet only part of the systemic green industrialization challenge. Four categories of systems can be identified, as follows: environmental systems and landscapes; infrastructure; inter-sectoral and inter-ministerial systems; and value chains.

ENVIRONMENTAL SYSTEMS AND LANDSCAPES

Environmental assets, such as water courses, are inherently systemic. Rain falls in a particular region, from which it may be collected or from which it might flow through riverine channels over large distances. These courses may span very large areas, characteristically crossing a number of national boundaries. The Niger River, for example, is longer than 4,000 kilometres, its wide basin of tributaries covering nine riverine nations, as it runs from the mountains of Guinea to the Niger-Delta region of Nigeria (figure 4.10).

FIGURE 4.10 TRANSBOUNDARY WATER BASINS: WEST AFRICA'S NIGER RIVER

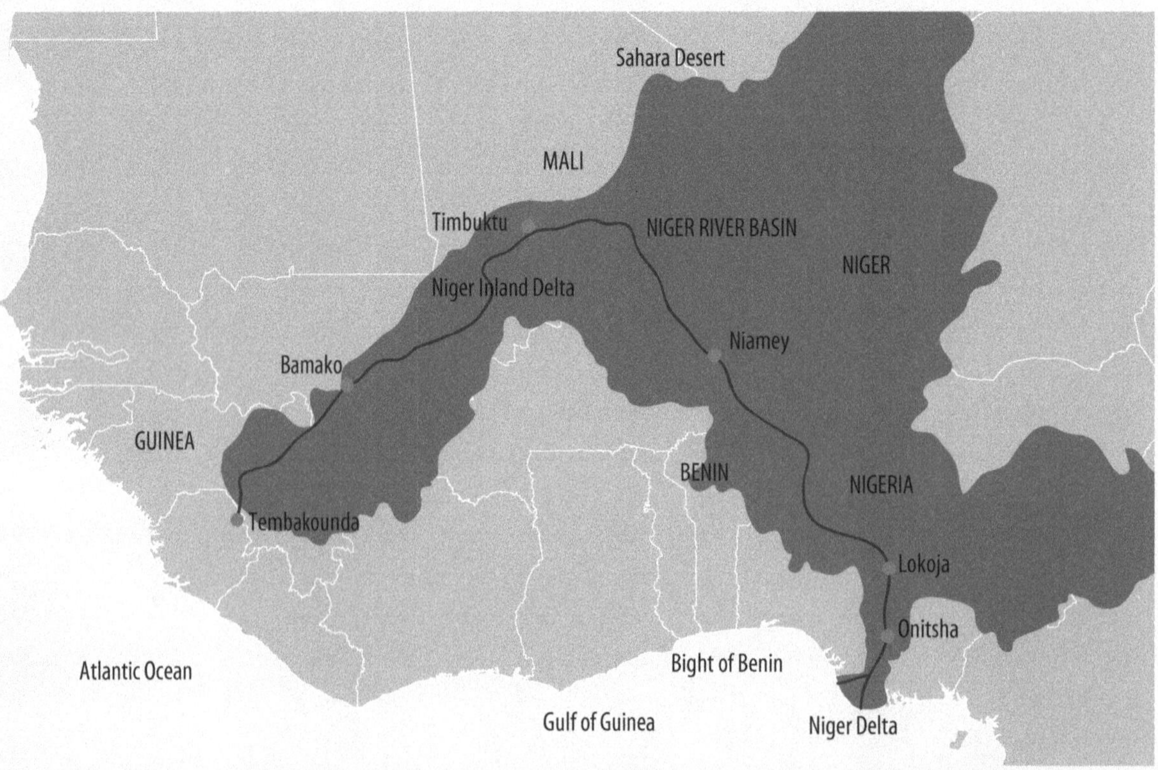

SOURCE: WIKIPEDIA.

Africa has 63 transboundary river basins, covering 64 per cent of the continent's land area and containing 93 per cent of its total surface water resource (UNEP, 2010). It also has major transboundary aquifers, such as the Nubian Sandstone Aquifer under Chad, Egypt, Libya and Sudan.

Water resource users come from households, fisheries, agriculture, industry, mining and infrastructure. Because water is a finitely constrained resource, its use in one part of the system affects its use in another part. Similarly, waste effluents released into the river at a particular place will have an effect on many other sectors and uses downstream. Groundwater exhibits similar problems of shared use and effects.

The water system is not only riverine but also involves seas and oceans, which offer resources for a range of competing activities. Hence, an increasing number of economies target the Blue Economy for income-generating opportunities and handle the systemic uses and abuses of seas and oceans (as noted for the AU Blue Economy Strategy, and as described for Mauritius in Chapter 6). Maintaining the integrity of these environmental assets against industrialization is a major challenge that cannot be met at the individual establishment level alone. Their management necessarily has to be systemic.

INFRASTRUCTURE

The same systemic approach is needed for many infrastructural inputs into production. Consider, for example, the central, eastern, southern and western coast-to-interior corridors being developed across Africa (figure 4.11). These projects are viable only when they operate at a systemic level, crossing countries and sectors. Hence, because the challenge is to promote green infrastructure and to provide infrastructure that promotes the greening of industry, infrastructural greening necessarily requires a systemic response, bringing together governance, politics, economics and practical management.

The green industrialization challenge crosses not only national borders but also individual sectors.

INTERSECTORAL AND INTERMINISTERIAL SYSTEMS

The green industrialization challenge crosses not only national borders but also individual sectors. Although decoupling in an individual factory can be seen as a focused challenge, and similarly the greening of a farm a challenge of greening agriculture, in almost all cases the greening of industrialization will require actions that cut across sectors. The problem with meeting this cross-sectoral agenda is that it generally cuts across ministerial and bureaucratic silos, too—for example, the global value chain (GVC) involved in the export of processed fruit and vegetables (figure 4.12).

Crops are produced in the agricultural sector (involving the Ministry of Agriculture), but they require inputs from the domestic manufacturing sector (Ministry of Industry), from imports (Ministry of Trade) and from knowledge-intensive institutions in the national system of innovation (Ministry of Education). Their outputs feed into the logistical sector (Ministry of Transport) and may involve government-approved certification (various ministries). Some of the output goes to the domestic market (regulation of retail) and

FIGURE 4.11 MAJOR INFRASTRUCTURAL AND DEVELOPMENT CORRIDORS, AFRICA, 2015

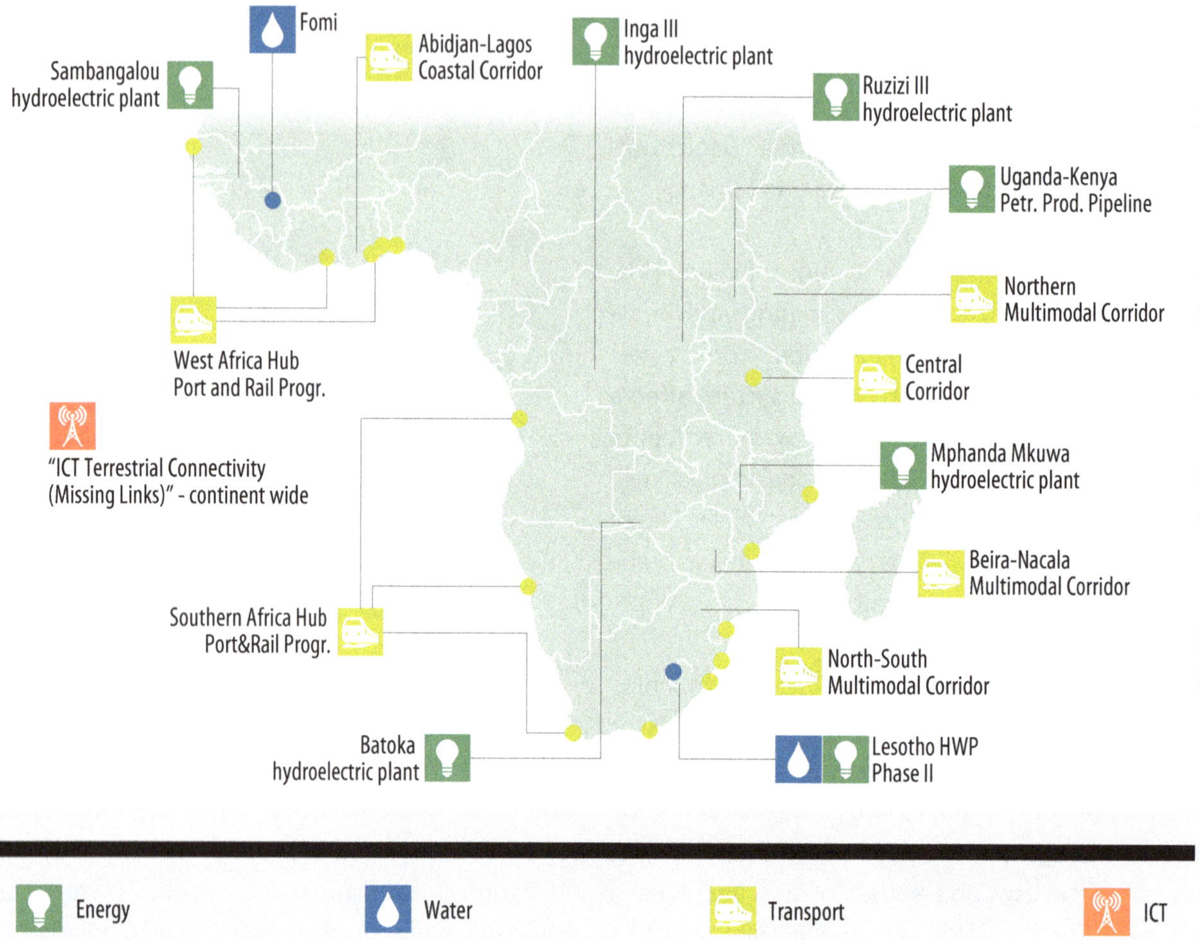

SOURCE: WORLD ECONOMIC FORUM (2015).

some into export markets (Ministry of Trade and Export Promotion). All this requires coordinated, systemic greening along the value chain—cutting across sectors and ministries (Chapter 6)—and at the establishment level.

VALUE CHAINS

In the remainder of this chapter we concentrate on the value chain system, a key arena for resource allocation in production. The value chain describes the full range of activities required to bring a product or service from conception, through the different phases of production (involving a combination of physical transformation of inputs and the incorporation of various producer services), delivery to final consumers and final disposal after use (see figure 4.12, although it does not include recycling and restitution of the environment after product use).

The increasing importance of value chains in recent decades follows from the growing division of labour that became pronounced in the last quarter of the 20th century, primarily specialization of businesses. Specialization means that firms focus on those capabilities ("core competencies") in which they have distinct strengths and in which they benefit from barriers to entry from other firms. All other activities are outsourced up the chain to suppliers or down the chain to users.

FIGURE 4.12 THE PROCESSED FRUIT AND VEGETABLE GLOBAL VALUE CHAIN

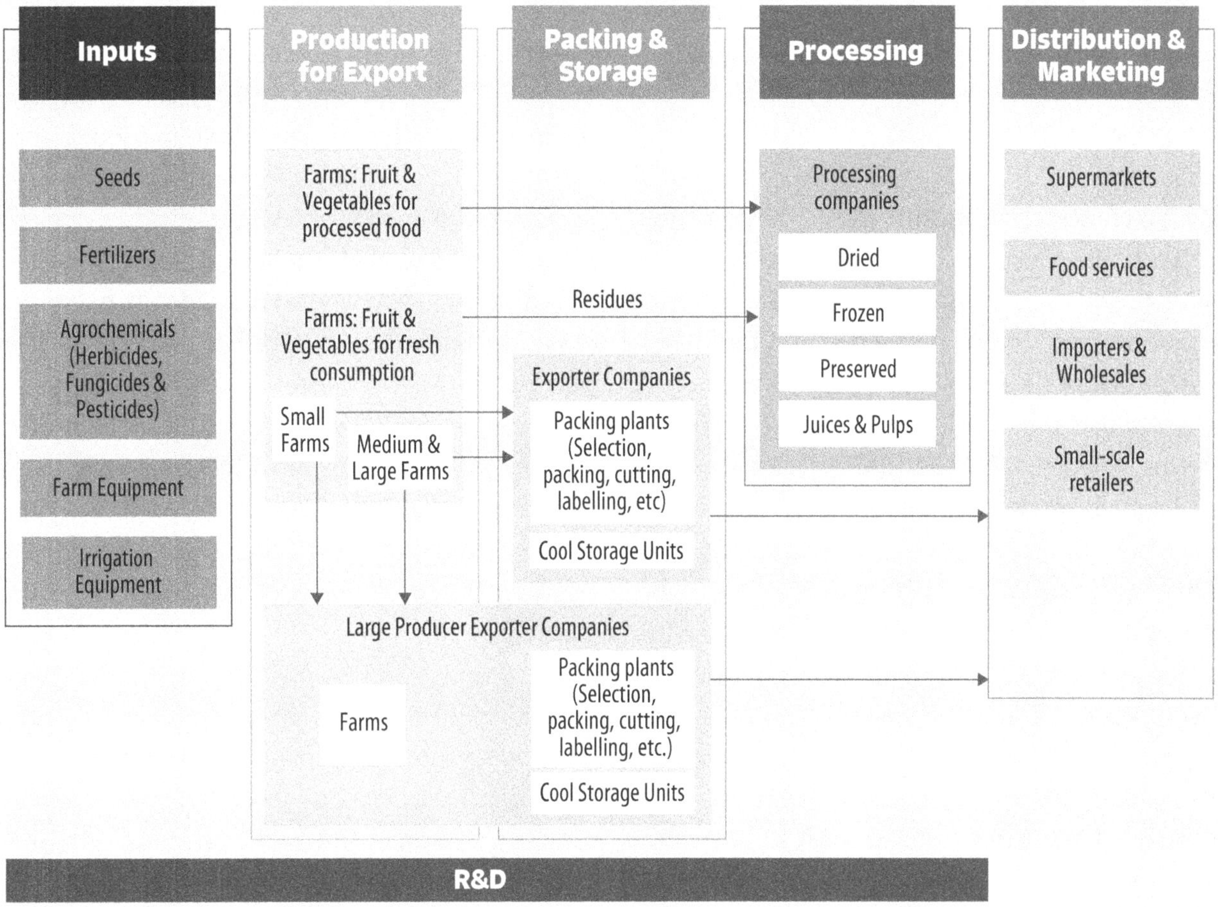

SOURCE: GEREFFI AND FERNANDEZ-STARK (2011).

From the early 1970s—and particularly after the mid-1980s, when China entered the global economy—this fragmentation and outsourcing took an increasingly global form, leading to the dispersion of manufacturing around the globe and the growing geographical separation of production from consumption. This pattern of global outsourcing, building on competencies in the emerging economies, but driven by the needs of large firms and retailers in advanced economies, underwrote the surge in the developing world's share in global manufacturing value added and trade. Unlike most Asian economies (especially China), which have benefited from this global dispersion of production, African economies have reaped these benefits far less.

By 2012, more than two thirds of global trade in goods and services was in intermediate products and services. The World Trade Organization estimated that a quarter ($5 trillion out of $19 trillion) of global trade in 2010 involved double-counting, that is, the value of intermediate products traded directly across national borders and indirectly, through subsequent incorporation in final products (UNCTAD, 2013; UNECA, 2014). As Chang (2015) notes, this flow of resources and revenue within GVCs represents a huge concentration of profits and power within the large multinational firms that can accrue technological dominance, brand recognition and access to low-cost capital because of the large scale at which they operate. The rising share of trade in these large firms and the associated movement of revenue between different jurisdictions raises vital questions about where corporate profit and turnover should be taxed.

This trade occurs along two different types of GVC (Kaplinsky and Morris, 2015). The first type is "vertically specialized chains", in which the different components can be produced in parallel, transport costs are relatively low and intermediate products do not degrade. These are largely characteristics of manufacturing and service value chains, in which the value added gained from the developing country component often is small. For example, the Apple iPhone4 was exported from China at a free on board price of $175 but incorporated only $6.50 of value added in China; the remainder consisted of imported intermediate components (Xing and Detert, 2010). The second type of GVC is "additive value chains", in which the various stages of production are necessarily sequential, transport costs are high and intermediate products may degrade. These value chains are mainly in the resource sector (agriculture, minerals and metals, and energy).

From the African perspective, whereas two thirds of GVC trade is in vertically specialized chains, its contribution to African exports is less than one quarter, much of that in Egypt, Mauritius and South Africa. The overwhelming share of African exports is in additive, commodity-based GVCs; thus, their greening is particularly important in greening African economies.

Value chains are a vehicle for promoting green and inclusive industrialization in three main ways.

Any chain is only as strong as its weakest link. Production occurs along the entire supply chain, and effective greening therefore requires action within each of these links if the entire chain is to function as desired. Moreover, evidence on the ground shows that production almost always crosses sectors. Hence greening is a systemic challenge and requires actions along the whole value chain, as evidenced in research by Kemp et al., (2013) on the energy efficiency of crop-drying technologies in the cassava chain in Nigeria and the maize chain in Kenya. The findings show clear signs of more energy-efficient investments being made in crop-drying methods. If energy use in the value chain as a whole is considered, however, drying technologies represent only a trivial component. The energy wasted in inefficient logistics (for example, dirty diesel combustion in the trucks hauling produce from farm to drier)— in part, a result of subsidized fuel—is far more than any marginal gains in the crop-drying component and has largely been ignored in the greening policy agenda.

Traditionally, industrial policy has focused on developing supply capabilities; however, the character of supply chains—including their "greenness"—is shaped by final market demand. In many advanced economies, final markets demand the greening of value chains, and that is increasingly the case for middle-income markets in Africa and other emerging economies, a process sharpened by the rapid advance of global supermarket chains in Africa and elsewhere. Thus, although traditional industrial policy has focused on the growth of supply capabilities, the value chain lens forces the greening agenda to respond to the demands of different final markets (box 4.7). Because Walmart acquired MassMart (a South African retailer expanding quickly throughout Africa) in 2012, the US behemoth will likely increasingly require the greening of its African supply chains.

Because markets drive the structure of systemic supply chains, one must understand how value chains are governed (Gereffi, Humphrey, and Sturgeon, 2005). This may involve a mix of regulations (producers that fail to comply cannot be included in the supply chain) and incentives (achieving the chain goal is rewarded with higher

BOX 4.7 THE GREENING OF WALMART'S SUPPLY CHAIN IN CHINA

In 2009, Walmart announced the development of a worldwide Sustainability Product Index, which began with a survey to be completed by all Walmart suppliers. The survey consisted of 15 questions about energy use, climate impact, material efficiency, natural resource usage, and local community involvement. The surveys fed into the "Sustainability Index Consortium", an open platform database that allowed for analysis of the information collected from Walmart's 100,000 suppliers.

By 2012, 500 suppliers and 107 product categories had participated in the index. At a Global Sustainability Milestone Meeting in Beijing in 2008, Walmart's chief executive officer announced plans to expand participation to 70 per cent of suppliers by 2017, making clear that failure to participate in the index would lead to removal of the firm from Walmart's supply chain.

SOURCE: KAPLINSKY AND MORRIS (2014).

BOX 4.8 FOUR SETS OF STANDARDS WIDELY OBSERVED IN GVCS

- *Corporate standards internal to the chain.* They typically address quality, cost and delivery procedures and, increasingly, environmental processes. They specify the requirements of the lead firm (at the buying end of the chain) for supplier firms to ensure systemic chain competitiveness.
- *Industry standards.* They are industry specific or relevant across a range of sectors, such as ISO9000 on quality and ISO14000 on environmental management.
- *Standards set by governments.* They include food safety and energy efficiency, and those set by international bodies include the EU "farm-to-fork" food standards and vehicle emission standards.
- *Standards designed by civil society.* They include labour standards, organic standards and Fairtrade certification.

SOURCE: AUTHOR'S COMPILATION.

prices). The greening of chains thus necessarily requires the governance of performance along the whole chain, and chain participants are characteristically required to meet a series of complex standards, such as with the Forest Stewardship Council's certification in the timber, wood and furniture value chain (Chapter 6). Four major drivers of greening standards in GVCs are corporate standards, industry standards, government standards and standards inspired by civil society organizations (box 4.8).

The three characteristics of value chains—their systemic nature, the links between production structures and final markets, and the governance of production along the chain—have to be addressed in green industrialization. Their practical significance is shown in many of the greening case studies in Chapter 6.

4.5 KEY STAKEHOLDERS IN THE GOVERNANCE OF VALUE-CHAIN GREENING

Understanding who does what in greening establishments and systems is important if a green industrial policy agenda is to be successful. In the analysis of GVCs this is referred to as "chain governance" (Gereffi, Humphrey, and Sturgeon, 2005), but this concept of governance can be used to analyse the implementation of greening in all of the four sets of systems identified in the earlier section "Entry points to embed greening in industrialization". Essentially, two sets of chain governors exist—internal and external.

Internal chain governance is exercised by actors within the chain. In private sector–driven chains, these governors are firms, generally the "lead firms". In state-driven chains, the key decision makers include the managers of these state enterprises.

The role played by lead firms is critical in an increasing number of GVCs, including that of the greening agenda. Final market demand forces key actors in the chain to drive green standards systematically both down and up their value chains (for example, Forest Stewardship Council certification). In many GVCs, these lead firms are transnational corporations, particularly in chains in which African producers participate. In other cases, particularly in the more industrialized low- and middle-income economies, the lead firms may be locally or regionally owned.

The motivation for lead firms to pursue a greening agenda is not just a response to state regulation but also a strategy to maximize profit by reducing costs (for example, energy), penetrate more lucrative market niches (such as organic markets) and avoid reputational damage tied to poor environmental or social practices. Walmart's greening of its value chain to save costs, Tesco's greening of its horticultural value chain to avoid reputational damage, and Shell's greening of its Niger River Delta operations to maintain its social licence to operate are all examples of lead firms driven strictly by commercial interests to behave according to more ethical or environmental principles.

Not all lead firms pursue active greening, however, nor is a strong green vision of corporate leaders necessarily reflected in events on the ground. Moreover, lead firms selling in lower-income markets, in which consumers are less demanding of green credentials, have less incentive to drive greening.

The nation state generally is the prime external chain stakeholder with the capacity to green systems, often through a mix of pricing decisions, regulations and incentives. Pricing reflects the government-determined cost of key environmental inputs, notably water and energy. Subsidies for high-carbon inputs (such as fossil-fuel energy) obviously are detrimental to a greening agenda; conversely, forcing producers to pay for environmental externalities, such as pollution, and subsidizing the price of green inputs, such as renewable energy, facilitate greening.

Regulations may affect process standards in production, for example, by requiring chain participants to achieve certain minimum conditions for effluents and by placing limits on, for example, water abstraction. Regulations may also affect product characteristics—for instance, contaminant levels in foodstuffs.

Incentives constitute a series of "carrots" to persuade firms to green their operations and include

BOX 4.9 GLOBAL STANDARDS—RAPID GROWTH IN COVERAGE AND DEMAND

The world has more than 400 eco-labels, most relating to agriculture and forestry. Eco-labels are usually voluntary, and help consumers identify products that satisfy certain environmental standards so far as their production is concerned. In 2012 the 16 largest initiatives covered total estimated trade of $31.6 billion, of which 40 per cent was coffee, 22 per cent cocoa, and 15 per cent palm oil. A total of 9 per cent of forested area has been certified as being managed in ways which satisfy sustainability standards.

In the early years, global civil society was key in setting standards and exerting influence over the private sector to ensure compliance. In the past decade, however, the private sector has shown much greater leadership and involvement in, for example, industry-led dialogue and cooperation, broad governance of criteria, and systems for compliance monitoring. Most standards cover either environmental or social criteria, with a few combining the two. The most recent standards cover a single crop or commodity, such as sugar.

SOURCE: POTTS (2014).

financial advantages and tax relief for new investment. In some cases governments provide support to use business service firms to assist the greening of operations along the chain.

Foreign governments are a further potential source of governance that affects GVC greening. They set the regulations that determine market entry and, hence, the character of the supply chains in producing countries. Increasingly, governments in high income nations, such as the United States and regional blocs such as the European Union, set market-entry standards that determine the green content of supply chains, particularly for the agricultural and resource sectors, which account for the bulk of Africa's exports.

Global civil society organizations are a further pressure point promoting the greening of value chains. Their power comes from their capacity to threaten non-compliant multinational firms with reputational damage. An alternative strategy by civil society has been to engage big firms in a collective attempt to raise standards and certify best practice. Examples of multi-stakeholder platforms involving civil society and transnational firms include the Roundtables on Sustainable Palm Oil, and Soy, and the Better Sugar Initiative.

A final set of stakeholders relevant to deploying green and inclusive industrialization includes international agencies and bilateral trade schemes that actively promote GVC greening. Unlike state-led governance, which is predominantly implemented through mandatory regulations, this form of governance provides incentives to greening, generally in the form of direct assistance and training to producers in the chain, such as UNIDO's work to establish National Cleaner Production Centres (UNIDO, 2015b).

Box 4.9 describes the large number and spread of eco-labelling schemes. One consequence of this value-chain greening, especially where driven by lead firms, is that it frequently excludes small producers, especially women, for three reasons. The first is that participating in value chains that demand comprehensive, certified standards requires a minimum level of literacy, training and skills, and these attributes often are lacking in small-scale, poor and female-headed farms and enterprises. Second, certification often is costly and requires regular renewal; larger and formal-sector enterprises have the capacity to spread these fixed costs over larger volumes of output. Third, existing patterns of gender relations often systematically exclude females from greening programmes. For example, a recent study of greening and capacity expansion in the cocoa value chain found that virtually all of the support given to farmers along the chain was directed to men's activities, yet the key tasks that determined productivity and greening were undertaken by women (Barrientos, 2014).

In a few words, building an inclusive green economy is the work of governments, businesses and people together, and implementing green industrial policy requires consultation, communication and cooperation among them. The process for designing industrial policy is therefore as important as all the documents and evidence used to guide this agenda. As shown in the Economic Report on Africa 2014, governments need to create coalitions of different actors so as to advance the industrial policy agenda, with greening and inclusion at its core.

The final chapter in this work, on recommendations and policy frameworks, addresses the construction of these multi-stakeholder processes. First, though, in Chapter 5 we examine the costs of inaction through a modelling exercise; then in Chapter 6, to draw broader lessons, we review experience across Africa of plant-level decoupling and system-level greening.

4.6 REFERENCES

African Development Bank Group (AfDB). 2013. *At the center of Africa's transformation: strategy for 2013–2022.* Abidjan, Côte d'Ivoire.

———. 2015. *Transforming Africa through Modern Infrastructure.* Abidjan, Côte d'Ivoire: African Development Bank. http://www.afdb.org/fileadmin/uploads/afdb/Documents/Generic-Documents/PIDA%20brief%20closing%20gap.pdf.

———. 2015. *Feeding Africa.* Abidjan, Côte d'Ivoire: African Development Bank.

African Union. 2009. *Africa mining vision.* Addis Ababa.

African Union (2013). Agenda 2063. *The Africa we want.* Addis Ababa.

Barrientos, Stephanie. 2014. Gendered Global Production Networks: Analysis of Cocoa–Chocolate Sourcing, *Regional Studies.*

Bass, Steve. 2015. Pro-poor, inclusive green growth. Report for the Global Green Growth Institute. London: International Institute for Environment and Development.

Bello, O., A. Inyinbor, A. Dada and P. Oluyori. 2013. "Impact of Nigerian Textile Industry on Economy and Environment: A Review." *International Journal of Basic and Applied Sciences* 13:01: 98-106.

Bridle, Richard, Lucy Kitson and Peter Wooders. 2014. Fossil-fuel subsidies: a barrier to renewable energy in five Middle East and North African countries. Geneva: International Institute for Sustainable Development, Global Subsidies Initiative.

Chang, Ha-Joon. 2015. *Smart industrial policy for Africa in the 21st century.* Report for UNECA.

EIB. 2015. *Plan Maroc Vert,* PNEEI. European Investment Bank, Luxembourg.

EIZ. 2015. *Report on ZESCO Load Shedding. Prepared by the Engineering Institute of Zambia,* Technical Experts Team. September 2015. www.eiz.org.zm

Gereffi, Gary, and Karina Fernandez-Stark. 2011. "Global value chain analysis: a primer. Durham, NC: Duke University Center on Globalization, Governance & Competitiveness." http://www.cggc.duke.edu/pdfs/2011-05-31_GVC_analysis_a_primer.pdf. Accessed 22 November 2015.

Gereffi, Gary, John Humphrey and Timothy Sturgeon. 2005. "The governance of global value chains. Review of International Political Economy", vol. 12, No. 1 (February), pp. 78–104.

Global Apollo Program. 2015. www.globalapolloprogram.org

Government of the Republic of Kenya. 2015. *Kenya Green Economy Strategy and Implementation Plan (GESIP).* Nairobi.

International Energy Agency (IEA). 2014a. Africa Energy Outlook. *A Focus on Energy Prospects in Sub-Saharan Africa.* Paris.

———. 2014b. World Energy Outlook. Paris.

IEA. 2015a. *Energy Balances of non-OECD Countries,* International Energy Agency, Paris.

IEA. 2015b. Energy Balances for OECD Countries, International Energy Agency. Paris

ILO. 2016. Briefing Note. Green jobs and renewable energy: Low carbon, high employment. www.ilo.org/green-jobs-programme.

International Monetary Fund (IMF). 2015. Counting the Cost of Energy Subsidies. IMF Survey, July 17, 2015.

Jerven, M. 2013. *Poor Numbers: How we are Misled by African Development Statistics and What to Do About It,* Ithaca: Cornell University Press.

Kaplinsky, Raphael and Mike Morris. 2014. Developing industrial clusters and supply chains to support diversification and sustainable development of exports in Africa: composite report. Cairo: African Export-Import Bank.

———. 2015. "Thinning and thickening: productive sector policies in the era of global value chains." *European Journal of Development Research,* 11 June, pp. 1–21. doi:10.1057/ejdr.2015.29.

Karikari, K., K. Asante and C. Biney. 2006. "Water Quality Characteristics at the Estuary of Korle Lagoon in Ghana." *West African Journal of Applied Ecology* 10: 73-79.

Kemp, René, John O. Adeoti, Jacinta Ndichu, Abiodun E. Obayelu, Julian Blohmke, Raphael Kaplinsky and Kevin Urama. 2013. Diffusion strategy of green technology and green industry in Africa. A study of renewable energy technology market and energy efficiency adoption in maize and cassava processing industries in Kenya and Nigeria. Final report of study for Korea Energy Economics Institute and United Nations Industrial Development Organization. Maastricht, Netherlands: United Nations University--Merit.

King, David, John Browne, Richard Layard, Gus O'Donnell, Martin Rees, Nicholas Stern, Adair Turner. 2015. A GLOBAL APOLLO PROGRAMME TO COMBAT CLIMATE CHANGE, Centre for Economic Performance. http://cep.lse.ac.uk/pubs/download/special/Global_Apollo_Programme_Report.pdf. Accessed October 2015.

Potts, Jason, Matthew Lynch, Ann Wilkings, Gabriel Huppé, Maxine Cunningham and Vivek Voora. 2014. *The State of Sustainability Initiatives Review 2014: Standards and the Green Economy*. Geneva: International Institute for Sustainable Development, and London: International Institute for Environment and Development.

Roberts, D. 2008. "Thinking globally, acting locally – institutionalizing climate change at the local government level in Durban, South Africa." Environment and Urbanization, 20(2), 521-537.

Roberts, D. and S. O'Donoghue. 2013. "Urban environmental challenges and climate change action in Durban, South Africa." *Environment and Urbanization*, 25(2), 299-319.

Shelagh, and Laurie van der Burg. 2015. "Fossil fuel subsidy reform in sub-Saharan Africa: from rhetoric to reality." Working paper. London: New Climate Economy. http://newclimateeconomy.report/misc/working-papers.

Southern African Development Community. 2012. *Regional infrastructure development master plan: Executive Summary: August 2012*. Gaborone, Botswana: SADC. http://www.sadc.int/files/7513/5293/3530/Regional_Infrastructure_Development_Master_Plan_Executive_Summary.pdf.

South African Government. 2012. National infrastructure plan. http://www.gov.za/issues/national-infrastructure-plan.

———. 2015. Expanded public works programme. http://www.gov.za/about-government/government-programmes/expanded-public-works-programme.

United Nations Conference on Trade and Development (UNCTAD). 2013. *Trade and Development Report, 2013: Adjusting to the Changing Dynamics of the World Economy*. Geneva: UNCTAD.

United Nations Development Programme (UNDP). 2011. Paving the way for climate-resilient infrastructure: guidance for practitioners and planners. New York.

United Nations, Economic Commission for Africa (UNECA). 2014. Dynamic industrial policy in Africa. *Economic Report on Africa*. Addis Ababa.

UNEP. 2006. Report on Atmosphere and Air Pollution. African Regional Implementation Review for the 14th Session of the Commission on Sustainable Development. Nairobi.

UNEP. 2010. *Africa Water Atlas*, Nairobi, United Nations Environment Programme.

———. 2011. *Decoupling natural resource use and environmental impacts from economic growth*. Nairobi. United Nations Environment Programme.

United Nations Educational, Scientific and Cultural Organization (UNESCO). 2009. *World Water Development Report 3 (WWDR3):Water in a Changing World*. Paris.

———. 2012. *World Water Development Report 4 (WWDR4): Managing Water under Uncertainty and Risk*. Paris.

———. 2015. *World Water Development Report 2015 (WWDR2015): Water for a Sustainable World*. Paris.

UNIDO. 2015a. *Manufacturing Value Added 2015*. United Nations Industrial Development Organization, Vienna.

UNIDO. 2015b. National Cleaner Production Centres. www.unido.org/en/ncpc20.htm

World Bank Group. 2015. *World Development Indicators 2015*. Washington, D.C.: World Bank Group. http://data.worldbank.org/sites/default/files/wdi-2015-frontmatter.pdf.

World Economic Forum. 2015. *Africa Strategic Infrastructure Initiative Project Overview: Accelerating Infrastructure Development in Africa*. Geneva, World Economic Forum.

Xing, Yuqing, and Neil Detert. 2010. "How the iPhone Widens the United States Trade Deficit with the People's Republic of China." ADBI Working Paper No. 257. Tokyo: Asian Development Bank Institute.

4.7 ENDNOTES

1 The AU has launched, for example, preparation of the African Integrated Maritime Strategy 2050, which aims to harness the assets and opportunities represented by Africa's vast oceanic and coastal resources, sometimes referred to as the Blue Economy.

2 Our search for data on industrial pollution found one overview of air pollution problems resulting from all human activity (UNEP, 2006) and a few journal articles about industry-related pollution problems in specific countries (for example, Bello et al., 2013 for Nigeria; and Karikari et al., 2006 for Ghana).

CHAPTER 5

ALTERNATIVE PATHWAYS FOR AFRICA: BUSINESS AS USUAL OR A GREEN AGENDA?

5.1 TWO SCENARIOS FOR AFRICA

To map the motivating factors for green growth and green industrialization in Africa and, more specifically, to identify points of entry for green growth interventions, as introduced in the previous three chapters, the first step is charting the socioeconomic futures of Africa and its subregions. One way of thinking about the future is through the use of scenarios.

The two scenarios developed for this analysis are designed to stimulate answers to questions such as, what will happen if we continue in a business as usual (BAU) fashion? What if we switch to a green agenda (GA)? In other words, what will happen if current growth trajectories continue, with uneven patterns of development and sporadic approaches to natural resource, waste and energy management? Alternatively, what could happen if Africa's industrialization was greened, using targeted improvements to urbanization, energy developments, population growth and changes to the very basis of our economies?

The two scenarios—BAU and GA—explore alternative trajectories for Africa from 2015 through 2050:

- **BAU** is a scenario portraying a continuation of current patterns and trends. The forecasts under BAU illustrate how the current development trajectory will affect different sectors, highlighting areas of concern.
- The **GA** is a scenario that models policy interventions in a range of sectors. Together, these interventions are intended to model a structural shift in the development trajectory of the continent towards a greener, more inclusive economic growth pattern than under BAU.

The GA scenario generates far better outcomes for key development indicators, especially per capita gross domestic product (GDP) and exports, and sees deeper and faster cuts in numbers of people in poverty, relative to the BAU scenario (figure 5.1). These findings strongly suggest that GA will bring more sustainable and inclusive benefits over the period (boxes 5.1 and 5.2).

The BAU and GA scenarios use Africa's subregions as a basis for analysis, with some illustrative country examples. The global context, too, is important, and the discussions on systemic drivers and some of the more central BAU scenarios relate Africa to the rest of the world on key aspects of green growth and industrialization. The methodology is explained in box 5.3 with detail in Annex 1.

... what could happen if Africa's industrialization was greened, using targeted improvements to urbanization, energy developments, population growth and changes to the very basis of our economies?

FIGURE 5.1 BAU AND GA—GDP PER CAPITA, EXPORTS PER CAPITA AND POVERTY LEVELS, AFRICA, 2015–2050

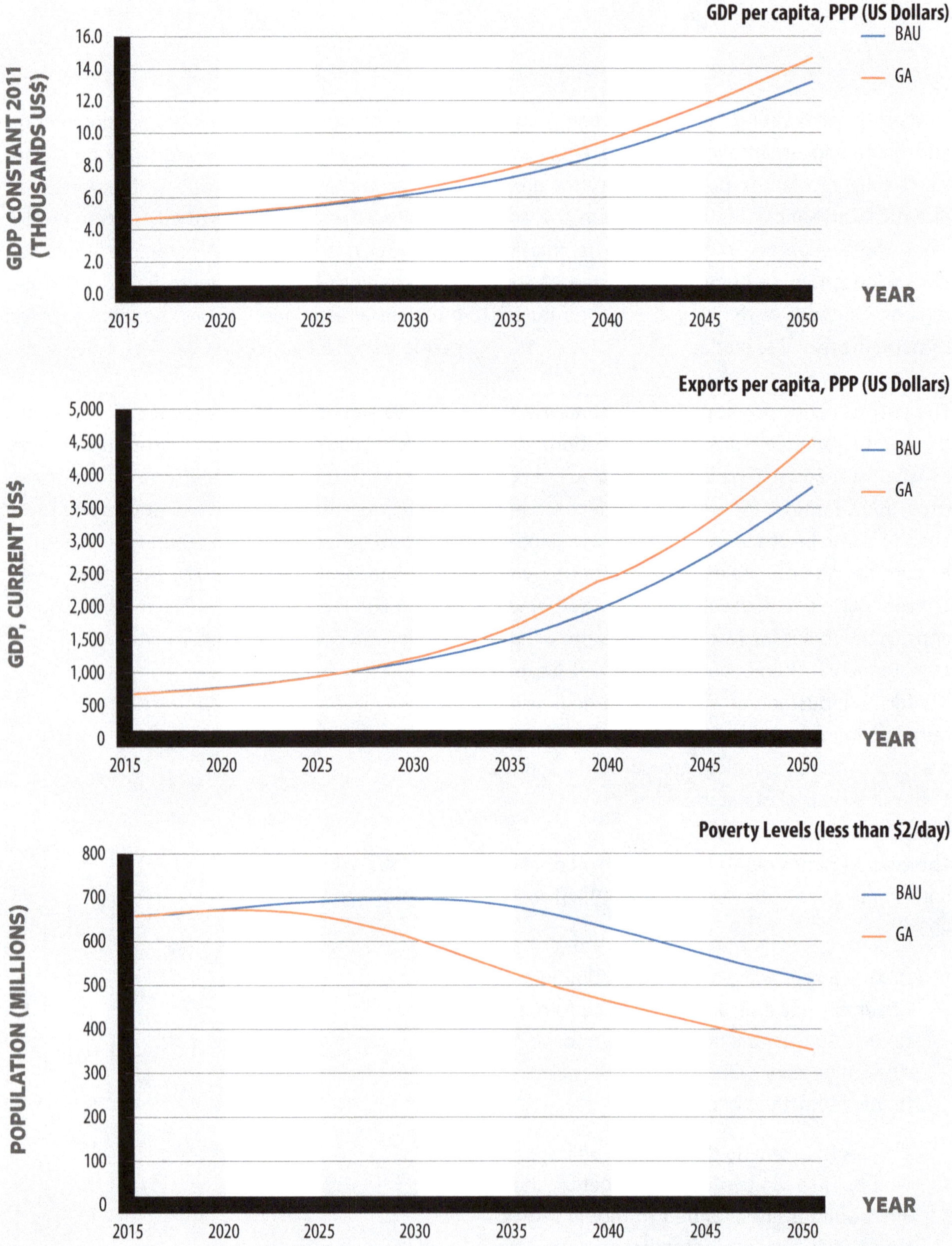

SOURCE: ONEWORLD, ADAPTED FROM INTERNATIONAL FUTURES (2015).

NOTE: BAU = BUSINESS AS USUAL; GA = GREEN AGENDA; GDP = GROSS DOMESTIC PRODUCT; PPP = PURCHASING POWER PARITY.

BOX 5.1 SUMMARY OF BAU SCENARIO

BAU	Rapid population growth continues, especially in East and West Africa; 65 per cent of the population will be urbanized by 2050. The majority of expected population growth occurs in urban areas. The foundation for the "demographic dividend" (box 5.4) is set but not realized by 2050. Growth in jobs is slower than growth in the working-age population. Economic growth is greatest in those subregions with the highest levels of population growth and urbanization. Growing infrastructure deficits check economic growth. Integration with global markets through trade and global and regional value chains remains low, as does intra-African regional integration. Water demand increases faster than population growth. Poor infrastructure, management, pollution and high climate variability are additional strains. Cooperation over shared resources—such as land (for example, transfrontier conservation areas), river basins and lakes shared by more than one country—is difficult, given low regional integration and strong competition for scarce supply. Essential resources cannot support average economic growth rates of 4–5 per cent a year. Energy demand heavily outstrips growth in supply. Investments do little to close the gap. Climate change and competition exacerbate water scarcity and reduce returns on hydropower and other investments. Substantial growth in renewable energy occurred, but dependence on fossil fuels increases. Shortfalls are met by price-volatile, high-GHG emitting imports. Skills gaps widen: the informal sector contributes 80 per cent of the labour force. Agriculture remains the primary employer but lags in its contribution to GDP. Agricultural yields remain lower than in other developing regions, disincentivizing farm investments. Climate volatility drives yields down further. Investments in food processing and storage are needed more than ever.
Climate change impacts	Droughts and extreme temperatures increase water scarcity. Hydropower production is lowered by 40 per cent in the worst-affected areas. Climate impacts on water and energy intensify resource competition—felt for the first time in "water-abundant" basins. Soil moisture declines, reducing yields. Rainfall increases, bringing flooding to urban areas. Periods between disasters shorten, increasing capacity pressure. Frequent and prolonged droughts bring sustained food insecurity and greater malnutrition. Fuel imports drive up emissions, as do unchecked land clearing and increased agricultural production.

BOX 5.2 SUMMARY OF THE GA SCENARIO

GA	Regional integration and infrastructure investments improve relative to BAU in that water resource governance is enhanced and regional trade increased. Policy implementation to limit pollution and to increase disaster risk preparedness makes water scarcity more manageable because all of the controllable scarcity factors are addressed. Growth and progress in agricultural transformation improve. Rising global competitiveness increases exports, and regional integration reduces reliance on imports. All relevant aspects of agro processing value chains are incentivized. Energy investments see major increases, including access to and mobilization of new funding sources for renewable energy. Greater carbon-market participation occurs, creating a revenue stream to finance green energy and technology. An enabling environment takes shape, including governmental green procurement programmes. Power purchase agreements are premised on informed trade-offs—for example, between water required for energy versus water required for expanded irrigation. Investments in energy increase by 20 per cent, and generation per capita increases by 30 per cent. Water data collection informs trade-off analysis. Energy demand still outstrips supply, but investments in energy production are accelerated, reducing fuel import dependence. Population growth is still rapid, but fertility rates start to fall as more sophisticated urban populations increase contraception use. Adding value to agriculture is incentivized, expanding the GDP while building urban skills which facilitates a transition to other manufacturing and services. Agricultural yields increase quickly as a result of intelligently scaled conservation agriculture, accelerated through incentives that target middle-tier small farmers. Climate impacts—for example, on soil moisture and nutrients and on water—are mitigated through conservation agriculture.
Climate change impacts	Improved coping capacities reduce water scarcity impacts 30 per cent. Load shedding from hydropower resulting from droughts and competing demands is cut 90 per cent. Agricultural yields improve rapidly as conservation agriculture raises soil moisture. Growth is inclusive, as middle-tier small farmers multiply the effect.

SCENARIO PARAMETERS

History has taught us that industrialization results in structural change. Although many of the shifts are welcome (poverty alleviation, more jobs), others may not, resulting in disruption and unintended consequences for the environment and for society (pollution, water scarcity and energy supply deficits, for example).

Each scenario is thus developed around the sectors most likely to be affected by, and to affect, industrialization in Africa. Those sectors—food and agriculture, water, energy and mineral extraction—are also central to Africa's economic growth and livelihoods. They operate within wider systems: the global economy, the global green agenda, continental economic growth and regional integration, population, urbanization and employment.

The interactions between sectors and the broader systems are complex, with high interdependencies. Water, for example, is a critical renewable resource and highly sensitive to rapid population growth and urbanization. In many parts of Africa, it is also a generator of electricity (hydropower), and its availability to the food sector is a critical success factor in increasing agricultural value added and in advancing industrialization across

BOX 5.3 SCENARIO-BUILDING METHODOLOGY

To build the alternative scenarios, a meta-systems approach was necessary, with interactions and numerous different levels of association between sectors. The two scenarios were developed using the International Futures (IFs) model for Africa and, where necessary, drawing on other international data and expert opinions to triangulate and address data discrepancies.

The IFs model is a large, long-term, integrated global modelling system that can create different scenario outcomes through linkages between subsystems (agricultural, demographic, economic, energy, environmental and sociopolitical). It is especially useful for modelling the potential success and size of effect of green growth policy interventions because of its integration of the agriculture (food security), energy, human health and water components into a representation of larger socioeconomic and environmental systems. IFs provides a way of thinking about the future, revealing intervention options that will allow Africa to achieve its human development goals within a sustainable pattern of economic growth that includes the renewable resource base.

The numerous linkages in the IFs model allow users to do the following:

- Examine the long-term impacts (until 2050) of a BAU approach.
- Explore how the widespread adoption of an aggressive green growth agenda could enable the continent to achieve higher, more inclusive economic and social development.
- Compare different outcomes to illustrate the benefits, costs and trade-offs in pursuing different political and economic agendas.

Comparisons are drawn with the global green economy scenarios developed for the United Nations Environment Programme (UNEP) for its Green Economy Report (UNEP, 2011) by the Millennium Institute, known as the T-21 model.

Models are, of course, only abstractions that simplify reality; they are tools to help think about future options. They also are highly dependent on the assumptions made and on the quality and quantity of data, which are difficult to obtain in much of Africa. Projections of the future by IFs should not, therefore, be taken as predictions of how an issue, country or region will evolve.

the continent. A similar story is true for energy. These are "high-pressure" sectors that can also yield socioeconomic opportunities throughout the wider system—with multiple co-benefits.

Consequently, compelling arguments exist for Africa to adopt an agenda that reduces the pressure on key resources, evidenced in the BAU scenario, through green growth while stimulating more inclusive economies and promoting infrastructure development as outlined in GA scenario. The continent, with its nascent industrialization, is well placed to do so.

BOX 5.4 UNDERPINNING CONCEPTS

Natural capital and ecosystem services

Natural capital—a fundamental, if undervalued, part of the global economy—comprises ecosystem assets (such as fresh water) and natural resources (such as fossil-fuel deposits) (Dickson et al., 2014) that, according to the United Nations (UN) Convention on Biological Diversity, account for at least 40 per cent of the world's economic activity and meet 80 per cent of the needs of the poor. These assets generate a range of essential ecosystem services that exist only as a function of the extent and condition of the ecosystem.

A useful UNEP (2007) definition provides clarity on the concept of natural capital and its components: "Natural capital includes land, minerals and fossil fuels, solar energy, water, living organisms, and the services provided by the interactions of all these elements in ecological systems." Those assets, in turn, enable the flow of ecosystem services, or the benefits that people derive from the ecosystem, including provisioning services (food and water), regulating services (flood and disease control), cultural services (recreation) and supporting services (nutrient recycling). Natural resources are a driver and a possible constraint of economic growth. The higher the GDP, the higher the demand for natural resources; growing demand leads to higher production, which depletes stocks. Declining stocks, on the other hand, reduce potential medium- to long-term production from natural resources, potentially constraining economic growth (UNEP, 2011).

Renewable-resource scarcity

Scarcity of a renewable resource is defined by its high cost and limited availability to the user—because the resource has been mismanaged, is polluted, cannot reach the user because of inadequate infrastructure or is negatively affected by change or variability in the climate. Degradation of ecosystems is an important contributor to scarcity, as the resources of an ecosystem yield critical services; for example, water is an important ecosystem service that is less readily available in degraded ecosystems. In Africa, many ecosystems (including river basins) are transboundary—they are shared by more than one country (sometimes as many as 10). Inadequate regional integration thus also exacerbates scarcity through a lack of shared infrastructure for managing common resources, especially water.

Economic regional integration and resource scarcity

Economic integration in Africa's subregions, usually measured in volumes of regional trade, is critical to the continent's development and cross-border natural resource management, because

- Integration fosters transboundary water management and subregional energy planning and trade;
- Slow regional integration impedes Africa's participation in global value chains and their regional counterparts, both critical entry points for green industrialization; and
- Infrastructure, currently a very tight bottleneck, will benefit from greater investment as a result of closer regional integration.

The demographic dividend

Demographic dividend is defined as the acceleration in economic growth that results from a decline in a country's mortality and fertility rates and the consequent change in the age structure of the population. With more active citizens, fewer people to support and the right policy frameworks, a country could gain immediate benefits from an increase in the number of employed people, creating opportunities for faster economic growth through increased investment.

- Africa's population is expected to double by 2050, reaching 2.4 billion people, and the working-age population will continue to grow over the next few decades—laying the foundation for a demographic dividend.
- Economic growth in Africa has not, however, translated into improved living standards, higher education levels or better health care for the majority. A skewed distribution of benefits from growth, alongside continued high population growth, has slowed per capita gains and left many people in poverty.
- The benefits of a demographic dividend are neither guaranteed nor unlimited. Governments have a narrow window of opportunity to use strong social and economic policy to create employment opportunities and economic growth.
- A raft of policy interventions is needed to achieve a rapid decline in the birth rate, combining investments in human capital and poverty reduction, increases in education and health budgets, and much greater effort to widen access to family planning. (Bangladesh is an example of success along this path. Growth in the textile industry there has increased employment opportunities for women, who as they have gained increased economic independence, started to access family planning.)

The parameters for each scenario are the following, with jobs and infrastructure integral to each:

- *Renewable resources:*[1] How will the main stress multipliers, such as climate change and variability and environmental degradation, deplete essential renewable resources, particularly water? What is the combined impact from these and other stresses, such as increased demand from a rising population?
- *Energy:* With the huge gap between rising demand and current supply and its uncertain trajectory, what are the key trends for demand, supply and investment?
- *Agriculture:* What is its future, given rising pressures on land, growing climate impacts and its potential for contributing to rapid industrial growth?

Understanding the two scenarios and their implications requires an appreciation of the underpinning concepts and the linkages between them (box 5.4). For example, natural resource assets, such as aquifers, are fundamental to economies and livelihoods and are central to interpreting the scenarios, but water scarcity is as much about how people *invest* in and *manage* the resource as it is about how little or how much rain falls. Further, transboundary water governance—important for dealing with water scarcity—is needed, given the large number of shared water basins, and it is better enabled in those subregions that display economic integration through trade, for example, yet again highlighting the role of water in economic management and growth. Finally, although a demographic dividend from burgeoning urban populations is desirable, reaping that dividend is unlikely to be realized unless natural capital is conserved for providing vital ecosystem services.

SYSTEMIC DRIVERS AND SCENARIO SECTORS

Before considering each sector examined in the two scenarios, we should understand the main system dynamics in play from now until 2050: economic growth and regional integration, population growth and urbanization, and employment.

ECONOMIC GROWTH AND REGIONAL INTEGRATION

Economic growth across Africa is likely to come primarily from the service sector, with industrial growth in increments rather than a boom. Services are a vital stimulant of industrialization and structural transformation and, although economic growth rates will vary considerably among the five African subregions, the following assumptions and findings are universal:

- Economic growth is highest in those subregions experiencing the highest levels of population growth and urbanization.
- Growth in the service sector is both a result of and a catalyst for increasing industrialization and structural transformation, thus becoming increasingly important to African economies.
- Growth in that sector sees capabilities built in industries critical to manufacturing, such as transportation and logistics.
- Increased contributions to GDP from manufacturing suggest growth in industrialization in those subregions that have experienced increased growth in manufacturing .
- Productivity improvements in manufacturing and in its supporting industries promote further industrialization.
- Although the service sector can expand quite easily, manufacturing growth is constrained by wide infrastructure deficits, which increase production costs along the entire value chain.

The growth of the service sector is a mutually reinforcing driver for expansion and diversification of industries. Increasingly, manufacturing activities within a global value chain require participation in more complex and more standardized coordination and transport processes. The rapid growth of African services therefore bodes well for further integration into global value chains and for industrialization. Despite high rates of economic growth in the past decade, however, Africa starts from a low base on regional economic integration.

POPULATION GROWTH AND URBANIZATION

Africa has the highest rate of population growth in the world's primary regions, rising by 2.55 per cent annually in 2010–2015. After 2050, Africa is expected to be the only major region to still have fast population growth (UN, 2015). The population of the continent will double by 2050, and rates of urbanization will be the fastest in those subregions with the highest rates of population growth (UN, 2015). This trend is most evident in West and East Africa, where rising population numbers have provided an expanding workforce and increasing consumer demand—both key drivers of economic growth.

Population growth in Africa will continue beyond 2050, even with the forecast fall in the birth rate from 4.7 births per woman in 2010–2015 to 3.1 in 2045–2050. Although continued rapid population growth places heavy pressure on already scarce resources and service delivery, when combined with accelerated urbanization, growing numbers of working-age people have the potential to drive industrialization. More working-age people channelled into labour-intensive activities, coupled with declining fertility and mortality rates—in part through family-planning investment and political support—are needed to lay the foundation for a demographic dividend.

... growing numbers of working-age people have the potential to drive industrialization.

EMPLOYMENT

Africa's economic growth has translated into neither growth of employment opportunities nor higher quality of existing jobs:

- African countries are not creating jobs at the same pace as the growth in working-age population, hence rates of participation in formal employment are falling;
- Low levels of labour productivity and poor infrastructure are the main reasons for slow growth in manufacturing and rising unemployment;
- Africa's youth bulge, paired with the demographic shift towards cities, will place ever heavier demands on informal settlements, service provision, and political and social stability; and
- Continued high levels of informal employment will result in persistent vulnerability among much of the population, given that the informal sector accounts for 50–80 per cent of employment in Africa.

Although those factors paint a grim picture for African cities, if correctly harnessed a growing working-age population concentrated in urban centres has the potential to drive rapid economic growth[1], a trend seen recently in emerging economies, notably China. Africa has an opportunity to capitalize on this demographic dividend, in part by promoting inclusive growth, as envisaged by the African Development Bank's Strategy for 2013–2022 (AfDB, 2013).

RENEWABLE RESOURCES

Water and other renewable resources in Africa are in scarce supply, with a widening gap between supply and demand. The reasons are clear.

Africa's infrastructure deficit increases water scarcity. To meet the demand for water and sanitation across the continent, Africa needs to increase its \$3.6 billion annual investment in water infrastructure nearly four times (AfDB, 2013). Institutional weaknesses are reflected in inefficiencies at local and national levels, inadequate attention to technology choice, low pump density, restrictive maintenance systems and the lack of a supply chain to maintain machinery (Barber, 2014).

Climate change and volatility intensify existing natural resource stresses. Extreme weather events, combined with changing temperature and precipitation patterns, decrease the availability of water where and when it is needed most (Petrie, et al 2014). Vital economic and livelihood sectors—in particular, agriculture and energy (hydropower)—are water dependent. Increased water scarcity and the frequency of extreme events (such as drought) have serious ramifications for food security, which, in turn, has vast implications for human health.

Continued low levels of regional integration undermine transboundary water management as countries sharing water systems see more value in protecting what they regard as national interests than in cooperating with each other to maximize shared benefits. Africa has 63 of the world's 263 shared basins, which cover about 64 per cent of the continent (UNEP, 2010). Most basins are shared by only two countries, but some are shared by many more. Of the 13 basins worldwide shared by five to eight riparian nations, 4 are in Africa. The Congo, Niger, Nile and Zambezi rivers are shared by 9 to 11 countries. Improved cooperative water governance is a necessity and will enable enhanced energy production, improved agricultural yields, critical infrastructural development and greater resilience to climate change.

Rapid population growth sharply increases demand for water. Population growth, coupled with economic development, raises water demand for domestic, agricultural and industrial uses, which in turn increases effluent output. As African populations continue to grow and industrialize, the supply of renewable resources will come under increasing pressure (Dubey and Narayanan, 2010; Juma, et al., 2014).

A burgeoning middle class places additional stress on the water supply. Africa's urban household incomes are twice those of rural households, and urban households make greater demands on services such as piped water (Barber, 2014). Households connected to water pipes use, on average, three times more water per capita than do unpiped households. Access to water is thus tightly linked to household income.

ENERGY

Historical trends in energy demand and supply highlight a similar pattern to that for renewable resources—a significant infrastructure deficit, underinvestment (relative to growing demand) and population pressure. Without a change in the pace of investment, the gap between supply and demand will widen further, with effects on health, education, economic growth and food security. The following circumstances are the leading gap-wideners.

Population growth is the main driver for energy demand throughout Africa. Population growth stimulates demand for energy and the associated services it provides for social and economic development, such as heating, lighting, mobility, manufacturing and industrial production.

Higher incomes and increasing industrialization fuel demand for energy. When countries can meet the energy needs of their citizens and enterprises, they become wealthier, more resilient and enabled to advance health and human development.

Energy access remains low across Africa. Economic growth has not led to universal energy access. In Central, East, Southern and West Africa, more than 620 million people live without access to electricity (IEA, 2014). High poverty levels are directly linked to the type of energy consumed: except in South Africa, wood and charcoal are the largest fuel source, mainly for heating and cooking. The pressure placed on forest resources is unsustainable—forests cannot renew themselves at the pace necessary to meet growing demand, resulting in serious repercussions for surrounding ecosystems and livelihoods.

Exploitation of renewable energy is rising, but currently supply cannot satisfy demand. Africa starts from a low base on renewable energy and hydropower exploitation and needs time to catch up with global trends and local demand. Current renewable energy sources constitute only 1 per cent of grid-based capacity (Africa Progress Panel, 2015). Hydropower has seen recent expansion, but investment returns are already under pressure as a result of climate change and competing development demands, such as irrigation.

Installed capacity figures understate the energy deficit. The amount of power available to consumers often is far less than total installed capacity, mainly because of poor maintenance of power stations, leading to inefficiencies in grid operation and unstable supply. Further, a lack of reliable fuel supply (such as natural gas) and insufficient transmission capacity lower the capacity in operation. Transmission and distribution losses cut the supply to end users by as much as 20 per cent in some countries, and the loss rate of electricity transmission in Central, East, Southern and West Africa is more than double the world average (IEA, 2014).

AGRICULTURE AND FOOD

Although an enhanced agricultural sector is pivotal to poverty alleviation and food security in Africa, it is a somewhat neglected sector in many African countries.

Africa's agricultural output consistently lags behind that in other developing regions. The Green Revolution of the 1960s and 1970s boosted crop yields in Latin America and Asia, based on irrigation, mechanization, chemical fertilizers and high-yield varieties. In Africa, however, few farmers have been able to capitalize on those advances because of limited irrigation; poor infrastructure; severe soil degradation; the high cost of fertilizers; and inadequate extension services, farmer-credit schemes and seed-distribution networks. Most governments have not paid enough attention to agriculture, consequently failing to meet the Maputo targets of investing 10 per cent of their budget in agriculture. Africa's yields are less than half of those in Asia and about one fourth of the continent's potential (NEPAD, 2013).

High population growth and urbanization place increasing pressure on the production of staple crops. Households increasingly rely on buying their food rather than producing their own, making them dependent on markets and increasing their vulnerability to fluctuations in food and energy prices. This shift offers a big opportunity for domestic agricultural value chains because rising domestic demand will require expansion of domestic agroprocessing activities, as well as a wide range of associated services in transport, storage and packaging.

Food security concerns are further challenged by climate change. Africa is the continent most vulnerable to climate change, given its current levels of water scarcity, highly variable rainfall, high average temperatures, poor infrastructure and heavy reliance on rain-fed agriculture.

Historically low productivity and land-use levels are being redressed, but the pace of change is not fast enough to meet the demands of growing populations and emerging agro-industries. Measured from a base year of 2005/2007, an estimated additional 51 million ha of arable land area will become available for cultivation in Central, East, Southern and West Africa by 2050 (Alexandratos and Bruinsma, 2012), the majority in Central Africa, West Africa and East Africa. This land is put to other uses, however, such as grazing and woodlands, so transforming it into cropland is not cost free.

Despite increases in output, agriculture has a declining share in African economies, as services and manufacturing increase. Africa relies heavily on agriculture for its contribution to GDP (37 per cent), to exports (40 per cent), to employment (70 per cent), and to the food and energy needs of the roughly two thirds of Africans who depend on subsistence farming for their livelihoods (Cilliers, Hughes and Moyer, 2011). Agriculture's declining share of GDP, as services and manufacturing become more central to economic development, is increasing rural–urban migration and placing further stress on urban infrastructure, housing settlements and service provision.

THE GLOBAL GREEN AGENDA AND AFRICA

The world is in an era of unprecedented transition. As a result of intense, human-driven development, global warming is raising temperatures at unprecedented levels that are fast approaching a critical threshold, or the point of no return. Extreme events are increasing in frequency and intensity, and sea levels continue to rise, with horrific prospects for the world's coastal regions and low-lying small islands.

Unemployment, particularly under-employment and informal employment, is rising alarmingly in developed and developing countries at a time when the problems linked to rapid urbanization, such as pollution and poorly provisioned services, are hitting the urban poor the hardest.

The global population is set to increase from 7 billion people (as of 2011) to 9 billion by 2050, at a time when the problem of feeding current populations and eradicating poverty remains unsolved. For the first time in recorded history, more than half the world's population lives in urban areas, and cities now account for 75 per cent of energy consumption (UNEP, 2011). Simultaneously, ecological scarcities are seriously affecting the foundational sectors that supply the world's food: forests, fisheries, freshwater and agriculture (UNEP, 2011). Unemployment, particularly under-employment and informal employment, is rising alarmingly in developed and developing countries at a time when the problems linked to rapid urbanization, such as pollution and poorly provisioned services, are hitting the urban poor the hardest (UNEP, 2011).

The need for a new way forward has, arguably, never been so great. Favourable economic development is high on every politician's agenda, and now the world believes that such development is much more achievable through green growth. Although traction for the green economy has grown steadily since the Rio +20 conference held in 2015, attended by world leaders, and a follow on to the first global sustainable development conference in Rio in 1995, was certainly a marker year for green growth.

The Paris Agreement on climate change (December 2015) cemented the world's evolving green growth agenda. Importantly, this agreement, concluded at the 21st Conference of the Parties (COP) under the United Nations Framework Convention on Climate Change (UNFCCC), came soon after the Sustainable Development Goals of 2015 were adopted to promote sustainable development as a means of addressing the still-abundant needs of the bottom of the social and economic pyramid. Kick-starting the 2030 Agenda for Sustainable Development, the Sustainable Development Goals offer the world an opportunity to reframe economic policy. The core elements lend focus to building and creating green economies and to growth that is inclusive, comprising sustainable consumption and production, socially equitable outcomes and investments for environmental sustainability (UNEP, 2015), such as climate-resilient and natural resource–friendly infrastructure. Those topics are at the heart of this chapter's scenario analysis, which identifies possible growth pathways for Africa. Similarly, the focus on the enabling institutions' policies and incentives that will enable the 2030 Agenda (chapter 2) applies to the policy recommendations for Africa that emerge from the scenario analysis.

Although the recent traction for green growth—also evidenced in mainstream global policy dialogues, such as G20 communiques—has likely stemmed from disillusionment with the ability of prevailing economic systems to deliver what is needed most, the growing body of evidence of environmental risks, resource scarcities and associated social disparities points to a new way forward (UNEP, 2011). Africa in particular has an advantage in accelerating its participation in the global green agenda, primarily because of its unique position, due to lagging levels of industrialisation relative to the rest of the world, of being able to leapfrog through how it invests in infrastructure, urbanizes and accelerates its uptake of renewable energy.

The following two scenarios have been developed specifically for Africa by OneWorld Sustainable Investments (OneWorld) using the International Futures (IFs) model developed by the Pardee Center for International Futures at the University of Denver, although BAU models occasionally contextualize Africa within global scenarios.

5.2 THE BAU SCENARIO

By 2050 at the latest, water and energy will be in alarmingly short supply, and investment in supply will have failed to meet growth in demand. Population is the main driver of this deficit. Still, water and energy demand will tend to increase faster than the population (because demand will also increase from industry, agriculture and domestic consumption, with rising incomes and urbanization).

Water use in North Africa offers an extreme example of the growing water scarcity that other subregions of Africa, too, will face (figure 5.2), with water use far in excess of renewable water resources. This increases pressure on other resources, such as aquifers, for which data are seldom available and which need to be recharged by rainfall. Parts of the continent rely on inter-basin transfers, which are another unsustainable solution to closing the gap between demand and supply.

Population growth in Africa is the fastest in the world, with total numbers expected to double by 2050. More than half the global population growth (54 per cent) between now and 2050 will be due to the growing number of Africans, who will increase from about 1.2 billion people in 2015 to almost 2.5 billion in 2050. This steep increase stems from declining infant mortality rates, life expectancy gains and still-high fertility in many poorer coun-

FIGURE 5.2 WATER USE AS A PERCENTAGE OF RENEWABLE WATER RESOURCES, NORTH AFRICA, 2015–2050

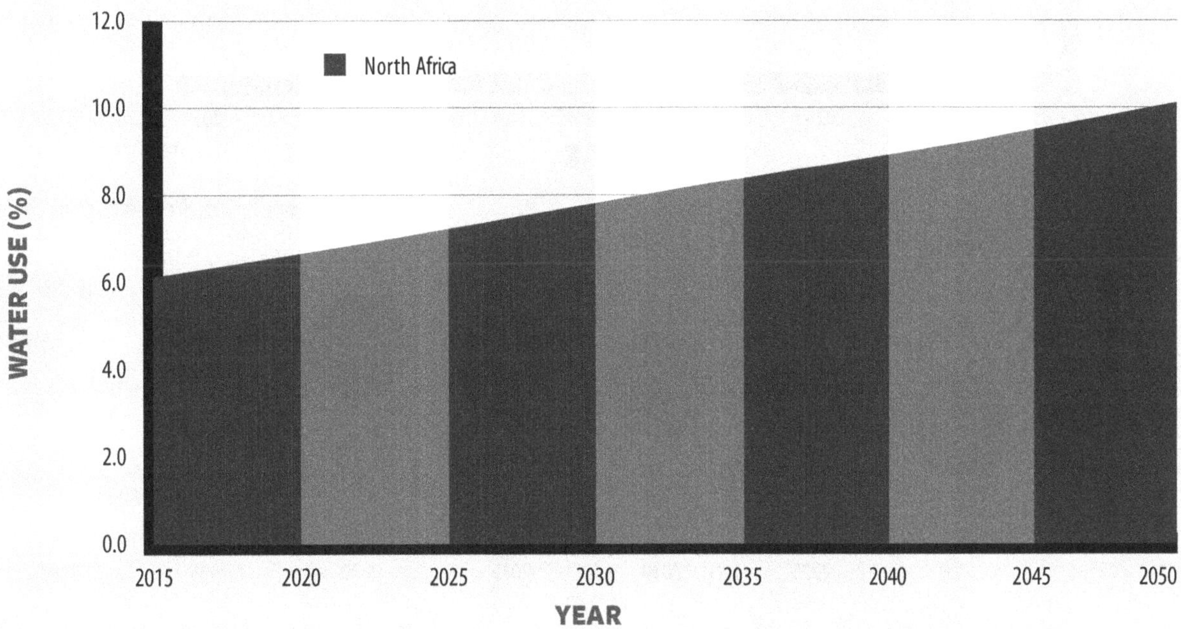

SOURCE: ONEWORLD, ADAPTED FROM INTERNATIONAL FUTURES (2015).

tries. The majority of this growth will happen in East and West Africa (figure 5.3, upper panel), shifting the demographic balance of the continent.

The majority of Africa's expected population growth will be in urban areas, with the urban population reaching more than 55 per cent of the total by 2050 (figure 5.3, bottom panel). Urbanization growth will be highest in West Africa, taking that subregion's urban share of population to nearly 70 per cent by 2050. Central, East, Southern and West Africa is expected to account for 17 per cent of the global urban population by 2050 (PRB, 2015).

Population growth and urbanization will present challenges and opportunities for each subregion. West Africa's demographic dividend will be concentrated in urban areas and, as discussed in Box 5.4 on the demographic dividend, could power economic growth and industrialization (figure

FIGURE 5.3 BAU POPULATION GROWTH AND URBANIZATION, 2015–2050

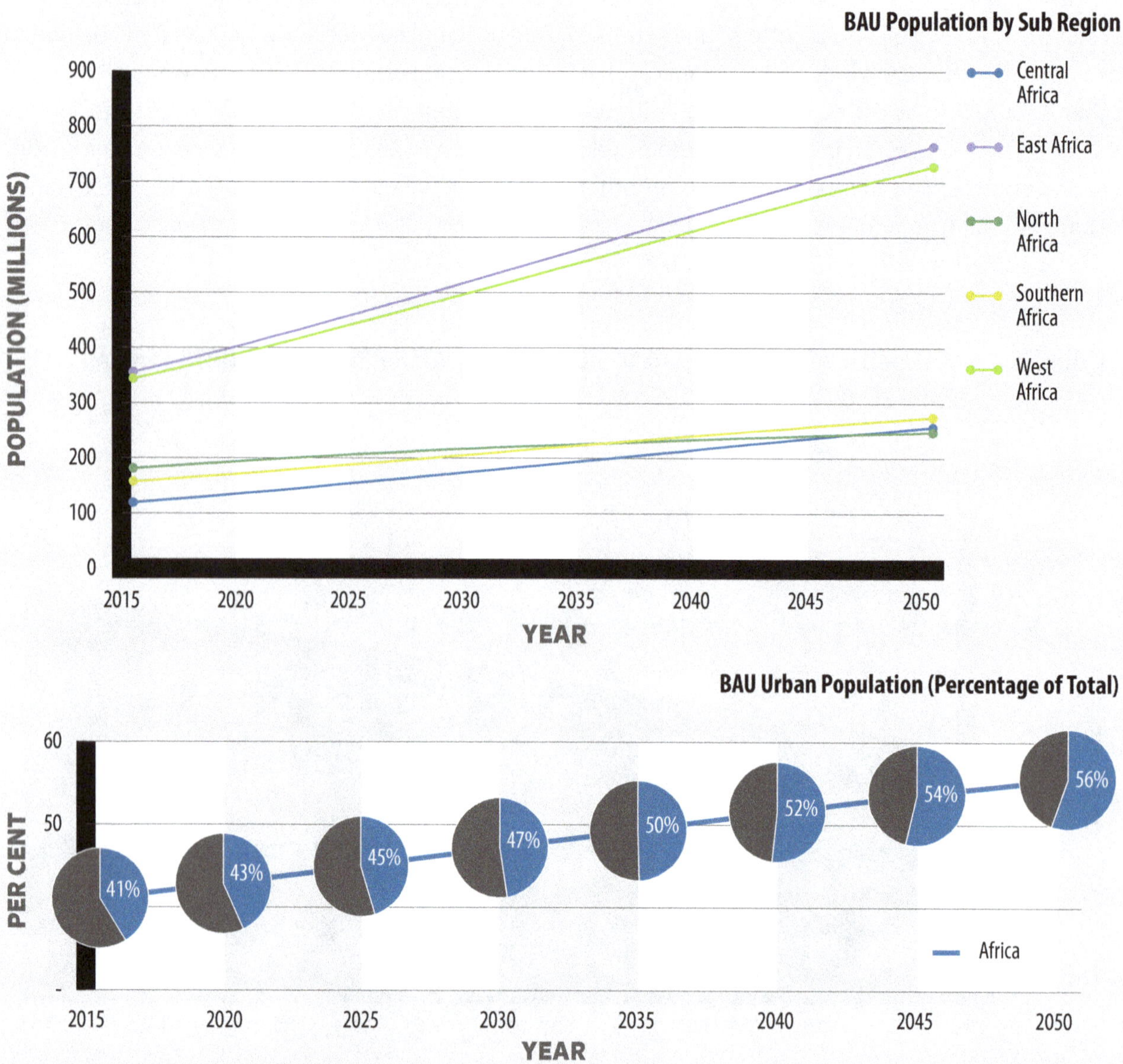

SOURCE: ONEWORLD, ADAPTED FROM INTERNATIONAL FUTURES (2015).

NOTE: BAU = BUSINESS AS USUAL.

5.4, upper panel). By contrast, East Africa will lag behind on its urbanized population share by 2050 because of it is relative un-urbanized. East Africa's rural majority will translate into slower growth in manufacturing and a continued reliance on agriculture in the medium term (to 2025) (figure 5.4, bottom panel).

FIGURE 5.4 BAU VALUE ADDED BY SECTOR-WEST AND EAST AFRICA, 2015–2050

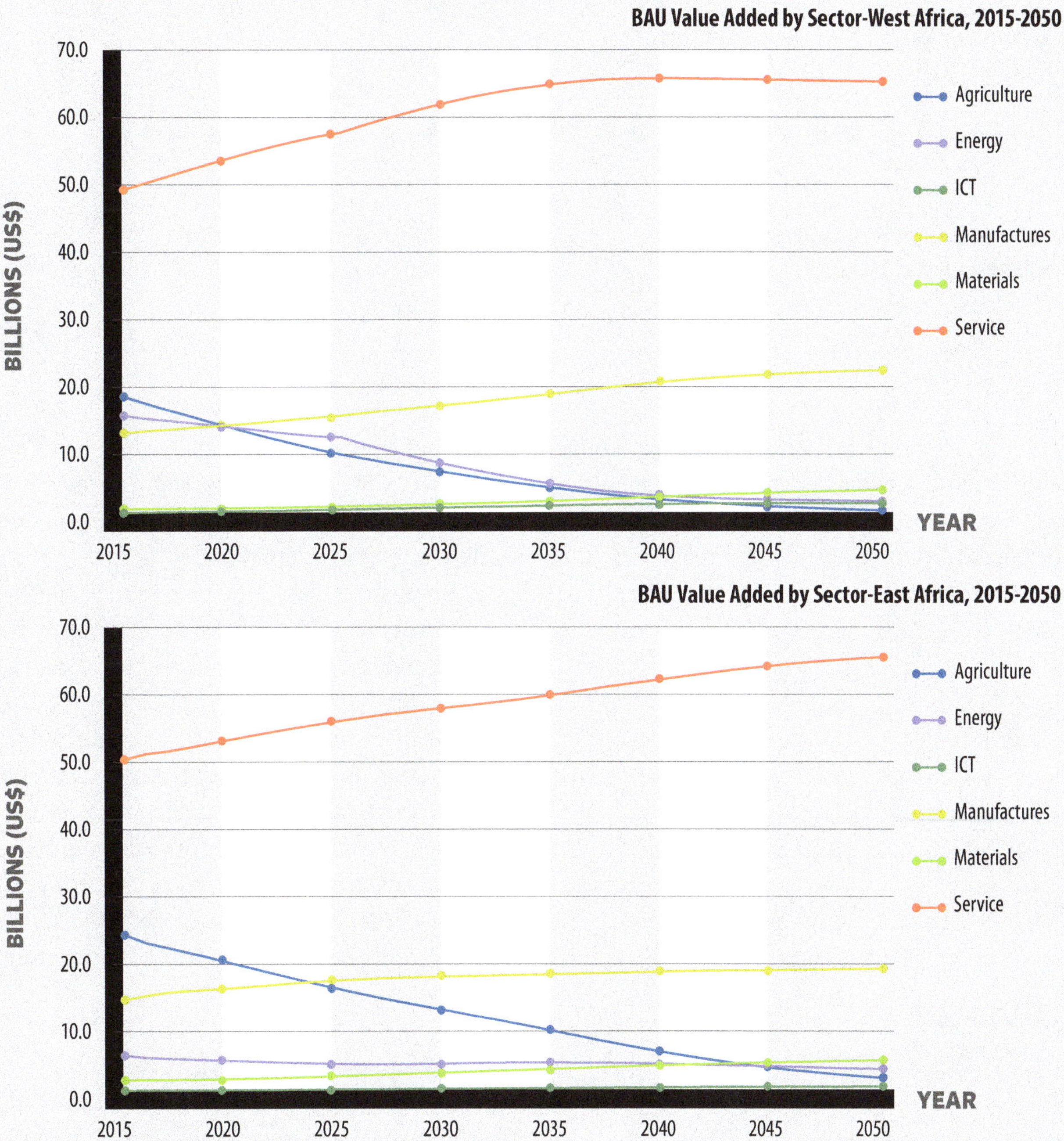

SOURCE: ONEWORLD, ADAPTED FROM INTERNATIONAL FUTURES (2015).

NOTE: BAU = BUSINESS AS USUAL; ICT = INFORMATION AND COMMUNICATIONS TECHNOLOGY.

FIGURE 5.5 BAU DEMOGRAPHIC DIVIDENDS, AFRICA AND SELECTED ECONOMIES

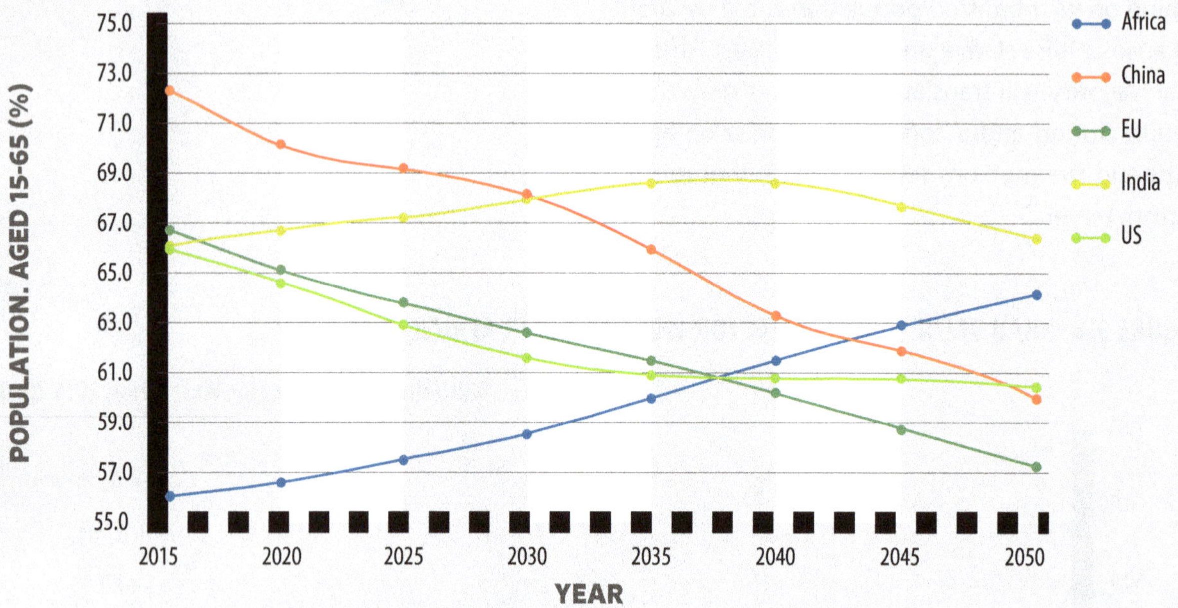

SOURCE: CILLIERS, HUGHES, AND MOYER, (2011).
NOTE: BAU = BUSINESS AS USUAL.

Although economic growth is strong in West Africa and parts of Central Africa, income per capita will not double for30 years, while the proportion of people living in poverty will remain high, at 30–50 per cent on average across countries.

Potentially good news for Africa's large proportion of vulnerably employed is the anticipated steady decline in the share of people who are informally employed.

Benefits of the demographic dividend will not be felt before 2050, although declining fertility and mortality rates and a growing working-age population establish its foundation. Africa's demographic transition is atypical, starting substantially later than demographic shifts in Asia, Europe, Latin America and North America (figure 5.5). In Africa, by 2050, more than half the population (64 per cent) will be of working age. Africa is expected to reach its peak share of working-age population by 2090 (65 per cent), meaning that the continent will most likely reap the benefits of the demographic transition—which depend on strong support for family planning and rapidly declining fertility rates—only in the second half of this century (Drummond et al., 2014).

Africa will not, however, create jobs at the same rate as the working-age population expands. Under BAU, the 10–24-year-old age group will make up more than 30 per cent of the Central, East, Southern and West Africa population in 2050 (PRB, 2015), and the majority of Africa's new jobs will come from service industries, in line with global employment trends. Although projections for Africa for 2050 (OneWorld, 2015) paint a picture of structural transformation from rural, agrarian activity to urban, industrial employment, poverty will not decrease through increased employment because the infrastructural investment will continue to fall short.

Potentially good news for Africa's large proportion of vulnerably employed is the anticipated steady decline in the share of people who are informally employed (figure 5.6). Growth in formal employment will translate into more stable and regular income, employee rights and benefits, operation within regulatory frameworks, and greater incentives for skill development and upward mobility. Expanding the formal sector should lead to gains in data quality for employment numbers, income levels and occupational capacities, which in turn strengthen the ability of states to formulate interventions, for example in labour market reforms, and to be held accountable.

Improvements in formal employment depend, however, on the success of the demographic transition. Without the forecast growth in services and manufacturing, the excess labour resulting from agriculture's decline will result in higher rates of vulnerable employment, worsening an issue that is already critical.

Economic growth will be fastest in subregions with the strongest population growth and urbanization. Population growth in West and East Africa in the next 35 years will far outpace that in all other subregions. By 2050, West Africa is predicted to overtake North Africa in the percentage of total

FIGURE 5.6 BAU INFORMAL LABOUR AS A PERCENTAGE OF TOTAL LABOUR FORCE, AFRICA, 2015–2050

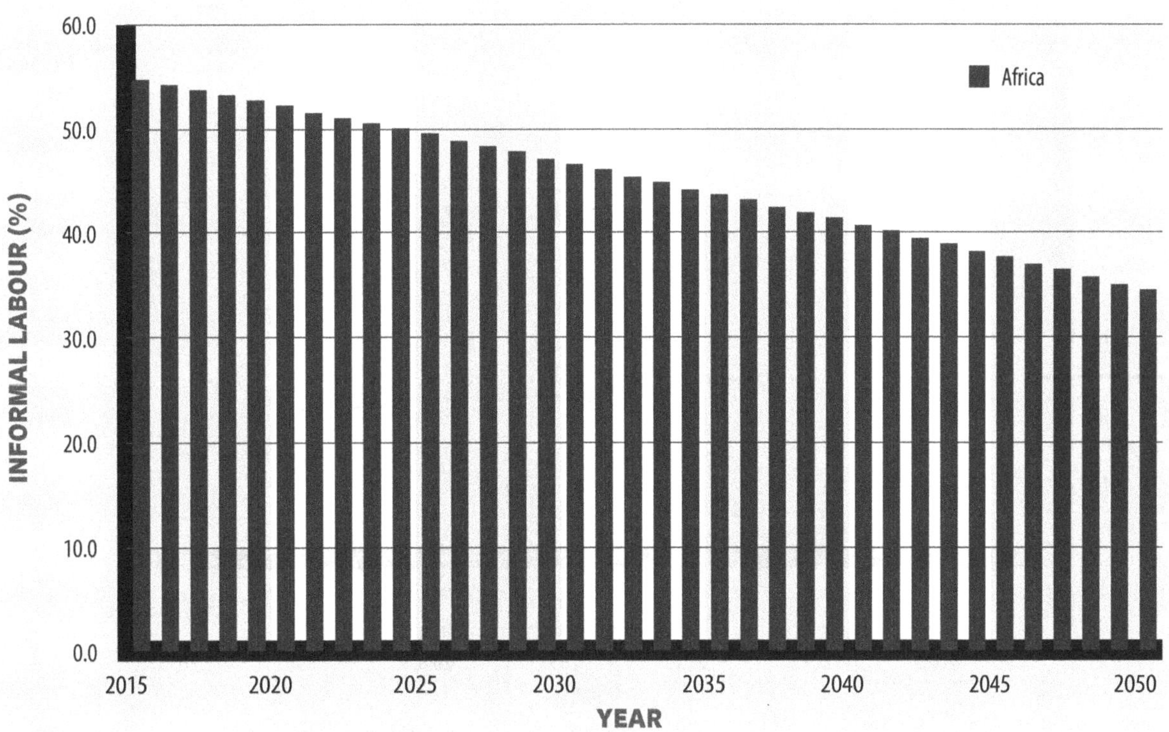

SOURCE: ONEWORLD, ADAPTED FROM INTERNATIONAL FUTURES (2015).

NOTE: BAU = BUSINESS AS USUAL.

FIGURE 5.7 BAU GDP, AFRICAN REGIONS, 2015–2050 ($ PER CAPITA, PPP)

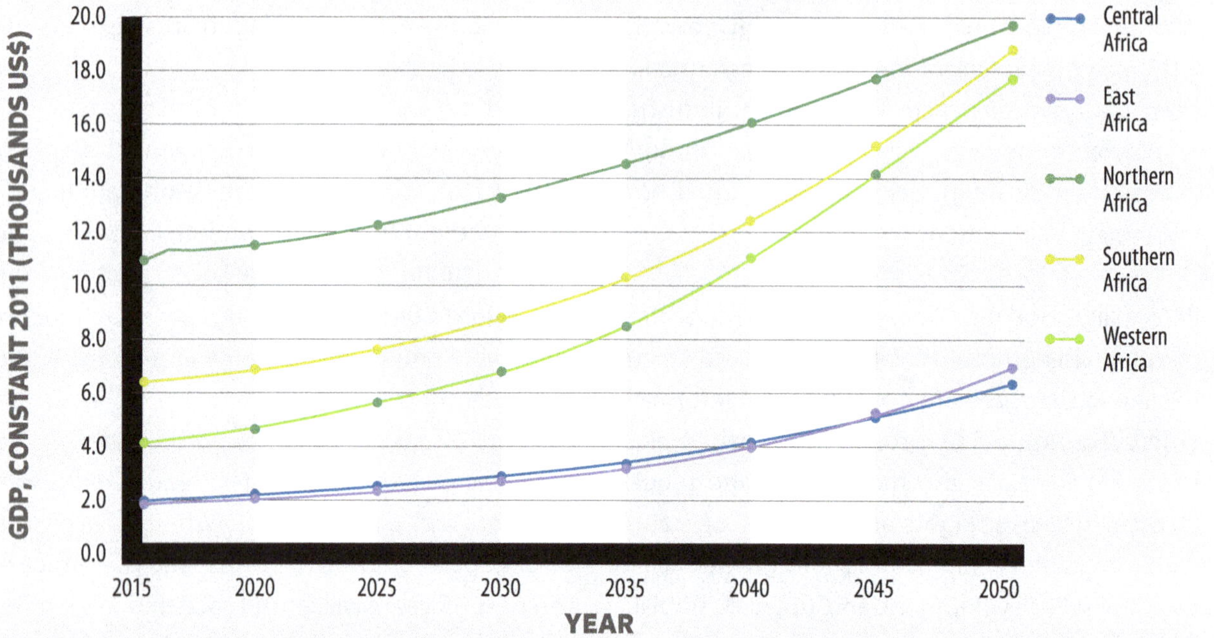

SOURCE: ONEWORLD, ADAPTED FROM INTERNATIONAL FUTURES (2015).

NOTE: BAU = BUSINESS AS USUAL; GDP = GROSS DOMESTIC PRODUCT; PPP = PURCHASING POWER PARITY.

FIGURE 5.8 BAU INFRASTRUCTURE INVESTMENT SHORTFALL, AFRICA, 2015–2050 (% OF GDP)

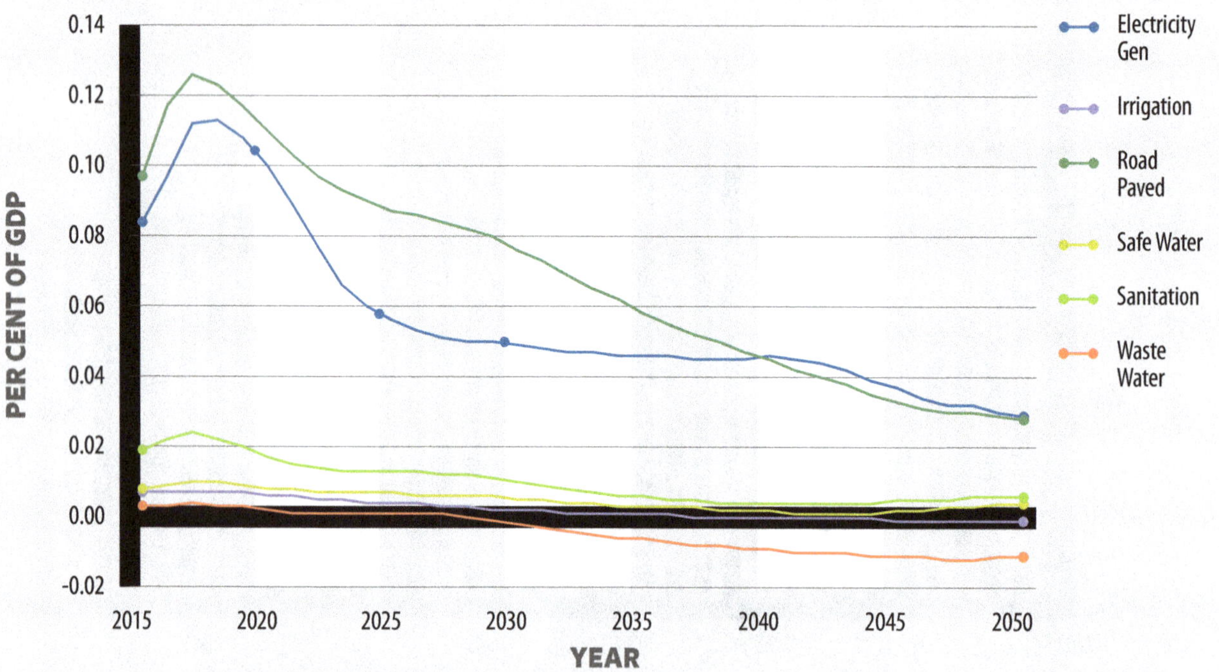

SOURCE: ONEWORLD, ADAPTED FROM INTERNATIONAL FUTURES (2015).

NOTE: BAU = BUSINESS AS USUAL.

population living in urban areas. That demographic shift, from the South and North to the East and West, will parallel an economic shift, as East and West Africa are also projected to grow fast economically. West Africa will experience higher levels of urbanization than will East Africa, leading to greater levels of industrial growth and thus higher GDP per capita. The predicted emergence of West Africa as an engine of growth underscores the transformational power of population growth when paired with urbanization (figure 5.7).

Growing infrastructure gaps will crimp economic growth. Across the continent, the largest deficits in infrastructure investment required are in paved roads and electricity generation (shown as the investment shortfall as a share of GDP; figure 5.8). Although investment in infrastructure increases considerably under the BAU scenario, the continent is still starting from a low baseline. Central, East, Southern and West Africa's road network is 204 km per 1,000 square km against a world average of 944 km (AfDB, 2010). This places a great burden on industrial growth, making it more expensive to source raw material inputs and to get final products to market.

Integration with global markets will remain low. The channels for integration are trade, global and regional value chains, and regional integration. An important signal, or predictor of low regional integration, is agriculture's inability to become a fully leveraged sector, or to mature (OneWorld, 2015). Other signals include continued low levels of cooperation in transboundary water management and the gap in infrastructural investment.

IMPLICATIONS FOR AFRICA'S RENEWABLE RESOURCES, ENERGY AND AGRICULTURE

If unchecked, growth in Africa's population, infrastructure deficit and unemployment, coupled with erratic economic growth that does not create jobs and alleviate poverty, will minimise Africa's ability to realise the demographic dividend and will increase pressure on water, energy and food security. The combined impact on Africa's endeavours to industrialise will be largely negative.

Not only do a rising population, urbanization and inadequate infrastructure stress water systems. Pollution, low maintenance, weak management, and high rainfall variability as a result of climate change also strain them.

RENEWABLE RESOURCES

Not only do a rising population, urbanization and inadequate infrastructure stress water systems. Pollution, low maintenance, weak management, and high rainfall variability as a result of climate change also strain them. Governance is an increasing problem, as cooperation over shared resources is becoming harder without close regional integration and given competing demands between sectors and countries.

Already low infrastructural investment relative to demand will decline even further in Africa's subregions. Compared with GDP, which continues to grow, overall public investment in water infrastructure will continue declining, even as demand for water climbs steeply because of population pressure. Despite currently heavy investment in Central and North Africa for "megaprojects" in transport, energy and mining, the expected challenges of meeting water security are not reflected

FIGURE 5.9 BAU PUBLIC WATER AND IRRIGATION INFRASTRUCTURE INVESTMENT AS A PERCENTAGE OF GDP, AFRICA, 2015–2050

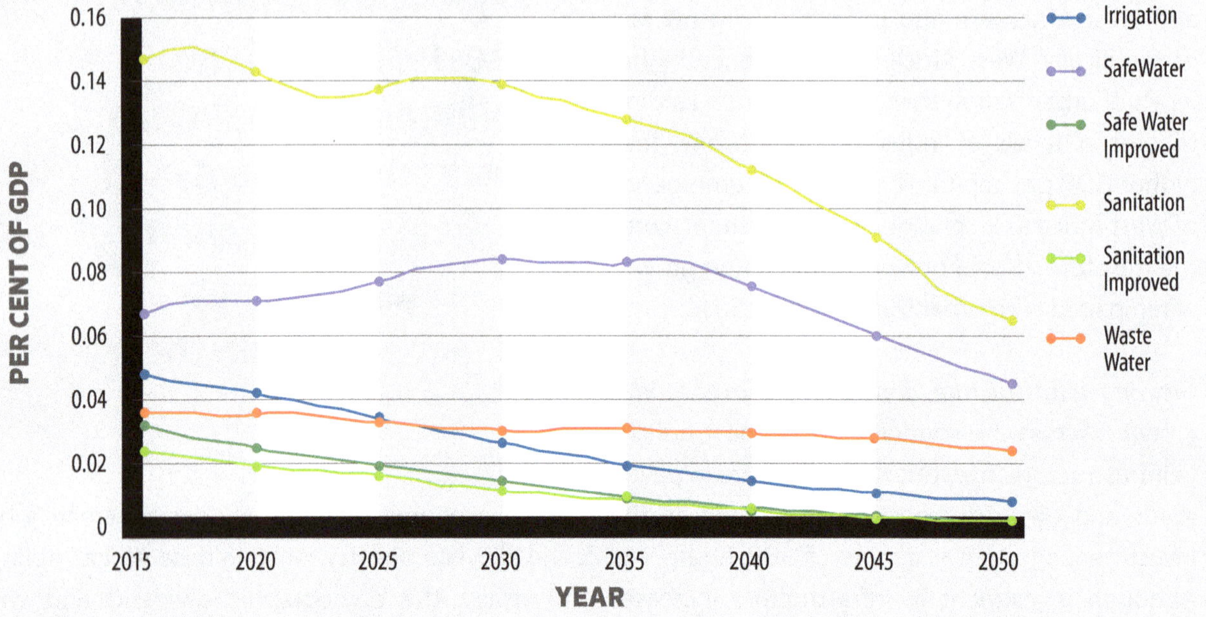

SOURCE: ONEWORLD, ADAPTED FROM INTERNATIONAL FUTURES (2015).

NOTE: BAU = BUSINESS AS USUAL.

FIGURE 5.10 BAU WATER USE AS A PERCENTAGE OF RENEWABLE WATER RESOURCES, 2015–2050

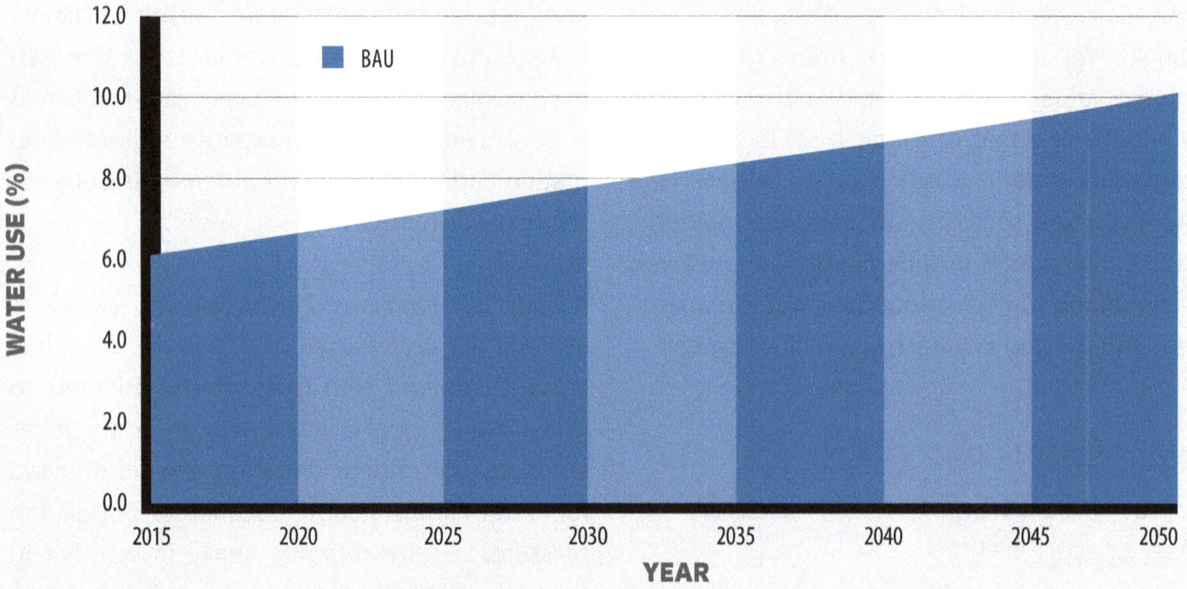

SOURCE: ONEWORLD, ADAPTED FROM INTERNATIONAL FUTURES (2015).

NOTE: BAU = BUSINESS AS USUAL.

in the volume of planned investment (figure 5.9). As a report on infrastructure development concludes, "Water and waste management presented a sector needing more investment, as it will play a critical role in the near to medium, and long-term future of the continent and world at large" (Deloitte, 2014). Thus, despite continued strong foreign investment in Africa, the lack of water-infrastructure investment points to impacts for subregional water consumption in the long term, such as that predicted for North Africa, particularly Egypt, which is expected to see a decrease of 75 per cent in per capita water availability by 2100 (UNEP, 2006).

Along with population growth, expected climate change impacts will accelerate the rate of environmental degradation, further undermining efforts to conserve renewable resources. For a global average temperature increase of 1.5–2 degrees Celsius, countries close to the equator will experience a likely increase of 4–5 degrees, which seriously jeopardizes existing farm systems and cropping patterns. Land already under pressure from rising populations and industrialization will be further hurt by the changing climate.

Areas particularly vulnerable to high rainfall volatility, such as East Africa, will see steep falls in returns on investment and, concomitantly, increasing energy insecurity in hydropower-dependent regions. Variation in the provision of energy will increase as hydrological cycles become disrupted, primarily because of poor water-systems management. Overall water use as a proportion of renewable water resources will continue rising (figure 5.10).

With expected changes in the amount, timing, form (rain, snow) and intensity of precipitation, as well as changes in water flow within watersheds, renewable water resources are expected to decrease in predictability and in the ability to renew themselves. Competing demands for water resources in Southern Africa, coupled with climate change, will seriously stress water governance in a subregion that shows the lowest level of regional integration on the continent. For example, scenarios developed for hydropower production in the Zambezi basin show that electricity generation from major hydropower plants could decline by 10–20 per cent by 2050, as a result of increasing temperatures and expanding irrigation, which combine to increase water abstraction, evaporation and evapo-transpiration (Spalding-Fecher et al., 2014).

... renewable water resources are expected to decrease in predictability and in the ability to renew themselves.

Water quality will be badly compromised. Compared with other world regions, Central, East, Southern and West Africa already has the lowest coverage of piped water, and more than - more than 40 percent of all people (321 million) without a source of improved drinking water live in sub-Saharan Africa (UNDESA, 2012). Rapid population and economic growth are increasing the demand for water for domestic, agricultural and industrial uses, which will raise effluent output. Water quality across Africa will therefore deteriorate by 2050 because of increasing effluent from wastewater and nutrients (fertilizers/pesticides) from agriculture, with potentially irreversible consequences for biodiversity and human health. Rapid urbanization and increased water consumption mean that demand will rise at double the pace of population growth, heightening competition for this resource and increasing the possibility of sociopolitical tensions.

ENERGY

As with water, energy demand will outstrip supply, exacerbating energy access and security and slowing poverty eradication. Nigeria, with the fastest growing population in Africa, will see a rise in energy demand accounting for most of the increase in energy demand in the West African subregion (figure 5.11, top panel). That country alone accounts for more than one quarter of total Central East, Southern and West Africa energy demand (figure 5.11, bottom panel).

FIGURE 5.11 BAU ENERGY DEMAND, AFRICAN SUBREGIONS AND NIGERIA, 2015–2050 (BILLION BARRELS OF OIL EQUIVALENT)

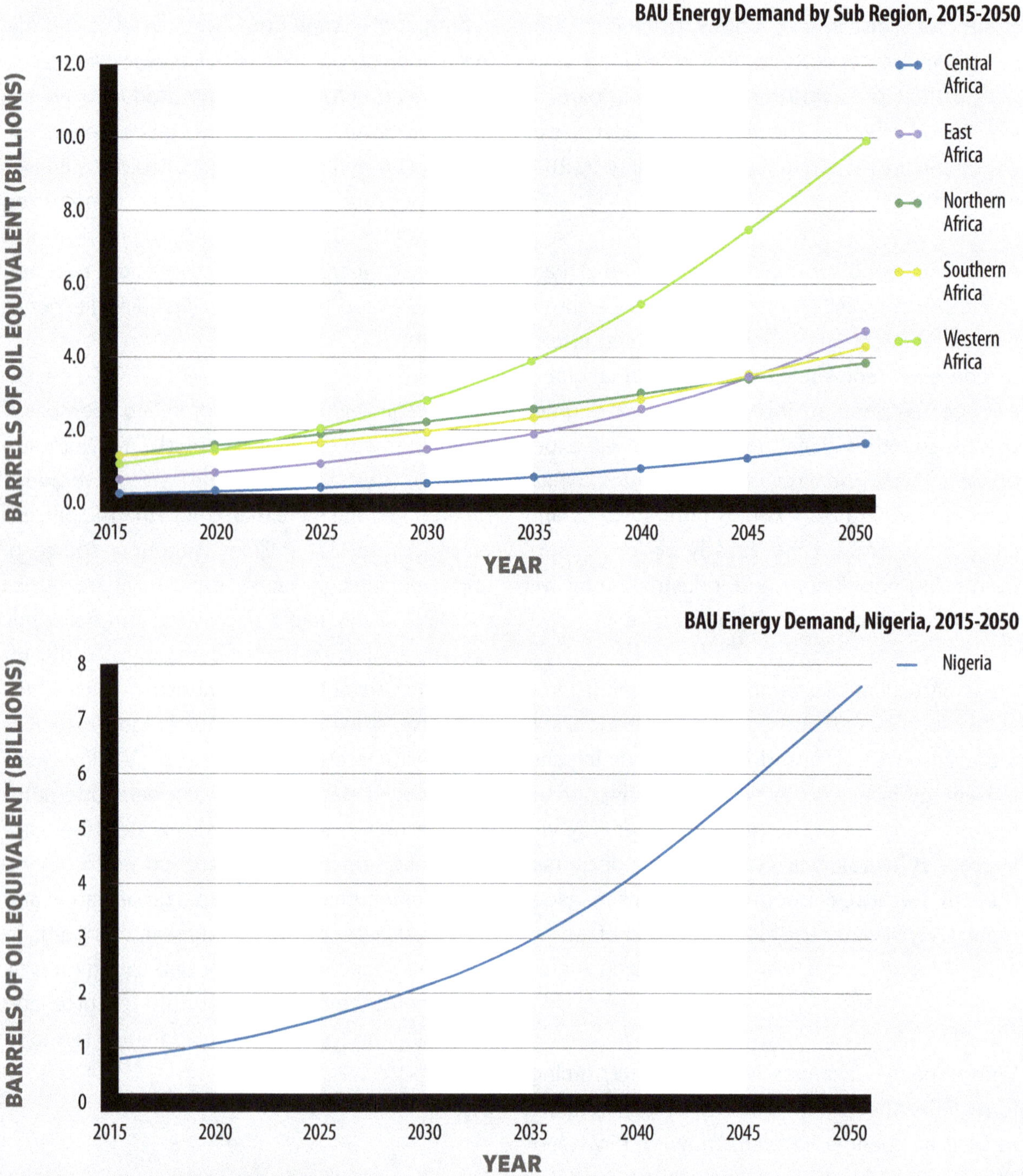

SOURCE: ONEWORLD, ADAPTED FROM INTERNATIONAL FUTURES (2015) AND IEA (2014).

NOTE: BAU = BUSINESS AS USUAL.

FIGURE 5.12 BAU ENERGY PRODUCTION, AFRICA, 2015–2050

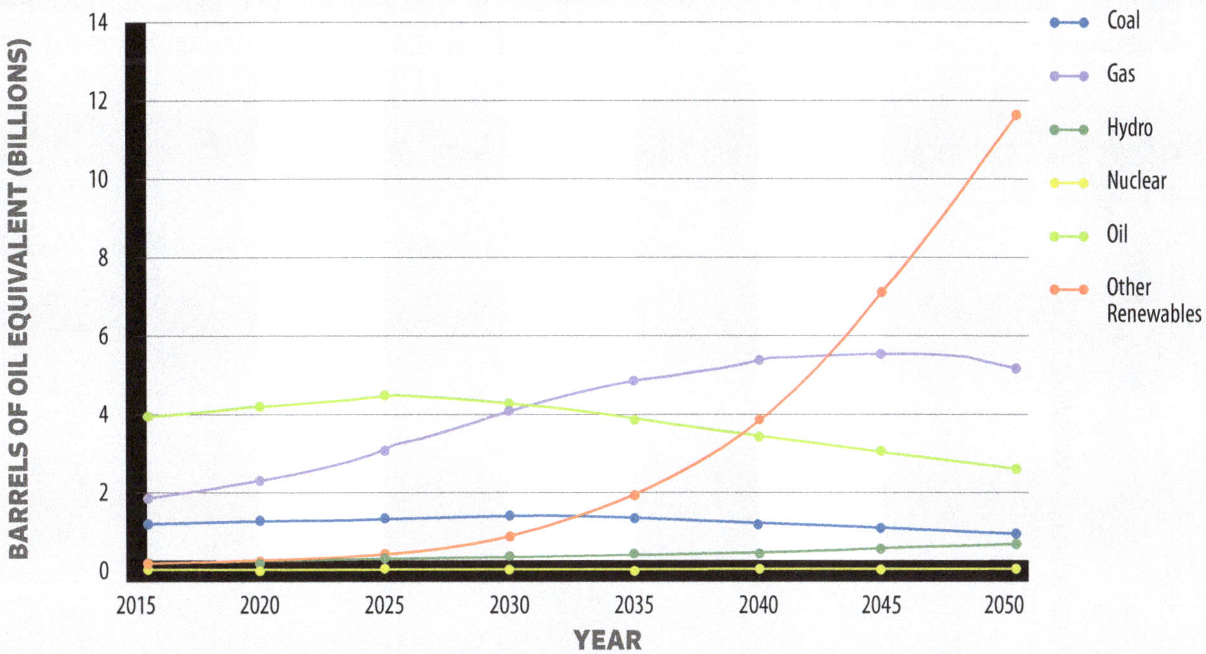

SOURCE: ONEWORLD, ADAPTED FROM INTERNATIONAL FUTURES (2015).
NOTE: BAU = BUSINESS AS USUAL.

The Democratic Republic of the Congo (DRC) and Ethiopia are forecast to become the ninth and tenth largest countries in the world by 2050, with populations of 194 million and 165 million, respectively (PRB, 2015), adding to the increasingly higher energy demands expected of the Central and Eastern subregions.

The access rate to electricity will stay low and will fall further by 2050, particularly in Central, East, Southern and West Africa. Although, globally, nearly 1 billion people will gain access to electricity by 2050, half a billion will remain without it (27 per cent of Africa's population) (IEA, 2014). Worryingly, the share of Central, East, Southern and West Africa's population without access to electricity will increase—the only region in the world where this will happen.

The gap between energy demand and electricity supply will widen. Electricity consumption will climb (consumption is expected to grow about 4.5 per cent a year due to population and industrial growth) as the middle class expands and countries industrialize, placing further pressure on generation, transmission and distribution systems. Demand for electricity will continue to outstrip supply, even assuming a BAU increase in investments in renewables and diversification of the fuel mix, with an attendant rise in electricity generation (figure 5.12) and decentralized energy policies that encourage off-grid power. Four-fifths of Africa's population now rely on biomass (straw, charcoal and firewood) to meet their energy needs; people in rural areas form the majority of those without access to electricity (Africa Progress Panel, 2015). By 2050, 1 billion tonnes of wood a year will be needed to meet demand for energy use (IEA, 2014).

Although large investments are forecast for expanding transmission lines by 2050, extensions still fall short of need. The gaps create huge shortfalls in the electricity system, particularly in rural areas, because of inefficiencies in grid operation, insufficient transmission capacity and losses in distribution.

Figure 5.13 shows total annual electricity use and share of energy imports in demand, measured in gigawatt hours (GWh). Annual electricity use

FIGURE 5.13 BAU TOTAL ELECTRICITY USE AND ENERGY IMPORTS, AFRICA, 2015–2050

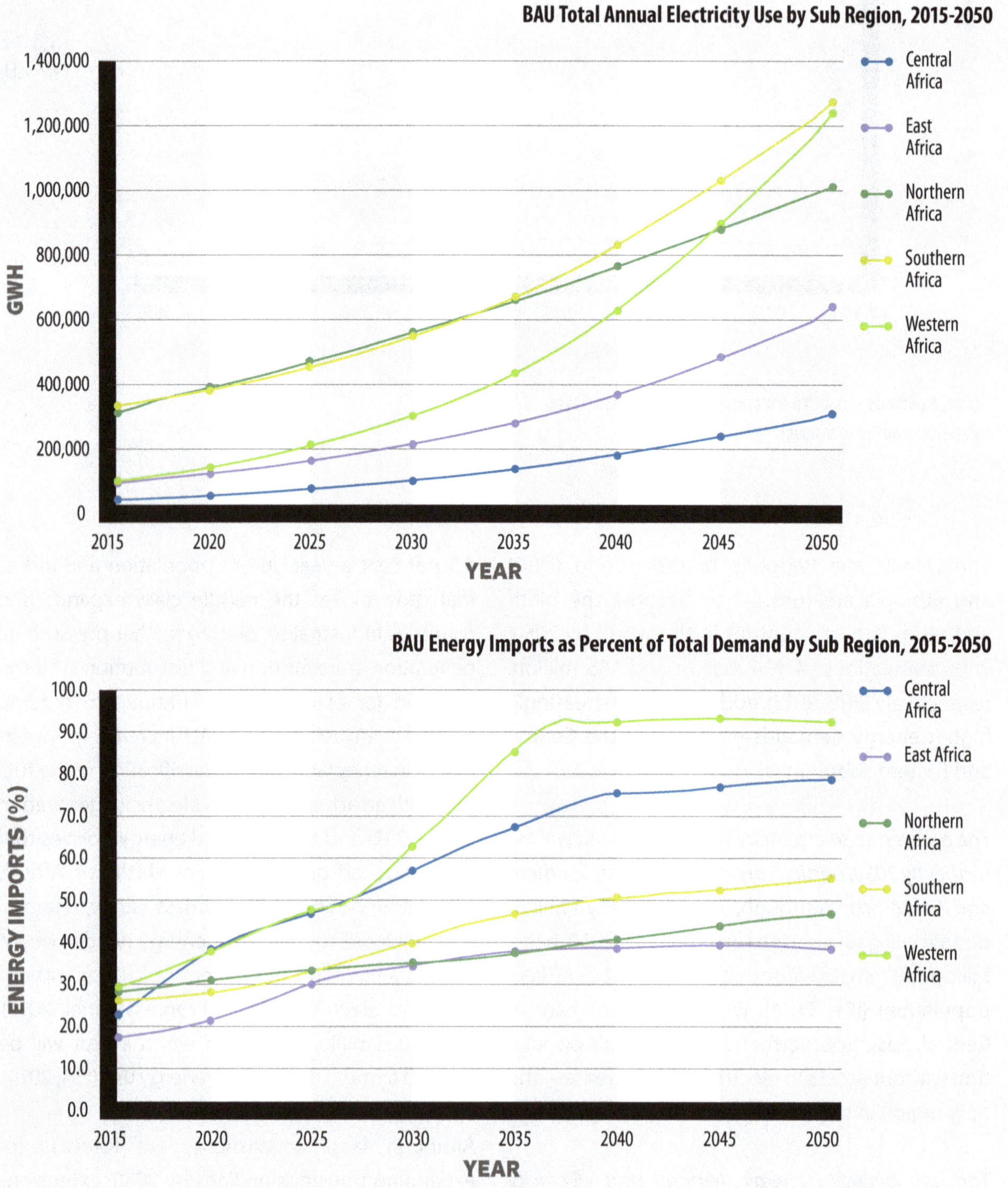

SOURCE: ONEWORLD, ADAPTED FROM INTERNATIONAL FUTURES (2015).

NOTE: BAU = BUSINESS AS USUAL

FIGURE 5.14 BAU AGRICULTURAL PRODUCTION, AFRICA AND SELECTED ECONOMIES, 2015–2050 (MMTS)

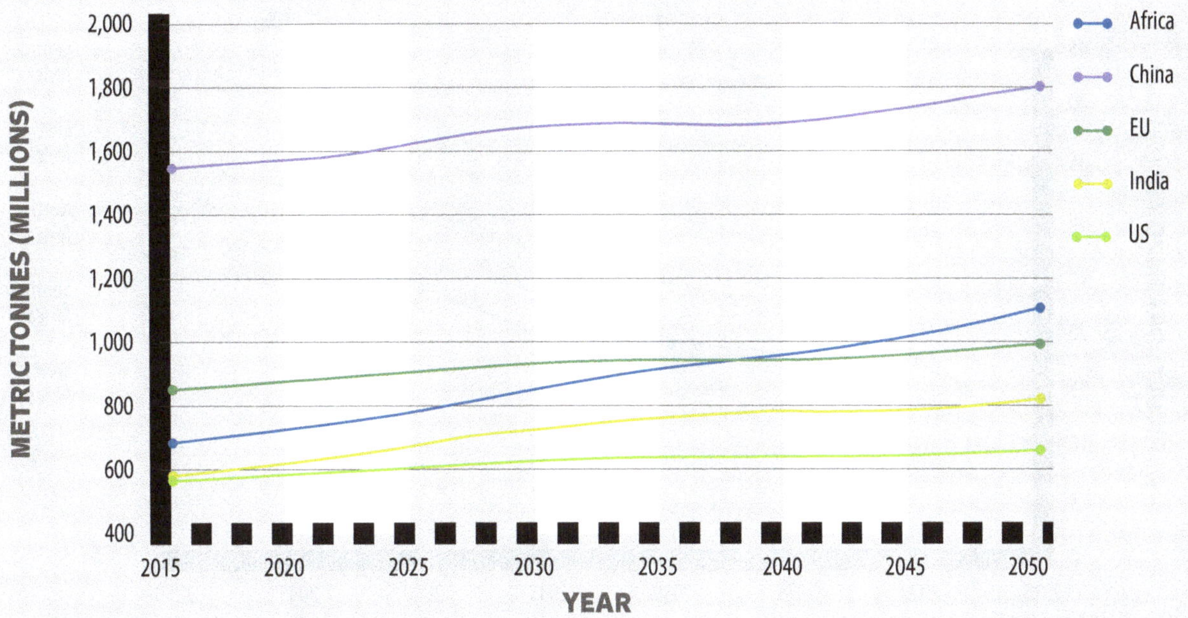

SOURCE: ONEWORLD, ADAPTED FROM INTERNATIONAL FUTURES (2015).

NOTE: BAU = BUSINESS AS USUAL; EU = EUROPEAN UNION; US = UNITED STATES.

is projected to soar in all subregions. Southern and North Africa start from a higher base (having higher electrification rates), but consumption will rise commensurately with predicted energy investments in all subregions (OneWorld, 2015) except West Africa—a population explosion node—where total annual electricity use already dramatically outstrips electricity production and shows a gap that widens sharply. Similar trends are occurring in Central, East and Southern Africa, where annual electricity use already surpasses production (net of losses) (OneWorld, 2015). Consumption is directly related to economic growth and will surge with accelerated economic growth in some countries and with upward trends in the extraction and consumption of commodities.

In this scenario, Africa's reliance on imports of fossil fuels as a share of demand will widen dramatically as countries attempt to close the supply–demand gap (figure 5.13). Fossil-fuel imports are regional and international. Regional imports are primarily from hydropower and coal-based electricity production, sometimes through bilateral power purchase agreements and in some instances through regional power grids. International imports tend to be concentrated in fuel oils—such as oil, gas and diesel—as well as in related technologies, particularly generators.

AGRICULTURE

Agricultural production will increase across the continent by 2050 as labour productivity, land under cultivation, irrigation infrastructure, and technology transfer (from developed and emerging economies) all expand or improve. Africa could outpace India, the United States, and the European Union in terms of agricultural output (figure 5.14). This is largely because of Africa's relatively untapped land and water resources.

Despite significant improvements in West and East Africa, the growth in agricultural yields will quickly

FIGURE 5.15 BAU AGRICULTURAL IMPORTS AS A PERCENTAGE OF DEMAND, BY SUBREGION, 2015–2050

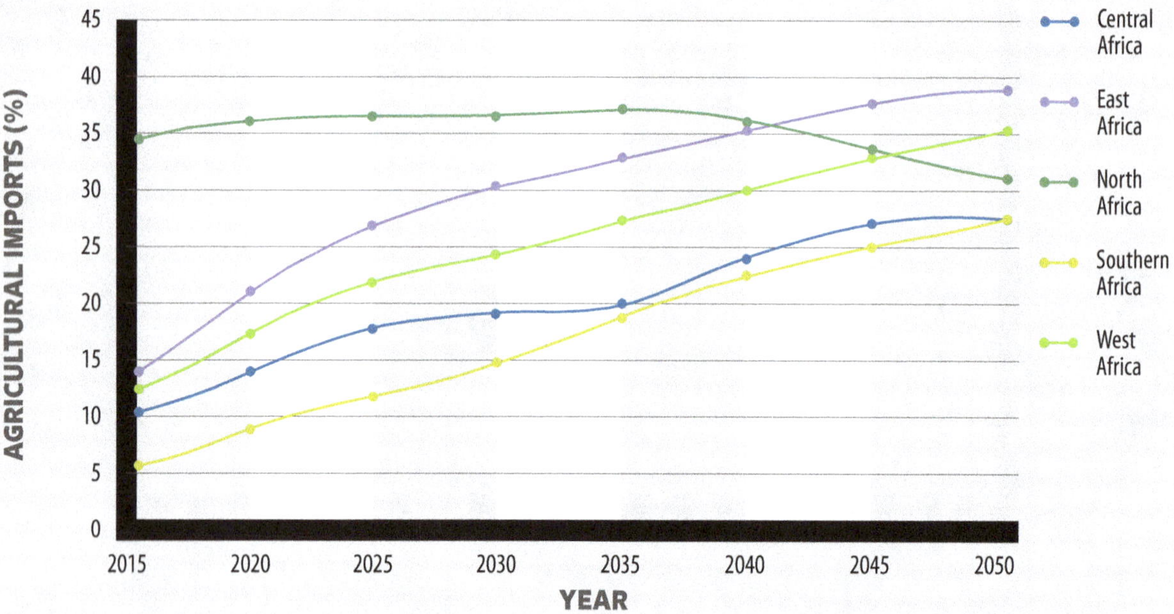

SOURCE: ONEWORLD, ADAPTED FROM INTERNATIONAL FUTURES (2015).

NOTE: BAU = BUSINESS AS USUAL.

be outpaced by population growth in those areas, driving an increase in agriculture imports and raising dependency (figure 5.15).

Stresses on food security will push people to migrate to Africa's urban centres, as well as to developed countries. Increased migration will further compound issues of poverty, violence and unemployment in Africa's cities, with the potential to destabilize the continent and undermine any advances made towards socioeconomic goals.

THE AFRICAN AND GLOBAL BAU SCENARIOS: SOME SIMILARITIES AND DIFFERENCES

Under the T-21 World Model (UNEP, 2011), BAU is modelled on the assumption that current trends will continue—that is, high energy use and emissions and unsustainable exploitation of renewable resources, with minor progress in shifting to a green economy—much along the same lines as the Africa BAU scenario. Global pressure on natural resources increases as GDP grows worldwide, and that slows the rate of growth. Higher water stress, lower soil quality and fossil-fuel price volatility all affect GDP negatively under the global BAU, lowering indicators such as the Human Development Index.

The global BAU scenario for water is similar to Africa's in that demand and consumption increase (reaching 70 per cent above current values), with corresponding reliance on groundwater reservoirs and streams well in excess of sustainable withdrawal. Global agricultural yields also increase with steady growth between now and 2050, with 36 per cent growth in crop production value between 2010 and 2050, improving average nutrition by 7 per cent by 2050.

In this global model the service sector shows the fastest growth, but agriculture remains a significant employer (at 32 per cent). As with Africa, largely because of population growth, primary energy demand will grow by more than 57 per cent by 2050. Increases in production of fossil-fuel, nuclear and renewable energy will meet demand (in that order, by size). Thus, the share of fossil fuels in global energy consumption remains at 81 per cent. That does not bode well for Africa's climate future, given that the continent is already suffering the consequences of global warming induced by fossil fuel–producing greenhouse gas emissions. Of additional concern to Africa's BAU scenario (in which growing energy demand and increasing deficit are met by imports of fossil fuels), the global scenario projects oil supplies peaking soon after 2030, driving up the price sharply.

Under the global BAU scenario, resource consumption is unsustainable in any geographical location. Africa's infrastructure and industrialization deficit sets it apart from most other regions, however. In all three sectors, Africa's is a story of underexploited resources with great potential to harness water, develop abundant renewable energy resources and improve lagging agricultural production. Moving on all three fronts could galvanize unprecedented levels of industrialization but only by greatly scaling up infrastructure investment.

Africa is at a crossroads. Economic growth in some of its countries is among the highest in the world, typically as a result of oil and gas rather than systemic and structural economic change. In commenting on the so-called African growth tragedy and the Africa rising discourses, Chang found deficiencies in both: "Africa is neither structured for underdevelopment nor has it suddenly entered a new golden age" (Chang, 2015). His report argues that policies, especially industrial policy, have the potential to make a significant difference to the continent's future. Africa's natural resource barriers, coupled with the socioeconomic challenges highlighted under a BAU scenario, mean that African countries have serious grounds for integrating industrial policy and green economy by adopting an inclusive green growth agenda.

5.3 THE GA SCENARIO

The green agenda (GA) scenario is characterized by deeper industrialization, faster economic growth and speedier progress towards Africa's transformation relative to the BAU scenario. Productivity increases and numbers in poverty decline faster than under BAU.. Green growth policies become the new "business as usual", decreasing resource intensity and rebuilding Africa's ecosystem services. Inclusive growth is promoted, increasing employment and skills, enhanced natural capital and opportunities for small or medium-sized enterprise development. Socioeconomic indicators improve as Africa becomes more globally competitive, with increased exports and less reliance on imports. More of the economy circulates within the continent, as domestic production grows to meet expanding consumer demand and intraregional trade deepens. Businesses in the formal sector and multinational companies safeguard their licences to operate by adopting sustainable practices and cooperating with their communities, which ensures equitable allocation of limited resources.

Targeted policy interventions and enhanced participation in global value chains yield solid gains. Indeed, a critical success factor is setting priorities because not everything can be done at the same time, given the known inadequacies in African systems and sectors. The GA scenario highlights the benefits of such targeted interventions cascading through the system.

The GA scenario is a variant of the BAU model that originates from the IFs Model (OneWorld, 2015, box 1). The assumptions underpinning the GA are in box 5.5.

BOX 5.5 THE VARIABLES UNDERLYING THE GA SCENARIO

The interventions modelled in the GA provide critical insight into the interventions most likely to have a positive effect on Africa's development trajectory, both overall economic development and the equitable distribution of benefits; and into the magnitude of intervention needed to generate a sizeable shift within the economy.

In the GA scenario, three critical sectors for intervention stand out— water, energy and agriculture . For each sector, the following interventions are targeted for maximum effectiveness.

RENEWABLE RESOURCES

Under the GA scenario, total water demand increases relative to the BAU, mainly as a result of industrial demand. By sector, municipal demand from household users registers no change under the GA (figure 5.16, top panel). Although that seems unrealistic—per capita income and human development indicators under the GA increase, stimulating water demand as access to water infrastructure increases and the middle class expands—the imperative to allocate water for industrialization will supersede domestic demand in a trade-off. Similarly, agriculture shows a slight increase in water demand under the GA relative to BAU, which aligns with the boost in agricultural investment and production by 2030, followed by a decline to a level lower than BAU projections by 2050.

Although agricultural water demand may not increase substantially under the GA relative to BAU (given the gain in yields on greater *efficiency* rather than *quantity* of water use), we should expect municipal demand to increase relative to BAU (given rising household incomes under the GA) and thus water demand to be even higher than in the BAU scenario.

		GA interventions, 2015–2050
Water	Renewable water supply increases by 100 per cent	This estimate is based on rainwater harvesting potential calculated by the International Centre for Research in Agroforestry (ICRAF) and the United Nations Environment Programme (UNEP) ((2005) for nine Eastern and Southern African countries. The minimum potential increase in water resources from widespread installation of rainwater harvesting equipment is 500 per cent. The estimate is downscaled because of regional differences in precipitation and is validated by global best practice examples—for example, in Australia and Germany.
Energy	Energy production costs fall by 5 per cent a year from 2015–2050	This estimate is based on predicted world renewable energy price declines—the cost of electricity from solar photovoltaic cells has fallen 50 per cent since 2010 (10–15 per cent a year) and is predicted to fall a further 40 per cent over the next 4 years and by 60–80 per cent over the next 20 years (IRENA, 2015; Pollin, 2015). The estimate is also based on steady declines in renewable energy production costs in South Africa. Since the onset of that country's renewable energy procurement programme, electricity costs from wind, solar photovoltaic and concentrated solar power (CSP) have fallen by an average of 25 per cent over three years (Eberhard, Kolker and Leigland, 2014). For our purposes, the annual decrease has been cut from 10–15 per cent to 5 per cent because of assumed higher production costs in less developed markets.
	Energy generation capacity per capita increases by 400 per cent	Estimate is based on two factors: 1 The increase it would take to bring Africa (currently 0.14 kWh per person) up to the present-day average energy generation capacity per capita of Brazil, China and India (0.5 kWh per person) by 2050; and 2 Projections in Greenpeace's Energy Revolution Scenario for a 500–700 per cent rise in electricity generation in Africa by 2050, lowered to account for population increase (Greenpeace, 2015).
	Energy investment in hydropower increases by 300 per cent	Estimate is based on projections in Greenpeace's Energy Revolution Scenario for a 200–300 per cent increase in hydropower energy investment by 2050 (Greenpeace, 2015).
	Energy investment in renewables increases by 3,000 per cent	Estimate is based on projections in Greenpeace's Energy Revolution Scenario for a 2,000–3,000 per cent increase in renewable energy investment by 2050 (Greenpeace, 2015).Estimate is in line with Pollin's (2015) projections for global clean renewable energy growth by 2035 (3,000 per cent growth globally).
Agriculture	Land equipped for irrigation increases by 60 per cent from 2015–2050	Estimate is based on two factors: 1 Alexandratos and Bruinsma's (2012) projections of land under irrigation by 2050, by region, ranging from a 23 per cent increase (South Africa) to a 39 per cent increase (West Africa) under BAU; and 2 Foster and Briceno-Garmendia (2009) estimate that full development of all economically feasible irrigation schemes (dam based and small scale) would double irrigated land under cultivation. With the full potential for expansion in mind (100 per cent), estimates in the GA scenario assume accelerated agricultural and infrastructure investment (Alexandratos and Bruinsma, 2012) but still take into account the historical trend of low investment in large-scale irrigation.
	Agricultural investment rises by 450 per cent from 2015–2050	Branca et al., (2012) estimate that the financing gap for agriculture (crops only) is $7.25 billion a year, cumulatively about $250 billion by 2050 (a 400 per cent increase). Including livestock, the figure increases to $400 billion by 2050 (a 660 per cent increase). Estimates cited here were selected from the 400–660 per cent range, based on aggressive agriculture-focused development.
	Agricultural losses fall by 50 per cent (because of inefficiencies, waste, crop failure, and so forth) from 2015–2050	Gustavsson (2011) estimates Central, East, Southern and West Africa food losses and waste at 160 kg per person a year, the vast majority lost in harvest, post-harvest and processing activities. Estimation of the GA trend is based on Central, East, Southern and West Africa reaching current levels of South and South-East Asian production and processing efficiency by 2050, equivalent to a 50 per cent decrease in losses.
	Road network density increases by 670 per cent by 2050	Estimate is based on the assumption that the planned expansion of major road networks under the Programme for Infrastructure Development in Africa (PIDA) is implemented by 2050, that is, from the current 10,000 km to 60,000–100,000 km, a 500–900 per cent increase.

BOX 5.5, CONTINUED THE VARIABLES UNDERLYING THE GA SCENARIO

	GA anticipated effects, 2015–2050
Water	In the GA scenario, water supply is estimated at 98 per cent higher than the BAU level in 2050 because of the following policy initiatives that, out of necessity, simultaneously and rapidly address the water infrastructure deficit and related ecological issues in Africa. With these interventions, Africa could realistically start to double its water supply as it makes a concerted effort to catch up with water access in other global regions: ▸ Widespread adoption of technologies such as rainwater harvesting; ▸ Increased investment in water treatment facilities for recycling and reuse; ▸ Land degradation addressed, and ecosystems within high-water-runoff areas (that act as critical water towers for river basins) restored; ▸ Investment in ecological infrastructure (protecting and restoring wetlands, removing alien invasive species, establishing riparian buffer strips, and so forth); ▸ Improved knowledge and resource management of groundwater resources; ▸ Increased investment in water infrastructure to improve access and efficiency; and ▸ Improved regional cooperation for equitable allocation and abstraction of shared water resources. ▸ East and West Africa offer the most potential for increases in rainwater capture. They are also the two regions with the fastest population growth and likely increasing rainfall trends in the next 50 years.
Energy	Relative to the BAU figures, renewable energy production under GA increases significantly as Africa aggressively accesses valuable, local renewable resources and reduces its dependence on fossil fuel production and imports: ▸ Renewable energy production in 2050 is 58.4 per cent of total production under BAU but 92.8 per cent of total production under the GA. ▸ Fossil-fuel production in 2050 is 8.74 per cent of total production under BAU but 1.86 per cent of total energy production under the GA. ▸ Total electricity production is 962 per cent higher than the BAU level in 2050. ▸ Energy import as a proportion of demand is 13 per cent lower than the BAU level in 2050.
Agriculture	Relative to the BAU levels in 2050, the GA levels are as follows: ▸ Agricultural production per capita is 103 per cent higher. ▸ Agricultural yield per hectare is 114 per cent higher. ▸ Agricultural exports as a share of GDP are 2,485 per cent higher. ▸ Dependence on agricultural imports is 91 per cent lower. ▸ Value added in agriculture is 98 per cent higher. ▸ Access to rural roads is 66 per cent higher.
Environment	Relative to the BAU levels in 2050, the GA levels are as follows: ▸ Forest land use is 1.1 per cent higher. ▸ Annual carbon emissions for the continent are 60.5 per cent lower. ▸ Precipitation change from carbon dioxide emissions is 7.8 per cent lower. ▸ Temperature change from carbon dioxide emissions is 10.7 per cent lower.
Economy and development	Relative to the BAU level, share or index in 2050, the corresponding GA figures are as follows: ▸ GDP per capita is 11 per cent higher. ▸ Exports per capita are 18.6 per cent higher. ▸ Informal GDP share is 16.9 per cent lower. ▸ Poverty levels ($2 per day) are 30.8 per cent lower. ▸ Calories per capita are 7.6 per cent higher. ▸ Democracy Index is 1.4 per cent higher. ▸ Economic Freedom Index is 1.2 per cent higher. ▸ Gender Empowerment Measure is 2.5 per cent higher.

Industrial demand for water will increase under the GA relative to BAU as the manufacturing base expands. Under GA, export promotion policies targeted towards agro-industry will greatly affect demand for water, as demand for raw agricultural inputs increases and as agricultural processing and higher value added activities grow.

FIGURE 5.16 BAU AND GA—WATER DEMAND AND WATER AVAILABILITY, AFRICA, 2015–2050

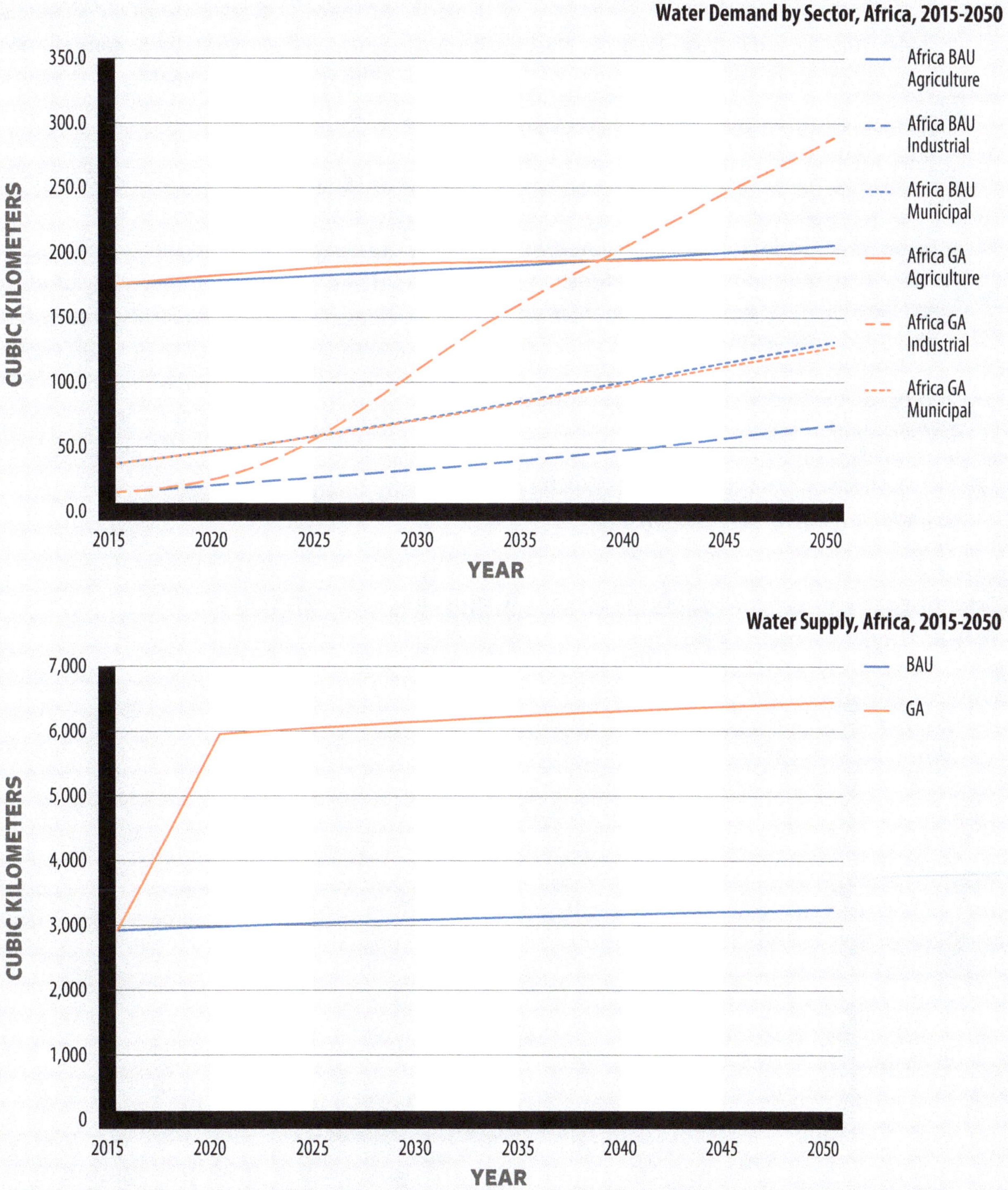

SOURCE: ONEWORLD, ADAPTED FROM INTERNATIONAL FUTURES (2015).

NOTE: BAU = BUSINESS AS USUAL; GA = GREEN AGENDA.

As water demand increases, water-scarce regions in Africa will need to scale up interventions to increase water supply. Under GA, water supply doubles, improving significantly relative to BAU because of the following efforts:

- Widespread adoption of technologies such as rainwater harvesting;
- Increased investment in water treatment facilities for recycling and reuse;
- Land degradation tackled, and ecosystems restored within high-water-runoff areas that act as critical water towers for river basins;
- Investment in ecological infrastructure (protecting and restoring wetlands, removing alien invasive species, establishing riparian buffer strips, and so forth);
- Improved knowledge and management of groundwater resources;
- Increased investment in water infrastructure to improve access and efficiency; and
- Improved regional cooperation for equitable allocation and abstraction of shared water resources.

The success of these interventions varies among regions, but East and West Africa—the two regions that will experience the highest population growth rates and increasing rainfall trends within the next 50 years resulting from climate change—offer the most potential for increases in rainwater capture.

Given water's integral role in socioeconomic development, improvements to the water supply cascade throughout the system, stimulating knock-on effects for food security, energy production and industrial growth. UNEP (2013) estimated that increased investment in improved natural resource management and land restoration would save 242 billion tonnes of water by 2030 in South Africa, translating into a 1.1 per cent decrease in the country's water stress index from BAU.

FIGURE 5.17 BAU AND GA—FOREST LAND AREA, AFRICA, 2015–2050 (HECTARES)

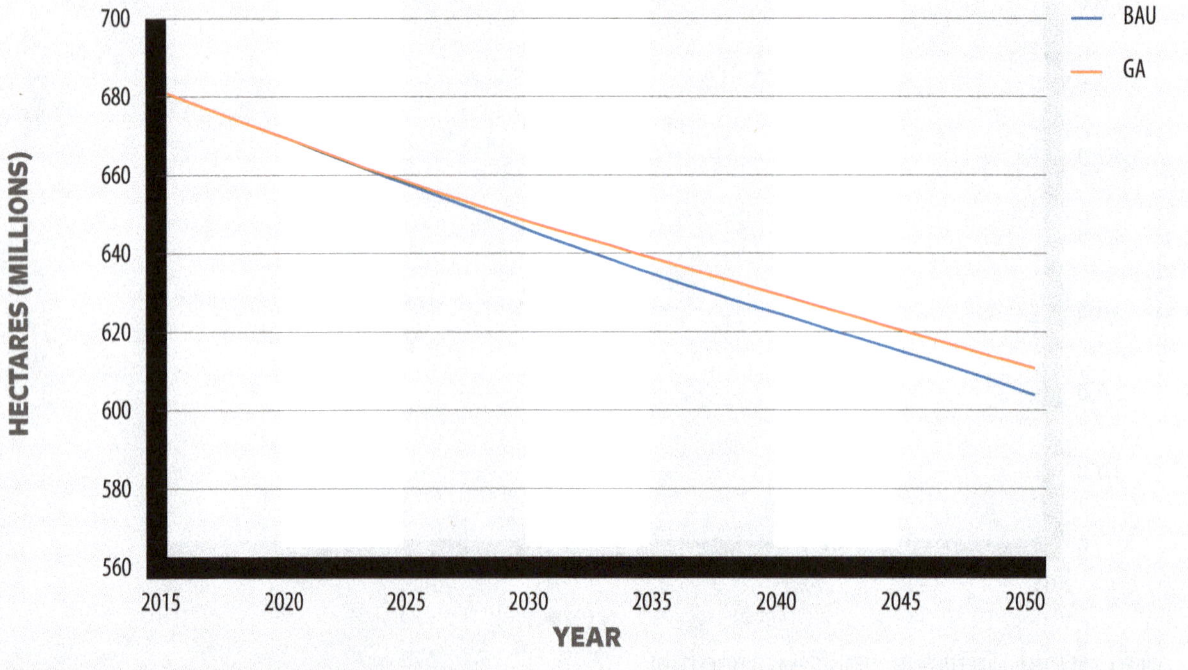

SOURCE: ONEWORLD, ADAPTED FROM INTERNATIONAL FUTURES (2015).
NOTE: BAU = BUSINESS AS USUAL; GA = GREEN AGENDA.

Improvements in water supply will become increasingly important with a changing climate. Each of the interventions under the GA also helps to reduce vulnerability to climate impacts.

The rate of deforestation slows relative to BAU, with policy interventions and increased investment in energy generation, agricultural production and associated infrastructure. Gains in energy production—which under the GA are entirely from renewable energy, including hydropower—and in energy access will increase consumption of clean energy. Consumption of bioenergy (primarily wood and charcoal) will fall, as access to the grid expands. Agricultural yields under the GA are higher primarily as a result of improved production techniques and technologies in land under cultivation, rather than an expanded area under cropping, which relieves some of the pressure to deforest for agricultural expansion. Those two GA interventions—in power and agriculture—reduce deforestation relative to BAU, and the gap between the two scenarios widens (figure 5.17).

ENERGY

Renewable energy generation capacity, abetted by, for example, green procurement programmes and falling costs, grows steeply and narrows the supply–demand gap. It reduces the heavy reliance on fossil-fuel production and imports seen in BAU (figure 5.18).

Based on variables applied to the GA scenario, access to electricity improves significantly relative to BAU (OneWorld, 2015). These results are in line with similar modelling exercises for the continent. UNEP's (2014c) assessment of the effect of green investment in Burkina Faso found that investment in renewable energy would increase electricity supply by 140 per cent in 2050, compared with BAU, with the share of renewables in the energy mix increasing from 20 per cent to 60 per cent.

AGRICULTURE

In the GA scenario, huge increases in productivity result from an aggressive greening of Africa's agriculture and expansion of irrigation, reducing dependence on rain-fed agriculture. Yields increase substantially relative to BAU.

Consumption of bioenergy (primarily wood and charcoal) will fall, as access to the grid expands.

Recent green economy modelling exercises have shown similar results, albeit on a smaller scale. Scenario modelling for Kenya's green economy transition found that agricultural yields improved by 15 per cent by 2030 compared with BAU (UNEP, 2014a), and similar modelling in Senegal saw agricultural production pick up relative to BAU as a result of improved agricultural techniques and increased uptake of advanced technologies (UNEP, 2014b). In South Africa, green investments in agriculture are modelled to increase yields by 23.9 per cent under a scenario in which the government allocates 2 per cent of GDP to green sectors (UNEP, 2013).

The projected increase in yields under the GA generates much-improved agricultural production per capita in terms of tonnes produced per hectare, enhancing food security in part through lowering dependence on food imports (figure 5.19). Major increases in yields enable the continent to feed its fast-growing population and capitalize on its comparative advantage, as it expands as an exporter of high value added agricultural products and agricultural raw materials.

FIGURE 5.18 BAU AND GA—RENEWABLE ENERGY AND FOSSIL-FUEL PRODUCTION, AND FUEL IMPORT DEPENDENCE, 2015–2050

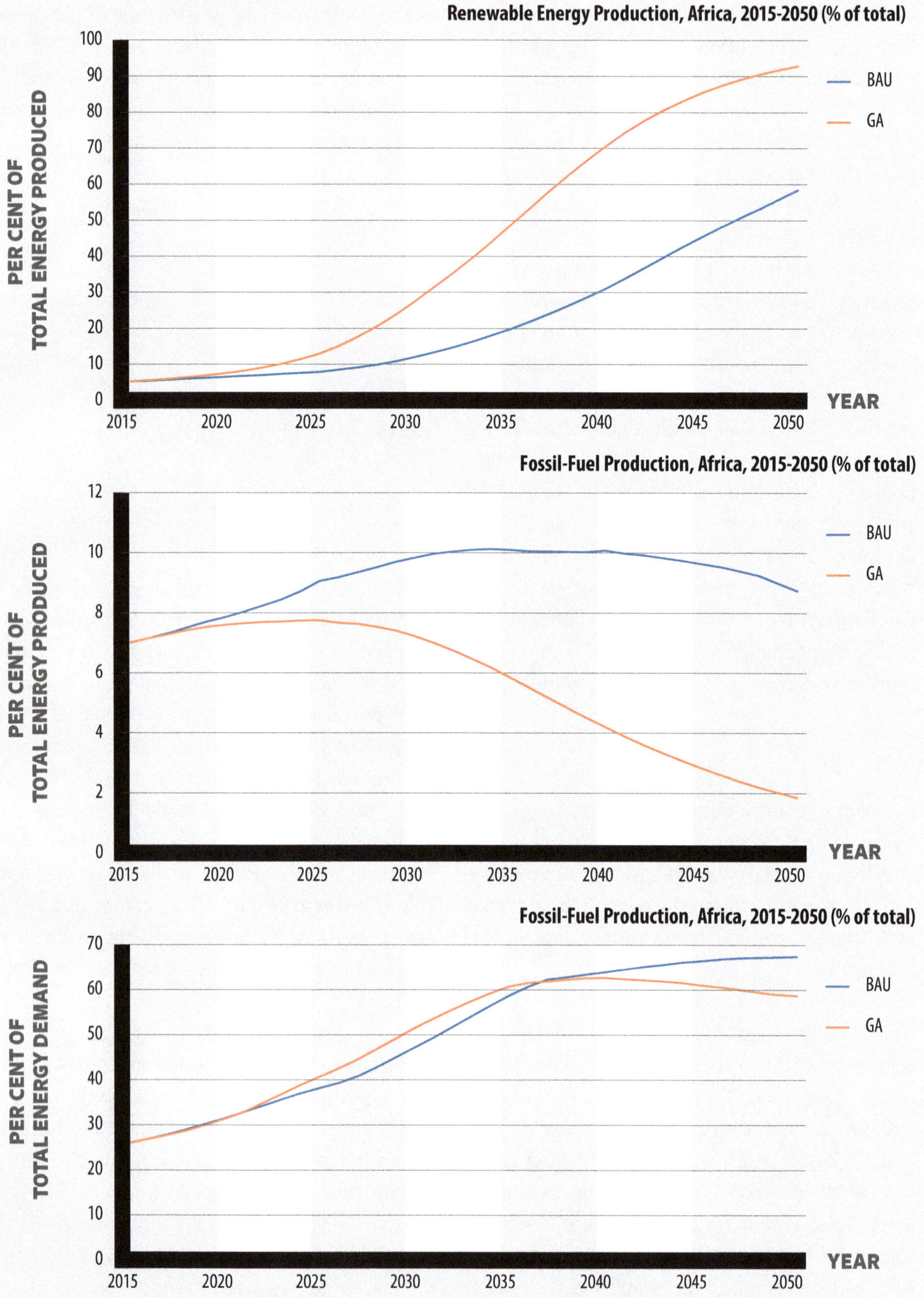

SOURCE: ONEWORLD, ADAPTED FROM INTERNATIONAL FUTURES (2015).

NOTE: BAU = BUSINESS AS USUAL; GA = GREEN AGENDA.

One outcome is a dramatic increase in agricultural exports and, although these start to level off in around 2045, a positive contribution to GDP is made under GA relative to under BAU (figure 5.20, right panel).

Studies around the developing world highlight that medium-sized farmers are more likely to improve resource efficiencies and adopt new technologies because they farm at a scale at which doing so makes economic sense. Their operations also are often inclusive of small farmers who help to improve productivity and maintain economies of scale (Sheahan and Barrett, 2014). The socioeconomic benefits of a green agenda are so apparent that the argument for not following a green industrialization pathway is weak.

Africa's accelerated irrigation expansion under the GA improves productivity and helps to mitigate the negative impacts of climate change. Under climate scenarios for higher temperatures and drier conditions, an important response in Africa's already dry areas, is to expand irrigated areas to supplement rain-fed production.

Agricultural output will increase even more with accelerated uptake of technologies, increased labour productivity and sustainable water management. Currently underexploited arable land (with low yields largely because of underutilization of water resources and of available land) provides the opportunity for leapfrogging to more sustainable and more inclusive agricultural development pathways. Unprecedented access to new research and technologies from successful "green revolutions" in Asia and Latin America, if harnessed, can accelerate the pace of change.

The combination of interventions in management of renewable resources, accelerated renewable energy generation and increased productivity across the agricultural sector—including through light manufacturing—have cumulative socioeconomic benefits. Those benefits include helping to realize the demographic dividend, substantially enhancing the transition from the informal to formal labour sector, strengthening infrastructure investment and broadening the base of economic growth.

POPULATION AND EMPLOYMENT

Central, East, Southern and West Africa's current fertility decline is slower than in other regions (including North Africa) that have already undergone a fertility transition and reaped some of the economic benefits, although the region faces un and under employed youth problems. Accelerating the fertility decline—as under GA—is essential, both to decrease Africa's dependency ratio and to realize the demographic dividend faster.

Widespread implementation of multisectoral GA interventions will hasten Africa's fertility transition, with enormous system-wide benefits. Better access to electricity and clean water leads to higher incomes, falling infant mortality rates, and upward trends in physical, social and knowledge capital. The overall effect is greater political and economic stability, a critical factor in reducing birth rates further.[3]

The transition towards the formal economy—with its increase in services and manufacturing as a share of GDP and a decline in informal labour as a

Currently underexploited arable land ... ... provides the opportunity for leapfrogging to more sustainable and more inclusive agricultural development pathways.

FIGURE 5.19 BAU AND GA—YIELD, PRODUCTION PER CAPITA AND IMPORT DEPENDENCE, 2015–2050

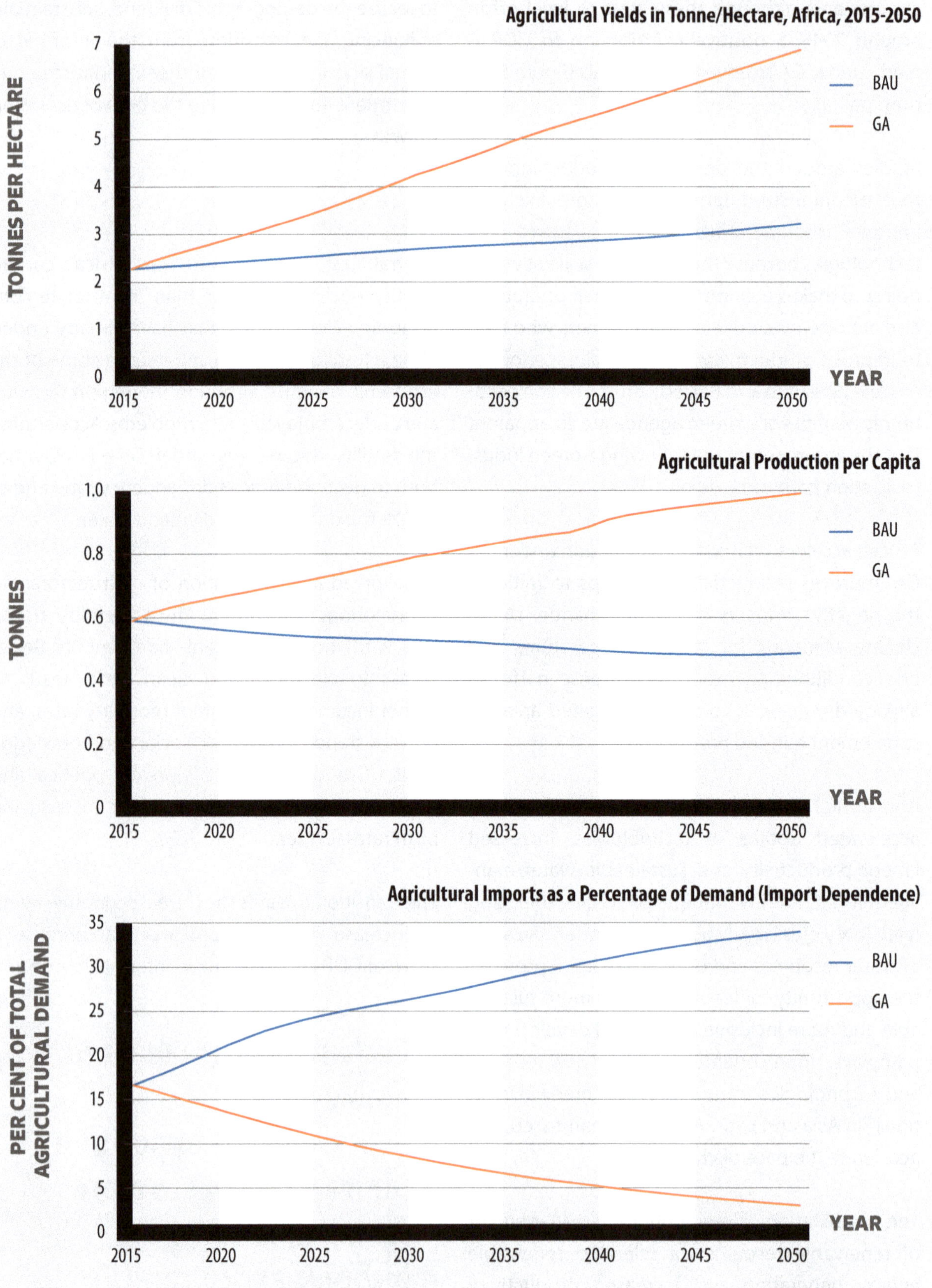

SOURCE: ONEWORLD, ADAPTED FROM INTERNATIONAL FUTURES (2015).

BAU = BUSINESS AS USUAL; GA = GREEN AGENDA.

FIGURE 5.20 BAU AND GA—VALUE ADDED IN AGRICULTURE AND AGRICULTURAL EXPORTS, 2015–2050

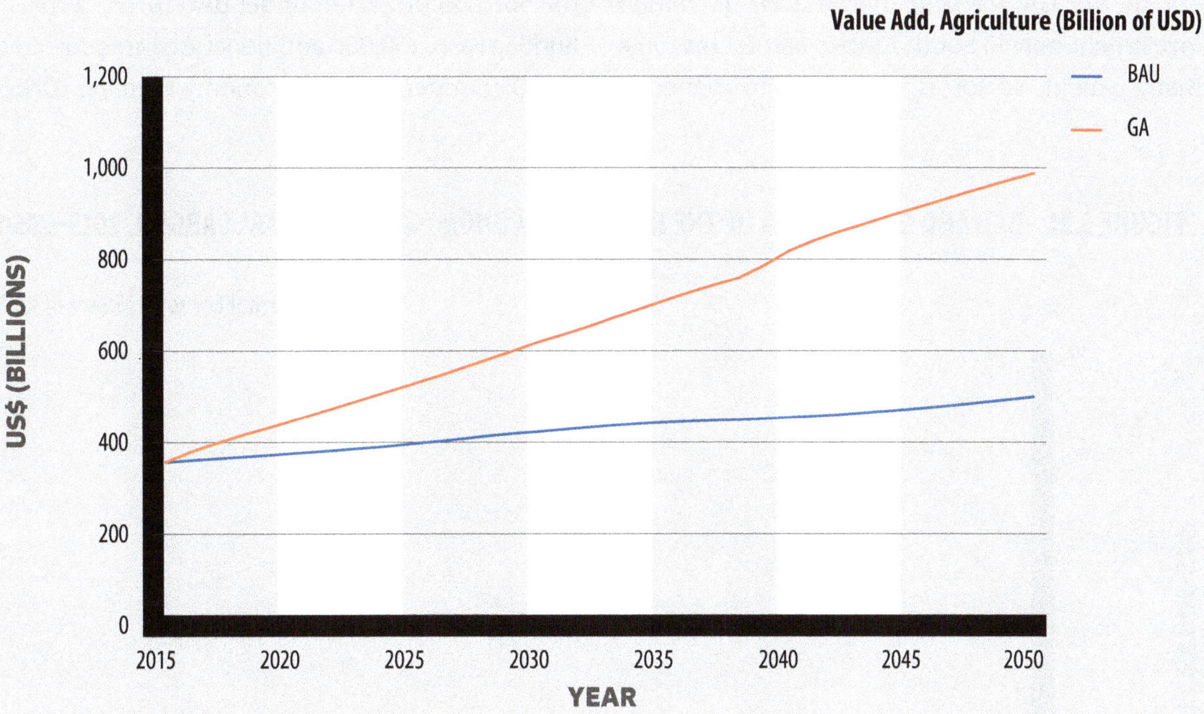

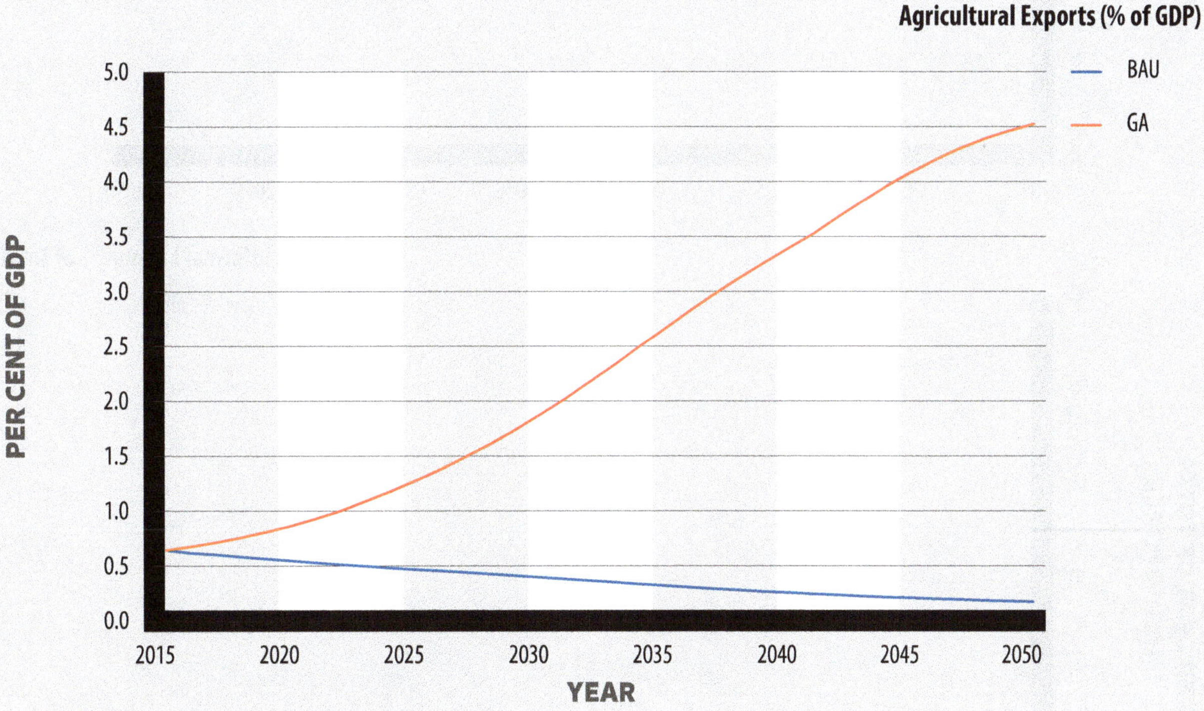

SOURCE: ONEWORLD, ADAPTED FROM INTERNATIONAL FUTURES (2015).

NOTE: BAU = BUSINESS AS USUAL; GA = GREEN AGENDA; GDP = GROSS DOMESTIC PRODUCT; USD = US DOLLARS.

share of the workforce—is an important co-benefit of the GA scenario (figure 5.21). Increased investment only in South Africa's natural resource management sector is projected to generate 701,000 new formal-sector jobs by 2030, up from the 568,000 projected under BAU (UNEP, 2013). In Burkina Faso, 160,000 additional jobs are projected by 2050 under a green economy scenario (UNEP,

FIGURE 5.21 BAU AND GA—SHARES OF THE INFORMAL ECONOMY AND INFORMAL LABOUR, 2015–2050

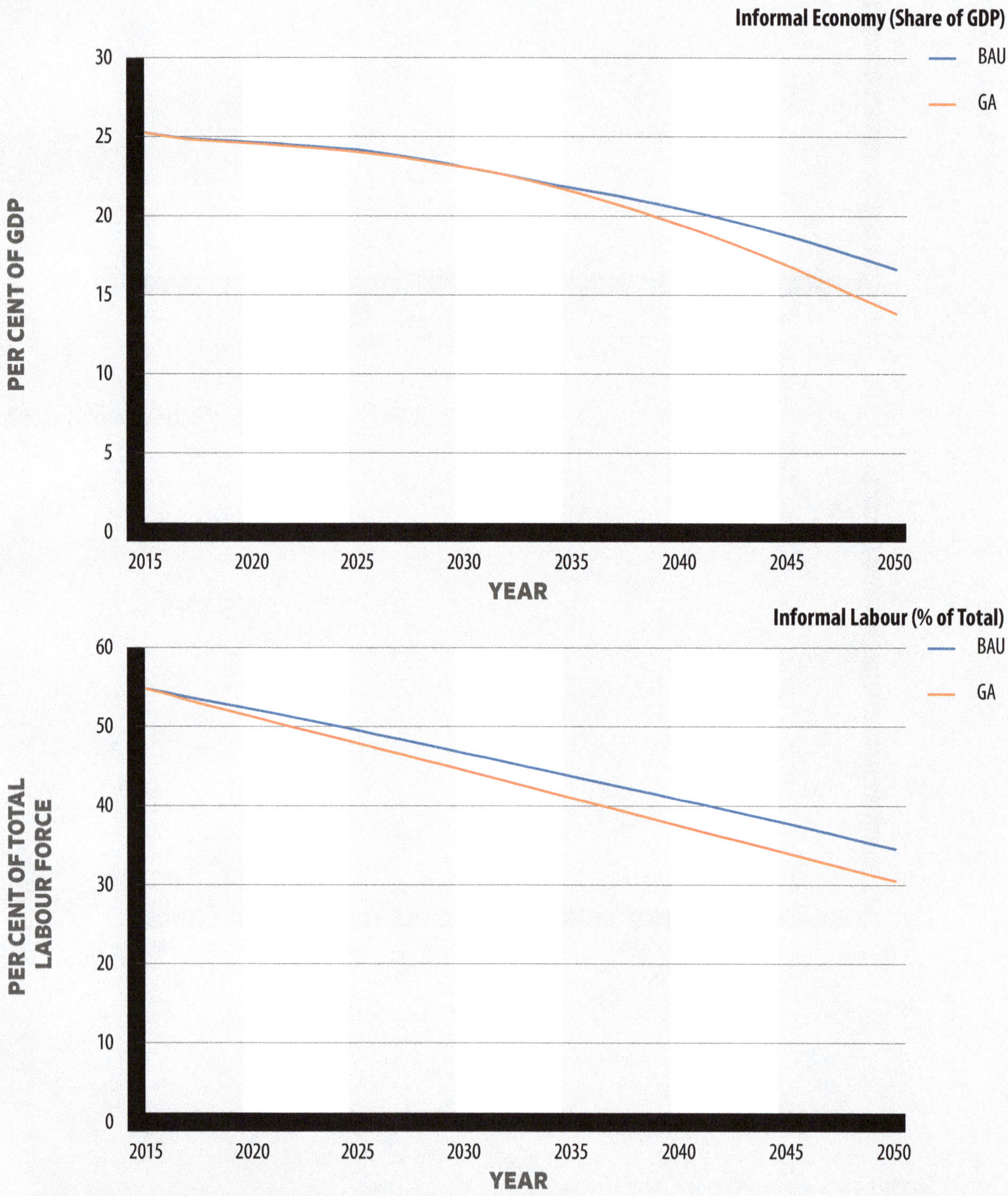

SOURCE: ONEWORLD, ADAPTED FROM INTERNATIONAL FUTURES (2015).

NOTE: BAU = BUSINESS AS USUAL; GA = GREEN AGE

FIGURE 5.22 BAU AND GA—ACCESS TO RURAL ROADS, 2015–2050

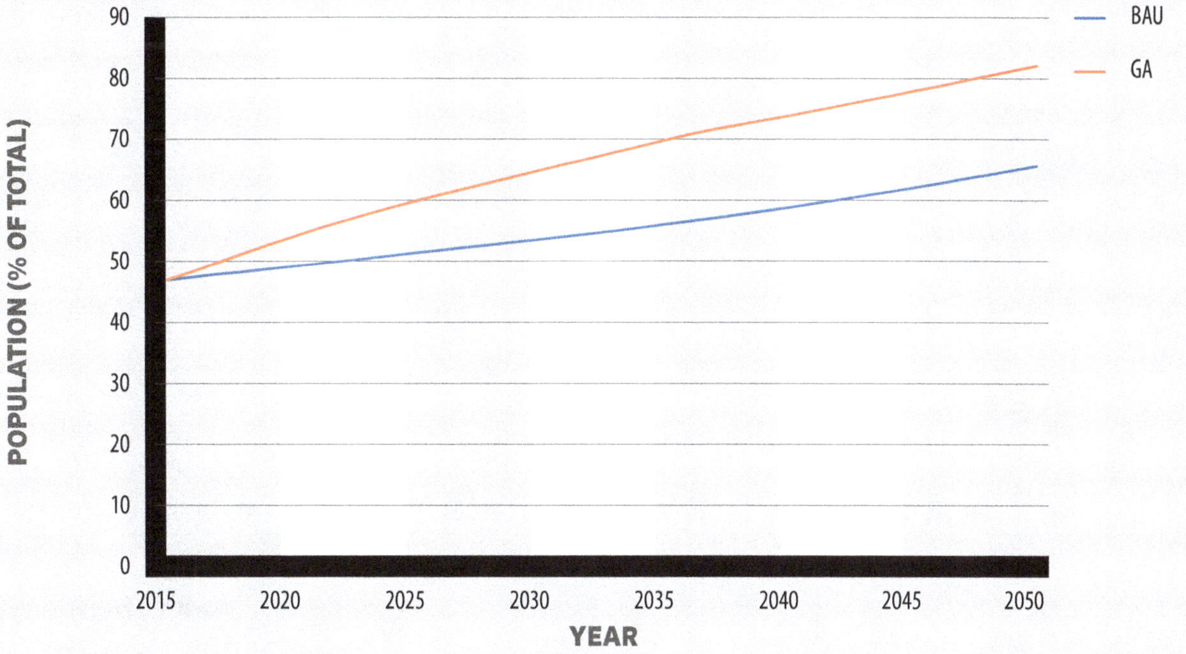

SOURCE: ONEWORLD, ADAPTED FROM INTERNATIONAL FUTURES (2015).
NOTE: BAU = BUSINESS AS USUAL; GA = GREEN AGENDA.

2014c). Senegal's renewable energy sector is estimated to generate between 7,600 and 30,000 new jobs by 2035 (UNEP, 2014b).

ECONOMIC GROWTH, DEVELOPMENT AND INFRASTRUCTURE

The cumulative result of the interventions will boost GDP per capita growth and exports per capita. (The Ethiopian eco-industrial case study in Chapter 6 provides early evidence of this trend.) With this growth in GDP per capita, poverty levels (measured at less than $2 per day) decline significantly under the GA scenario compared with BAU (see figure 5.1).

These results are in line with the findings of several green economy assessments (UNEP, 2014a, b, and c). UNEP (2014a) found that Kenyan GDP growth under a green economy scenario was 12 per cent higher in 2030 than under BAU, with an additional 3.1 million people shifted above the poverty line.

Expenditure on research and development increases dramatically in the GA from the BAU scenario (from 0.4 per cent to nearly 2 per cent of GDP by 2050) (OneWorld, 2015), bringing benefits in improved technology uptake and facilitating, for example, a robust shift to more productive agriculture resulting from improved agro-processing.

Africa's GA scenario infrastructure investments increase road networks (figure 5.22), improving market access and trade, thereby helping to increase Africa's participation in regional and global value chains.

The cumulative results of adopting a green agenda and green industrialization pathways are positive for many of the continent's develop-

FIGURE 5.23 BAU AND THE GA—INDICES FOR DEMOCRACY, ECONOMIC FREEDOM AND GENDER EMPOWERMENT, 2015–2050

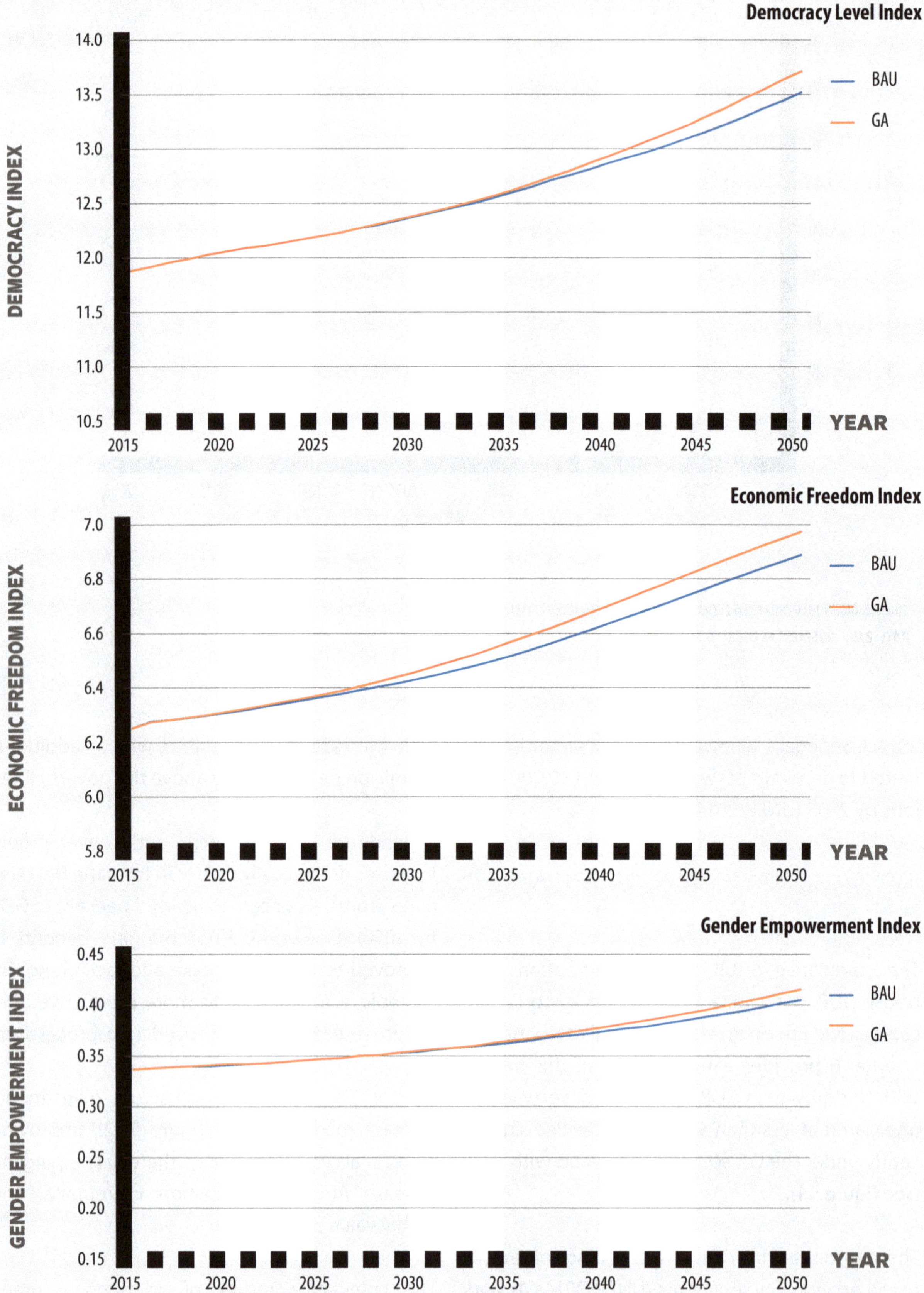

SOURCE: ONEWORLD, ADAPTED FROM INTERNATIONAL FUTURES (2015).

NOTE: BAU = BUSINESS AS USUAL; GA = GREEN AGENDA.

ment indicators, reflecting co-benefits to society, including gains in democracy, economic freedom and gender empowerment—all of which improve more under the GA than under BAU (figure 5.23).

THE GA SCENARIO AND THE GLOBAL GREEN INVESTMENT SCENARIO: SOME SIMILARITIES AND DIFFERENCES

Some of the assumptions and outcomes of the GA scenario are comparable to the global green investment scenario (G2) developed under the T-21 World Model (UNEP, 2011), particularly green investments showing positive outcomes and trends across the social, economic and environmental spectrum.

G2 provides an opportunity to contextualize Africa's green growth globally. Africa's GA scenario outcomes are aligned with those of G2 (the broader assumptions are similar), although some drivers and baselines differ, sometimes greatly, particularly with respect to Africa's infrastructure and industrialization deficits and far lower greenhouse gas emissions. G2 represents a similar strategy to the GA scenario for Africa of embedding green investments and enabling a policy framework into long-term commitments (UNEP, 2011).

The GA is aligned with the G2 assumption that 2 per cent of global GDP channelled into green investments will yield 10 per cent growth in global GDP, gradually over time, with positive social and environmental benefits. As with the GA scenario, G2 prioritizes sectoral policy targets that position the world to better absorb the impacts of climate change and volatility.

G2 emphasizes energy and climate change. The GA also prioritizes energy investments, particularly renewables, to address three key issues: Africa's massive energy infrastructure and resource deficits; paucity of enabling conditions for Africa to industrialize; and diversion of energy reliance from hydropower investments (given their decreasing returns because of environmental and climate impacts and increased competition for water) and from fossil-fuel imports (which are price volatile, expensive and environmentally unfriendly). In addressing these issues the GA recognizes that Africa needs a reliable and adequate energy supply to industrialize, and that it has a tremendous opportunity to leap-frog by prioritizing green energy investments using its vast, renewable resource base. This is a cornerstone of Africa's green industrialization pathway.

Although G2's promotion of investment in key ecosystem services and low-carbon development slightly slows economic growth in the short to medium term, growth is faster and more sustainable further out. The African and global green scenarios are more resilient than the modelled' BAU scenarios, driven by lower emissions from clean energy investments, reduced dependence on volatile fuels and more efficient and sustainable use of natural resources. The GA also prioritizes—by necessity—investments in Africa's rainwater harvesting and storage infrastructure, in transport networks and in improved agricultural land-use practices.

Under the GA scenario, water scarcity becomes manageable even though water demand increases because each of the factors contributing to scarcity is addressed simultaneously with the greening of the massive, new infrastructure investments.

In agriculture and its industrialization, G2 argues that green investments should be allocated to agriculture more predominantly where that sector is a major driver of economic and social development (UNEP, 2011). This is true for most of Africa, which houses the majority of the world's least developed countries. G2 shows that in these cases, investments in more sustainable agriculture could increase yields and production, improving nutrition and food security and paving the way for agro-industrialization.

The GA for Africa makes similar assumptions with attractive returns, noting though that the infrastructure deficit must be bridged—urgently. The GA includes irrigation expansion, improved water access, greener farming practices and the incremental investments (organic fertilizer, pest control, and food processing) that G2 considers.

Cumulatively, these investments improve crop productivity under both scenarios. In G2, annual incremental investments of about $198 billion increase productivity by 17 per cent in 2050 (UNEP, 2011). Both G2 and the GA show positive trends for value added in agriculture: it increases to 9 per cent relative to BAU in 2050 under G2, mainly because of G2's higher yield per hectare estimate in the medium to longer term.

Gradual social and environmental gains also are seen in both G2 and the GA. Under the global BAU scenario, investments drive faster economic growth than the green alternatives in the short term (in terms of total and per capita GDP), with only marginal differences on the social side (poverty, employment and nutrition). Matters are very different in the medium to longer term: G2 and the GA both outperform BAU in economic and social development. Both of these green scenarios also have lower negative impacts on the environment, such as energy intensity, water use and natural capital footprint, which contributes to their faster medium to longer term economic growth.

The final positive trend observed and compared is inclusive growth, particularly employment. Under G2, economic development in a global green economy pushes employment up to 4.9 billion, or 3–5 per cent above BAU. Under GA, Africa's urban population continues to grow at a similar pace as under BAU, but a greater share are employed because of green industrialization, growth of jobs, and local enterprise development.

Increased industrialization and services also facilitate the transition towards the formal economy in Africa (see figure 5.21). They are important co-benefits of the GA scenario, which also stem from greater investments in renewables, climate-resilient infrastructure, resource-use efficiencies, land restoration and new green enterprises. (This point is backed by global case studies and to some extent by the country case studies in Chapter 6.) The cumulative return of all these investments will be millions of new jobs and inclusive growth across the continent.

5.4 SOME CONCLUSIONS: THE IMPORTANCE OF THE ENABLING ENVIRONMENT

Africa is sitting on a "'gold mine", as one of the few major regions left with viable natural resources and abundant opportunities for economic growth and industrialization. Pursuing a green agenda with urgency—BAU shows the huge resource depletion possible in a mere 35 years—can create the right enabling environment.

One critical enabler is infrastructure, an arena in which Africa needs huge investments; green industrialization will be impossible without them. BAU demonstrates that investments of this scale must be greened to harness and protect critical renewable resources and to stimulate inclusive growth and employment. Without the right enabling environment, however, the deficit in Africa's infrastructure investments will continue to grow alarmingly. With increasing weaknesses in unsustainable infrastructure (because it is neither climate resilient nor resource efficient), the deficit will remain a threat to Africa's growth prospects.

The costs to renewable resources of the green agenda are steep, but they can be met. A green agenda raises questions of trade-offs, but it also demonstrates how Africa can control and mitigate many of the factors threatening growth. The continent can even adapt to climate change, whose cause is largely not attributable to Africa (figure 5.24), if serious thought and focused action are applied to building resilience. Applying lessons from global examples of best practice and regional successes can help African countries improve water resource management, mitigate the economic and social impacts of extreme events, and access international and domestic sources of climate finance.

The most important condition for success is, arguably, improved governance across Africa at national, regional and subregional levels. Africa's 16 landlocked countries depend on their neighbours with coastlines for many resources, such as access to ports, markets and skills. Investors, particularly the private sector, depend on sustainable market access and secure natural resources to ensure a return on their stake. Intercountry dependencies and shared resources often mean that potential investors have too little control over too many variables. To secure the interests of investors and the rights of citizens, African governments must tackle the infrastructure deficit within a framework of regional cooperative governance.

Better governance and investment decisions require governments to prioritize among the trade-offs linked to the resource demands of competing development claims, particularly among sectors and countries that share resources. Understanding trade-offs may help countries overcome the current inertia on transboundary and regional cooperation, which often is driven by the need to protect perceived vested national or sectoral interests, and which may well be less than the shared benefits of cooperation. Analysis of the trade-offs and shared benefits requires a longer term view in weighing the possible outcomes of development decisions: water is available now for expanding hydropower and irrigation, but will that still be true in 2050 if populations grow as forecast? Will greening new infrastructure accelerate the pace of investment, or will the related expense outweigh this benefit over the long run?

Adopting the green agenda may seem a trade-off for some, but it is not. Focused and incremental pursuit of the GA has obvious direct and indi-

FIGURE 5.24 ANNUAL CARBON EMISSIONS, AFRICAN SUBREGIONS AND GLOBAL REGIONS (BILLION TONNES PER YEAR)

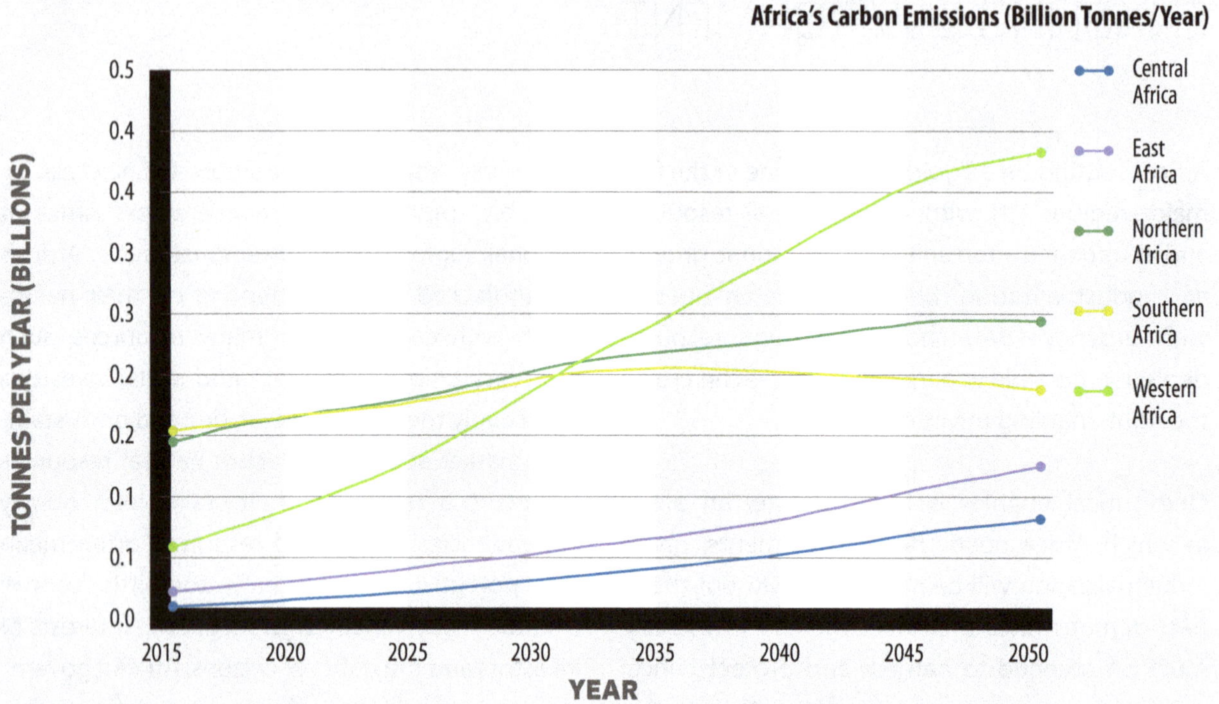

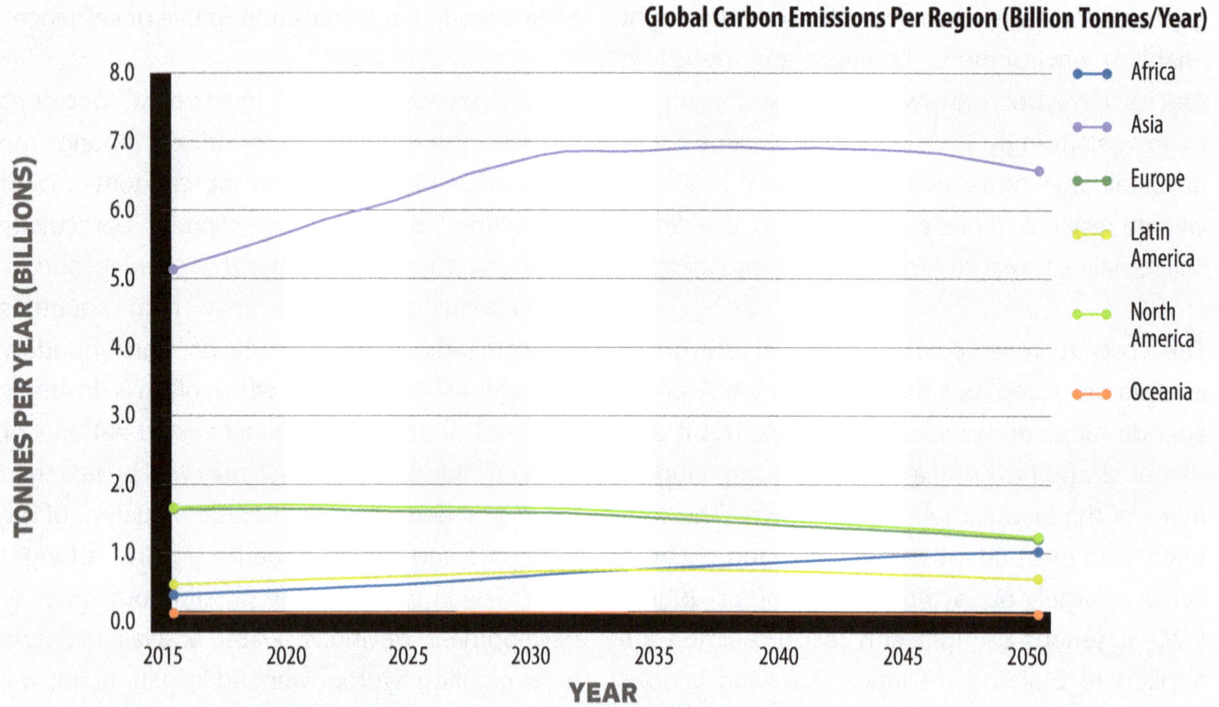

SOURCE: ONEWORLD, ADAPTED FROM INTERNATIONAL FUTURES (2015).

rect benefits. Although a detailed cost-benefit analysis is unavailable, the GA scenario strongly suggests that greening industrialization does not come at too high a cost and, in particular, supports the assertion in the UNEP global green investment scenario that investment of 2 per cent of GDP generates an attractive 10 per cent increase in GDP (UNEP, 2011).

BAU generates a different set of costs. Current growth pathways not only pose a threat to economic growth and industrialization but also fail to make serious progress towards meeting objectives related to job creation, inclusivity, human development and environmental protection—all key components of the Sustainable Development Goals.

The GA implies—and requires—a substantial upfront investment to realize longer range goals. In return the GA offers a pathway on which benefits increasingly outweigh costs (because of the far-reaching direct benefits and co-benefits from implementing the GA), while ensuring that the continent is well on its way to structural transformation through green industrialization.

In other words, the green agenda moves Africa well beyond protecting its natural resource endowments; it also produces highly desirable economic co-benefits, including poverty alleviation. It demands a set of actions to take governments beyond BAU, however, and requires a close alignment of policy measures with that agenda.

Ethiopia is an excellent example of a country that combines complex policies that link greening, infrastructure, industrialization and climate resilience (Chapter 6). The country's internationally acclaimed Climate Resilient and Green Economy framework maps its broader strategy, in which industrialization is key. The government's quest to increase textile exports aligns with its zero waste and zero pollution policies by establishing eco-industrial parks. This alignment will, for example, help to ensure that wastewater treatment is part and parcel of manufacturing activities.

Aquaculture in Nigeria provides an alternative, market-driven example of inclusive growth through a resource-efficient, agro-industrial value chain that has improved its resource efficiency and incorporated indigenous knowledge to expand market share and promote inclusive employment (Chapter 6).

Although every country is different, applying to the whole continent the inclusive green growth principles inherent in Ethiopia's green framework could set Africa on a green industrialization course with a wide range of benefits, including higher growth, lower poverty levels, more sustainable resource management and realization of the demographic dividend—important shifts given projected severe population pressure and rapid urbanization.

Achieving such outcomes requires bold steps mapped coherently. The GA scenario (and UNEP's global green investment scenario) offers guidance on policy interventions and incentives. If implemented well, monitored closely and enforced tightly, they show great promise in setting African countries on a high-return investment path. A clear, well-articulated policy is essential to promote Africa's green industrialization agenda, but it needs complementary work on integrated approaches to greening water, energy and agriculture. A vital component is to tackle together investments in greening these sectors to manage related interdependencies and effects and to realize their collective importance for socioeconomic well-being because the whole is greater than the sum of its parts. Both scenarios highlight the rapidly expanding urban populations (expected to accompany Africa's high population growth) across the continent. Urbanisation is shown to exacerbate Africa's existing water, energy and food security challenges, emphasising the particular importance of integrated approaches to greening Africa's cities.

WATER

Africa has little choice but to optimally use whatever water it has at its disposal to benefit society, the economy and the environment. Multiple infrastructure investments are needed by the public and private sectors. Climate change demands that all new water infrastructure be developed according to climate-resilient standards. Other issues include transboundary, national and sectoral governance, as well as trade-offs in allocating water among development priorities. A heavy investment is thus needed in trade-off analysis between sectors and countries that quantifies the social, economic and environmental benefits and consequences of water-reliant development that will also be affected by climate volatility and change. Governance and institutional arrangements may have to be revised to enable effective implementation of the decisions resulting from such analysis.

Water resource development and greater water-use efficiencies need stronger incentives.

African countries have opportunities to reduce water scarcity and improve quality. They range from improved transboundary water management and governance to engaging everyone—municipalities, businesses, SMEs and households—in water conservation and harvesting, for example, through rainwater harvesting at the household and industry levels.

Water resource development and greater water-use efficiencies need stronger incentives. Depending on how they are structured, such incentives could lead to pricing the true cost of water, a source of revenue necessary in the longer term to finance other important interventions, such as restoration of degraded land and removal of alien invasive species.

ENERGY

Scaling up renewable energy sources predicates both the GA and G2 and is one of the cornerstones of Africa's industrialization. Without energy, Africa cannot industrialize and as the other options are finite, too expensive and volatile price-wise (imported fossil fuels, nuclear) or decreasingly available (hydropower), renewables are the logical choice. Africa has several country success stories (Chapter 6) to build on. Green procurement programmes, tailored to a country's circumstances, can improve energy access, stimulate more locally generated electricity, yield important water-resource benefits and reduce dependence on increasingly unreliable hydropower and fossil-fuel imports. Central to achieving this progress has been the big drop in renewable energy costs, which is expected to continue.

Green procurement programmes must be matched to the way a country does business, which varies. Although South Africa has had unexpected success in increasing its renewable energy supply in a short space of time, incorporating the private sector, mitigating the energy crisis is the country and generating new jobs and community benefits (Chapter 6), the approach taken was feasible because the country has a robust financial services sector and highly engaged foreign and local investors. Inclusive growth has been a major benefit from the widespread growth in renewable energy in Kenya and South Africa, with strengthened participation of small and medium-sized enterprises, substantial job creation and increases in foreign investment and local content (local manufacturing of renewable energy technology components, local jobs and community benefits).

Green procurement programmes can and should be incentivized; as shown in South Africa (Chapter 6), the cost to governments and consumers can be little or nothing, making it an extremely attractive policy option. Governments need to guarantee power purchase agreements and, if the cost of renewables is maintained at a lower price than the cost of alternative electricity production, as is currently the case for South Africa, furnishing those guarantees is not onerous.

The challenge is to replace "'free" energy sources, such as biomass, with renewable fuels. Poorer groups, however, may be unable to afford to pay the true cost of energy (or of water). This means that the full costs of fossil fuel extraction, such as coal in South Africa, or the associated external environmental costs such as degraded land from biomass collection, are currently often not factored into tariffs and this is difficult to adjust, particularly in poorer areas. . Social protection measures may be needed as an interim solution to shift people's consumption out of high-carbon energy (and reliance on free water). Alternative sources of income through diversified livelihoods are key, and the agriculture sector provides a short- to medium-term opportunity, particularly through value add processing from raw materials produced in the agriculture sector.

AGRICULTURE

Decisions for agriculture must be considered in conjunction with those for water and energy. The co-dependence between these sectors and with people's health and livelihoods—particularly in urban centres—is high.

Although the GA for agriculture suggests a group of interventions, ultimate growth in this sector is likely to be driven by world food demand and purchasing power. Relative to other hungry regions around the world, Africa has underused land and water resources that even include untapped access to rain-fed pasture (Alexandratos and Bruinsma, 2012). Moreover, agricultural production has a finite capacity to increase financial returns; intensive studies over recent years, across Asia and Africa, reveal that agricultural production is limited at around 3,000 calories per person (Choudhuri, 2016), meaning that agroprocessing, an important sector value add, is critical to optimising the potential of the sector . Africa thus has the opportunity to generate surplus food and earn export income, but the continent must ready itself to meet the external demand from countries where resources are exhausted and populations go hungry. This calls for government investment in skills, technology, institutions, infrastructure, appropriate policies and accountability mechanisms.

Africa must prepare for that demand by proactively determining a sustainable means of delivery that is at once socially, economically and environmentally fruitful. Some investment options to achieving the GA are as follows:

- *Expand climate-resilient water infrastructure.* Steps to raise irrigation capacity, for instance, although often private (that is, by commercial farmers), are in fact national and sometimes transboundary decisions that call for evaluation of water availability and competition from alternative uses, such as hydropower. Still, irrigation is an important infrastructural investment that increases the reliability of yields. Increased rainwater harvesting—a critical assumption under the GA scenario—will also require private investment (at household and industry levels), but achieving the scale needed is possible only with public incentives. The feasibility of this solution lies in its simple technology, knowledge of the environmental and economic benefits, and robust research on biophysical aspects such as climate. The short to medium goal is reduced water scarcity, and then sustained supply. The intervention potentially also has a longer range benefit of delivering catchment- or even basin-level water security.

- *Green agriculture.* Including green irrigation schemes, aggressive greening of agriculture is achievable through heightened efficiencies (reduced pre- and post-harvest waste and crop losses), more efficient water use and improved land-use practices. A welter of policy interventions is required, such as enhanced extension services and technology support and secure tenure rights for land users. These moves call for government investment in skills, institutions, technology support, appropriate policies and accountability mechanisms.

- *Attract investment to value added agriculture.* Improved yields from green agricultural processes and expanded irrigation should spur greater investment in light manufacturing in the sector, especially given current low levels of agroprocessing. Creating an enabling environment will further promote those investments, in the form of better market access, improved standards and adherence procedures, and facilitated regional and international export growth. Value added agriculture, as in the Nigeria catfish case study (Chapter 6), has some of the greatest sectoral potential—beyond reaping the food security benefits—to generate inclusive growth along local supply chains and regional and global value chains.

GREENING URBANIZATION

Population growth and rapid urbanization present a primary opportunity—and challenge—for Africa as it sets about securing sustainable economic growth into the future. Cities—key engines of economic growth, job creation and innovation and major contributors to global warming and environmental problems—are at the heart of the transition to a green global economy (Hammer et al., 2011). Mayors from around the developed and developing world agreed at an OECD Urban Roundtable held in 2009 that because the well-being of cities will be intimately tied to promoting environmental and social inclusion through economically stimulating activities, cities will be fundamental to advancing green growth (Hammer et al., 2011). One of the mayors' arguments, central to a theme of this chapter that energy is a cornerstone of green industrialization, is that urban form matters: lower urban density is a driver for higher energy consumption for electricity and transportation. This, among other factors—such as feeding fast-growing urban populations and ensuring reliable access to safe water—makes careful planning imperative.

Many African cities bring some of the continent's deficits together and into sharp focus, including poor infrastructure (energy, water and sanitation), dirty air (local air pollution from transport, kerosene and paraffin), un- and underemployment, paucity of food, and social inequality. In overburdened cities (some of which are already megacities, with populations of more than or fast approaching 10 million) and in growing cities that can cope now, as well as in emerging cities, these challenges require urgent resolution. The BAU scenario highlights the need to green urbanization in Africa quickly; the GA scenario provides hope that doing so will deliver green growth through strengthened synergies between economic, environmental and social inclusion policies. Effective urban policy will fit into place one large piece in the puzzle of the enabling environment for Africa's industrialization. It may even deliver more on green growth than wider economic approaches, such as deeper industrialisation, simply because cities—as centres of skills, innovation and opportunity—are well placed to deliver concentrated eco-innovation, scaled-up green infrastructure, and green skills for the economy.

5.5 REFERENCES

Africa Progress Panel. 2015. *Power, People, Planet: Seizing Africa's Energy and Climate Opportunities. Africa Progress Report 2015.* Available from http://www.africaprogresspanel.org/wp-content/uploads/2015/06/APP_REPORT_2015_FINAL_low1.pdf.

African Development Bank (AfDB). 2010. Infrastructure deficit and opportunities in Africa. *Economic Brief.* vol. 1 (September). Available from http://www.afdb.org/fileadmin/uploads/afdb/Documents/Publications/ECON%20Brief_Infrastructure%20Deficit%20and%20Opportunities%20in%20Africa_Vol%201%20Issue%202.pdf.

———. 2013. *At the Center of Africa's Transformation: Strategy for 2013–2022.* African Development Bank Group. Available from http://www.afdb.org/fileadmin/uploads/afdb/Documents/Policy-Documents/AfDB_Strategy_for_2013%E2%80%932022_-_At_the_Center_of_Africa%E2%80%99s_Transformation.pdf.

AfDB and World Wildlife Fund (WWF). 2015. African ecological futures 2015. Available from http://www.afdb.org/fileadmin/uploads/afdb/Documents/Generic-Documents/xwwf_african_futures_report_english-lo-rez.pdf.

African Union) (AU). 2010. *Programme for Infrastructure Development in Africa (PIDA): Interconnecting, integrating and transforming a continent.* Addis Ababa, Ethiopia. Available from http://www.afdb.org/fileadmin/uploads/afdb/Documents/Project-and-Operations/PIDA%20note%20English%20for%20web%200208.pdf.

Alexandratos, Nikos, and Jelle Bruinsma. 2012. *World agriculture towards 2030/2050: the 2012 revision.* ESA Working Paper No. 12-03. Rome: FAO. Available from http://www.fao.org/docrep/016/ap106e/ap106e.pdf.

Barber, D.A. 2014. Africa's poor water infrastructure draws big investments. AFK Insider Online. Available: http://afkinsider.com/77623/africas-poor-water-infrastructure-draws-big-investments/

Branca, Giacomo, Timm Tennigkeit, Wendy Mann, and Leslie Lipper. 2012. *Identifying opportunities for climate-smart agriculture investments in Africa.* Rome: FAO. Available from http://www.fao.org/docrep/015/an112e/an112e00.pdf.

Chang, Ha-Joon. 2015. *Smart industrial policy for Africa in the 21st century.* Paper prepared for UNECA. Addis Ababa, Ethiopia.

Choudhuri, S., and G. B. Dixie. 2015. "A cool tool or flashy toy? The agricultural transformation matrix." Paper prepared for the World Bank. Washington, D.C.

Cilliers, Jakkle, Barry Hughes and Jonathan Moyer. 2011. *African Futures 2050.* Institute for Security Studies. Pretoria, South Africa. Available fromhttps://www.issafrica.org/uploads/Mono175.pdf.

Deloitte. 2014. *Deloitte on Africa: African construction trends report 2014.* Available fromhttps://www2.deloitte.com/content/dam/Deloitte/za/Documents/manufacturing/za_africa_construction_trends_2015_10032015.pdf.

Dickson, B., R. Blaney, L. Miles, E. Regan, A. van Soesbergen, E. Väänänen, S. Blyth, M. Harfoot, C. S. Martin, C. McOwen, T. Newbold and J. van Bochove. 2014. *Towards a global map of natural capital: Key ecosystem assets.* Nairobi, Kenya: United Nations Environment Programme.

Drummond, Paulo, Vimal Thakoor and Shur Yu. 2014. "Africa rising: harnessing the demographic dividend." International Monetary Fund (IMF) Working Paper No. WP/14/43. Available fromhttps://www.imf.org/external/pubs/ft/wp/2014/wp14143.pdf.

Dubey, B., and A. S. Narayanan. 2010. Modelling effects of industrialization, population and pollution on a renewable resource. Mathematics Group, Birla Institute of Technology and Science, Pilani, India. *Nonlinear Analysis: Real World Applications*, vol. 11, No. 4: 2833–2848. Available fromhttps://www.researchgate.net/publication/242999317_Modelling_Effects_of_Industrialization_Population_and_Pollution_on_a_Renewable_Resource.

Eberhard, Anton, Joel Kolker and James Leigland. 2014. *South Africa's Renewable Energy IPP Procurement Program: Success Factors and Lessons.* Washington, D.C.: World Bank Group, Public-Private Infrastructure Advisory Facility. Available from http://www.gsb.uct.ac.za/files/PPIAFReport.pdf.

Foster, Vivien, and Cecelia Briceno-Garmendia, eds. 2009. *Africa's Infrastructure: A Time for Transformation.* Paris: Agence Française de Développement, and Washington, D.C.: World Bank. Available fromhttps://openknowledge.worldbank.org/handle/10986/2692.

Greenpeace. 2015. *Energy [r]evolution: a sustainable world energy outlook 2015*. Greenpeace International, Global Wind Energy Council, and Solar Power Europe. Available fromhttp://www.greenpeace.org/international/Global/international/publications/climate/2015/Energy-Revolution-2015-Full.pdf.

Gustavsson, Jenny, Christel Cederberg, Ulf Sonesson, Robert van Otterdijk and Alexandre Meybeck. 2011. *Global Food Losses and Food Waste: Extent, Causes and Prevention*. Study conducted for the International Congress SAVE FOOD! at Interpack2011, Düsseldorf, Germany, by the Swedish Institute for Food and Biotechnology (SIK), Gothenburg, Sweden, and FAO. Rome: FAO. Available fromhttp://www.fao.org/docrep/014/mb060e/mb060e.pdf.

Hammer, Stephen, Lamia Kamal-Chaoui, Alexis Robert and Marissa Plouin. 2011. *Cities and green growth: a conceptual framework*. OECD Regional Development Working Paper No. 2011/08. Paris: OECD Publishing. Available from http://dx.doi.org/10.1787/5kg0tflmzx34-en.

International Centre for Research in Agroforestry (ICRAF) and United Nations Environmental Programme (UNEP). 2005. *Potential for Rainwater Harvesting in Africa: A GIS Overview*. Available from http://www.unep.org/pdf/RWH_in_Africa-final.pdf.

International Energy Agency (IEA). 2014. *Africa energy outlook: a focus on energy prospects in sub-Saharan Africa*. World Energy Outlook Special Report. Paris, France: OECD/IEA. Available fromhttps://www.iea.org/publications/freepublications/publication/WEO2014_AfricaEnergyOutlook.pdf.

International Labour Organization (ILO). 2013a. *Assessing current and potential green jobs: the case of Mauritius*. Policy Brief. Geneva: ILO. Available fromhttp://www.ilo.org/wcmsp5/groups/public/---ed_emp/---emp_ent/documents/publication/wcms_184298.pdf.

———. 2013b. *Sustainable Development, Decent Work and Green Jobs*. International Labour Conference, 102nd Session. Geneva: ILO. Available fromhttp://www.ilo.org/wcmsp5/groups/public/@ed_norm/@relconf/documents/meetingdocument/wcms_207370.pdf.

International Renewable Energy Agency (IRENA). 2015. *Renewable power generation costs in 2014*. Abu Dhabi, United Arab Emirates. Available fromhttp://www.irena.org/documentdownloads/publications/irena_re_power_costs_2014_report.pdf.

Juma, Dauglas Wafula, Hongtao Wang and Fengting Li. 2014. Impacts of population growth and economic development on water quality of a lake: case study of Lake Victoria Kenya water. National Centre for Biotechnology Information (NCBI). *Environmental Science and Pollution Research International*, vol. 21, No. 8, pp. 5737–5746. Available from http://www.ncbi.nlm.nih.gov/pubmed/24442964.

May, John. 2012. *West Africa: the demographic dividend is not a given*. Global Health Policy Blog. Center for Global Development. Available from http://www.cgdev.org/blog/west-africa-demographic-dividend-not-given.

New Partnership for Africa's Development (NEPAD). 2013. *Agriculture in Africa: Transformation and Outlook*. Available fromhttp://www.un.org/en/africa/osaa/pdf/pubs/2013africanagricultures.pdf.

OneWorld Sustainable Investments (OneWorld). 2015. Accessed and adapted from the Frederick S. Pardee Center for International Futures (IFs), Josef Korbel School of International Studies, University of Denver. Available from http://pardee.du.edu/access-ifs

Petrie, Belynda, Arthur Chapman, Amelia Midgley and Ruth Parker. 2014. *Risk, vulnerability and resilience in the Limpopo River Basin: climate change, water & biodiversity - a synthesis*. Compiled for USAI D Southern Africa Resilience in the Limpopo River Basin (RESILIM) Program by OneWorld Sustainable Investments Cape Town, South Africa. Available from https://www.usaid.gov/sites/default/files/documents/1860/Risk,%20Vulnerability%20and%20Resilience%20in%20the%20Limpopo%20River%20Basin%20-%20A%20Synthesis%20(1).pdf

Pollin, Robert. 2015. *Greening the Global Economy*. Cambridge, MA: MIT Press.

Population Reference Bureau (PRB). 2015. *2015 world population data sheet: with a special focus on women's empowerment*. Population reference manual. http://www.prb.org/pdf15/2015-world-population-data-sheet_eng.pdf.

Sheahan, Megan, and Christopher B. Barrett. 2014. "Understanding the agricultural input landscape in sub-Saharan Africa: recent plot, household, and community-level evidence." World Bank Group Policy Research Working Paper No. 7014. Africa Region, Office of the Chief Economist.

Spalding-Fecher, Randall, Arthur Chapman, Francis Yamba, Hartley Walimwipi, Harald Kling, Bernard Tembo, Imasiku Nyambe and Boaventura Cuamba. 2014. "The vulnerability of hydropower production in the Zambezi River Basin to the impacts of climate change and irrigation development." *Mitigation and Adaptation Strategies for Global Change*, pp. 1573–1596. doi:10.1007/s11027-014-9619-7.

United Nations (UN) Department of Economic and Social Affairs, Population Division (DESA). 2015. *World population prospects: the 2015 revision*. UNDESA Working Paper No. ESA/P/WP.241. New York.

United Nations Environment Programme (UNEP). 2006. *African regional implementation review for the 14th session of the Commission on Sustainable Development* (CSD-14): Report on climate change. Available fromhttp://www.un.org/esa/sustdev/csd/csd14/ecaRIM_bp1.pdf.

United Nations Environment Programme (UNEP). 2007. *The Fourth Global Environment Outlook – Environment for Development Report.* Available from http://www.unep.org/geo/geo4/report/geo-4_report_full_en.pdf

———. 2010. *Africa Water Atlas. UNEP Division of Early Warning and Awareness, Nairobi, Kenya.* Available from-http://www.unep.org/pdf/africa_water_atlas.pdf.

———. 2011. *Towards a Green Economy: Pathways to Sustainable Development and Poverty Eradication.* Nairobi, Kenya. Available fromhttp://www.unep.org/greeneconomy/Portals/88/documents/ger/ger_final_dec_2011/Green%20EconomyReport_Final_Dec2011.pdf.

———. 2013. *Green economy modelling report of South Africa: focus on natural resource management, agriculture, transport and energy sectors. Nairobi, Kenya.* Available from https://www.environment.gov.za/sites/default/files/docs/greeneconomy_modellingreport.pdf.

———. 2014a. *Green economy assessment report: Kenya. Nairobi, Kenya.* Available from http://www.unep.org/greeneconomy/portals/88/documents/KenyaGEassessment.pdf.

———. 2014b. *Green economy assessment study : Senegal. Nairobi, Kenya.* Available from http://www.un-page.org/files/public/content-page/green_economy_assessment_study_senegal_unep.pdf.

———. 2014c. Integrated assessment of the impacts of green investment and policy reforms in Burkina Faso.

———. 2015. *Building inclusive green economies in Africa: experiences and lessons Learned 2010–2015.* Nairobi, Kenya. Available fromhttp://www.unep.org/greeneconomy/Portals/88/documents/GEI%20Highlights/EC_AFRICA_SYNT-REPORT_FINAL_10FEB-c.pdf.

5.6 ENDNOTES

1 In these scenarios the focus is primarily on water because water is the resource on which every other sector depends, to a greater or lesser extent. Water scarcity, even in subregions with good rainfall, is set to continue across Africa, largely because of weak infrastructure. Average water availability per person in Africa is 5,720 cubic metres a year, compared with a global average of 7,600.

2 This is because urban centres connect people to economic opportunity and the kind of jobs that can provide them with a pathway out of poverty.

3 Causality works in both directions. Improved socioeconomic indicators beget lower birth rates, which will amplify progress in other sectors, creating a virtuous circle that can shift the development trajectory even further beyond the GA scenario. That scenario illustrates the effect of slower population growth as it flows through the International Futures (Ifs) system model. Nowhere is this more evident than within the economic and development indicators and environmental indicators, as declining fertility rates relieve some of the pressure on natural resources and service provision.

ANNEX 1

FIGURE 1 THE MODULES AND HIGH-LEVEL CHARACTERIZATION OF LINKAGES BETWEEN MODULE COMPONENTS IN THE IFS

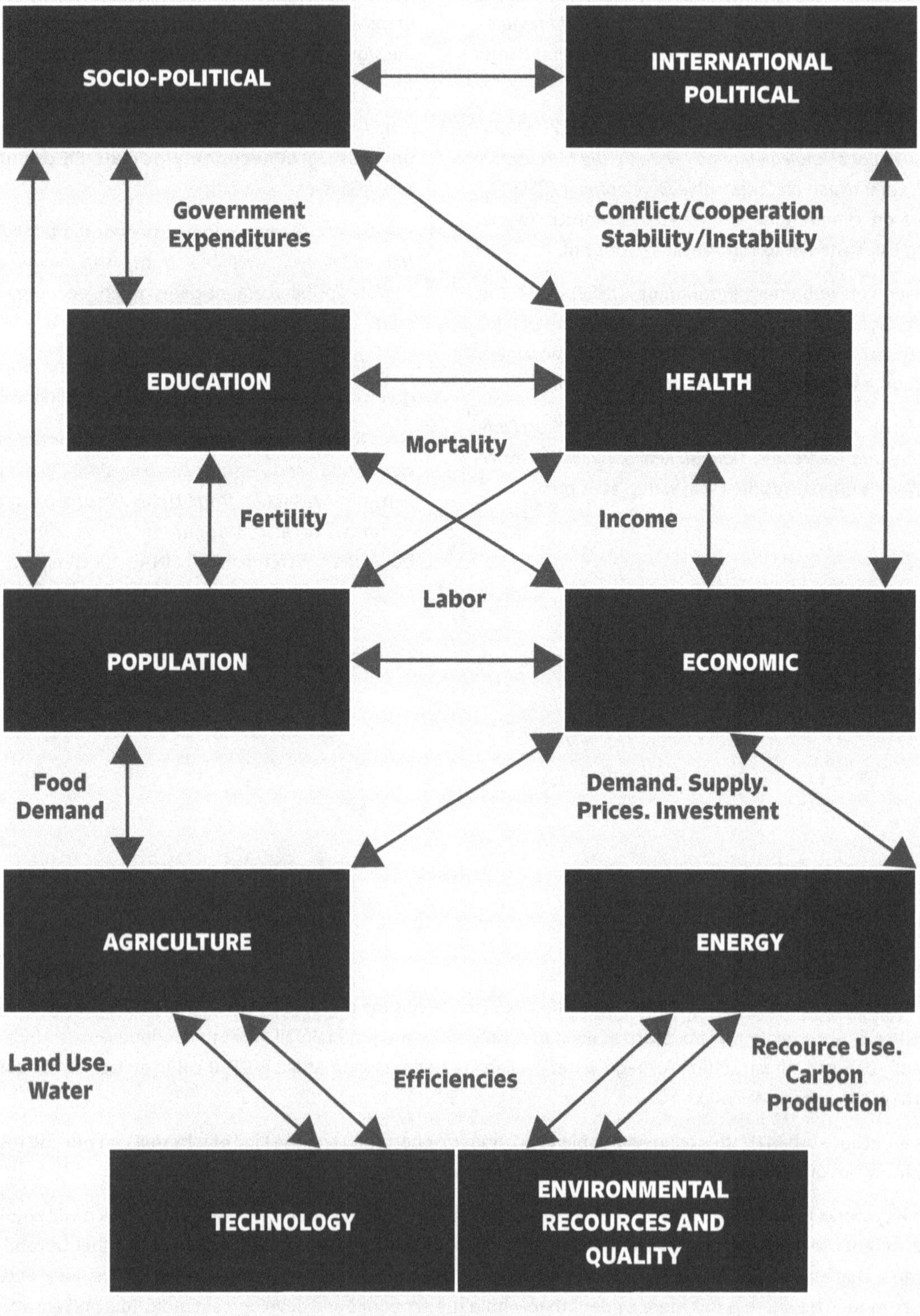

SOURCE: HUGHES (2006).

SCENARIO DEVELOPMENT METHODOLOGY

The numerous linkages in a model like IFs, which is only an abstraction of a much larger set of interlinkages, evolves over time as economists better understand the linkages in the real economies of countries. Typically, those linkages focus on distinguishing the proximal and distal drivers of an outcome (for example, poverty).

CAUTION WITH IFS MODELLING

Models are huge abstractions and simplifications of reality, and all models, by definition, are wrong. Projections by IFs of the future are wrong in that they should not be used as accurate statements of how an issue, country or region will evolve into the future. No one can predict the future. Nevertheless, because of its rich specification and long history of development with well-accepted socioeconomic and environmental relationships, a model can be used as a tool to help think about the future. IFs is used in this context to undertake forecasts using known relationships, with confidence levels surrounding the exact nature of these relationships varying dependant on the quality and quantity of data and the extent to which the model accommodates for context-specific issues.

CHAPTER 6

PROGRESS IN THE GREENING OF AFRICA'S INDUSTRY

A business-as-usual (BAU) industrialization trajectory in Africa not only reduces the rate of growth in the medium to long term but is also unsustainable (Chapter 5). Africa consequently has no real choice if it is to industrialize but to promote the greening of industry—a sometimes difficult path. It will require painful changes in the pricing system (for example, charging users for the externalities involved in energy and water production and in the cost of cleaning up pollutants), which will need appropriate compensatory mechanisms for poorer consumers and producers. However, as this chapter will show, much—not all—industrial greening provides short-term positive returns alongside longer term gains, and some involves heavy upfront costs. Greening also will require changes in attitudes throughout the population, not just the industrial sector.

... much—not all—industrial greening provides short-term positive returns alongside longer term gains, and some involves heavy upfront costs. Greening also will require changes in attitudes throughout the population, not just the industrial sector.

None of these choices are unique to Africa. All economies that pursue a green path of industrialization face the same or similar challenges, but recordable progress is possible even in the short term. In many cases where industry is operating at high levels of inefficiency, industrial greening need not involve short-term trade-offs with slower growth. Instead, greening will enhance productivity and the rate of economic growth. When designed right, greening should also promote social and economic inclusion rather than continued inequitable patterns of growth.

This chapter presents, in 14 case studies, concrete examples of multiple win-win outcomes of green growth and industrialization in Africa. They show that substantial progress has already been made, and that these experiences are replicable across sectors and economies throughout the continent. We lead off with examples of plant-level greening, followed by systemic, sectoral (including agro-industry, energy, water, manufacturing and resource extraction), and then inclusive examples, and we round off with findings on the importance of governments and regulation in greening.

This distinction and links between establishment- and system-level greening were described in Chapter 4, in which we identified three critical systemic components to the green growth agenda: coordinated efforts across sectors; cross-border coordination and decision-making; and coordinated action along the entire value chain. This last component brings transnational corporations (TNCs) and large local firms into the picture because a major driver to greening is consumer demand in final markets, as buyers seek assurance that environmental and social standards have been met along the entire supply chain.

The following examples are based on visits by the ECA team to African countries in late 2015, and comparative evidence drawn from desk research.

6.1 PLANT-LEVEL GREENING

The market has often led to resource de-coupling in African industry (in which output continues to grow but at lesser impact on resource use and the environment), but policy has also been important at this micro-level of industrial greening, as seen in the following two examples.

NATIONAL CLEANER PRODUCTION CENTRES AND THE LEATHER INDUSTRIES OF UGANDA

The United Nations Industrial Development Organization (UNIDO) and the United Nations Environment Programme (UNEP) launched the National Cleaner Production Centre Programme in 1995 with 8 centres, 2 in Africa (Tanzania and Zimbabwe); by 2015 the programme comprised 60 centres worldwide, 14 in Africa.

A recent UNIDO assessment of a dozen industrial plants targeted in five African countries shows successful decoupling accompanied by high economic benefits. Across food, textiles, leather goods, bottled drinks and chemicals, these results show win-win outcomes from the greening of industry. In each of the plants, there are very significant material savings and pollutant reductions, resulting in considerable financial savings (UNIDO, 2015). Resource-efficient and cleaner production (RECP) is a way to achieve such outcomes. RECP includes the application of preventive management strategies that increase the productive use of natural resources, minimize generation of waste and emissions, and foster safe and responsible production. The following example illustrates those gains. (Many similar examples can be sourced at www.unido.org/cp.)

Leather Industries of Uganda Ltd. (LIU) is a private limited liability company established by the Aga Khan Development Network that processes raw hides and skins through to their finished state in Uganda. It has an installed capacity to process 1,000 pieces of raw hides and 5,000 skins per day and exports 95 per cent of its produce around the world. LIU consumes some 600 cubic metres of water a day, releases 99 per cent of the consumed water as effluent and generates about 2,000 kg of solid waste a day, which has to be eliminated. Driven by the objectives of addressing pressing environmental challenges and increasing productivity and competitiveness, LIU decided to implement RECP in the entire processing factory (UNIDO, 2015).

This investment in cleaner production to prevent pollution and reduce resource consumption has proved more cost effective than continuing to rely on increasingly expensive end-of-pipe solutions. Since 2010, RECP in LIU has led to a savings of $2,236,450 against investment of $1,676,121, which represents a healthy return of 133 per cent over five years.

LIU has been able to achieve these improvements as a result of the commitment of top management and team spirit from employees. Notably, cleaner production methods have been instituted in the tanning yard and dye house; in effluent treatment; in waste, energy and chemical management; and in water use (table 6.1). Those changes have also resulted in improved occupational health and safety. The RECP "primer", accompanying calculator and further case studies are at www.recpnet.org, www.unido.org/cp and www.unep.fr/scp/cp, respectively.

TABLE 6.1 LEATHER INDUSTRIES OF UGANDA LTD.: CLEANER PRODUCTION METHODS ADOPTED

Action	Benefits		
	Economic investment ($)	Annual economic savings ($ per year)	Environmental effect
Water management			
Install new drums to replace worn-out, leaking drums	22,000	10,000	Reduced chemical loss
Wastewater management			
Construct a secondary wastewater treatment plant	297,860	500,000	Reduced pollution load and better environmental legal compliance
Materials management			
Recycle chrome and tanning bath solutions	50,000	13,700	Reduction in the chemical pollution load of the effluent
Energy management			
Install iron sheets with translucent sheets in the beam house and tanning yard	280	300	Reduction in input costs
Install energy savers for all lights and security lights	320	8,000	Reduced energy consumption
Raise the main water supply tank and use gravity instead of electric pumps to supply water to the factory	4,000	48,434	Reduction of energy used for pumping water
Solid waste management			
Obtain equipment to process animal feed from by-products and waste Ensure proper treatment and disposal of organic waste	50,000	2,736	Legal compliance; reduced soil and water contamination; odour management; improved aesthetics; reduced public complaints; income generation from sale of feed

SOURCE: UNIDO (2015).

The environment-friendly approach to leather tanning has resulted in conservation of natural resources, such as water and energy, as well as control of environmental pollution through reduced chemical consumption. With better awareness of its effects on the environment, LIU is looking for further cost-effective solutions to conserve natural resources and reduce waste. Some of the possible measures include reducing land requirements for the sludge disposal area by directly applying the sludge on land as fertilizer; reduction of water wastage; using energy more efficiently and reducing energy needs through more efficient processing; and adopting better technologies, such as automated switches on drums.

TRANSFER OF ENVIRONMENTAL SOUND TECHNOLOGY PROJECT IN THE SOUTH MEDITERRANEAN REGION

This project, too, exemplifies what can be achieved through clean production methods. Led by UNIDO's Green Industry Initiative, MED TEST (Transfer of Environmentally Sound Technologies) addresses land-based sources of pollution within industrial hot spots of the South Mediterranean, as part of its Strategic Action Plan (SAP-MED). MED TEST involves a comprehensive diagnosis of enterprise needs, the key outputs of which are to identify and adopt new practices, skills and management approaches, enabling the company to hone its steps to sustainable production.

By 2015, the MED TEST approach had been implemented in 43 companies in six manufacturing sectors in three countries—Egypt, Morocco and Tunisia. In each sector, many resource-efficiency measures and cleaner technology investments have been adopted, including management systems (for example, ISO 14001) that integrate the environmental dimension. The results for Tunisian companies are in table 6.2.

TABLE 6.2 IMPROVED PRODUCTION PRACTICES, 15 COMPANIES, TUNISIA

Company	Size[1]	Investments [USD/year]	Savings [USD/year]	Water Savings [%]	Energy Savings [%]
Food & Beverage Sector					
Générale Industrielle Alimentaires Slama (GIAS)	493	191,200	133,700	12	17
Société de Conserves Alimentaires du Cap Bon	50-250	98,139	73,639	44	9
Tunisie Lait	308	827,410	746,638	16	13
Société de Boissons du Cap-Bon (SBC)	119	56,331	75,454	22	21
Société Nouvelle de Boissons (SNB)	202	29,200	194,600	12	14
Centrale Latiere du Cap nord (CLC)	547	484,945	546,903	13	19
Textile Sector, Finishing					
Teinturerie et Finissae Mediterraneenne (TFM)	55	1,264,645	491,860	56	10
Gartex	185	76,200	67,200	19	15
Megastone	150	76,500	55,600	10	30
Traitex	60	181,800	111,836	19	39
Garment Dyeing Servic	80	139,000	91,300	24	7
Star Wash	40	37,500	28,000	30	14
Leather Sector, Tanneries					
Tanneries Megisserie du Maghreb (TMM)	180	523,000	446,800	14	15
Société Moderne des Cuirs et Peaux (SMCP)	35	287,000	97,200	22	3
Tannerie du Nord Utique (TNU)	50	184,000	125,000	8	70
Total		**4,456,870**	**3,286,530**		

[1] number of employees, 2009

Estimated Environmental Benefits			
Water Savings [m³/year]	**Energy Savings [MWh/year]**	**BOD5 Reductions [tons/year][2]**	**COD Reductions [tons/year][2]**
650,00	**25,083**	**1,610**	**2,762**

[2] BOD5 and COD are ways of measuring organic pollution in the water supply.

SOURCE: UNIDO (2012).

6.2 SYSTEMS-LEVEL GREENING—FORESTS, FARMS AND FOODS

Many green challenges require changes beyond the plant level and at the broader system level—crossing sectors, national borders and value chains—for which we now present examples. Systemic greening is driven by a combination of regulations and final demand (chapter 4). It invariably requires the "governance" of systems greening by one or a few key stakeholders—in some cases, government; in others, a lead firm.

The majority of Africa's population lives in rural areas, and agriculture remains the continent's largest employer. Agriculture is a major source of livelihood for the poor. Greening of the agricultural chain thus has a critical environmental and developmental effect across the continent.

Three examples—timber and wood products, agro-processing and fish farming—show the potential for win-win outcomes because value chain greening offers prospects for entering high-income and niche markets. The importance of final markets in value chain greening diminishes, however, when the final market destination shifts from high- to low- and middle-income markets.

THE TIMBER AND WOOD VALUE CHAIN

Timber and its array of final products form one of the most widespread land-use sectors in Africa and offer multiple livelihood opportunities to millions of African people and enterprises. Forestry is important in greening the global economy, largely because it is a major carbon sink, and deforestation is a big contributor to global carbon dioxide emissions. The pressures on global forestry arise from a mix of non-market demand for household use and of timber commercialization, feeding into national and global markets. Figure 6.1 shows how this value chain spans a range of service, processing and manufacturing subsectors.

Given its importance in all these areas, forestry's importance to greening is unsurprising. Forests also provide a wide range of non-market functions, such as stemming soil erosion, regulating climate and water processes and providing a harbour to enormous reserves of biodiversity.

Forests also provide a wide range of non-market functions, such as stemming soil erosion, regulating climate and water processes and providing a harbour to enormous reserves of biodiversity.

One key driver of forestry's greening comes from high-income markets, in which consumers—individuals or governments—increasingly insist on greening in this value chain. Certification by the Forest Stewardship Council (FSC) provides access to the higher margin niche markets in those economies; it requires systemic greening and a "chain of custody" to verify greening throughout the chain (box 6.1).

In forestry, we can see a clear link between the character of final market demand and pressure

FIGURE 6.1 THE FORESTRY AND TIMBER VALUE CHAIN

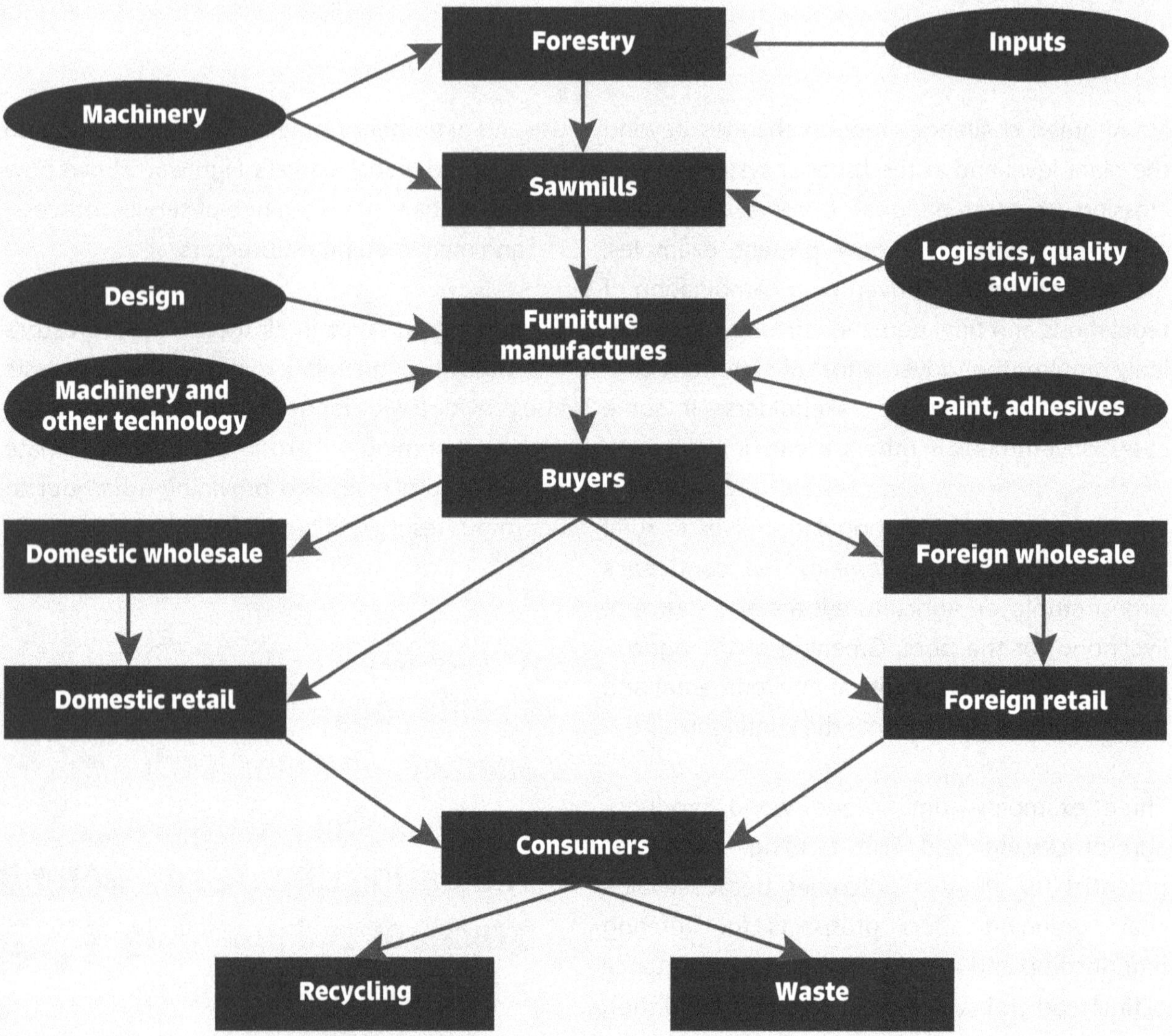

SOURCE: KAPLINSKY, R. AND M. MORRIS (2001).

to drive systemic greening along the chain, but many markets do not exert this greening pressure. Although consumers and governments in high-income economies are increasingly sensitive to social and environmental concerns, the same is not always so in low- and middle-income markets. Take Gabon, for example. Its timber and wood value chain had become a major exporter to the European Union (EU)—historically its dominant market—but from the mid-1990s, rapid demand growth in China led to its supplanting the EU as that market; by 2010, exports to China were, by volume, three times those to the EU. The nature of demand in China (figure 6.2), however, was such that it led to a relative de-greening of the Gabonese timber and wood value chain.

BOX 6.1 FOREST STEWARDSHIP COUNCIL

The FSC was founded in 1993 as an international non-profit organization to support environmentally appropriate, socially beneficial and economically viable management of the world's forests. The creation of an international labelling scheme for forest products provides a credible guarantee that the product comes from a well-managed forest.

The need for such a scheme arose from pressure groups, consumer bodies, indigenous people's movements, environmentalists and governments concerned about the destruction of the world's natural forests and the plethora of unsupervised and poorly based claims that wood products were "environmentally friendly".

The FSC consists of a diverse group of representatives from environmental and social groups, the timber trade and the forestry profession, indigenous people's organizations, community forestry groups and forest-product certification organizations from around the world. Certification takes place through independent, profit-making certification bodies, accredited by the FSC and operating throughout the world, which are evaluated and monitored to ensure their competence and credibility. Certifiers assess forests' operations against a predetermined set of standards developed by the council. This allows wood to be sold in the market as "certified" wood, bearing the FSC trademark logo.

To ensure that all products manufactured from timber reflect this certification, accredited organizations conduct inspections all along the supply chain to verify chain-of-custody systems for products from certified forests. FSC claims that this provides the consumer with a guarantee that the product has come from a forest that has been evaluated and certified as being managed according to agreed social, economic and environmental standards (www.fscoax.org). In many cases, the global lead firms have become the active drivers of high standards through the value chain of demands emanating from civil society. Business takes on responsibilities for ensuring adherence with high environmental and social standards, which typically would be assigned to the state. The state is seen as less well placed to enforce such social and environmental regulations, however, because of weak governance and limited administrative resources.

SOURCE: KAPLINSKY AND MORRIS (2014).

FIGURE 6.2 EUROPEAN AND CHINESE BUYERS' REQUIREMENTS—WOOD LOGS

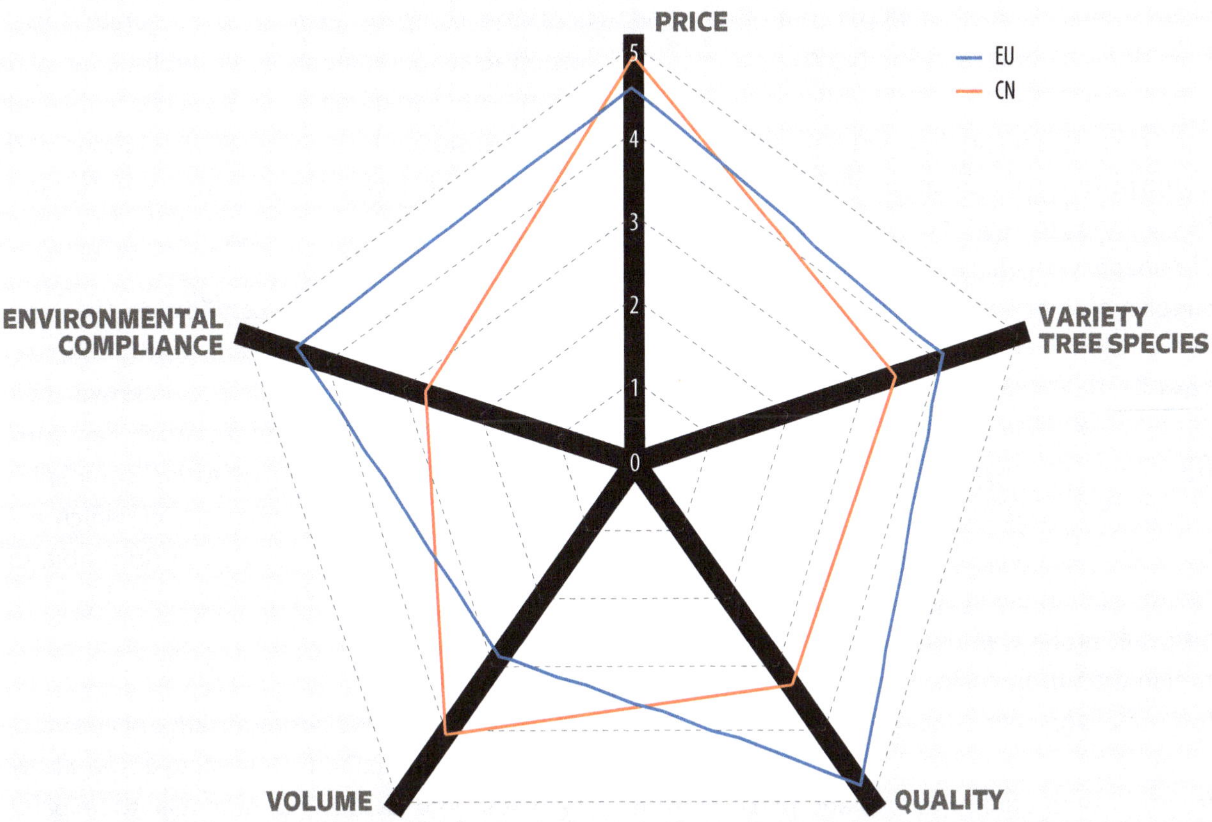

SOURCE: KAPLINSKY, TERHEGGEN, AND TIJAJA (2011).

NOTE: 1 = NOT IMPORTANT; 5 = VERY IMPORTANT.

THE GHANAIAN TIMBER VALUE CHAIN[1]

Successful greening in the Ghanaian timber supply chain has involved four main actors: two timber buyers in the United Kingdom (UK), a timber supplier in Ghana and the Global Forest and Trade Network (GFTN) of the World Wide Fund for Nature (WWF).

Travis Perkins, the UK's number one supplier of building and construction materials, had been criticized by civil society organizations (CSOs) for sourcing wood to be used in major government building projects from suppliers with poor sustainability practices. Work on the renovation of the historic Parliament buildings in London heightened the level of interest and concern about the origin and quality of the wood to be used. The UK government requires that all state-run construction projects use materials from sustainable sources. One of Travis Perkins' biggest suppliers, Timbnet Silverman, the largest importer of hardwood in the UK, sources 40 per cent of its wood from Ghana (Emmet and Sood, 2010).

Samartex Timber and Plywood is a company with a long history in the Ghanaian timber industry and has a long-standing business relationship with Timbnet Silverman. The company is now the lead supplier of sustainable timber in Ghana.

The GFTN is a WWF initiative to pressure large construction corporations to source wood materials from environmentally sustainable supply chains. The GFTN creates links between global corporations and local timber suppliers that are committed to creating green supply chains. The network also uses an independent auditor to certify each firm in the supply chain, according to responsible forest management principles.

In response to public criticism and pressure from shareholders to become more environmentally friendly, Travis Perkins and Timbnet Silverman began seeking solutions to green their supply chain. They pressured Samartex to transform its timber-sourcing practices in Ghana in return for an increase in the price and quantity of wood bought by Timbnet Silverman. In 2004, Samartex signed an agreement with WWF to become the first certified sustainable timber supplier under the GFTN. Since Samartex's successful certification, eight other timber suppliers in Ghana have undergone audits for certification.

GFTN, with the help of the United States Agency for International Development (USAID) and the UK Department for International Development, coordinated and funded the technical assistance required for greening Samartex's supply network. Samartex greatly reduced the amount of damage caused by poor timber felling and hauling practices. The company also built new roads and provided new hauling equipment to reduce the environmental impact of transporting timber. In addition to transforming its environmental practices, the company developed corporate social responsibility agreements and established a joint forum with communities in the area, aimed at finding sustainable development solutions and educating the locals about sustainable forestry practices.

After Samartex received its certification, the company's orders increased $2 million from global timber-supply companies wishing to improve their sourcing practices for tropical timber. Samartex has served as a model for Ghanaian companies looking to achieve GFTN certification, which are largely motivated by the paucity of firms able to meet the increasing demand for sustainable tropical hardwood.

This case study shows the importance of adopting a systemic approach to the greening of the whole chain and the associated potential to expand exports into higher yield niche markets. Pressure for greening was exerted in final markets, and the drivers of this greening process reflected cooperation between foreign lead firms, CSOs and government procurement rules.

Before an industrial plant can be established, a company now must show an environmental and social impact assessment and an environmental and social management plan.

AGRIBUSINESS IN CÔTE D'IVOIRE

In 2011, Côte d'Ivoire adopted a strategy to cut its poverty rate by half and to achieve middle-income status by 2020. It has also given increasing prominence to green growth and, in 2013, established a Directorate for Green Economy in the Ministry of Environment. Before an industrial plant can be established, a company now must show an environmental and social impact assessment and an environmental and social management plan. The Chamber of Commerce and Industry of Côte d'Ivoire has been active in promoting green industrialization.

Growth in the country's gross domestic product (GDP) has been high in recent years, and real GDP per capita increased by 25 percent over the three years 2012–2014, accompanied by a hike in private investment, which grew by 118 per cent over the same period. Côte d'Ivoire is one of the most industrialized economies in Africa, with more than 5,000 industrial enterprises in 2013 which contributed 26 per cent of GDP. The target is to increase that share to 40 per cent by 2020. Manufacturing is dominated by agribusiness, which accounts for 75 per cent of all industrial activity.

Côte d'Ivoire is Africa's largest producer of cocoa, cashews, coffee and rubber; the second-largest of crude palm oil; and the fourth-largest of cotton and pineapples. Processing is low, however, except for crude palm oil and cocoa (table 6.3), which indicates there is major potential for further industrialization through crop processing.

TABLE 6.3 MAIN AGRICULTURAL PRODUCTS, CÔTE D'IVOIRE

Agricultural products	Production 2012–2013 (thousand tonnes)	Rank (in Africa)	Processed domestically (%)
Cocoa	1,671	1	30
Cashews	500	1	5
Crude palm oil	392	2	100
Cotton	350	4	<5
Rubber	290	1	<5
Coffee	104	1	<5
Pineapples	60	4	<5
Mangoes	47	7	<5

SOURCE: MINISTRY OF INDUSTRY, CÔTE D'IVOIRE.

Agricultural crops traded globally are seeing a drive towards green agribusiness, primarily because of final export markets, especially the private sector (mainly leading trans-national corporations (TNCs) selling under global brands). This trend is also present in Côte d'Ivoire. For example, for Nestlé Côte d'Ivoire, greening is not driven by philanthropy but is necessary to ensure that the company maintains access to the high-quality inputs it needs for selling in global final markets. With this rationale, the firm is working with more than 60 cooperatives and more than 28,000 farmers in the Nestlé Cocoa Plan (NCP), under which the company provides training to farmers in its supply chain to improve productivity, the quality of their cocoa, and health and safety on their farms.

The NCP follows a Triple Bottom Line Agenda, combining economic, environmental and social sustainability. The environmental bottom line is addressed through a programme of replanting, with more than 900,000 new seedlings distributed in 2014. Replanting helps to prevent deforestation of new land. Even the plastic bags used for the plantlets are recycled. The NCP also targets social sustainability, and Nestlé ensures that farmers are certified by UTZ or Fairtrade. Nestlé also has put in place a Child Labour Monitoring and Remediation System (CLMRS) that involves 22 cooperatives nationally. Through CLMRS, community liaison officers from farming communities identify the children most at risk and, to combat child labour, the company is building or refurbishing 40 schools. Finally, the company has signed the Women's Empowerment Principles, a partnership between the United Nations Global Compact and UN Women, which is dedicated to gender equality and women's empowerment. From 2013 to 2014, the share of women in decision-making positions in NCP in Côte d'Ivoire's co-ops and farmer organizations grew from 4 to 10 per cent.

Agricultural crops traded globally are seeing a drive towards green agribusiness, primarily because of final export markets, especially the private sector ...

A second agri-TNC, Olam Côte d'Ivoire, sees green industrialization as an opportunity for lower production costs, by which value chain greening reduces the company's environmental impact and lowers reputational risk. Environmental impact is a standard part of Olam's due diligence for new investments and acquisitions, particularly factories or plantations. The company measures its resource use intensity—greenhouse gas emissions and water use in factories—and uses this information to decouple its operation. Olam is affiliated with the Fair Labour Association, which audits Côte d'Ivoire's cocoa supply chains.

A third company, the locally owned Société Ivoirienne de Productions Animales (SIPRA), has developed a major business in poultry production and feed. It has followed an environmental compliance policy since 2012 as a condition for funding from the International Finance Corporation (IFC). SIPRA also developed an environmental and social charter, and an environmental and social action plan, with help from the IFC. Continued IFC financing is linked to the action plan, for which SIPRA produces an annual monitoring report. SIPRA has rationalized its outlets to bring them closer, thereby avoiding costly, time-consuming long-distance transport.

Two of the three agribusinesses show the influence of final market demand on the greening of value chains, while the third demonstrates the power of international funding agencies like the IFC to demand high standards. All three lead firms see a strong alignment between green industrialization and competitive advantage.

Hundreds of fish farms now supply live fish transported through a network of specialized market "queens and mamas"—the network of women acknowledged as the people with the skills to expand and manage these markets by building on a pool of indigenous knowledge.

AGRO-LED INDUSTRIALIZATION: CATFISH FARMING IN NIGERIA

Nearly two decades ago, Nigerian rivers and lakes were producing fewer and fewer catfish—a premium fish product in Nigeria—at a time when demand was increasing. Freshwater fish accounts for approximately 33 per cent of the value and about 14 per cent of the volume of fish consumed in Nigeria. Food consumption patterns have also been shifting, and by 2006, fish consumption exceeded meat consumption in the country (Dixie and Ohen, 2006).

A Nigerian entrepreneur, Ade Alakija, responded to rising demand by studying aquaculture and starting a catfish farming business, Durante Fish Industries Limited, which originally sourced catfish stock and water-recycling systems from Holland. The firm refined the farming systems while selling catfish and subsequently diversified into selling feed, fingerlings, and other varieties of fish, including tilapia (although catfish is still the primary fish product). Throughout this process, Durante built the foundation for a new farming sector, making continuous improvements and expanding into different activities within the catfish value chain. Durante is a fully integrated business that, in addition to fish products, offers a full range of services, including advisory services and franchise systems to mid-scale farmers. It is one of Nigeria's leading fish-farming businesses (NRI, 2014).

Greening the supply chain has taken place gradually in response to unreliable supplies of energy and water, and a cost-driven need for power, transport and water efficiencies. Durante shifted away from tank culture to pond and cage culture because of power cuts and water constraints. The firm has invested great effort in increasing the energy efficiencies of its fish-farming processes and systems and in introducing water-recycling features (NRI, 2014). Durante found ways of transporting live fish to distribution points along routes frequented by business people on their way home, cutting the need for energy-intensive, costly refrigerated vehicles while expanding the market.

Women are important for the catfish supply chain. Other Nigerian entrepreneurs have started to introduce and refine catfish-farming systems, such as flow-through systems and cage farming. Hundreds of fish farms now supply live fish transported through a network of specialized market "queens and mamas"—the network of women acknowledged as the people with the skills to expand and manage these markets by building on a pool of indigenous knowledge. The products are consumed in restaurants or cooked at home. Offshoot businesses have been created in catfish drying, carried out by micro-businesses around Lagos, using renewable energy

The aquaculture sector in Nigeria produces about 250,000 tonnes of farmed catfish, generating aggregate farm gate income of approximately \$500 million a year, as well as an equivalent amount in the value chain. The water-recycling systems are yielding attractive rates of return: they have a capital cost of \$150,000 and a payback period of 18–24 months. Analytical studies and support to increase market access were conducted by the IFC, USAID, the World Bank, and the Food and Agriculture Organization of the United Nations (FAO), and that helped this new industry to emerge.

High rates of urbanization, population growth and a growing middle class continue to boost the market for catfish. These growth trends are expected to continue (see the scenarios in Chapter 5). Important market linkages have been established, thus generating inclusive economic growth as profits and benefits circulate throughout the local economy. Women, as the market and Buka-café "queens" in Nigerian social structures, are among the primary beneficiaries. A USAID-funded study found that for every 10 tonnes of catfish produced, seven jobs are generated, six of them for women (Dixie and Ohen 2006). By 2006, the catfish industry had generated an estimated 15,000 jobs, a figure that is estimated to have nearly tripled since (Dixie, personal communication, 2015).

What began as one firm seizing a market opportunity has grown into a new, thriving industry that capitalizes on indigenous expertise, seeks continuous improvements in greening the value chain and is experiencing a growing level of dynamism and competitive advantage. It is a highly replicable model of agro-led industrialization, home grown in Africa. Greening is evident through the industry's search for greater water, energy and transport efficiencies and its use of sustainable technologies in private-led enterprise development. It is a useful example of how local economic growth can be achieved through a green approach to agri-food industrialization which needs to be central to African economic growth, and feeding of urban populations.

6.3 THE ENERGY SECTOR

The energy sector is not just a vital foundation for productive employment throughout Africa. Energy access and cost play a major role in people's health, consumer welfare and inclusive development. Here, too, win-win outcomes between greening and inclusive growth are possible to observe—in the production of biofuels in Malawi and renewable energy in Kenya, Morocco and Rwanda. Examples from Nigeria and South Africa demonstrate the vital role of government in framing policy to draw private investment into the renewable energy sector.

BIOFUELS IN MALAWI

The transport sector plays a key role in Malawi's national development. As a land-locked country, Malawi depends greatly on land transport to move people and goods, and fuel is 10 per cent, by value, of the economy's imports. Transport costs in Malawi are the highest among countries in the Southern African Development Community (SADC). They account for up to 56 per cent of landed import costs and 30 per cent of export costs, increasing the cost of imported consumer goods and hurting Malawi's regional trade competitiveness. More than 70 per cent of internal freight traffic and 99 per cent of passenger traffic is handled by road transport. The average consumption of petrol and diesel in the transport sector is 1 million litres a day, making it the largest sectoral consumer of liquid fossil-fuel energy. Transport accounts for 3.8 per cent of the country's energy consumption and 43 per cent of its commercial energy consumption (Government of Malawi, 2015).

The hike in oil prices in 1973 that threatened to derail economic growth triggered investment in ethanol blending in Malawi. A second oil-price shock in 1979 provided a further incentive. Coupled with the outbreak of the civil war in Mozambique, whose seaport provided access to imported commodities, Malawi suffered an unprecedented crisis of shortages of refined petroleum products. This shortage generated social unrest, loss of people's time in long queues for fuel, and significant losses of income, especially for farmers and for small and medium-sized enterprises.

The government believed that these shocks amounted to a national security crisis. It considered diversifying its sources of petrol and modes of supply to be critical in establishing greater energy security. The government further demanded that the National Commission for Science and Technology consider the local production of ethanol-blended fuel. (This coincided with similar initiatives in Brazil and Zimbabwe.) Private sector firms, especially the sugar companies, were challenged to seize the opportunities for investment in such blending. One outcome was a national biofuel policy that involved a public–private part-

[The government] ... considered diversifying its sources of petrol and modes of supply to be critical in establishing greater energy security.

nership from the outset. The government set the policy framework and provided the incentives and infrastructure, within which the private sector could respond. The leading investor was Press Corporation Limited, a publicly listed company incorporated in Malawi.

The feedstock for bio-ethanol is molasses, a byproduct from sugar production. The first ethanol plant was built by Press Corporation in 1982, with a final blending ratio of 10 per cent, and in 2004, they opened a second plant, with a combined total capacity of 18 million litres a year. However, currently, both plants operate at 50 per cent of capacity, as a result of inadequate molasses feedstock, much of it imported from neighbouring Mozambique. The blending ratio today is 20 per cent, which constitutes the maximum ratio that does not require mechanical adjustment of the engine (nor technicians to fit the required conversion kits to vehicles). In Malawi, fuel prices are regulated by an automatic pricing mechanism, with the price of ethanol linked to that of fossil fuels.

The Malawi government commissioned a second study on the possibility of vehicles running purely on ethanol, which was carried out by the National Commission for Science and Technology. The results, submitted to the government in 2012, concluded that vehicles can indeed run on 100 per cent ethanol. With an increasing shift towards ethanol blending in the liquid fuel use of Malawi, the current relationship between fuel imports and ethanol use (figure 6.3) is likely to change, even with an increasing number of car owners and users in the country.

The long-standing government policy commitment presents a sound business case for private sector investment in ethanol production and blending. Press Corporation also seeks deeper integration in the liquid energy value chain, and is in partnership with Puma Energy Malawi to distribute liquid fuels in the latter's filling stations. Puma has become the launch pad for commercializing 100 per cent ethanol use in cars. This includes an advisory service for consumers seeking to buy cars that rely on ethanol.

FIGURE 6.3 FUEL IMPORTS AND ETHANOL PRODUCTION TRENDS, MALAWI (1000 BARRELS PER DAY)

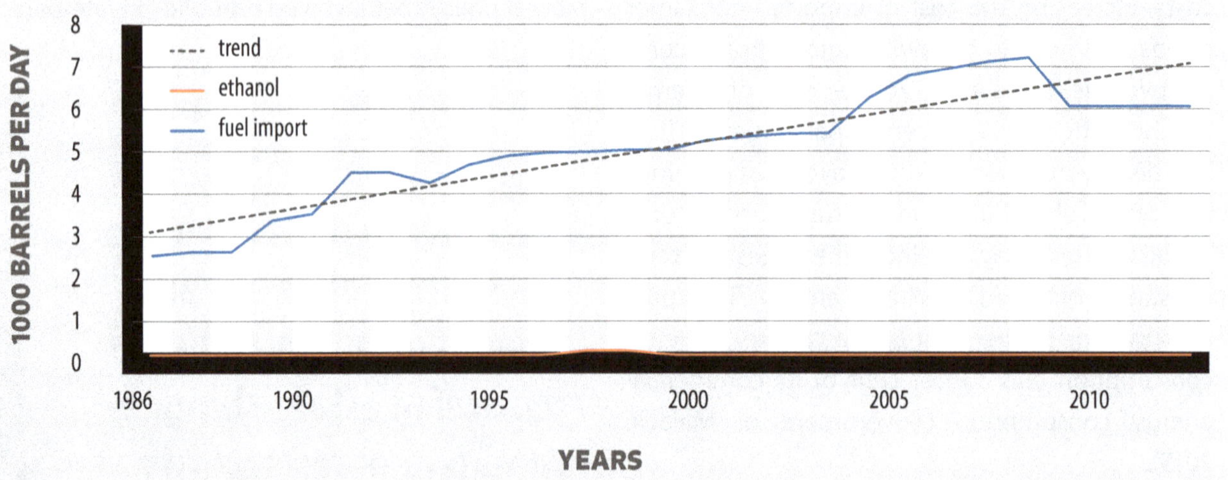

SOURCE: EIA (2015).

In the run-up to the Paris Climate Summit, the Government of Malawi announced plans to expand bio-ethanol production from 18 to 40 million litres/year under its climate mitigation plan (Government of Malawi, 2015).The government's goal is to alter the current trajectory of greenhouse gas emissions from liquid fuels, which are projected to increase from 290,000 to 420,000 million tons of carbon dioxide equivalents between 2015 and 2040. The ambition is also to increase bio-diesel production from 2 million to 20 million litres a year so that 5–7 per cent of all vehicles will be running entirely on ethanol by 2020.

However, because ethanol production is restricted by a shortage of feedstock, the government has established a Greenbelt Initiative to encourage sugar cane production by smallholders, using contract farming arrangements that safeguard the interests of smallholders in a buy-back scheme. The long-term interest of the government is to steadily wean farmers off tobacco production, which had been the country's major cash crop, because tobacco's export value is declining and the domestic market is small. More than 4,200 ha of sugar cane are expected to be developed using smallholder-grower schemes in partnership with Press Corporation.

The development of ethanol as a green feedstock is an attempt by the government to improve fuel security and create viable incomes for smallholders. By pegging the price of ethanol to the price of oil, these objectives can be met without raising the cost to consumers, even in times of low oil prices. Meeting these greening objectives in ethanol production, however, requires integration along the chain (ethanol production, distribution and car conversion), as well as systemic coordination between the agricultural and industrial sectors. Government regulations and strategic policymaking have been the principal drivers of this value chain greening.

The long-term interest of the government is to steadily wean farmers off tobacco production, which had been the country's major cash crop, because tobacco's export value is declining and the domestic market is small.

SOLAR ENERGY IN RWANDA[1]

Rwanda has made impressive headway in inclusive growth over the past decade. Under the Economic Development Poverty Reduction Strategy (EDPRS, the economy has grown at an average 8 per cent a year, which has translated into a fall in inequality, a significant reduction in absolute poverty and an increase in life expectancy from 43 to 64 years (WHO, 2016).

The government recognizes the importance of mainstreaming climate change—not only in its Vision 2020 and EDPRS 2 but also in its sectoral strategies. It introduced the National Strategy on Climate Change and Low Carbon Development in 2010/11 to mainstream climate resilience and low-carbon development into key sectors. Its long-term strategy, "Vision 2050", aims to transform Rwanda into a developed country, with a strong service sector, low unemployment and low poverty rates. This strategy also envisages that agriculture and industry will have a minimal negative impact on the environment, operating sustainably and enabling Rwanda to be self-sufficient in basic necessities (Republic of Rwanda, 2011).

FONERWA (the national environment and climate fund) was established in 2012 as the engine for green growth in Rwanda. It attracts and streamlines climate finance with the national strategy and leverages private investment for low-carbon initiatives. Putting FONERWA into operation has been a strategic move to facilitate access to international climate finance, especially Fast-start Finance for adaptation. Under the National Strategy for Climate Change and Low Carbon Development (2011), there is a programme of action focusing on the Low Carbon Energy Mix Powering the National Grid. The programme proposes the introduction of renewable energy feed-in tariffs and the promotion of public–private partnerships. Another programme of the National Strategy encourages small-scale energy installation, especially in rural areas, to promote access to electricity and reduce dependence on wood fuel. Rwanda intends to use public funds to serve as the guarantee for investment in electricity-generation projects and to introduce terms that will attract private investment in energy (Republic of Rwanda, 2013).

The government sees electricity generation as a critical factor for socioeconomic development and the main vehicle for diversifying the economy. It aims to achieve 70 per cent access to electricity by 2017—a substantial increase from 19 per cent in 2012—and to increase electricity-generation capacity more than tenfold, from 100 megawatts (MW) in 2012 to 1,160 MW by 2017. The estimated investment needs are at least $500 million a year. About $200 million a year is planned to come from the public sector and $300 million from the private sector (AfDB, 2013).

The programme proposes the introduction of renewable energy feed-in tariffs and the promotion of public–private partnerships. Another programme of the National Strategy encourages small-scale energy installation, especially in rural areas, to promote access to electricity and reduce dependence on wood fuel.

To achieve these objectives, the government envisages two main scenarios: accelerated and delayed. The former would need investment of approximately $4.2 billion from 2013 to 2017 (an annual $845 million). The latter requires an estimated $2.5 billion for 2013–2017 ($510 million a year), which would then continue at the rate of $550 million a year (AfDB, 2013). Potential sources of financing for this expansion include electricity tariffs, government budgets, development partners, the private sector and revenue from the Rwanda Energy Group.

The strong direction taken by government policy has provided the framework for a range of investments. One is a solar field funded by Gigawatt Global, Norway's Investment Fund for Developing Countries (Norfund) and Scatec Solar and backed by US President Obama's Power Africa Initiative. The $23.7 million project is the first utility-scale, grid-connected, commercial solar field in East Africa. The field generates 8.5 MW and has increased Rwanda's power-generation capacity by 6 per cent. Construction began in February 2014 and was completed by July. It produced an estimated 15 million kilowatt-hours in its first year, sending power to a substation 9 km away. The solar field is linked to a central server in Oslo, Norway, and can be monitored remotely via the Internet. The project is built on land owned by the Agahozo-Shalom Youth Village, whose mission is to care for Rwanda's most vulnerable children orphaned before and after the genocide. This lease provides the biggest source of income to the six-year-old village, currently home to 512 young people, who are offered schooling and extracurricular activities (Guardian, November 23rd 2015).

Rwanda's progress in renewable energy is embedded in a larger, systemic framework that invests in the provision of inclusive, decentralized production of green energy technologies. This programme is driven primarily by the Rwandan government but seeks to build into its development greater private sector participation. International agencies and external support—regional and global—are important components of this greening programme.

MOROCCAN SOLAR ENERGY

A large concentrated solar power plant was completed in central Morocco, near Ouarzazate in 2015. Covering the equivalent of 35 football grounds and generating 160 MW in phase 1, it works by concentrating heat from the sun using parabolic mirrors to generate heat in turbines, from which electricity can then be generated.

Morocco is the only North African country with virtually no fossil-fuel resources. In 2009 the country imported 97 per cent of its energy needs, at a cost to the state of Dh62 billion ($6.2 billion) a year. With rapid growth in energy demand, Morocco needed to take a decisive step in a new direction (Financial Times, 23 November 2015).

The driving force behind this investment has been the commitment of the government to use its enormous solar potential. A specialized agency was set up, MASEN, the Moroccan Agency for Solar Energy. This first phase of the project, Noor-Ouarzazate, will be followed by two further phases, which together should take capacity to 500 MW, enabling Morocco to obtain more than 40 per cent of its electricity from renewable sources by 2020.

Funded by a consortium including the EU, the World Bank, European Investment Bank, African Development Bank (AfDB), Germany's Kreditanstalt für Wiederaufbau and Agence Française de Développement, it has been built by a Saudi Arabian construction company. Projects like that at Ouarzazate could also offer a secure supply of renewable energy to neighbouring Europe, especially Germany, where nuclear power is being phased out.

GEOTHERMAL ENERGY IN KENYA

Only 16 per cent of Kenya's population currently has access to electricity, and demand outstrips supply. The national grid is unreliable and costly, in part because hydropower is frequently interrupted by drought and is, in the long term, vulnerable to climate change. Geothermal power has the potential to provide reliable, cost-competitive power with a small carbon footprint. If the ambitious target of producing 5,000 MW from geo-thermal sources by 2030 is achieved, this form of energy from east Africa's Rift Valley could power 15 million homes (Guardian November 22nd, 2013).

Geothermal resources in Kenya are along the Rift Valley and have estimated potential of 7,000–10,000 MW at 14 prospective sites. Kenya has been leading other countries in the region by complementing investment in Olkaria's geothermal power plants with policies designed to make this energy transition as efficient as possible. The country's links to other geothermal countries, especially Iceland, have also enabled knowledge sharing to improve technologies, geothermal training and education.

By 2015, the 70 per cent state-owned Kenya Electricity Generating Company (KenGen) had built three plants to exploit the Olkaria geothermal resources. Kenya aims to acquire 5,530 MW of geothermal power (26 per cent of total power generating capacity) by 2030, making it the largest source of clean energy. As a share of national power, by 2030 geothermal power in Kenya could reach the same level as in the world leader, Iceland (CDKN, 2014).

The government has been the main driver of investment in geothermal energy, and it formed the Geothermal Development Company (GDC) following agreement of the 2006 Energy Act to assume the high upfront risks of exploration and deployment. The government is providing considerable financing for the programme through budgetary allocations and infrastructure bonds. It has provided $399 million for the three ongoing projects and has helped facilitate loans. For the three projects, a combination of grants and loans have been committed from the World Bank $222 million, the European Investment Bank $204 million, and AfDB $120 million. The GDC is designed to become financially self-sustaining by generating revenues from the sale of energy, progressively relieving the government of the burden of funding. GDC's projections indicate that it will require investment of $2.57 billion in the next 10 years, $1.52 billion from accrued revenues (Ngugi, 2012).

Investments in geothermal power are embedded in a wider programme to increase foreign investment. Kenya Electricity Generating Company (KenGen) and independent power producers (IPP) are projected to raise $12 billion for investment in several power plants, whereas GDC, supported by the government, will raise $6 billion. A considerable investment gap of more than $18 billion remains, however in the power sector. A key concern for investors is whether these projects are bankable, in terms of project viability and risk. In an attempt to ease investors' anxieties, the government has liberalized the exchange rate and created an independent judiciary.

The government provides incentives in the form of full cost recovery of investment through power purchase agreements, steam supply agreements, feed-in-tariff policies and government guarantees. Another undertaking is a commitment to $166 million in partial risk guarantees to reassure investors concerned about state-owned electricity use and its obligations towards them. Further, Kenya has structured its geothermal power-generation prices to afford a reasonable return to private investors and adequate funds for the government entities.

Finally, KenGen receives carbon credits from the World Bank's Community Development Carbon Fund for investing in renewable energy, since it displaces higher carbon sources in the national grid (World Bank 2013). The fund pays KenGen a premium on the credits, but in return requires that part of the revenue from the credits be used for social co-benefits. The money from the sale of carbon credits is used to build schools and finance training to educate students in the skills required in tapping geothermal energy, which has stimulated investment from the private sector.

The expansion of green geothermal energy in Kenya is driven by the state, and supported as a systemic initiative by a range of complementary policies, including those designed to attract foreign direct investment. Still, the government's long-term aim is that green energy will involve strong participation from the private sector.

TRADE-OFFS AND CHOICES FOR ENERGY IN NIGERIA[1]

The government has pursued strategies to promote greener industrialization, even though no formal green industrialization policy exists. Energy security is perhaps the most critical challenge to industrialization in Nigeria, green or otherwise. The government employs a mix of instruments to decouple economic growth from environmental pressures, including command and control regulations and self-regulation by industries.

Shortage of electricity remains the critical bottleneck to industrialization. With levels of power generation of just over 4,000 MW and demand exceeding 10,000 MW, Nigeria faces a huge gap. The Renewable Energy Master Plan intends to increase the share of renewable energy in electricity production from the current 13 per cent to 23 per cent by 2025 and 36 per cent by 2030. Although the government plays a major role in defining such a strategy, in practice the difficulties faced by major industries in securing energy for their activities mean that a significant expansion of coal-fired electricity supply is under way, alongside long-standing reliance on diesel-fuelled generators.

The government of Nigeria recently announced measures to stimulate demand for renewable energy in electricity production and distribution, under the National Renewable Energy and Energy Efficiency Policy, which entered into force in 2015. The government has adopted a renewable energy feed-in tariff (REFIT), which requires electricity-distribution companies to source 50 per cent of their total electricity from renewable energy producers. In addition to assuring a market for renewable energy, REFIT has established guaranteed prices through 20-year power purchase agreements that provide stable income and returns on investment. Tariffs offered are technology specific, varying by renewable energy source and by scale. For automatic integration into the grid, REFIT targets electricity generated from small plants of 1–30 MW. Plants greater than 30 MW will be subject to competitive bidding. By 2020, it is hoped that growth in renewable energy generation will be achieved through additional capacity in solar (387 MW), wind (412 MW), small hydro (675 MW) and biomass (526 MW). Were it to be achieved, this new capacity would make a significant contribution to energy availability, as it compares with total installed capacity of 7,500MW, and average generating capacity of 3,800MW. Different regions in the country have been mapped and allocated REFIT quotas based on their comparative energy potentials.

Investors have shown strong interest in the renewable energy and efficiency sector. The solar sector has received a major boost ...

For the Nigerian biofuel industry, the government has developed a biofuel program to avoid distorting food production and food security. The Nigerian Biofuel Programme is led by the Nigerian National Petroleum Company, with the goal of helping the domestic ethanol fuel industry to take off. As with Malawi, the programme aims to blend up to 10 per cent of fuel ethanol with gasoline to attain an E10 blend. The programme aspires to achieve 100 per cent domestic production of biofuels consumed in Nigeria by 2030.

Investors have shown strong interest in the renewable energy and efficiency sector. The solar sector has received a major boost with the November 2015 announcement by Access Infra and Quaint Global Energy Solutions of a \$100 million solar project of 50 MW capacity. Dangote Group Cement Plc, a large Nigeria-owned cement company, established its sustainability strategy in 2015 to coincide with the company's expansion into other regions of Africa. This strategy aims to "attain carbon and dust emission resource efficiency performance in line [with], or above, peers in the industry, and implement a reliable and systematic assurance and sustainability reporting system" (dangote.com).

The Nigerian government is adopting a broad approach towards energy provision. Coal-based energy is expected to rise significantly to 2040 (IEA, 2014), but the government has simultaneously introduced policies designed to achieve greater energy decoupling through the industrial sector and to expand the production of renewables. The government is the driving force, given the scale of the challenges faced and the gap between current capacity and untapped demand.

BENEFITS OF RENEWABLE ENERGY DEVELOPMENTS IN SOUTH AFRICA

A combination of skills, markets, resources and pragmatic policy instruments are accelerating uptake and investment in renewable energy in South Africa, offering a sustainable opportunity for mitigating the energy crisis in the country and the related economic fallout.

Renewable energy resources (solar, wind, and biomass) are abundant in the country, which is partly why the National Development Plan, launched in 2012, included a 21 per cent target for renewable energy supply by 2030. Budgetary constraints and rising electricity tariffs for households, however, meant that this target had to be achieved at no cost to the government or to electricity consumers. A highly pragmatic policy instrument was needed. The result was a green procurement programme designed to provide significant incentives to private investors seeking new markets, to integrate the financial services sector (which is relatively robust in South Africa) and to ensure rural development and community benefits.

Competitive energy pricing has been made possible by steep price falls in renewable energy technologies globally, and the procurement programme's competitive rolling-bid process.

The Renewable Energy Independent Power Producer Procurement Programme (REIPPPP), was launched in 2011. Having completed its fourth round in 2015, it has channelled substantial private expertise and investment into grid-connected renewable energy at competitive prices (Eberhard, et al., 2014), at no additional cost to consumers. Government expenditure is limited to off-take and tariff guarantees (underwriting part of the risk). The processes followed by government have transferred other major risks to the private sector (high penalties for underperformance, Environmental Impact Assessments, technical assessments, expensive bid bonds, and so forth), thus discouraging more inexperienced energy companies from putting forward proposals. The government has also encouraged the financial sector to develop the skills needed to support the major role to be played by domestic energy firms..

Competitive energy pricing has been made possible by steep price falls in renewable energy technologies globally, and the procurement programme's competitive rolling-bid process. Although round 1 in 2012 did not see much in the way of competitive pricing in bids, in subsequent rounds, greater competition meant that project selection could focus on the top projects in price, technology and socioeconomic benefits.

This investor-friendly programme has realized valuable social and economic benefits. South Africa's Council for Scientific and Industrial Research (CSIR) (2015) found that these renewable energy investments had created $400 million in financial benefits, including the following:

- A large increase in foreign direct investment (FDI) in South Africa—of the cumulative $20 billion total investment between rounds 1 and 4, 28 per cent was foreign, amounting to 85.8 per cent of all FDI in 2014;
- A large contribution to decentralized energy delivery—South Africa is now the 10th biggest solar market in the world for installations of less than 5 MW, which offers a shift towards more decentralized energy delivery models;
- Reduced load shedding;
- Reduced carbon emissions (by the equivalent of 4.4 million tonnes of carbon dioxide);
- Creation of 109,000 jobs (and more to come)—the renewable energy sector is expected to create 462,000 jobs by 2030;
- A manufacturing boost—the new solar photovoltaic plant in Durban employs 160 people, and the solar tower facility in Atlantis employs 200;
- Stimulation of research and public–private partnerships, establishment of research chairs and centers for renewable and sustainable energy studies at South Africa's top universities and the Battery Research Unit at the CSIR, funding by the government and private sector of the RE Technology Centre to train technicians to service renewable energy projects;
- Communities' ownership of 10.5 per cent of renewable energy projects (the required minimum is 2.5 per cent);
- Expected net income of $290 million over 20 years; and
- $1.1 billion in goods and services to be procured by 2030 from Black Economic Empowerment (BEE) suppliers.

Since the first request for proposals in 2011, local content requirements for project bids have grown, resulting in the emergence of new manufacturing activities in renewable energy components. In the photovoltaic industry, for example, local content (measured by share of total project spending) increased from 53 per cent in round 1 to 65 per cent in round 2. The trend is expected to continue. As REIPPPP continues, price competition is expected to level out, increasing emphasis on higher local content contributions for winning bids. In response, solar manufacturers have set up bases in South Africa, increasing employment from 13,000 full-time employees in round 1 to 26,000 in round 4. International investors are increasingly viewing South Africa as a potential manufacturing hub and entry point into the nascent renewable energy sectors of other African countries.

Critically, the success of REIPPPP, particularly in considerably lowering the cost of entry for renewables, is also stimulating the development of other IPP models in South Africa (and replicable outside the country). An entrepreneurial renewable energy company, Tombolo Energy, is developing the IPPs that underpin decentralized renewable energy models. The company's vision is to build localized energy networks by creating agreements directly with municipalities and large consumers. It is building on precedents established by innovative power agreements in the country, such as that between Amatola Green Power and Nelson Mandela Bay Municipality, a deal that includes a 20-year off-take agreement with BHP Billiton South Africa for renewable energy credits.

Another spin-off is the establishment of a local wind turbine manufacturing plant that brings world-recognized German technology developed by Aerodyn GmbH to Cape Province, South Africa, under licence to manufacture locally. The company, I-WEC, is a joint venture between two local entities, Tawk Energy (40 per cent) and IWECON (60 per cent). In addition to creating jobs for local economies (2 people employed for every single turbine produced), I-WEC's local manufacture of wind turbines and blades will be exported to neighbouring countries and reduce the impact of exchange rate volatility for developers.

The renewable energy developments in South Africa over the past five years reach far and range wide, to include new jobs and skills, circulation of financial benefits in local economies, improved national and local energy security, emission reductions, foreign investment, and welcome changes to the regulatory environment—not least of which is the facilitation of decentralized energy generation. With market demand for renewable energy going from strength to strength and rising local and foreign investment, every indication is that the central role of renewable energy for green industrialization—and its co-benefits—will ratchet up.

6.4 THE WATER SECTOR

THE TRANSBOUNDARY CUBANGO-OKAVANGO RIVER BASIN

The Okavango River Basin is in Southern Africa, spans the three countries (Angola, Botswana and Namibia) and provides water for a population of some 922,000 in the immediate region—a figure expected to increase to more than 1.67 million people by 2025 (OKACOM, 2015). Because of its relatively pristine state, the basin is of global interest, and the Okavango Delta, in the Botswana portion of the basin, is the third-largest designated wetlands site on earth, recognised as such by the international Ramsar Convention. The delta, as a major global tourist attraction, is a hefty contributor to Botswana's economy, generating $866 million a year in tourism income (Murphy, 2013). It is also a source of diverse livelihoods (such as farming, fishing, tourism services, and basket weaving) for the many ethnic groups dependent on it.

As one of the world's largest inland water systems, the basin is a critical shared natural resource for its riparian countries. The Okavango River is the only exploitable perennial river that flows through countries of Botswana and Namibia ...

As one of the world's largest inland water systems, the basin is a critical shared natural resource for its riparian countries. The Okavango River is the only exploitable perennial river that flows through countries of Botswana and Namibia (OKACOM, 2015). It is also a rich but fragile source of biodiversity and is of regional and global importance.

Although Botswana derives significant socioeconomic benefits from the basin, Angola has the largest portion of it, with 48 per cent of the basin's area; Botswana has 15 per cent and Namibia 37 per cent. The source of the Okavango is in the Angola highlands, so Angola's development decisions have fundamental consequences for the downstream riparian countries. Since Angola's civil war ended in 2002, the country has become increasingly dependent on water abstraction from the Cubango-Okavango River System as a means to boost economic growth and enhance the livelihoods of its population (SAIIA, 2014). Although permanent water scarcity does not threaten the basin overall, the river swells and contracts with regular, periodic flooding; economies and tourism are heavily dependent on the basin's biodiversity. Regular flooding is an essential event for the delta because it supports the ecological system that provides the foundation for tourism, biodiversity and livelihoods.

The Okavango Watercourse Commission (OKACOM) was set up in 1994 to provide a vehicle for joint management and coordination. Through promoting regional cooperation and sharing benefits, OKACOM aims to reduce unsustainable activities in all three countries and prevent development activities that exceed the constraints of the system, while enhancing the ecosystem services of the basin for the benefit of all riparian countries (OKACOM, 2015). The institution strives to deepen cooperation to ensure that the three countries define and respect those system thresholds, or the upper limits of sustainable abstraction.

Although donor funding supports OKACOM, cooperation is primarily attributable to the political will of all three countries. Historical political alliances have formed trust, which is still a key success factor, primarily because those alliances encourage a shared vision among the countries, facilitating water policy in a way that preserves the ecological integrity of the basin and protects the system's socioeconomic benefits. One example of important transboundary cooperation is that all three countries have ratified the UN Framework Convention on Climate Change, the UN Convention on Biological Diversity, the UN Convention to Combat Desertification and the Southern African Development Community (SADC) Revised Protocol on Shared Watercourses; Botswana and Namibia have also ratified the Ramsar Convention (OKACOM, 2015).

Still, the cooperative basis on which the basin is managed is under threat from three drivers: climate change and the consequent increased variability in rainfall and water flows; population pressure: and economic expansion.

Still, the cooperative basis on which the basin is managed is under threat from three drivers: climate change and the consequent increased variability in rainfall and water flows; population pressure: and economic expansion. They are systemic drivers of change that, together, could destabilize political alliances, as countries believe that they have no choice but to focus more on their national interests. Solutions require adoption and alignment of green policies by all the riparian countries. Those policies include climate change adaptation plans; compatible water, environmental and development plans; innovative approaches to payment for ecosystem services; and pre-emptive conflict management. Thus, trade-off analyses and consultations must deepen further and consider the long-term nature of costs and benefits flowing from choices made today.

Management of this water basin is inherently systemic, crossing national boundaries and affecting the growth of the services and agricultural sectors. The drivers of coordinated intergovernmental action are a proactive concern for this ecosystem, which is vulnerable to climate change and over-abstraction. The key governance bodies of this systemic response are governments rather than the private sector.

GREENING THE MARITIME CHAIN IN MAURITIUS

Greening the maritime chain in Mauritius is progressing well. Policy initially was a response to comply with international standards for marine safety and pollution prevention, but it has matured into a strategic vision for how the maritime system can provide multiple green development opportunities. The sector accounts for more than 10 per cent of Mauritian GDP, and its constituent subsectors—of which tourism and hospitality are the most important—span a range of sectors, including fishing, transport, agriculture and services (figure 6.4). The maritime sector provides many jobs and is an important driver of inclusive development.

Critical to the vision that drives government policy is its green identity, observable in a range of individual policy initiatives, including the exploration and exploitation of hydrocarbons and minerals from the seabed, the hospitality sector, fisheries, renewable energy, marine technologies, international transport and the provision of water for sustainable agriculture.

The green maritime vision was catalysed by proactive adherence to a set of green standards and conventions from the International Maritime Organization (IMO), notably the following:

- The International Convention for the Safety of Life at Sea (SOLAS) 1983, which defines minimum standards for the construction, equipment and operation of ships. They cover aspects such as design specifications for oil tankers and carriage of cargoes, including dangerous goods. A flag state—a state in which a vessel is registered—has to ensure compliance with a series of environmental requirements for ships operating under its jurisdiction. SOLAS also has a port state control provision, through which contracting governments can inspect ships of other

FIGURE 6.4 OCEAN ECONOMY AS A PERCENTAGE OF GDP, MAURITIUS

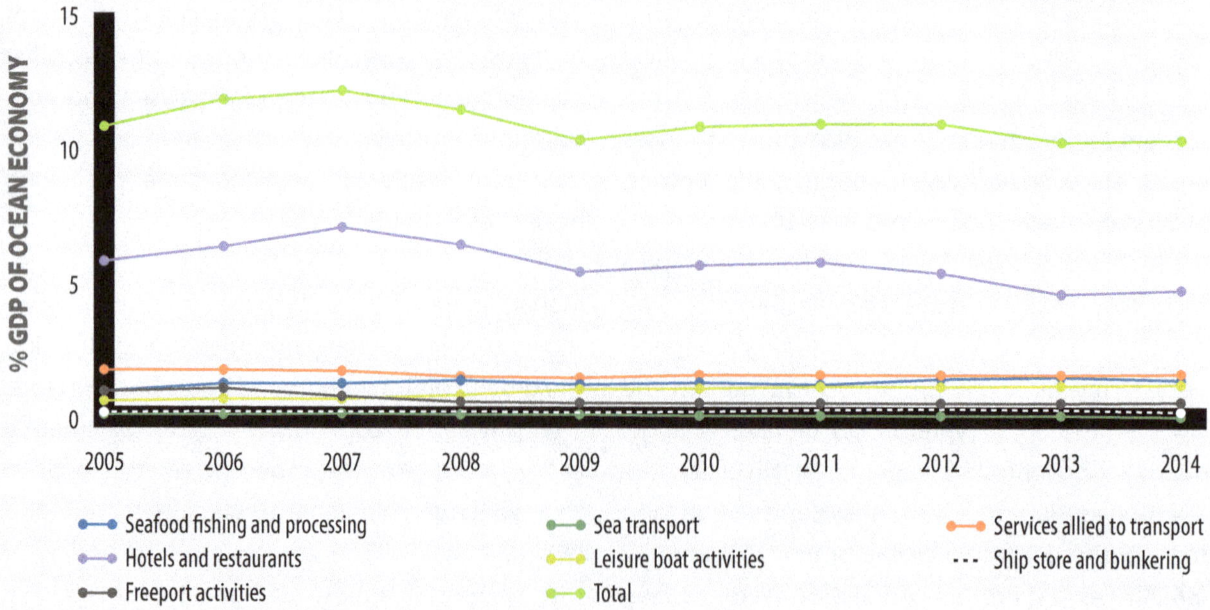

SOURCE: STATISTICS GOVERNMENT OF MAURITIUS, ECA ANALYSIS (2015).

contracting states in case of doubt regarding non-compliance. This power of inspection has provided a growing source of revenue to Mauritian port-based companies.

- The International Convention for the Prevention of Pollution from Ships (MARPOL, short for "marine pollution") 1973, which defines regulations aimed at preventing and minimizing pollution from ships. It covers pollution that is accidental and that happens through routine operations, such as pollution by oil, sewage, garbage and noxious liquid substances from ships.

- The Convention on Standards of Training, Certification and Watchkeeping for Seafarers (STCW) agreed in 1978, which defines basic requirements for mariners. Countries must at least meet these standards. STCW is crucial in building the required skills and capabilities and increasing employability in important marine sectors, such as general provisions, the engine department, master and deck departments, and emergency, occupational safety and medical care and survival departments.

Compliance with the IMO and similar standards has led to significant progress in greening the maritime transport chain. Some of the green practices that have emerged include using energy-efficient engines and less polluting fuels to control nitrogen oxide and sulphur oxide particulates and other noxious emissions, waste management methods, and skill- and capability-building standards to ensure safety at sea and green stewardship of the sea. These developments have resulted in Mauritius being included in the IMO's "white list" of 127 nations that are in full compliance with the regulations. (Countries not on the list may find their ships denied entry into ports, detained or subject to very close inspection.)

Beyond the marine sector are its linkages to the economic hinterland. The country's export-oriented industrial sector feeds into global and

Some of the green practices that have emerged include ... ... standards to ensure safety at sea and green stewardship of the sea

regional value chains; 84 per cent of exports go to high-income economies, such as those in the EU. This requires environmentally compliant transport chains, particularly for ships flying the Mauritian flag, which has now gained a strong international reputation for complying with high standards in environmentally sensitive global maritime trade. Those green credentials have allowed Mauritius to become a platform for ship registration, trans-shipment, fuel storage, ship repairs and related activities, allowing it to take full advantage of its oceanic location.

Mauritius has therefore seen a shift from environmental compliance as a response to IMO standards to adoption of a green vision for managing its ocean resources—the "Blue Economy". This vision is supported by legal, strategic and policy frameworks, such as those that follow:

- **Maurice Ile Durable (MID).** This strategic framework embraces five development pillars: energy, equity, employment, education and environment (the "five Es"), aiming to sustainably harness the social, ecological and environmental landscape of Mauritius.

- **The Ocean Economy Roadmap.** This document outlines how the Blue Economy will be harnessed sustainably. It covers mid- and long-term priority areas and enablers.

- **Related laws.** Those laws include the National Oil Spill Contingency Plan; Environment Protection Act; Marine Pollution Bill; Port Master Plan; Fisheries and Marine Resources Act; National Coast Guard Act; Maritime Zones Act; and Continental Shelf Act. Each targets a green agenda—not just as an act of compliance but as a strategic area for sustainable income growth and employment.
- **Greening agendas.** They are supported by government subsidies to the Mauritius Maritime Training Academy, which aims to boost the stock of skills and employability of young people in the marine sectors.
- **Resource mobilization.** One aim is to develop the Port Louis Harbour into a regional maritime hub for services such as fish processing, maritime transport and ancillary businesses.

The greening of the Mauritius maritime chain is systemic, not just in spanning the different economic maritime subsectors but also in greening logistics in export-oriented global value chains. The driver initially came from the government's desire to comply with international conventions and standards, as discussed, but increasingly the commercial benefits flowing from the greening of the maritime system have attracted a wide range of private actors.

Focusing on the higher returns in green niche markets, private firms—national and foreign—are seizing those opportunities and pursuing corporate strategies that provide for sustainable growth and profits and that create jobs throughout the economy (in the maritime-related hospitality sector, for example). A holistic approach is required to implement this vision and has led increasingly to policies among the Ministry of Ocean Economy, Marine Resources, Fisheries, Shipping and Outer Island; the Ministry of the Environment, Sustainable Development and Disaster and Beach Management; and the Mauritius Ports Authority. The government has been central to the design of this strategic vision and of associated policy, such as the Ocean Economy Roadmap. The private sector is increasingly pivotal to implementation.

6.5 THE RESOURCE SECTOR: WATER AND SUSTAINABLE MINING IN SOUTH AFRICA

South Africa is a water-stressed country. It is projected to experience a 17 per cent gap between water demand and supply by 2030. The risks associated with this growing gap and the pressures on supply from unprecedented environmental impacts are becoming a major concern to businesses in the country. Leading companies are increasingly recognizing that current approaches to water management are no longer sufficient, and those companies are waking up to the challenge that responsibility for water management cannot be left solely to government.

One corporate initiative is the annual South Africa Water Report, part of the international Carbon Disclosure Project (CDP) Report that summarizes annual surveys of the way business is addressing major environmental issues. Fifty-eight of the 100 top companies listed on the Johannesburg Stock Exchange took part in the 2014 survey. The Carbon Disclosure Project (CDP) Water Report indicates that a large number of companies experienced detrimental water-related impacts during the previous 12 months, including declining water quality, flooding and drought, government regulation of discharge volumes, increased water stress and high water prices. The CDP Water Report also illustrates some of the response strategies that companies are putting in place to address water-related risks and impacts, and it highlights examples of how companies are partnering with non-governmental and governmental bodies in water stewardship.

Historically, most of South Africa's industrial development and wealth are associated with extractives. Mining accounts directly for about 9 per cent of the country's GDP (19 per cent if related activities are included), about 50 per cent of the country's merchandise exports, and 35 per cent of the value of the Johannesburg Stock Exchange (CDP, 2014). Mining employs half a million people directly and another half a million indirectly, accounting for 1 million of the 8 million people formally employed in South Africa.

Coal mining is the largest contributor to mining value added. In 2013, 72 per cent of South Africa's primary energy consumption came from coal, and that is unlikely to change much in the decades to come, primarily because of the country's lack of investment in alternatives. South Africa is the fourth-largest producer of coal globally, and with more than 100 years of proven coal reserves remaining, coal is set to remain a valuable resource if the current business-as-usual scenario continues. Coal mining imposes severe demands on water resources, given its huge uptake of water and its pollution impacts, so it is an important challenge for greening (albeit partial greening because coal is the least green source of energy), with water efficiency and pollution management important entry points.

One coal mining company—Exxaro Resources Limited—provides an example of how the corporate sector can green its activities. Established in 2006, Exxaro is one of the largest diversified resource groups based in South Africa. Listed on the Johannesburg Stock Exchange, its current business interests span Australia, South Africa and the Republic of the Congo. Its capital expenditure programme is dominated by the coal-based business in South Africa, from which it produces more than 39 million tonnes of coal a year. The firm employs more than 7,500 full-time employees, with about the same number employed by contractors. Of its full-time employees, 17 per cent are women, compared with the industry average of 11 per cent.

Exxaro's business is based on a "five capitals model" (natural, human, social, manufactured and financial), which seeks a balanced approach to sustainable growth. The company considers sustainability not as a separate objective but as an input into and an outcome of its operations. It seeks to add value to these capitals throughout the lifetime of every mining operation, with the intention of leaving each area holistically richer after mine closure. Each stage of the mining value chain, referred to as the resource-to-market business model, is thus designed to leave a cumulative net positive effect.

For Exxaro, water is a strategic natural resource, critical to its business. It therefore promotes water resource management with this consideration built into its plans. Exxaro has launched initiatives to conserve water at all sites, adopting an overall strategy to manage water-related risks, minimize impacts, and operate through reduction, reuse and recycling. It participates in the CDP Water Disclosure Project surveys. Exxaro has partnered with the government's Department of Water and Sanitation and the Chamber of Mines through a steering committee to set water-use efficiency targets for the mining sector. The company achieved all its 2013 targets, which included 5% savings in potable water used, a cut in water intensity, and an increase in the proportion of water re-used and re-cycled over the previous year.

Exxaro has also prepared a water conservation plan that supports the national water strategy to ensure equitable distribution of water resources while enabling business growth and promoting sustainable use. The company seeks to enhance the protection and improvement of water quality by ensuring that the water discharged from its operations is of the same quality as or better than the original consumed. This informs the company's policy and strategy on mining and wastewater management in preventing pollution; in minimizing environmental impacts; and in maximizing water reuse and reclamation, responsible water discharge and disposal, and water treatment.

The company has developed a management standard on water for mining and industrial use that articulates its commitment to implement integrated water and waste management plans. The standard applies to the full lifecycle of a mine, including planning, construction, decommissioning, closure and rehabilitation. The water management programme entails water-use and related risk issues—from security of supply for operations to water efficiency and water-cost management—and manages those components within the framework of current and expected regulatory requirements.

In addition to three- to five-year goals, Exxaro pursues aspirational goals that include becoming self-sufficient in operational water needs and becoming a leader in water technology solutions. Its research and development department, with the University of the Free State, is evaluating innovative passive water treatment systems as a long-term solution to water management, including post–mine closure.

This example of a corporate commitment to environmental stewardship reflects the interplay of systems, markets and chain governance. Exxaro recognizes the need to focus on the whole value chain. It shows how green industrialization can be driven by a nationally owned lead firm that is responding to concerns expressed in financial markets about the nature of its environmental impact. It also shows the complexity of the greening challenge because it illustrates the challenge of greening an intrinsically high-carbon, non-green economic activity.

6.6 MANUFACTURING EXPORTS: ETHIOPIA'S HAWASSA ECO-INDUSTRIAL PARK (OQUBAY 2015)

Ethiopia has had annual GDP growth of 10.5 per cent from 2005-2014 (WDI, 2015). Although its economic take-off has been based on agriculture, it has recently focused on manufacturing for sustaining rapid growth and structural transformation. The country also has focused on long-term infrastructure, in particular energy, and transport to which it has allocated almost 60 per cent of its capital budget. In 2015, Ethiopia set a goal to achieve fourfold growth of manufacturing output by 2025, which entails attracting new investment and industrial infrastructure.

Ethiopia is a latecomer to industrialization—and to industrial parks. In 2015 it had four industrial zones, three of them foreign-owned. The Eastern Industrial Zone at Dukem, the Lebu Industrial Zone which is owned by Huajian Group and Modjo Industrial Zone owned by George Shoe. Only one Industrial Park is owned by the government; the Bole Lemi Industrial Zone. Hawassa Industrial Park is situated 275km south east of the capital. While these parks have created 11,000 jobs, they have generated insignificant export earnings to date. The government decided that its 2025 vision must be based on a thorough understanding of industrial parks and investment promotion. It thus commissioned policy research on industrial parks, with a focus on countries that have used industrial parks for industrial catch-up, notably China, the Republic of Korea, Singapore and Vietnam in Asia, and Mauritius and Nigeria in Africa. The state is the driver of the industrial park programme, and the lead organizations are the Ethiopian Investment Commission and the Industrial Parks Development Corporation.

Ethiopia has targeted manufacturing for its industrial parks, focusing on priority sectors. Choice of investor is based on a close understanding of final markets and the role played by lead firms in the value chain. Initial engagement started with the two largest US buyers in the textile and apparel industry. The 10 leading Asian manufacturers were then approached, with the intent of building a vertically integrated value chain, including production of high-quality cotton (ginning, spinning and weaving), establishment of fabric mills and output of garments. The country also aims to attract a network of support industries and accessory manufacturers.

Ethiopia has targeted manufacturing for its industrial parks, focusing on priority sectors.

Understanding the nature of the industry and the requirement of the clients has been essential. Construction of this specialized industrial park—Hawassa Eco-Industrial Park—was started in mid-2015 to host the leading firms, to be completed in nine months. The location was selected because of the competitive labour cost, skills and physical infrastructure. The design of the park has been focused on the needs of the lead buyers in global textiles and apparel. The layout and design of buildings draw from the latest standards developed in the industry, such as those established by the US Customs authority after the September 11, 2001, terrorist attacks, to ensure security of trade, and safety at work, after the fire disasters in Bangladesh textile factories in April 2013. A one-stop government service has been introduced to cut red tape and improve the business environment. The China Civil Engineering Corporation, a leading construction company is building the park as a turnkey "design and build" project. Efforts are being made to generate positive spill-overs by integrating the industrial park with the city of Hawassa and contribute to a stronger service sector. Studies are being conducted to design resource-efficient housing units, to accommodate local workers.

The Hawassa Eco-Industrial Park is nested within Ethiopia's green economy strategy. Ethiopia has also sought to leapfrog global competition by using the green identity of the park to provide a competitive advantage over rivals from Bangladesh and China. The green industrial park recycles water, uses LED (light-emitting diode) and intelligent lighting systems, plants trees, and uses natural ventilation and lighting. To achieve zero pollution—and making it one of the first such industrial parks globally to do so—the park has adopted state-of-the-art "zero liquid discharge" technology, reflecting its similar reliance on 100 per cent renewable energy. Ethiopia is just completing Africa's first electric-driven railway network, from the capital Addis Ababa to the port of Djibouti, and a spur will be constructed to link Hawassa with this mainline, to ease transport from the industrial park.

All future industrial parks in Ethiopia are to be green, and will be based on the design of Hawassa Eco-Industrial Park. Even before formal opening in early 2016, Hawassa has registered 100 per cent occupancy and by 2017 will have 60,000 workers (75 per cent of them expected to be female), and with gross export earnings of $1 billion anticipated. Of the 10 leading international firms investing in Hawassa, two manufacturers each come from India and Hong Kong; one each from Sri Lanka, Indonesia, Taiwan and China; and a couple are local firms. Ethiopia aims to employ 2 million workers in a dozen export-oriented industrial parks by 2025.

Hawassa Eco-Industrial Park aims to show how targeted manufacturing investment in a world-class green industrial park will generate manufacturing jobs, increase export earnings, build production capabilities and generate spill-overs to the domestic economy. It is hoped that the success of the programme will follow from a deep engagement with and understanding of the requirements of final buyers. In the case of Hawassa, the Ethiopian government early recognized commercial and economic rewards to greening the value chain as an instrument of competitive advantage. Understanding the global value chain and the structure of each industry and focusing on lead firms has been challenging but is proving essential for obtaining commitment.

6.7 INCLUSION AND GREENING

Africa faces a dual challenge of promoting green and more inclusive forms of industrialization (chapters 3 and 4). Those efforts usually require discrete but complementary top-down actions by governments. Some cases exist, however, in which a natural, market-led and bottom-up co-evolution of development occurred, as with the Kumasi Hub recycling project in Ghana.

Enterprises have tended to evolve into specialized operations or producers, and some small engineering workshops emerged, producing new or reconditioning old parts.

MAKING, MENDING, REPAIRING—GHANA'S MECHANICS IN KUMASI (SCHMITZ, 2015)

Africa's biggest recycling hub, in Ghana, illustrates the strength of a circular economy that seeks to reuse and recycle valuable metals and machinery. This vehicle repair and metal-working cluster in Suame, a constituency in the Kumasi Metropolitan district, is remarkable for its scale and the technical skills available. Recycling has been practised here for more than 30 years and involves huge numbers of people working in individual enterprises that, together, have the ability to mend and re-build old vehicles.

The collective effect of the thousands of small workshops is remarkable (Schmitz, 1990). This agglomeration of small producers and traders, known locally as the Magazine, coalesced in part because of the unavailability of imported materials and spare parts, which necessitated people to repair and recycle—in particular, cars, lorries and small buses. Local workshops found ingenious ways to prolong the life of vehicles. Enterprises have tended to evolve into specialized operations or producers, and some small engineering workshops emerged, producing new or reconditioning old parts. None of these workshops could have existed in isolation, but together they achieved an impressive collective efficiency that helped to stop the transport system from collapsing.

In the 1980s, the Suame Magazine provided earnings to approximately 40,000 people; 30 years later, some 200,000 work there, in perhaps 12,000 businesses. Earnings in the cluster are a little better than in most other parts of the local economy. Some entrepreneurs have become rich, employing dozens of apprentices.

The cluster has specialized to cope with the challenge of electronics—which on new vehicles control the windows, door locks, fuel injection and other functions—and greater ease in importing spares. Although the skills base of the cluster lies primarily in mechanics, some workers have acquired skills in electronics; a few work at the larger workshops, but more are self-employed, providing their electronics expertise to other workshops. For example, an electronic diagnostic—to identify where the problems lie—costs 50 cedis ($12.50). Sometimes the repair can be rectified by replacing faulty components (bought from specialized traders); sometimes the electronically controlled part is replaced by a mechanically controlled part.

Second-hand reconditioned engines are widely available in the cluster. Lorries and cars are stripped down and then reassembled with reconditioned parts—or, where required, with new parts, such as plugs, gaskets or piston rings. A problem that seems unsurmountable for one workshop may become an opportunity for another.

The Suame cluster of recycling businesses was not established, nor has it been driven, by green objectives. Planetary boundaries and resource depletion are not subjects for discussion among members of this cluster. Instead, the concerns are focused on making a living or a profit by offering cost-effective transport solutions for the local market. Recycling is a mere by-product of such concerns.

Local scarcity and poverty are thus the drivers of recycling in Ghana. What is special about Suame is that local enterprises do more than just collect, sort and sell materials. They deepen the value chain by remaking a finished product from recycled materials or by providing a complete service. Thus, although Ghana's capital city Accra has a cluster of auto-parts traders in Abossey Okai, Kumasi has a cluster of both traders and makers in Suame, making the Magazine particularly interesting from the perspective of resource efficiency and urban livelihoods.

LOCAL CONTROL AND INCLUSION IN GREENING THE FORESTRY SECTOR (IIED 2015)

The forestry sector is important for green industrialization through different types of interventions, such as greening forest-related value chains and establishing sustainable forest management. When locally controlled forest enterprises implement those interventions, many benefits for inclusion arise. Such local control can offer a viable solution to address complex demands on forests during industrialization by helping local businesses transform their activities better to meet market opportunities. Local control helps them, for example, secure land and resource tenure; form larger coalitions and achieve economies of scale and the power of collective bargaining more easily; invest in programmes that strengthen business know-how; and revitalize technical extension services and deliver local and global public goods.

Many initiatives around the world are shifting towards a more local approach to generate inclusive livelihoods and respond to weak governance in the forestry sector. The Forest Governance Learning Group (FGLG) initiative is an informal alliance of 10 in-country groups of partners, including 7 from Africa (Cameroon, Ghana, Malawi, Mozambique, South Africa, Tanzania and Uganda). The FGLG thematic areas focus on strengthening forest rights; supporting small forest enterprises; encouraging trade in legal forest products; and advocating for pro-poor climate change mitigation and adaptation through forestry.

For example, in Cameroon, the FGLG took actions to increase the rights for very small forest enterprises to access, process and market forest products.. It made forest governance more effective by involving all stakeholders, certifying forest products, increasing employment via local processing, fighting corruption (through new anti-corruption cells) and supporting environmental decentralization in giving a greater role to civil society. In Malawi, the FGLG consortium of partners has aimed to bridge the gap between the well-designed forest policy and its weak implementation on the ground, formal recognition of the "illegal" charcoal trade, and strengthening village based management of local forests and associated revenues (Mayers 2014, Sibale et al., 2014).

The Forest and Farm Facility (FFF), hosted by FAO (Food and Agriculture Organization of the United Nations), works with FGLG to encourage investment in locally controlled forestry. The facility recognizes four preconditions to attract investment into forest enterprise: secure commercial tenure; solid business capacity; sound technical extension; and effective producer groups. The FFF works by strengthening forest farm producer organizations, operating through global, regional and national federations, representing more than 200 local forest and farm producer organisations, with more than 40 million members. In terms of business development by forest farm producers, more than 100 enterprises now produce for a wide range of markets- timber, bamboo, rattan, textiles, fisheries, fruit juice, honey, craftwork, nuts, cinnamon and cardamom and other non-timber forest products. Business takes time to develop and service provider organisations play a key role in helping enterprise develop and grow, as do international exchanges amongst forest enterprises, from which new technical or business practices are transferred (Macqueen et al., 2015).

As with Ghana's recycling cluster, this example from local forest enterprise shows that inclusion can be integrated into green industrialization through a locally grounded strategy—here, as part of a wider programme of linking local initiatives across African forestry. It also shows how such integration can be achieved by linking producers to potential investors and to the enabling institutions, such as those which secure land rights, and offer technical support, required to draw in such investment.

Business takes time to develop and service provider organisations play a key role in helping enterprise develop and grow, as do international exchanges amongst forest enterprises, from which new technical or business practices are transferred (Macqueen et al., 2015).

The key stakeholders in the inclusive greening of the timber value chain are governments in Africa and Asia, cooperating closely with international and local civil society organizations (CSOs). Market forces alone seem unable to facilitate the inclusive greening of these and similar chains; hence, the change calls for a combined approach.

6.8 SYSTEMIC GREEN INDUSTRIALIZATION: LESSONS FOR GOVERNMENT

We observed at the start of this chapter the significant gains to be realized from discrete investments in greening at the level of individual manufacturing establishments in Africa. Although the examples given were all drawn from manufacturing, greening gains could similarly be evidenced in agriculture and services.

The greening challenge cannot be limited to these micro-interventions, though; to be successful, green industrialization must necessarily target the greening of systems. Systemic greening may span sectors, countries and value chains, but because it involves complex interconnections, we must understand the primary drivers to systemic greening and the key stakeholders who make it possible.

Table 6.4 summarizes the evidence of the 14 case studies in this chapter. Each shows systemic processes at work. In some cases the systems cross national boundaries, such as the Cubango-Okavango River Basin. They may also cut across economic sectors (the water and marine sector, agro-forestry and agri-food processing, bio-ethanol, the Cubango-Okavango River Basin) and ministries (Kenyan geothermal, Ethiopian industrial parks). Characteristically, these greening case studies also cut across value chains (forestry, the resource sector and industrial eco-industrial parks).

Three primary drivers of green industrialization stand out. In the case of public goods, such as infrastructure—energy and water— incentives, investment and government vision are critical and are the primary driver of systems greening, as with the renewable energy examples and the marine sector in Mauritius. In some cases, the vision is driven by governments acting in concert, as with the Cubango-Okavango River Basin. By contrast, in the productive sector, the primary drivers of green industrialization are final markets, in which consumer demand, environmental activism by CSOs and government regulations force greening along the value chain. There are also good examples of publicly funded programmes which have helped firms achieve major improvements in resource use efficiency and cuts in pollutant discharge.

A variety of primary stakeholders are involved in these cases. As with the drivers of greening, in the infrastructure sector governments (often aided by external donors) are responsible for requiring industrializing along green lines. Where market pull is the primary driver, the key implementers are lead firms (not always foreign owned, as can be seen from the examples of Exxaro in South Africa, SIPRA in Côte d'Ivoire and Dangote in Nigeria), sometimes responding to pressure from, or cooperating with, international CSOs.

A green industrialization agenda cannot, in short, be pursued by one set of stakeholders alone. CSOs, government, the private sector (domestic and foreign) and development partners and funders must act in concert.

The lessons from these case studies help to define the policy options and recommendations for promoting green industrialization in Africa. As seen from table 6.4, the government will always be a key player in setting the wider vision, putting in place consistent and credible incentives for private investment, ensuring delivery of key public goods—energy and water—and creating a shared platform for stakeholders to build a green agenda

TABLE 6.4 MAJOR STAKEHOLDERS AND DRIVERS IN SYSTEMIC GREENING

Case study	Systemic component	Greening drivers	Greening stakeholders
Timber value chain—Gabon and Ghana	Greening from forest to consumer	Consumer pressure in high-income final markets and CSOs	Lead TNC buying firms and local and foreign domestic producers
Agribusiness in Côte d'Ivoire	Greening of value chains	Final markets in high-income economies; foreign donor conditions.	Lead TNC and local firms
Catfish farming in Nigeria	Greening of fish supply chain	Local consumers; urban demand	Small entrepreneurs testing new processes
Bio-ethanol in Malawi	Coordination between retail, industrial and agricultural sectors	Government policy	Mainly government, with growing private sector participation
Rwanda renewables	Government policy and investment fund	Government policy	Commercial investors in solar, with strong state backing
Kenya geothermal	Combined government policy, crossing ministries and sectors	Government policy; foreign donors	Mainly government, with growing private sector participation
Nigerian renewables	Systemic approach towards energy decoupling and renewable production	Government policy	Mainly government, with growing private sector participation
South Africa renewable energy	Combined government policy	Falling photovoltaic-cell prices; high demand for energy; funders ready to invest	Government-set framework for investor opportunities, multiplying jobs and economic benefits
Cubango-Okavango River Basin	Cross-border water management; integration of agricultural and service sector needs	Governments aware of fragility of ecosystem and risks to commercial exploitation of resources	Intergovernmental action
Mauritian Blue Economy	Systemic approach towards marine and water sector	Government policy	Mainly government, with growing private sector participation
Exxaro resource sector	Greening of water in the value chain	Market pressure and corporate commitment	Domestically owned lead firm
Hawassa Eco-Industrial Park	Greening of the value chain	Competitive advantage in export markets	Government, with mainly foreign-owned lead firms
Recycling in Ghana's vehicle industry	Greening through supply and service activities	Foreign exchange and spare parts shortages	Thousands of small informal enterprises, working as a cluster
Inclusion in forestry	Inclusion in value chain; cooperation across national borders	Government policy; CSOs; market pressure	Government, private sector and CSOs

SOURCE: AUTHOR'S COMPILATION.

NOTE: CSO = CIVIL SOCIETY ORGANIZATION; TNC = TRANSNATIONAL CORPORATION.

together. Equally clear is the importance of CSOs, external donors and the private sector to this endeavour.

In the final chapter, this report considers the steps required to turn a vision of green and inclusive industrialization into reality—a feat that entails cooperation among the many stakeholders.

6.9 REFERENCES

African Development Bank Group. 2013. *Rwanda - Energy Sector Review and Action Plan*. Abidjan.

CDP. 2014. *South Africa Water Report*. Park Town, National Business Initiative, and London, Carbon Disclosure Project.

Climate and Development Knowledge Network. CDKN. 2014. *Nationally Appropriate Mitigation Action (NAMA) to accelerate geothermal power: Lessons from Kenya*. http://cdkn.org/wp-content/uploads/2014/12/Kenya-IS4.pdf

CSIR. 2015. *Financial benefits of renewables in South Africa in 2015*. Centre for Scientific and Industrial Research, Energy Centre. South Africa.

Dixie, Graham and Susana Ohen. 2006. *The Market for Catfish and other Aquaculture products in Nigeria*. Washington DC, USAID.

Eberhard, A., J. Kolker and J. Leigland. 2014. *South Africa's Renewable Energy IPP Procurement Program: Success Factors and Lessons*. Washington DC, World Bank Group.

Emmet, Stuart and Vivek Sood. 2010. *Green Supply Chains. An action manifesto*. Chichester, John Wiley.

Financial Times. 23 November 2015. How Morocco's King Mohammed VI secured priority for renewables.

Government of Rwanda. 2000. *Vision 2020*. Kigali.

Government of Rwanda. 2011. *Green growth and climate resilience: National strategy for climate change and low carbon development*. Kigali.

Government of Rwanda. Ministry of infrastructure. 2011. *National Energy Policy and strategy*, Kigali May 2011

Government of Rwanda. 2013. Second Economic Development and Poverty Reduction Strategy

(EDPRS2)

EIA (Energy Information Administration). 2015. US Energy Department, on https://www.eia.gov. Accessed January 2016.

IEA. 2014. *Africa Energy Outlook*. Paris, International Energy Agency.

Guardian newspaper. November 22nd 2013. *Kenya's energy revolution: full steam ahead for geothermal power*

Guardian newspaper. November 23rd 2015. *How Africa's fastest solar power project is lighting up Rwanda*.

IIED. 2015. *Four ways to support locally controlled forestry*. London, IIED. http://www.iied.org/four-ways-support-locally-controlled-forestry-benefit-people-planet

Kaplinsky, R. and M. Morris. 2001. *A Handbook for Value Chain Research*, Brighton, IDS.

Kaplinsky, R., A. Terheggen and J. P. Tijaja. 2011. "China as a Final Market: The Gabon Timber and Thai Cassava Value Chains", *World Development*, Vol. 39, No. 7, pp. 1177-1190

Kaplinsky, R. and M. Morris. 2014. *Developing Industrial Clusters and Supply Chains to Support Diversification and Sustainable Development of Exports in Africa*, Cairo: African Export Import Bank.

Macqueen, Duncan, Anna Bolin and Martin Greijmans. 2015. Eds. *Democratising forest business: a compendium of successful locally controlled forest business organizations*. London, IIED.

Mayers, James. 2014. *Social justice in forests: gains made and tactics that work. A report from the Forest Governance Learning Group*. London, IIED.

Murphey MJ, "Botswana's Future Depends on the Protection of its Wildlife", Mmegi online, http://www.mmegi.bw/index.php?sid=2&dir=2013/March/Thursday7#sthash.Y3mSRA.Ue5BzVKi.dpuf.

Ngugi, Paul. 2012. "Financing the Kenya Geo-thermal Vision". Presented at "Short Course on Geothermal Development and Geothermal Wells", UNU-GTP and LaGeo, in Santa Tecla, El Salvador, March 11-17, 2012.

NRI. 2014. *Aquaculture in Africa – Unlocking the potential. 1st Interim Report*. Submitted by the Natural Resources Institute to Agricultural Technology Transfer, July 2014.

OKACOM (Permanent Okavango River Basin Commission). 2016. 'Fact Sheet for the Cubango-Okavango', http://www.okacom.org/okavango-fact-sheet

Oqubay, Arkebe. 2015. *Made in Africa: Industrial Policy in Ethiopia* Oxford, Clarendon Press.

Rwirahira, J. and S. Fisher. 2015. *Inclusive financing for low carbon resilient development in Rwanda*, IIED Country Report, IIED, UK.

SAIIA. 2014. *Water Governance and International Co-operation: Lessons from the Cubango-Okavango River System*. SAIIA Policy Briefing 121. December 2014.

Schmitz, Hubert. 2015. "Africa's biggest recycling hub?" November 2015. IDS blog. www.ids.ac.uk

Schmitz, Hubert. 1990. "Small firms and flexible specialization in developing countries." *Labour and Society* 15(3): 257-85.

Sibale, Bright, Robert Kafakoma, John Ngalande and Duncan Macqueen. 2014. *Forest Governance*

Learning Group – Malawi. Pushing for justice: opening up the governance of Malawi's forests. London, IIED.

UNIDO. 2015. *RECP Experiences at Leather Industry of Uganda,* UNIDO/UNEP. Accessed at www.RECPnet.org

UNIDO. 2012. *Towards green competitive industry. MED TEST. Transfer of Environmental Sound Technology in the South Mediterranean Region. Project Summary and Achievements.* Vienna, UNIDO.

WHO. 2016. Global health Observatory. http://apps.who.int/gho/data/view.main.680

World Bank. 2013. *Kenya's first Carbon Credits from Geothermal Energy Pay for Schools* http://blogs.worldbank.org/climatechange/kenya-s-first-carbon-credits-geothermal-energy-pay-schools

WDI. 2015. World Development Indicators. Washington DC, World Bank.

6.10 ENDNOTES

1 This case study draws on Kaplinsky and Morris 2014.

2 Case study based on Rwirahira, J. and Fisher, S. 2015. Inclusive financing for low carbon resilient development in Rwanda, IIED Country Report, IIED, UK.

3 Source: Personal interviews with representatives of key ministries as well as the Cement Manufacturer Association.

CHAPTER 7

POLICY RECOMMENDATIONS AND CONCLUSIONS

Africa's recent strong economic growth has not been matched by economic and social transformation, keeping the continent commodity dependent and reliant on the informal sector for jobs, with high inequality and poverty (ERA, 2014). Volatility in the prices of natural-resource and agricultural commodities has put at risk the economic and fiscal plans of many resource-dependent governments. Given the slowdown in the global economy over the past year and heightened concerns about financial stability, Africa's near-term economic growth is likely to be modest relative to its social development needs. The regions are also hit by different destabilizing factors, such as the severe dry spell in East and Southern Africa and security concerns (linked to political instability) in the Maghreb, Sahel, Horn of Africa and Central Africa.

Thus, turbulence in the global economy, worries about financial instability and Africa's vulnerability to these shocks give cause for a strategic rethinking of Africa's growth and broader development strategy.

As envisaged by recent Africa-wide strategies, economic structural transformation would permit a shift of resources into higher value activity—strengthening linkages with research and development and reinforcing regional integration—in a manner that supports greener growth. Green industrialization is the clearest route for Africa to pursue job-generating growth and develop high-value manufacturing and modern agriculture and services, which would bolster continental integration and promote sustainable development. Low-carbon development can trigger new investment opportunities and build the foundation to achieve a global economy that must keep average global warming to less than 2 degrees Celsius.

The past year has seen two landmark global agreements that align well with Africa's need to industrialize by generating greener, more inclusive growth. The first was the 21st annual Conference of the Parties (COP21) during the United Nations Climate Change Conference in Paris in December 2015. At COP21, all nations signed an agreement that—if the terms are carried out—will lead to a low-carbon economy and a shift away from fossil fuels. The agreement puts the global economy on course for a transformation of its energy systems, as all countries have pledged "to keep a global temperature rise this century well below 2 degrees Celsius and to drive efforts to limit the temperature increase even further to 1.5 degrees Celsius, above pre-industrial levels" (UNFCCC, 2015). All countries of the world have submitted plans laying out their intended contribution to achieving the global target of less than 2 degrees Celsius, and those plans will be subject to five-year review to ratchet up the ambition gradually. The second agreement—on the Sustainable Development Goals (SDGs), in September 2015—places equality, sustainability and universal basic needs at the heart of our common global economic strategy.

Green industrialization is the clearest route for Africa to pursue job-generating growth and develop high-value manufacturing and modern agriculture and services ...

Together, these global agreements set the stage for international and regional partnerships that can transform Africa's growth prospects.

Africa is blessed with abundant land, water, energy sources and natural capital, as well as a young and increasingly better educated population. Such abundance, when combined with capital investment, can generate the prosperity, employment and sustainability needed to achieve the promise laid out in the African Union's Vision 2063. Some African countries are making good progress, with a focus on water, energy and agriculture, systematically building low carbon and climate resilience into their plans and decision-making. Many, however, have yet to focus on how best to join the post-2015 momentum in climate and sustainability and use it to accelerate their plans for growth, structural transformation and sustainable industrialization. This year, 2016, is the ideal time to redesign long-term growth plans to deliver green and inclusive industrialization.

A low-carbon economic pathway must be followed globally if the world is to keep the mean global temperature increase to less than 2 degrees Celsius. A perspective to 2050 and beyond means that all countries should plan the route to deep de-carbonization to achieve 80 per cent emission cuts by 2050 and net zero carbon by 2070 (Sachs, 2015). African nations have contributed very little to global greenhouse gas emissions, and perhaps should not, therefore, be expected to take the lead on low-carbon development. African countries can stand back and watch others take the lead in building a green economy—or they can benefit from their current low-carbon position and leapfrog the process. Following the latter strategy means that many African economies can get it right the first time; infrastructure does not have to be retrofitted to make it climate resilient, and high dependence on volatile fossil fuels can be avoided, bringing significant co-benefits for health and energy security.

Africa's move to greener industrialization is not just a step towards meeting global carbon emission targets but a precondition for the continent to achieve sustainable and inclusive growth. The "Intended Nationally Determined Contributions", prepared by each country in advance of COP21, offer the ideal framework for the practical steps to take over the next 5 to 10 years, aligning with long-term goals of de-carbonization, building climate resilience and delivering sustainable development.

Africa can explore many productive ways to achieve green industrialization—starting with existing enterprises. Because of current high levels of waste and inefficiency at the plant level, supporting business to become more resource efficient provides multiple opportunities for win-wins. National Clean Production Centres show much promise in this domain, and there is much to be gained from collaboration with the joint programme led by UNIDO and UNEP

Working at the higher systemic level offers big opportunities to leverage the greening of supply chains, infrastructure and energy generation. Government plays a central role in this process, which must take a long-term perspective, looking out to 2030 and beyond. Policy stability and effective public institutions are key to creating credible incentives for the private sector, be they small and medium-sized enterprises (SMEs) or major transnational companies. Achieving inclusive greening means overcoming major externalities that make for market and governance failures while investing in new technologies and the research sector. Although government must take the lead role, it cannot hope to design, fund and achieve a green and inclusive economy alone. Government needs to build strong, long-term partnerships with business, civil society organizations (CSOs), community groups, municipal government, and financial and research sectors, understanding what each constituency can contribute, and where its interest lies.

This report has explored the strategic opportunities presented by Africa's situation in the post-Paris and post-SDG world. Now is a critical moment to rethink what has been achieved and the consequences for depletion of key resources, alongside Africa's slow record of translating growth into inclusive incomes and growth in jobs for the poor majority.

Chapters 1 and 2 revealed that Africa's double-digit economic growth of recent years rests on a weak foundation because of high levels of dependence on natural resources, for which the markets are volatile—especially oil, gas and minerals. Moreover, Africa relies heavily on the global economy, including for large and growing food imports, primarily because of low levels of regional integration. A strategic rethink across Africa's regions to achieve structural transformation should focus on building much stronger domestic and regional linkages, reducing impacts from climate change, and greatly improving use of renewable resources, particularly water and energy.

This year's report, with its focus on greening industrialization, continues the strong thematic approach of previous years' reports, which focused on how to achieve Africa's structural transformation and industrialization. The message of ERA 2016 chimes closely with the successful global meetings and agreements of 2015 and the traction gained in related global markets, such as renewable energy. Together, those global agreements and market shifts confirm a direction of travel for the global economy towards a low-carbon future based on green and inclusive growth. This conjunction of events—combined with Africa's limited industrialization, infrastructure, and low-carbon and sustainable development—provides an auspicious opportunity to mobilize Africa's leadership to be at the forefront of the economic transformations that all economies will have to follow.

This report has recognized the rising strain on all environmental resources as African economies develop and grow, and the need to generate better jobs and higher incomes for its citizens. Green and inclusive industrialization offers an ideal focus for addressing those challenges. Much of the impetus for green growth in other parts of the world has come from the need to cut greenhouse gas emissions. In Africa, however, for growth to be sustainable and inclusive, equal thought must be given to getting the best value from agriculture and its associated environmental base, and the extractive industries—oil, gas and minerals - which have been more of a curse than a blessing. Consider the impacts of uncertain and poorly managed water supply, on which life depends, and the rapid growth in fossil fuel–based energy demand. Well-shaped green growth measures can, however, offer good outcomes for all these challenges.

Worldwide, a growing number of countries have seen the green growth agenda not as an obstacle and a threat but as the next big opportunity for growth and transformation. They recognize that not only can green growth contribute to enhanced developmental outcomes, such as better health, and mitigate the harmful impacts of climate change and climate variability, but it also offers the potential to make growth more efficient by better use of scarce resources. Those countries stress the scale of co-benefits and synergies rather than trade-offs. Greening industrialization has the potential to create exports and jobs through developing green capital goods and services and, if designed with the needs of the majority population in mind, offers the promise of more inclusive patterns of development. It demands a shared approach to inclusion, green growth, industrialization and structural transformation, built on a model of regional integration that generates shared benefits for member countries. The concept of "decoupling" industrial growth from resource use helps to identify the scope for improving the efficiency with which these resources are incorporated in production. Evidence from a number of African countries shows that individual manufacturing establishments have been able to green their production in a way that has saved significant costs, ensured market access and increased profitability.

A valuable and systemic response to generating low-carbon industrial development would be for governments to set up eco-industrial parks.

The scenario analysis in Chapter 5 showed that the costs of not going down a green growth pathway are formidable and accelerate damage; a business-as-usual (BAU) approach to growth is quite clearly unsustainable. The bio-physical environment—land, water, soils, forests—will be unable to bear the stresses involved, while climate degradation will impoverish much of the rural population and drive people off the land. Although seemingly paradoxical, the economic strategy that pursues growth as an end in itself eats away at the very conditions that make sustained growth possible. A simulation analysis based on two modelling scenarios was conducted to show how the greening of growth helps avoid the very high costs of a BAU approach and is vital to ensuring that Africa's growth can meet its social, economic and environmental goals. A combination of bold measures and interventions is needed to shift growth to a more sustainable and inclusive pathway.

Through a series of case studies (Chapter 6), the report showed practical and successful experiences in the greening of individual establishments and of systems in a variety of African economies. In some cases the process has involved greening agendas that cut across sectors; in other cases they have spanned neighbouring economies, offering a regional perspective of mutual benefits stemming from improved and shared governance. The contribution made by a value-chain approach to greening is evident: the greening of a chain of suppliers rather than individual firms optimizes the opportunities for inclusive green growth. These case studies show that the greening of value chains requires coordination and governance that is, in different contexts, performed variously by lead firms, governments or other entities.

7.1 POLICY RECOMMENDATIONS

GREENING AFRICAN INDUSTRIALIZATION: FROM VISION TO TRANSITION

Turning a green vision into reality poses challenges similar to those in many other policy agendas. The breadth of the agenda for this transition is arguably greater, however, than that for any other that has faced African policymakers since independence. Simply put, continuing current trends along a BAU approach will prevent African economies from meeting their developmental goals. Such a BAU pathway will also challenge the very sustainability of growth. Marginal change in a few parameters will not be enough to shift resources to green growth—it requires a system-wide shift and a clear, consistent change in direction.

Given the enormity of this challenge, how can African economies bridge the gap between vision and reality? How can African countries make the most of their current low levels of carbon emissions per head, thinly spread infrastructural assets, and little value added for many of their commodities? Such attributes might be considered weaknesses in building a more sustainable and inclusive economy, but they can also be seen as strengths. Having less infrastructure means less investment is needed for its conversion to low-carbon and climate-resilient norms, fewer vested interests are dug into high-carbon activities, and current low levels of processing provide a lot of headroom for growth in value added. Africa's late industrialization offers many chances for leapfrogging to more effective, greener forms of industrialization that build on win-win synergies between inclusive growth and environmentally sustainable growth pathways (box 7.1).

THE PUBLIC SECTOR IN THE LEAD, WORKING CLOSELY WITH OTHER SECTORS

Responsibility for building a green, resilient economy lies primarily with government, as the collective vehicle for the interests of current and future citizens of the nation. Government must understand the nature of the challenges ahead, analyse the options, identify and plan with different stakeholders how best to achieve the outcomes they seek, and offer a platform and consistent policy to coordinate the actions of others.

The private sector is not very likely to do all that—nor should it be expected to. The different parts of business, government and civil society must work together, understand who is best placed to do what, and identify what market forces can and cannot achieve. Sometimes the tendency is to argue for either public or private measures;

Having less infrastructure means less investment is needed for its conversion to low-carbon and climate-resilient norms, fewer vested interests are dug into high-carbon activities, and current low levels of processing provide a lot of headroom for growth in value added.

BOX 7.1 STEPS TO GREENING INDUSTRIALIZATION

1. *Develop a green industrialization vision and strategy.* Building on industrial policy frameworks, processes and institutions elaborated in ERA 2013, 2014 and 2015, the greening strategy must be comprehensive. As shown in this report, the green challenges are systemic, crossing national, sectoral and enterprise boundaries. The strategy involves changes not just in the pattern of resource allocation in the public and private sectors but also in the behaviour of Africa's citizens.
2. *Translate this vision and strategy into policies.* These include shifts in government regulation, expenditure and fiscal measures. Unless those policies incorporate sanctions, though—positive incentives and negative penalties—they will be mere statements of intent and unable to deliver what is needed.
3. *Make sure that policies are "joined up" and reinforcing.* Although this step relies on a policy agenda that cuts across ministries and sectors, it also has to recognize that currently governance is generally built on a framework of silos, sectors and national boundaries.
4. *Attune policy ambition to delivery capability.* This step is needed because African economies vary enormously, including in human skill endowments and state administrative capacity. Too ambitious an agenda may blunt the capacity to deliver anything significant. On the other hand, if the policy agenda is not ambitious enough and the approach taken insufficiently consistent, the green growth agenda will be undermined. Regional entities are well placed to provide alignment and coherence to this agenda, as well as support and learning for national governments.
5. *Involve the full range of stakeholders in the design and delivery of policies.* Otherwise policies are unlikely to move beyond planning documents and the statute book.

in practice, though, the most effective greening of industrialization will take place when an effective partnership is built within countries and across borders. That means clarity, confidence and consistency among key parts of government and nations. Intergovernmental trust and trust between government and many different partners—large and small—is essential. Besides partnering with civil society and business, government must engage citizens in new ways of thinking and acting, such as developing a shared understanding of and approach to the environment. Initiatives that target dissemination of citizen-level environmental stewardship, such as local economies that minimize waste and pollution, are necessarily core components of a green growth agenda.

The COP21 outcome, as a global agreement designed to be delivered through decisive national actions, provides an added spur for African governments to take the lead in bringing their stakeholders together. Building on the Addis Ababa Action Agenda, international public finance is being mobilized in the form of contributions to the Green Climate Fund and to multilateral development banks, for investment in climate related actions. The African Development Bank (AfDB), for example, has announced a doubling of its climate change funding.

The loud and clear statement of policy direction stemming from the Paris Agreement should also unlock substantial amounts of private finance and investment that can now be targeted towards low-carbon investments. The challenge will be for

African governments to attract private investment in a way that aligns with their own objectives and to ensure that this mix of public and private investment facilitates inclusive, sustainable growth that achieves rising incomes and middle-income status over the next decade.

Hence, a credible, long-term and ambitious strategy must be laid out by government—through its planning process—and linked to expenditure and investment targets. Recent years have seen the emergence of strong African leadership in this area, which has demonstrated the importance of combining vision with the capacity to make things happen in practice (Oqubay, 2015). This demands a consistent approach that maps out the pathway to be followed—recognizing the sequencing necessary to make progress along that path—and that understands the costs of inaction. There is no substitute for leadership at the highest level of government to ensure that greening becomes a systemic approach, drawing on and bringing benefits to all sectors of the economy.

Inevitably, some political interests will not want such changes. Not everyone will gain from the reorientation of the growth path, and many will have to be persuaded to shift from a focus on BAU today—with little thought for the cost to be borne by tomorrow's generations—towards a pattern of growth that delivers a more sustainable future. Thus, necessary reforms must occur in phases and the costs to particular constituencies must be addressed. No single measure exists for achieving this greening of structural transformation. The solution must comprise an integrated set of actions in the fields of policy, regulation, price incentives, infrastructural investment, and research and development. Government systems will need retooling to account better for costs and benefits related to environmental and social inclusion and to the collection of data required to track progress with implementation.

For those African governments wanting to make progress down this pathway, the good news is that they can learn much from the experience achieved to date by colleagues in neighbouring countries and continents. Multiple platforms and support programmes now are aimed at accelerating progress through shared learning, from which leaders can take heart—UN-PAGE, the Global Green Growth Forum, the Green Growth Knowledge Platform, and the Green Economy Coalition, to name a few. Such peer-to-peer learning offers much potential for toolkits, partnerships, policy support and training opportunities.

African countries have widely different economic portfolios, depending on their size, natural resource assets, climate and other natural endowments, historical and cultural connections around the world, and human and institutional resources. Consequently, the policy choices they face will also be diverse. As the world transitions towards a low-carbon economy, big questions will arise regarding the future value of fossil-fuel reserves; optimal rates of depletion for oil, gas and coal; and how best to invest public revenues generated from those resources. Fulfilling the Paris Agreement implies the phasing out of high-carbon fuels and hence the falling value of fossil fuel reserves. Public revenues from such remaining reserves thus need especial care to diversify economic structures, construct badly needed infrastructure and build the human capacities that will be central to the low-carbon economies of the future. At the same time, the collapse in oil prices in 2014–2015 places complex demands on African economies, on one hand reducing the short-term economic drivers to de-carbonize and diversify growth , and on the other hand, reducing the funds for oil-exporting economies to finance the necessary economic transformations.

INFRASTRUCTURAL INVESTMENT: BUILDING FOR THE NEXT GENERATION

LANDSCAPE, SOILS, WATER AND BIODIVERSITY

A large share of Africa's people rely on the continent's infrastructure of natural capital—its land, soils, water and biodiversity. This natural infrastructure supports fish, crops, trees, wildlife, grazing livestock and other products of nature. Low farm productivity means continued dependence on imports for basic foodstuffs across the continent, even though Africa's farmers have the potential to feed the continent's people and to supply overseas markets. Poor linkages between agriculture and urban markets often have blocked the growth that could occur through the processing of many agri-food products for domestic consumption, revealing substantial room for improvement.

Incentives to manage resources sustainably are limited, property rights are weak and insecurity is rising. Large land acquisitions for commercial agriculture have demonstrated for many farmers the fundamental weakness of their rights when faced with powerful domestic and international interests.

A "modern" agricultural sector is often assumed to be large and commercial. Much evidence, however, shows that Africa's herders and smallholder farmers, particularly mid-level farmers, are highly responsive to new technologies and better market opportunities.

Africa's forests and grazing lands are the major source of carbon emissions, estimated at one quarter of the continent's greenhouse gas emissions. Mitigation actions include reforestation, increasing the organic content of soils and landscapes, taking a watershed approach to managing water and large dams, and providing incentives to invest in rehabilitating soils and vegetation. There is much innovation in mitigation actions, such as shown by combining simple soil conservation techniques with securing firmer rights over farmland and grazing (Reij and Winterbottom, 2014). More resilient high-carbon landscapes can be built by combining a local approach to landscape management with access to decentralized funds, recognizing the centrality of investment in institutions that support the livelihoods needed in a climate changing world (Hesse, 2015; IED-Afrique, 2015).

A "modern" agricultural sector is often assumed to be large and commercial. Much evidence, however, shows that Africa's herders and smallholder farmers, particularly mid-level farmers, are highly responsive to new technologies and better market opportunities. African governments that have fulfilled their commitments to the Maputo Declaration, in which they pledged 10 per cent of government expenditure to agriculture, have seen benefits in higher yields and bigger harvests. Greater investment in agriculture by governments that have fallen well short of this 10 per cent target could generate not only incomes for farmers and food to feed the cities but also the raw materials on which to base a more substantial industrialization effort.

WATER AND ENERGY

As shown by the case studies in Chapter 6, huge difficulties remain in delivering basic services essential to long-term economic growth and development—"hardware" and "software". Continental and regional plans, such as the Programme for

Infrastructure Development in Africa, estimate that $360 billion will be needed over 2012–2040 to build the necessary water, transport and energy infrastructure to deliver economic growth. Everyone now recognizes that energy supply is the foremost infrastructural challenge needed for green industrialization. The African continent's inability to provide a secure, guaranteed supply of electricity to big and small users is an enormous burden (APP, 2015).

It was therefore timely that African governments launched a joint plan at COP21—the Africa Renewable Energy Initiative—which aims to add an additional 10 gigawatts of renewable-energy capacity to the African energy sector by 2020 and an additional 300 gigawatts by 2030. African households, businesses and individuals are hungry for energy and willing to pay for secure supplies. As experience from Kenya and South Africa shows (Chapter 6), opportunities abound for efficient, scalable and cost-effective renewable-energy generation and for more efficient use of generated power. When the regulations are framed properly, economies can attract considerable private sector funding to invest in energy infrastructure. The credibility of government, its regulatory and policy measures (such as feed-in tariffs and green procurement programmes), and better provisions for remittance of profits abroad are key to bringing in such funds.

Infrastructure for sustainable water use and management is also critical, with security of the water supply coming under ever greater stress in many countries. Some watersheds are already fully exploited, and others will need careful management of trade-offs between competing uses, while the shared benefits of doing so are made explicit to sectors and countries. At present, the win-win opportunities of moving to more sustainable patterns of water use are not as apparent as for renewable-energy provision. Identifying those benefits is possible, though, given that much of Africa's water scarcity is attributable to inadequate infrastructure and governance, meaning that water often is available in the wrong place at the wrong time.

Attracting the public and private sector investments needed to overcome the obstacles is a further opportunity for Africa to leapfrog in the greening process: investments in water infrastructure (both "hardware" in the form of dams and "soft" in the form of ecosystems) will be attractive if governance and regional integration are boosted.

African households, businesses and individuals are hungry for energy and willing to pay for secure supplies. As experience from Kenya and South Africa shows ...

In all economies, infrastructural decisions require government to play a leading role, individually and in concert with regional partners. The scale of investment required and the long-term choices inherent in the location, design and construction of capital assets make such leadership a necessity. For example, given the expected phase-out of unabated fossil fuel use globally, governments must answer vital questions about the construction of large power generators and choice of fuels— oil, gas or coal. Some infrastructural investments demand that governments across a region engage in thinking about and planning new investments, such as big dams (in shared river basins) or regional power networks. Although much of the funding may come from multilateral or private financers, government must provide guarantees of the broader policy environment so that investors are confident that their returns are assured and not exposed to policy risk.

The poor status of infrastructure is estimated to depress firms' productivity by as much as 40 per cent, while exposing people to high risks from flooding and from inadequate water, shelter and sanitation. Infrastructural investment has a long life and hence must be designed with future conditions in mind. For that reason, ensuring that major infrastructural spending draws on an understanding of likely risks from climate change and aligns with a low-carbon future is of increasing concern. The water and hydropower sectors are particularly vulnerable to rainfall patterns over the next 30 to 50 years. In a wet future, expanding hydropower capacity makes sense, whereas in a drier future, having built capacity that cannot be used owing to drought would be very costly. Because development decisions also place investments and assets at risk, a sensible step in all climate and development scenarios is to diversify energy supply by exploiting readily available renewable resources as widely as possible. Consequently, assumptions must be made about likely climate and development futures to factor those risks into design choices today (UNDP, 2011).

Decisions taken now will determine patterns of economic growth such as urbanization, energy consumption and industrial development over the next 30 to 50 years. Getting them right will avoid the risk that infrastructural investments lock in a pattern of production that maintains high-carbon and natural resource–intense systems, exposing people (and infrastructure) to the impacts of greater climate vulnerability. If chosen correctly, infrastructural investment can facilitate growth in new buildings, industry, mass transit systems and energy technologies and encourage the inclusion of renewable-energy systems in building and urban infrastructure design (NCE, 2014).

URBANIZATION

Urban development is a particularly urgent item on the infrastructure and investment agenda for government. The continent's population is forecast to more than double from 1.1 billion today to 2.3 billion by 2050, of whom more than half will be living in towns and cities. Such rapidity of population growth is a central concern and a great opportunity: by 2020, 24 of the world's 30 fastest growing cities will be African (FAO, 2012). Economic growth and urbanization are closely linked. Industry offers employment, whereas cities connect people, knowledge and innovation. Many urban inhabitants of middle- and low-income nations, however, suffer very large (and mostly preventable) health burdens from urban pollution and are increasingly exposed to the risks associated with inadequate planning, poor infrastructure and weak provisioning of basic services, which frequently leads to conflict. The main cause is a lack of capacity in urban governments for planning, food security, pollution control, waste management and environmental health. Few city governments have much finance to address those problems and ensure effective regulation. For instance, health burdens often are exacerbated in the substantial informal settlements that house more than 60 per cent of the city's inhabitants (APHRC, 2014). Urban areas have heavy concentrations of air and water pollution from transport, households, businesses and industry.

Greening African cities is one of the cornerstones of Africa's green industrialization and is a further opportunity to leapfrog the process. Cities bring together social innovation and critical skills, but they also need scaled-up infrastructure to ensure food, water and energy security. They are a focal point for fuelling green industrialization if designed in an inclusive manner—for both the poor and the better off.

Urban areas are also major centres of economic growth, accelerating industrial development with skills, innovation and infrastructure. In Africa, a paramount task is that urbanization be greened—and quickly—through inclusive planning and implementation. Not doing so will result in lost opportunities and exacerbated stresses on urban populations, such as pollution and increased human insecurity. In the traditional model of urban expansion, industry often is pushed to city boundaries for practical reasons and to reduce the immediate impacts of pollution. Subsequently, increases in housing prices and jobs lead to the urban poor clustering around industrial areas or having to commute long distances. Thus, over time more people are exposed to higher pollution because industrial sites share the same neighbourhood as residential settlements and experience lower socio-economic development. The siting of industrial estates thus must be considered alongside social service provision, major transport links and energy and water systems.

As noted in 2014 by the High Level Panel of Eminent Persons on the Post-2015 Development Agenda, "cities are where the battle for sustainable development will be won or lost" (United Nations, 2013, p. 17). Consequently, attention must be paid to a wide range of municipal responsibilities, such as ensuring urban food security, especially for poorer neighbourhoods, establishing accountable and transparent means for acquiring urban land, setting urban land tax policy, securing municipal revenue streams for service delivery, inclusively planning new infrastructure, and protecting and greening public spaces. Clean air policies and integrated, green urban planning are key to reducing pollution and its adverse impact on human health, and to linking with wider energy choices, transport systems and industrialization options.

Monitoring performance and increasing compliance require data and information. Many local governments have few means to collect and process that data, however; hence some city governments work with federations of the urban poor and other civil society groups to draw on their skills, knowledge and perspectives. This model should be replicated. Mobile telephones offer an excellent way to "crowd-source" information about non-compliance with environmental standards, collect real-time data and access and provide information on extreme events, such as flash floods and wildfires. In the medium term, a reliable, simple system of data collection and indicators is important for African cities to identify their needs, plan their development and monitor their progress.[1]

THE POLICY TOOLKIT

LONG-TERM DEVELOPMENT PLANNING

Addressing Africa's pressing structural transformation and inclusive development challenges requires a coherent, integrated long-term development plan and associated frameworks. As emphasized in previous reports, to achieve better outcomes the development process has to be carefully planned. The changes to policy and practice required for promoting green industrialization and inclusive development are substantial and resources are limited, which means that thought needs to focus on how Africa can make better use of what it has.

Mobile telephones offer an excellent way to "crowd-source" information about non-compliance with environmental standards, collect real-time data and access and provide information on extreme events, such as flash floods and wildfires.

Decision-making cannot be left to market forces, nor can it rely on government acting alone. The interdependence of all elements can be dealt with better by creating a comprehensive development-planning framework rather than resorting to partial solutions. African countries and sub-regions have pervasive market and governance failures, so the information and coordination externalities involved in development can only be addressed when sectors, countries and stakeholders identify priorities and shared benefits, striking a balance between long- and short-term goals.

The interdependence of all elements can be dealt with better by creating a comprehensive development-planning framework rather than resorting to partial solutions.

The commitments in recent global and regional development frameworks offer tremendous opportunities to African policymakers for sustainable and green industrialization. The frameworks state the priority of tackling inclusion and environmental concerns. Exploiting the benefits of these initiatives, however, will require them to be integrated well within national planning frameworks. Africa's priorities are well reflected in the Sustainable Development Goals (SDGs), the Paris Agreement and the Addis Ababa Action Agenda, which should facilitate national buy-in and support for implementation.

Nevertheless, the broad scope of the SDG agenda—many goals, targets and indicators—means that policymakers will have to filter these components according to their own priority agendas while coordinating implementation of Agenda 2030 and 2063. At the same time, the inclusion of all nations—high-, middle- and low-income—in the SDGs may stimulate competition for an ever-shrinking pool of official development assistance. The Paris Agreement is conclusive on the amount of additional money needed to finance implementation although vague on where that money will come from. Policymakers in Africa must be mindful of these challenges and opportunities as they prepare for the transition to the new agenda.

MACRO POLICIES

Macroeconomic policy and the incentives driving it are key components of a green growth agenda. Beyond maintaining broad measures of price stability, predictable property rights and other macro policies that affect all investment, three fields of macro policy have particular relevance to the greening agenda.

The first is the pricing of water and energy. These two resources are critical inputs to the household and productive sectors. Their pricing not only affects the type and distribution of investment in the productive sector but also the distribution of income and patterns of social inclusion. Calling for higher prices that reflect the true environmental costs of these inputs is a politically sensitive issue, but it is a touchstone for green policy commitment. The "under-pricing" of water and energy can send adverse signals to users and severely distort consumption and investment choices.

For this reason (among others) several countries in Africa—including Angola, Egypt, Ghana, Kenya, Nigeria and Uganda—have sought to curb subsidies on fossil fuels (Whitley and van der Burg,

2015), incurring political pushback from rich and poor alike. In the short term, poorer groups will need protection from price increases (as when social protection measures are used to compensate for withdrawal of subsidies on fossil fuels, such as petrol and kerosene), but in the medium to longer term, firms and individuals need to move away from consumption of high-carbon energy. Key to making the case for subsidy reforms is to provide "clear, open and honest information on the scale of subsidies, their costs and impacts, who pays and who benefits, plans for reform, and complementary measures to be adopted" (op. cit.).

Equally, for decades, access to water often has been at little or no cost, especially for richer groups who can access water through piped supplies. By contrast, people living in informal settlements buy their water from street vendors, often paying prices more than 10 times higher. Water must be distributed more fairly to reduce waste and inefficiency and to offer incentives to conserve scarce supplies.

The second macro policy field concerns ways to address the adverse externalities arising from economic growth. A decisive approach is required that makes clear to producers their responsibility to internalize many of the costs of their operations that currently are externalized (such as effluent release into rivers and groundwater). Monitoring, regulation and sanctions of pollution incidents is the basic issue, along with measures to establish the norms, capacity and institutions to ensure a credible response. Pollution problems often are associated with informal activities, such as artisanal mining, that can generate much more destructive environmental spill-overs than activities of the formal sector. The informal sector must be brought into some form of government recognition, with the regulation of activity implied. Pollution outflows from many small and large industrial enterprises frequently are poorly regulated. Governments may be able to get better results through ensuring public access to information about standards and practice so that neighbourhood groups and civil society can add their voices to demand state action.

The third set of macro policy instruments is to achieve structural transformation. Typically, policy incentives and public investment must combine to steer the economy in specific directions to sustain appropriate forms of growth over the medium and long term (Chang, 2015). As noted by Oqubay (2015), the economic growth and transformation process has to be seen as shifting from one disequilibrium to the next, with the stresses and tensions so released helping to propel the structural changes. As we saw in Chapter 4, green structural transformation requires the development of systemic approaches to three types of green industrialization—moving out of polluting and out of energy- and water-inefficient sectors; decoupling water, energy and pollution intensity across the spectrum of productive activities; and expanding the green capital goods and services sectors. This systemic approach lies at the heart of green structural transformation.

Closely linked to it is the development of infrastructure that not only is green but that facilitates

... for decades, access to water often has been at little or no cost, ... through piped supplies. By contrast, people living in informal settlements buy their water from street vendors, often paying prices more than 10 times higher.

the greening of other sectors (such as off-grid infrastructure to enable decentralized growth of small and medium-sized enterprises). An additional and necessary accompaniment is to reorient research and technology organizations (including curricula in universities and other higher education institutions) to provide a suitable knowledge base for these broad pathways.

Most of this macro agenda is best pursued by national governments, with decentralized action led at the municipal and district levels. The systemic nature of much of the green transformation challenge, though, particularly for infrastructure, often requires cooperation across national borders. The United Nations Economic Commission for Africa, AfDB and the eight officially recognized regional economic communities (RECs) of the African Union—AMU, CEN-SAD, COMESA, EAC, ECCAS, ECOWAS, IGAD and SADC[2]—are well-placed to provide a platform for a coordinated response to the greening challenge.

Examples of shared concerns include food security, water management, transport infrastructure and regional power pools. Joint programmes within the RECs are critical to long-term management of scarce water resources, such as the many shared river basins in Africa and cross-border aquifers. The RECs also can help generate the flow of new ideas about investments and innovation, addressing capacity and technical deficits. The regional dimension is the connective thread that ties together new growth and sustainability, offering opportunities to learn and share experience with greening through strengthened regional integration.

GREEN POLICY INSTRUMENTS

Beyond macro policies are a raft of policies in each sector that will assist governments to roll out the green growth agenda. Those policies include establishment of eco-industrial parks, regulations for biofuel production and use, and feed-in tariffs, power purchase agreements, and green procurement programmes in energy. They also include technical support and training in fields such as geothermal energy, marine engineering and ecosystem management. Investment in better land management and integrated water resource management requires enabling institutions that provide secure rights to land, water and natural resources. In many African countries, property rights are uncertain, given the prevalence of legal pluralism, low levels of formal land registration, limited recognition by government of customary land rights, and weak rights associated with collective property, such as woodlands and pastures for grazing. If users are to invest in the long-term resilience of their lands and other resources, they need assurance that they will gain the benefits from such investment over generations to come.

BUILDING INCLUSION INTO GREENING INDUSTRIALIZATION

Africa's economic growth has not led to the broad spread of jobs, incomes and prosperity that many had hoped for. Although middle-class incomes and aspirations are multiplying for those individuals with the skills and education, a large and growing body of people have not reaped rewards from current growth patterns.

Designing policies and institutions requires making choices. Building a inclusive perspective into the way government provides support, funding and services can result in better distributional outcomes (box 7.2). Policies with that perspective emphasize the need to design processes that enable different groups to participate, recognizing the highly unequal access to power between the rich and the poor and between urban and rural groups.

BOX 7.2 DESIGNING POLICY AIMED AT GREEN AND INCLUSIVE DEVELOPMENT

1 *Focus on creating decent green jobs.* Seek out inclusive returns by considering local investments that create jobs with low energy, resource and financial costs, as alternatives or complements to capital-intensive, nationally driven investments. Identify opportunities throughout industrial lifecycles to boost job creation, as in renewable-energy programmes. Promote and enshrine skills upgrading and decent work in laws to increase the likelihood of such co-benefits. Explore opportunities in the informal economy, co-designing job creation with target communities.

2 *Recognize the limits of economic methodologies and market instruments.* Economic-valuation tools and cost–benefit analysis risk overlooking long-term value, distributional impacts and social and cultural goods and services. Market-based instruments such as cash transfers may provide safeguards, but their ultimate effectiveness depends on institutional capacity and accessible procedures being in place.

3 *Promote poor people's empowerment and address elite power.* Recognize power imbalances and ensure that policies and services are designed with and for local communities. Support the decentralization of natural resource access, use and governance to the community level wherever possible. Policies and services should recognize and address the influence of powerful elites and interests in blocking (to others) and capturing (for themselves) the benefits of green policymaking.

4 *Prioritize participation—especially of women and marginalized groups—in policymaking.* Policies should be co-designed with and for the target communities, especially women and vulnerable and minority groups. Develop participatory methodologies and invest in capacity building and education about greening. Provide specific skills training and childcare to help women benefit from opportunities in transitioning sectors, and promote equitable governance within the community.

5 *Support adaptive, context-specific and local policy approaches.* Recognize the influence of local sociocultural factors—not only laws and regulations—on the success or failure of interventions. Policies should be context specific (not "one size fits all") and capitalize on local opportunities. Successful outcomes often are achieved at local-authority scale by harnessing the dynamics and reinforcing the benefits of local change. Policies must be adaptive and flexible to changing circumstances and project outcomes.

6 *Consider spacing, timing and phasing.* The transition to a green and inclusive economy will not be smooth. Understand the geography of sectoral change: stranded assets, induced migration, job creation and losses and their associated opportunities and threats. Anticipate the timing of greening interventions, and consider phasing in policies to protect any communities vulnerable to changes in prices or regulations.

SOURCE: BASED ON RAWORTH, WYKES AND BASS (2014).

The box suggests multiple ways to broaden the benefits of a green policy agenda so that it builds on the knowledge and priorities of poor groups and provides them with better jobs, wider opportunities for training, and more secure assets and livelihoods. A conscious bringing together of the policy measures targeting inclusion and green industrialization can then deliver on all three policy imperatives of green growth, inclusive growth and industrialization (as shown in figure 3.4). Given the impact of climate change, attention must focus on building more resilience into land, food, water, shelter and energy systems so that damage from climate disasters does not reverse the gains of green, inclusive industrialization.

BUILDING PLATFORMS FOR LEARNING AND INNOVATION

International experience shows that the first critical steps in sparking innovation often are initiated by governments and other public bodies (Mazzucato, 2011). The key decisions in Africa's productive sector, however, are to a greater or lesser degree determined by the private sector—whether the large corporations, family businesses or many millions of small farms. The private sector, too, in all its diversity must be on board for the green growth journey.

The private sector, too, in all its diversity must be on board for the green growth journey.

Some lead firms that feed into final markets in high-income countries, for example, are already committed to greening their supply chains (although corporate policy visions are not always executed effectively). In some sectors, a key driver for greening is the pressure exerted by civil society groups. They often play an influential role in assisting producers, particularly small and marginalized producers, to develop their capabilities to take part in green growth.

Be that as it may, whoever initiates green innovation and implements greening in the productive sector will need help from universities and from research and technology organizations in a country's national innovation system. Hence, a critical component of the macro policy agenda is to develop a platform on which the public sector, the private sector, civil society groups and knowledge institutions can join together in greening growth. International experience shows that if the non-state parties are only brought into the picture at a late stage to implement government policy, progress will be patchy. They need to be involved in policy development—not just implementation—including within their own value chains.

National dialogues on what makes a Green Economy are important to kick-start local and national actions. Thus, for example, the Green Economy Coalition—a global network of diverse organizations from business, research institutes, trade unions, United Nations bodies and non-governmental organizations—has facilitated more than a dozen national, multi-stakeholder dialogues aimed at exploring how to build a greener, more inclusive economy (GEC, 2013). In Zambia a platform has been built bringing together the Ministries of Finance and of Lands, Natural Resources and Environmental Protection; the Organisation for Economic Co-operation and Development (OECD); and the AfDB; alongside civil society organizations and university researchers, to scope the local actions, policy measures and funding opportunities that could contribute to Zambia's Inclusive Green Growth Strategy (Banda and Bass, 2014).

Software for greening industrialization requires continued investment in the skills, networks and institutions essential, such as health and education, innovation capacity, business connections, and information and communications technology. Institutions—although invisible—are critical for achieving collective action at local, municipal and national levels. Several universities have been connecting to entrepreneurs to create innovation hubs in which new business can be supported by the ideas and technical skills of the research sector. These hubs for "incubating" new entrepreneurs are key to bringing practical science and technology into a growing green sector. Also needed is investment in the quality of officials in the public administration and public sector management to ensure high standards for probity and to address tax evasion and illicit financial flows (UNECA, 2013; 2014). Investment in data quality and availability often is neglected, despite its importance. One option could be to draw on the skills and energies of civil society and crowd-sourcing data as alternative means to monitor the environmental performance of large firms, as has been demonstrated by Ma Jun and the Institute of Public and Environmental Affairs in China.

Investment in data quality and availability often is neglected, despite its importance. One option could be to draw on the skills and energies of civil society and crowd-sourcing data as alternative means to monitor the environmental performance of large firms, ...

ENSURING SYSTEMIC GREENING: SUPPLY CHAIN MANAGEMENT

Greening the value chain requires change throughout the chain—all chains are only as strong as their weakest link. To achieve such greening, countries have an opportunity to learn from extensive global experience of supply chain upgrading in the industrial sector. Essentially, supply chain management was pioneered in the Japanese automobile industry in the 1960s and 1970s, which subsequently diffused widely through most industrial and service sectors, as well as in agricultural value chains (Kaplinsky, 2005). The central idea of supply chain management activities is that individual firms (or links in the chain) need assistance in adjusting to new forms of organization, both within their operations and in the way they relate to other firms.

Once firms see the benefits of upgrading their production processes, it becomes autonomous and dynamic. Government must provide the incentives that induce the upgrading and the support for training programmes to develop those capabilities, both within supplier firms and in the business services sector. Government support for efficiency improvements in the South African automobile sector provides a useful model of what can be achieved in a chain-greening programme. The key step was the demand from the lead auto assembling firms that all parts of their chains should upgrade. Then the government gave initial support for the business services sector to work with suppliers to help them meet the new requirements of the lead firms. These business services were subsidized in the early years of the programme, but once supplier firms saw the financial benefits of upgrading, it became self-financing.

The lesson for supply chain greening in value chains is therefore that governments induce this chain upgrading through subsidies, which then tail off as the greening begins to finance itself. Small firms, particularly in the informal sector or headed by women and other disadvantaged groups, may require greater incentives, and much can be learned from attempts to promote inclusion in Africa's horticultural global value chains.[3]

THE REGIONAL DIMENSIONS OF GREENING INDUSTRIALIZATION

Greening industrialization and the broader growth pathway have strong regional dimensions, with the RECs providing a foundation to support the structural transformation in five areas.

First, countries in each region face many common challenges that benefit from joint research, learning, reflection and coordinated action. Second, as described earlier, many shared resources cross boundaries and require a collective approach to be managed as a system, such as aquifers, wildlife, river basins and forest resources. Third, economies of scale and connectivity offer huge benefits in certain industries and areas of service provision, especially energy. Fourth, infrastructural investments make much more sense if planned regionally, such as transport links for enabling landlocked nations to access seaport facilities. Finally, differences in ecology and climate systems at a regional scale offer good opportunities for countries to specialize in specific areas of farm produce and processing for wider regional markets and distribution. An obvious example is West Africa, spanning humid, tropical coastal regions that produce oil palm, coffee, pineapples and bananas to the dry grazing lands and irrigated agriculture of the Sahel, which generates meat, rice and sugar.

FINANCING GREEN INDUSTRIALIZATION

Massive financial resources are needed to green Africa's industrialization. In the short term, it is likely to cost more than investment along BAU lines. No detailed figures are available for the continent, but global numbers give a clue: the New Climate Economy Commission reckons that, globally, the net incremental infrastructure investment needed for a low-carbon transition up to 2030 could be just $4.1 trillion if the investments are done well—equivalent to a 5 per cent increment over BAU. According to the NCE (2014), "between public and private sources, there is already sufficient capital available to finance a low-carbon transition. However, the ambiguity, inconsistency and lack of predictability in policy settings creates high government-induced uncertainty, especially for long-lived assets." Hence, establishing predictable regulation and associated policy are critically important in providing confidence to investors in low-carbon activity.

Financial resources will come from a mix of remittances, green bonds, diaspora bonds, domestic revenue, foreign investment, municipal finance, international climate finance and other sources. The signal to curb or even end fossil fuel dependence potentially releases a large source of predictable green finance. Fossil fuel subsidies around the world amount to approximately $600 billion a year. Some of that money could be diverted—through reforms to such subsidies—to finance the green agenda.

To make the best use of this mix of financial resources, some countries have set up a national funding mechanism that can receive climate-related finance and allocate funds to low-carbon and climate-resilient investments. The United Nations Framework Convention on Climate Change (UNFCCC) and the Green Climate Fund encourage countries to establish direct access modalities, such as "national implementing entities," to act as the principal conduits for global climate funds (Rwanda's National Climate Fund offers a good model). As of mid-2015, 20 countries had reported their entities to the Green Climate Fund, including 5 from Africa—Kenya, Namibia, Nigeria, Rwanda and Senegal. Given the fund's potential scale of financing, a vital task is for other African governments to register their agencies or government structures as recipients and managers.

The private sector has long been seen as an important source of climate finance, and there is now much greater focus on bringing sustainable development and green growth to the heart of corporate governance. An array of initiatives are emerging, alongside guidelines for green reporting and accountability mechanisms. Earth on Board, an embryonic initiative supported by the World Business Council for Sustainable Development (WBCSD) and the Cambridge Institute of Sustainability Leadership, aims to target corporate governance in multinational companies and those working in countries that urgently need to embark on green growth pathways.

Led by South African judge, Mervyn King, the King Reports have provided stimulus to corporate boards to change the way they govern. Although developed in South Africa, with implementation under the watchful eye of the Johannesburg Stock Exchange (JSE), the King reports are globally renowned and hence can influence corporate governance around the world. King III, the latest of these broadened the scope of evaluating ethical corporate behaviour, and has elevated "sustainability" to constitute the primary imperative not only for private firms, but also for public entities, non-profits, and civil society organisations. The report argues for a transformational shift in the way public and private entities integrate notions of sustainability within all facets of operation, and insists on new benchmarks for annual evaluation and reporting of non-financial performance indicators, for the benefit of consumers and shareholders.

Good news from growing global experiences—for example in leveraging private investment with relatively small amounts of public finance—can reassure countries embarking on the green agenda. Equity and debt financing by public institutions, especially development banks, has been a crucial catalyst of private investment, as have green bonds, feed-in tariffs and publicly sponsored insurance schemes that cover political and currency risk (Zadek, 2013). Moreover, middle-income countries are emerging as a rapidly growing source of green finance. Recent growth rates from investments originating in non-OECD countries (which grew from \$4.5 billion in 2004 to \$68 billion in 2011) surpassed similar investments by OECD countries in 2012. In 2013, China's investments in renewable energy at \$56.3 billion exceeded Europe's for the first time (UNEP, Bloomberg New Energy Finance, and Frankfurt School-UNEP, 2015) and the Asian Infrastructure Investment Bank (AIIB) will be a new potential source of investment for Africa.

African countries face differing financial opportunities and constraints. In middle-income nations such as South Africa, public resources raised through bond issues and fiscal measures can

The report argues for a transformational shift in the way public and private entities integrate notions of sustainability within all facets of operation, and insists on new benchmarks ... ... for the benefit of consumers and shareholders.

provide funds for key infrastructure and delivery of public goods in which the private sector is unlikely to invest. As noted by UNEP's Inquiry into the Design of a Sustainable Financial System (2015), public funds will inevitably be limited. Instead, governments will have to find ways of accessing private capital at scale, "with banking alone managing financial assets of almost US$140 trillion and institutional investors, notably pension funds, managing over US$100 trillion, and capital markets, including bond and equities, exceeding US$100 trillion and US$73 trillion respectively" (p. xiii).

Access to low-carbon energy could follow the model of mobile phones, with prepayment cards as a means to ensure cost recovery for investors.

In low-income countries, with their limited domestic resources, multilateral development banks and international development finance will likely continue playing a key role in funding infrastructural investment. Access to low-carbon energy could follow the model of mobile phones, with prepayment cards as a means to ensure cost recovery for investors. Curbing illicit financial outflows and promoting domestic resource mobilization are also critical.

Translating those developments into investments for Africa requires change at four levels.

AFRICA NEEDS TO TAKE CONTROL OF ITS ECONOMIC STRATEGY AND SET ITS OWN AGENDA

In seeking to benefit from green industrialization, African countries must determine their financing and green agendas with a view to attracting investments that target job creation, greater income generation and local content, while reducing resource scarcity. In doing so, Africa must look to its primary development partners and its own fiscal spending. For decades, African countries have relied heavily on traditional OECD Development Assistance Committee country support, and certainly those donors are major drivers behind green growth and climate change mitigation. Growing evidence, however, indicates that the BRICS countries (Brazil, Russia, India, China and South Africa) are taking the lead in investment, particularly in developing Africa's resources and infrastructure.

For example, the New Development Bank (NDB), often referred to as the BRICS Development Bank, is a multilateral development bank operated by the BRICS countries. NDB is an alternative to the existing United States– and European-dominated World Bank and International Monetary Fund. Alongside the new Asian Infrastructure Investment Bank, the New Development Bank could provide Africa with increased opportunity to manage the financing of its green growth agenda. On the home front, most African countries need to make adjustments to their fiscal arrangements and policies, with support from their RECs, the AfDB and regional development banks.

AFRICA NEEDS TO PLAY A DECISIVE ROLE IN REFORMS TO INTERNATIONAL TRADE AND FINANCE RULES TO ENCOURAGE GREEN GROWTH TRANSITIONS

The World Trade Organization has been largely silent in global climate negotiations, including COP21. Africa has demonstrated that it can have a strong and collective voice in the UNFCCC negotiations. The continent developed and evolved the African Common Position on Climate Change, mandated by the Committee of African Heads of State and Government on Climate Change and the African Ministerial Council for the Environment and implemented by the African Group of Negotiators. The position statement has helped to ensure that the interests of African countries are well represented in the global climate deal, and it shows what might be possible in influencing the international trade regime if African countries work together well on issues such as export subsidies. Equally, some of the current trade rules, supported by international development finance institutions, block the opportunities for industrial and economic gains from green investment and should be lobbied against. Progress must be made in high-carbon sectors, such as aviation and maritime transport, in which, to date, a global approach has been blocked.

FINANCIAL MARKETS NEED TO TAKE A LONGER TERM VIEW, WITH COMBINED MARKET-LED ACTIONS AND CLEAR, CONSISTENT POLICY

Much can be done to include environmental risks in credit ratings and ensure fuller disclosure of how investors price natural resources, such as water, carbon and energy. Again, inspiration can be drawn from an increasing wealth of experience. The CDP (called the Carbon Disclosure Project through 2012), designed to stimulate disclosure of environmental risk, launched a project to raise business awareness of water-related risk. In 2015 more than 617 institutional investors representing more than $63 trillion in assets supported this project (CDP, 2015).

Further, the reinsurance sector, led by major firms such as Munich Re Group (active in Africa) and Hannover Re, is heightening awareness of climate and natural-disaster risk. Through robust actuarial analysis, these institutions are able to understand the cost of these and related risks. Africa has the emerging Africa Risk Capacity facility, an insurance risk pool that aims to capitalize on the natural diversification of weather risk across Africa. This allows countries to manage their risk as a group in a financially efficient manner to respond to probable, but uncertain, risks. Nonetheless, as advanced countries' financial sectors remain largely resistant to reform, Africa's challenge will be to stimulate global reform while promoting reform in its own financial markets.

WHATEVER THE SOURCE OF FUNDING, PUBLIC AND PRIVATE FUNDS MUST REACH DOWN TO THE DECENTRALIZED LEVELS OF GOVERNMENT THAT CAN IDENTIFY MORE CONCRETE INVESTMENTS

Whether in building climate resilience, designing low-carbon energy systems, or practising sustainable landscape management, local voice and knowledge must be able to shape investments. Recent work in northern Kenya, Mali, Senegal and Tanzania demonstrates the great value to be gained from working with local government to harness local initiatives and institutions for designing resilient investments (Hesse 2015). Hence, government has to ensure that national funds operate according to clear guidelines for sharing resources allocated to local governance and implementation.

7.2 CONCLUSIONS

If African governments are to achieve structural transformation and sustainable development through greening industrialization, the state needs to play the leading role in setting out this agenda, providing leadership at the highest level, and offering a clear, credible and consistent policy framework. To shift from a business as usual pathway demands more than marginal changes to policy, investment, resource allocation, and the overall pattern of incentives. A step-change is needed not only in the vision and strategy laid out by government, but also in the quality of the partnership offered to the private sector, both small- and large scale. It requires a systemic approach across sectors, stake-holders and scales so the principal drivers of change are aligned behind a low carbon growth pathway. While this agenda might seem complex and difficult, there are good models being followed already in Africa, and neighbouring continents from which to seek inspiration and practical guidance.

Earlier chapters in this Report show that much of this can be achieved with win-win outcomes. But this will not always be the case, and painful choices and trade-offs will be inevitable. However, as seen in Chapter 5, greening of industrialization is a crucial and necessary requirement for growth to be sustained, not just in the long term but increasingly in the short and medium term as well.

African countries have the chance to take a forward role in achieving the structural transformation they seek, greening their economies, generating jobs, and showing the responsibility they take for long-term stewardship of the earth.

7.3 REFERENCES

APHRC (African Population and Health Research Center). 2014. *Population and Health Dynamics in Nairobi's Informal Settlements, Report of the Nairobi Cross-sectional Slums Survey (NCSS) 2012*, Nairobi: APHRC.

APP (Africa Progress Panel). 2015. *People, power, planet. Seizing Africa's energy and climate opportunities*. Africa Progress report 2015. Geneva, Africa Progress Panel.

Banda, Tasila and Steve Bass. 2014. "Inclusive green growth in Zambia: Scoping the needs and Potentials." International Institute for Environment and Development (IIED) Country Report February 2014. IIED London.

CDP (Carbon Disclosure Report). 2014. *South Africa Water Report*. Park Town, National Business Initiative, and London, Carbon Disclosure Project.

Chang, Ha-Joon. 2015. *Smart industrial policy for Africa in the 21st century. Addis Ababa*, UNECA.

FAO (Food and Agricultural Organization). 2012. Growing greener cities in Africa. Rome, FAO.

GEC. 2013. Real Green Economies. Report of the meeting at Wilton Park, February 2013. London, Green Economy Coalition.

Hesse, Ced. 2015. "Climate adaptation finds." Backgrounder, November 2015. International Institute for Environment and Development (IIED), London.

IED-Afrique. 2015. *Decentralizing climate funds in Senegal and Mali*. Bamako, and Dakar. Near East Foundation, IIED, and IED-Afrique.

Kaplinsky, Raphael. 2005. *Globalization, Poverty and Inequality: Between a Rock and a Hard Place*. Cambridge: Polity.

Mazzucato, Mariana. 2013. *The entrepreneurial state: Debunking public vs private sector myths*. Bath, UK: Anthem.

Monden, Yasuhiro. 1983. *Toyota Production System: Practical Approach to Production Management*. Atlanta: Industrial Engineering and Management Press.

New Climate Economy (NCE). 2014. Better growth, better climate: charting a new path for low-carbon growth and a safer climate, *2014 Report*. NCE, London.

Oqubay, Arkebe. 2015. *Made in Africa: Industrial Policy in Ethiopia*. Oxford: Oxford University Press.

Raworth, Kate, Sarah Wykes and Steve Bass. 2014. Securing social justice in green economies: a review and ten considerations for policymakers. Issue Paper. London: International Institute for Environment and Development.

Reij, Chris and Robert Winterbottom. 2014. *Scaling up regreening: Six steps to success. A practical approach to forest and landscape restoration*. Washington DC, World Resources Institute.

Sachs, Jeffrey D. 2015. Pathways to deep de-carbonization. 2015 Report. SDSN, IDDRI.

United Nations (UN). 2013. *A new global partnership: eradicate poverty and transform economies through sustainable development*. The Report of the High-Level Panel of Eminent Persons on the Post-2015 Development Agenda. New York.

United Nations Development Programme (UNDP). 2011. *Paving the way for climate-resilient infrastructure: guidance for practitioners and planners*. Official Proceedings of the International Conference: Strategies for Adapting Public and Private Infrastructure to Climate Change, San Salvador, El Salvador, 30 June 2010. New York: UNDP.

ECA (Economic Commission for Africa). 2013. Making the most of Africa's commodities: industrializing for growth, jobs and economic transformation. *Economic Report on Africa*. Addis Ababa.

———. 2014. Dynamic industrial policy in Africa. *Economic Report on Africa*. Addis Ababa.

ECA (Economic Commission for Africa). 2013. Making the most of Africa's commodities: industrializing for growth, jobs and economic transformation. *Economic Report on Africa*. Addis Ababa.

———. 2014. Dynamic industrial policy in Africa. *Economic Report on Africa*. Addis Ababa.

United Nations Environment Programme (UNEP). 2015. *Inquiry into the design of a sustainable financial system. The financial system we need: aligning the financial system with sustainable development*. The UNEP Inquiry Report. Geneva.

———. 2016. *Africa Regional Assessment Report*. GEO 6. Nairobi, UNEP.

United Nations Environment Programme (UNEP), *Bloomberg New Energy Finance, and Frankfurt School-UNEP*. 2015. Global trends in renewable energy investment 2015. Nairobi, Kenya OR Frankfurt, Germany.

United Nations Framework Convention on Climate Change (UNFCCC). 2015. Adoption of the Paris Agreement. Paris.

Whitley, Shelagh, and Laurie van der Burg. 2015. "Fossil fuel subsidy reform in Sub-Saharan Africa: From rhetoric to reality." Working Paper. London: New Climate Economy. Available from http://newclimateeconomy.report/misc/working-papers.

Zadek, Simon. 2013. "Reshaping the Political (Green) Economy." Journal of Corporate Citizenship, Volume 2013, Number 51, September 2013, pp. 5-16(12).

7.4 ENDNOTES

1 ERA 2017 will focus on urbanization in Africa and consequently address these issues and policy options in much greater depth.

2 The eight RECs are the Arab Maghreb Union (AMU); Common Market for Eastern and Southern Africa (COMESA); Community of Sahel-Saharan States (CEN-SAD); East African Community (EAC); Economic Community of Central African States (ECCAS); Economic Community of West African States (ECOWAS); Intergovernmental Authority on Development (IGAD); and Southern African Development Community (SADC).

3 http://www.capturingthegains.org

STATISTICAL NOTE

This year's *Economic Report on Africa* is based on the latest updated and harmonized data from a range of sources, including questionnaires developed by the authors. The main economic and social data variables are obtained from databases of the United Nations Department of Economic and Social Affairs (UN-DESA) and the International Labour Organization (ILO). Data from the statistical databases of the International Monetary Fund, Economist Intelligence Unit (EIU), United Nations Conference on Trade and Development (UNCTAD), World Bank and some government departments in African countries are also used. Previous years' data in the Report may differ from those in earlier editions, reflecting recent revisions.

The database of UN-DESA's *Global Economic Outlook* provides comparable data on growth in gross domestic product (GDP) for all African countries, except Seychelles and Swaziland, for which data are obtained from the EIU database. Real GDP growth rates are generated using country data, with 2010 as the base year. Subregional inflation rates for country groupings are weighted averages, with weights based on GDP in 2005 prices. Baseline scenario forecasts are based partly on Project LINK and the UN-DESA World Economic Forecasting Model.

To estimate the impact of the recent oil price shock on Africa's GDP growth, the Report uses the quadratic match-sum method to decompose low-frequency data (annual) to higher-frequency data (monthly). This method fits a local quadratic polynomial for each observation of the original series, using the fitted polynomial to fill in all observations of the higher-frequency series associated with the period. The quadratic polynomial is formed by taking sets of three adjacent points from the original series and fitting a quadratic function to ensure that the sum of the interpolated monthly data points matches the actual annual data points.

Social data are based on the latest data from the United Nations Educational, Scientific and Cultural Organization. Employment figures are from the ILO's Key Indicators of the Labour Market database. Data on trade (exports and imports) are from UNCTAD and the World Trade Organization.

Unless otherwise noted, the data cover 53 African countries (excluding South Sudan, owing to a lack of data). Countries are classified into geographical regions and into country groupings: oil importers, oil exporters, mineral-rich countries and mineral-poor countries. Country groupings are based on UNCTAD trade data for 2012 and 2013 (SITC 33 for oil and SITC 27+28+32+34+35+68+667+971 for minerals).

Geographical regions are North, Southern, East, West and Central Africa.

Oil exporters are those with oil exports at least 20 per cent higher than their oil imports and comprise Algeria, Angola, Cameroon, Chad, Congo Republic, Côte d'Ivoire, Democratic Republic of Congo, Equatorial Guinea, Gabon, Ghana, Libya, Niger, Nigeria and Sudan.

Oil importers comprise Benin, Botswana, Burkina Faso, Burundi, Cabo Verde, Central African Republic, Comoros, Djibouti, Egypt, Eritrea, Ethiopia, Gambia, Guinea, Guinea-Bissau, Kenya, Lesotho, Liberia, Madagascar, Malawi, Mali, Mauritania, Mauritius, Morocco, Mozambique, Namibia, Rwanda, São Tomé and Príncipe, Senegal, Seychelles, Sierra Leone, Somalia, South Africa, Swaziland, Tanzania, Togo, Tunisia, Uganda, Zambia and Zimbabwe.

Mineral-rich countries are those where mineral exports account for more than 20 per cent of total exports and include: Algeria, Benin, Botswana, Burkina Faso, Central African Republic, DRC, Djibouti, Equatorial Guinea, Eritrea, Guinea, Lesotho, Liberia, Mali, Mauritania, Madagascar, Mozambique, Namibia, Niger, Rwanda, Sierra Leone, South Africa, Sudan, Tanzania, Togo, Zambia and Zimbabwe.

Mineral-poor countries comprise Angola, Burundi, Cameroon, Cabo Verde, Chad, Comoros, Congo, Côte d'Ivoire, Egypt, Ethiopia, Gabon, Gambia, Ghana, Guinea-Bissau, Kenya, Libya, Malawi, Mauritius, Morocco, Nigeria, São Tomé and Príncipe, Senegal, Seychelles, Somalia, Swaziland, Tunisia and Uganda.

The thematic part of the Report uses primary data and information collected, harmonized and analysed by staff at the United Nations Economic Commission for Africa through questionnaires and some secondary sources. Interviews were conducted in 10 countries (Côte d'Ivoire, Gabon, Ghana, Kenya, Malawi, Mauritius, Morocco, Nigeria, Rwanda and South Africa). Additional information was also collected from some regional economic communities.

www.ingramcontent.com/pod-product-compliance
Lightning Source LLC
Chambersburg PA
CBHW061206240926
51846CB00006B/1130
* 9 7 8 9 2 1 1 2 5 1 2 6 5 *